Comparing Political Communication

Theories, Cases, and Challenges

This volume assesses the state of the art of comparative political communication research and considers potential ways in which it could and should develop. While cross-national studies were long neglected, twenty experts from Europe and the United States offer a unique and comprehensive discussion of the theories, cases, and challenges of comparative research in political communication. The first part discusses the fundamental themes, concepts, and methods essential in order to analyze the effects of modernization and globalization of political communication. The second part offers a broad range of case studies that illustrate the enormous potential of cross-national approaches in many relevant fields of political communication. The third part paves the way for future research by describing the most promising concepts and pressing challenges of comparative political communication. This book is intended to introduce new students to a crucial, dynamic field as well as to deepen advanced students' knowledge of its principles and perspectives.

Frank Esser is Assistant Professor of Mass Communication at the University of Missouri, Columbia. He was assistant professor at the University of Mainz, Germany, and visiting professor at the University of Oklahoma. His research centers around cross-national studies of journalism and political communication and has appeared in the *European Journal of Communications, American Behavioral Scientist,* and *Press/Politics.*

Barbara Pfetsch is Professor of Communication and Media Policy at the University of Hohenheim, Germany. She was a Fellow at the John F. Kennedy School of Government at Harvard University and at the Center for German and European Studies at Georgetown University. Her research interests focus on comparative analyses of political communication and the mediated public sphere.

Politics and relations among individuals in societies across the world are being transformed by new technologies for targeting individuals and sophisticated methods for shaping personalized messages. The new technologies challenge boundaries of many kinds – between news, information, entertainment, and advertising; between media, with the arrival of the World Wide Web; and even between nations. *Communication, Society and Politics* probes the political and social impacts of these new communication systems in national, comparative, and global perspective.

Comparing Political Communication

THEORIES, CASES, AND CHALLENGES

Edited by

Frank Esser
University of Missouri-Columbia

Barbara Pfetsch
University of Hohenheim

CAMBRIDGE
UNIVERSITY PRESS

PUBLISHED BY THE PRESS SYNDICATE OF THE UNIVERSITY OF CAMBRIDGE
The Pitt Building, Trumpington Street, Cambridge, United Kingdom

CAMBRIDGE UNIVERSITY PRESS
The Edinburgh Building, Cambridge CB2 2RU, UK
40 West 20th Street, New York, NY 10011-4211, USA
477 Williamstown Road, Port Melbourne, VIC 3207, Australia
Ruiz de Alarcón 13, 28014 Madrid, Spain
Dock House, The Waterfront, Cape Town 8001, South Africa

http://www.cambridge.org

First published 2004

Printed in the United States of America

Typefaces Minion 11/13 pt. and Centaur   System LATEX 2$_\varepsilon$ [TB]

A catalog record for this book is available from the British Library.

Library of Congress Cataloging in Publication Data

Comparing political communication : theories, cases, and challenges / edited by Frank Esser,
Barbara Pfetsch.
p.   cm. – (Communication, society and politics)
Includes bibliographical references and index.
ISBN 0-521-82831-7 – ISBN 0-521-53540-9 (pbk.)
1. Communication in politics – Comparative method.   2. Mass media – Political aspects –
Comparative method.   3. Communication in politics – Cross-cultural studies.   4. Mass media –
Political aspects – Cross-cultural studies.   I. Esser, Frank, 1966–   II. Pfetsch, Barbara.   III. Series.
JA85.C67   2004
320'.01'4–dc22   2004040653

ISBN 0 521 82831 7 hardback
ISBN 0 521 53540 9 paperback

Contents

II: CASES

III: PERSPECTIVES AND CHALLENGES

Contributors

Jay G. Blumler is Emeritus Professor of the Social and Political Aspects of Broadcasting at the University of Leeds, England, and Emeritus Professor of Journalism at the University of Maryland. A Fellow and Past President of the International Communication Association and a founding co-editor of the *European Journal of Communication*, he has written extensively on the mass media and politics, including "The Crisis of Public Communication" (1995, with Michael Gurevitch) and "The Third Age of Political Communication: Influences and Features" (in vol. 16 (3), 1999, of *Political Communication*, with Dennis Kavanagh).

Wolfgang Donsbach is Professor of Communication and founding director of the Department of Communication at the University of Dresden, Germany. He received his Ph.D. and his postdoctoral Habilitation at the University of Mainz. Prior to his current position he taught at the universities of Dortmund, Mainz, and Berlin. He was a Fellow at the Gannett Center for Media Studies at Columbia University, New York, in 1989–90, and Lombard Visiting Professor at Harvard University, Cambridge, in 1999. From 1995 to 1996 he was president of the World Association for Public Opinion Research (WAPOR), and from 2004 to 2005 he is president of the International Communication Association (ICA). He also served as chair of the International Association for Media and Communication Research (IAMCR) Psychology and Public Opinion section and of the ICA Political Communication division. He is managing editor of the *International Journal of Public Opinion Research*. His main research interests are in journalism, political communication, and media effects.

Frank Esser is assistant professor of mass communication at the University of Missouri, Columbia. He was assistant professor in the Institute fuer Publizistik at the University of Mainz, Germany, and visiting professor in the Department of Communication at the University of Oklahoma. His research interests center around cross-national studies of journalism and political communication. He received three top-paper awards at the annual conventions of the ICA (1996, 2001, 2003) and has published four books and various articles in journals such as *European Journal of Communication, Harvard International Journal of Press/Politics,* and *American Behavioral Scientist.*

Michael Gurevitch is professor in the College of Journalism at the University of Maryland. Prior to his current position he was on the faculty of The Open University in England. Besides his recent book, *The Crisis of Public Communication* (with Jay Blumler), he has published a large number of journal articles and book chapters and is co-editor of *Mass Communication and Society* (1977), *Culture, Society and the Media* (1982), and *Mass Media and Society* (1991, 1995, 2001). He served as associate editor of the *Journal of Communication* and is currently a member of the editorial board of *Journalism Studies.*

Daniel C. Hallin is Professor of Communication at the University of California at San Diego. His research interests include media and war, media and elections, the development of journalism as a profession, and comparative analysis of media systems, particularly focusing on the United States, Western Europe, and Latin America. He recently published, with Paolo Mancini, *Comparing Media Systems: Three Models of Media and Politics* (2004).

Christina Holtz-Bacha is Professor of Communication at the University of Mainz, Germany. After receiving her Ph.D. from the University of Muenster in 1978, she held positions as assistant professor at the University of Munich and full professor at the University of Bochum, Germany. She was visiting professor at the University of Minnesota in 1986 and a Fellow at the Joan Shorenstein Center on the Press, Politics, and Public Policy at Harvard University, Cambridge, in 1999. From 1998–2002 she was chair of the Political Communication division of the German Communication Association (DGPuK), and since 2002 she has been chair of the Political Communication division of the ICA. She published several books, including the *German Communication Yearbook*

(1999), *Wahlkampf in den Medien–Wahlkampf mit den Medien* (1999), and *Wahlwerbung als politische Kultur* (2001).

Hans J. Kleinsteuber is Professor of Political Science and Journalism at the University of Hamburg, Germany. He studied in Berlin and Medford, Massachusetts, and received his Ph.D. in 1975 from the Free University of Berlin. He was visiting professor at various universities in the United States, Canada, Australia, and Japan and is a member of the Euromedia Research Group since 1982. His research interests include media policy and political communication in comparative perspective. He published several books, including *Europa als Kommunikationsraum* (1994, with T. Rossmann), *Information Superhighway* (1996), and *Neue Medientrends in den USA* (2001).

Steffen Kolb studied media and communication sciences and political sciences at the universities of Leipzig and Aix-en-Provence. As research and teaching assistant at the University of Hamburg, Germany, he is completing his doctoral thesis on media coverage of leaded gas in comparative perspective. His research interests include intercultural communication, empirical methods, and political communication.

Hanspeter Kriesi is Professor of Comparative Politics in the Department of Political Science at the University of Zurich, Switzerland. After studies in sociology at the universities of Berne, Chicago, and Zurich, he became an assistant professor in sociology at the University of Zurich. Then he taught political behavior at the University of Amsterdam and Swiss politics and comparative politics at the University of Geneva. His research focuses on opinion formation in grassroots democracies, elections, social movements, the development of West European party systems and the European public sphere, and public participation in democratic systems.

Sabine Lang is Visiting Associate DAAD Professor of Politics at the Henry M. Jackson School of International Studies of the University of Washington, Seattle. Having finished her studies of political science in Freiburg, New York, and Berlin, she did her doctorate on the "Political Public in the Modern State" (published 2001). She was assistant professor in the Department of Political and Social Sciences at the Free University of Berlin and visiting Fellow at the Center of European Studies at the University of California, Berkeley. She published widely, particularly on political public sphere, mass media, and gender studies. In her current research project on mobilizing urban publics, she investigates changes of local publics in German and U.S. cities.

Paolo Mancini is Professor of Communication and Academic Director of the School of Broadcast Journalism at the Universitá di Perugia, Italy. He has published several books, including *Videopolitica* (1985), *Come Vincere le Elezioni* (1989), *Guardando il Telegiornale* (1991), and *Il Giornalismo e le Sue Regole* (1992). Many of his works appeared in international journals such as *Theory and Society*, *European Journal of Communication*, and *Journal of Communication*. His research concerns primarily political communication and comparative analysis of mass media systems. He recently published, with Dan Hallin, *Comparing Media Systems: Three Models of Media and Politics* (2004).

Pippa Norris is the McGuire Lecturer in Comparative Politics at the John F. Kennedy School of Government, Harvard University. A political scientist, her research compares election and public opinion, political communications, and gender politics. She has published more than thirty books, including *A Virtuous Circle* (2000), *Digital Divide* (2001), *Democratic Phoenix* (2002), *Rising Tide* (2003), *Electoral Engineering* (2004), and *Sacred and Secular* (2004) for Cambridge University Press.

Thomas E. Patterson is Bradlee Professor of Government and the Press in the John F. Kennedy School of Government at Harvard University. He previously taught for many years at Syracuse University, where he took a position after completing his Ph.D. at the University of Minnesota. His recent book *The Vanishing Voter*, published in 2002, is based on a study of the decline of citizen participation in U.S. elections. Earlier books include *Out of Order*, which was recipient of the American Political Science Association's Graber Award for the best book in political communication, and *The Unseeing Eye*, which was selected by the American Association for Public Opinion Research as one of the fifty most influential books of the past half century in the field of public opinion.

Barbara Pfetsch is Professor of Communication and Media Policy at the University of Hohenheim, Germany. She previously held a position as senior researcher at the Science Center Berlin for Social Research (WZB) and taught at the Free University of Berlin and the University of Mannheim. She was a Fellow at the J. F. Kennedy School of Government at Harvard University, Cambridge, and at the Center for German and European Studies at Georgetown University, Washington, D.C. Her research interests center on comparative analyses of political communication and on media and the public sphere. She published several books including *Politische Kommunikationskultur* (2003) and numerous articles and book chapters including "Political Communication Culture in the United States and Germany" (in vol. 6 (1), 2001, of *Press/Politics*) and "Government News Management" (in *The Politics of News: The News of Politics*, edited by D. Graber et al., 1998).

Patrick Rössler is Professor of Communication Science at the University of Erfurt, Germany, and serves as representative of the ICA in Germany. He received his Ph.D. from the University of Hohenheim, Germany, and was assistant professor in the Department of Communication at the University of Munich. His research interests concern political communication, media effects, media contents, and new media technology. He has published several books including *Agenda-Setting* (1997), *Online-Kommunikation* (1998, ed.), and *Theoretische Perspektiven der Rezeptionsforschung* (2001, edited with U. Hasebrink and M. Jäckel) and numerous journal articles in, among others, *Journal of Communication, International Journal of Public Opinion Research*, and *Communication Research*.

Rüdiger Schmitt-Beck is Professor of Politics and Political Communication at the University of Duisburg-Essen, Germany. His research interests center on comparative analyses of political communication, political participation, political culture, and election campaigns. His publications include *Do Political Campaigns Matter? Campaign Effects in Elections and Referendums* (2002, with D. M. Farrell), *Politische Kommunikation und Wählerverhalten. Ein internationaler Vergleich* (2002), and *Mass Communication, Personal Communication and Vote Choice – The Filter Hypothesis of Media Influence in Comparative Perspective* (in vol. 33, 2003, of *British Journal of Political Science*).

Robert L. Stevenson is Kenan Professor of Journalism at the University of North Carolina at Chapel Hill. He earned a Ph.D. from the University of Washington in 1975, where his academic adviser was Alex S. Edelstein. Since joining the University of North Carolina in 1975, he has been a Fulbright Senior Scholar in Mainz, Eric Voegelin Professor in Munich, German Academic Exchange Service Visiting Professor in Dresden, and assistant director of the American Journalism Center in Budapest. He is author of *Global Communication in the 21st Century* and *Communication, Development, and the Third World – The Global Politics of Information* and coeditor of *Foreign News and the New World Information Order*. He was associate editor of *Journalism Quarterly* and president of the regional Southern Association for Public Opinion Research.

David L. Swanson is Associate Provost and Professor of Speech Communication and Political Science, University of Illinois at Urbana-Champaign. His research concerns the social effects of mass communication, with particular attention to the role of media in politics. His scholarly work on these subjects has appeared in various journals and volumes in the United States, Europe, and Asia and includes "The Uses and Gratifications Approach to Mass Communication," "New Directions in Political Communication" (with D. Nimmo), and "Politics, Media, and Modern Democracy" (with P. Mancini).

Werner Wirth is Professor of Empirical Communications at the University of Zurich, Switzerland. He previously taught as Professor of New Media and Online Communication at the University of Munich, Germany. He has edited three books and published numerous book chapters and journal articles in different areas, including media exposure and media effects research, infotainment, online research, and empirical methods.

Thomas Zittel is John F. Kennedy Memorial Fellow at the Minda de Gunzburg Center for European Studies at Harvard University, Cambridge. He studied political science and German and holds an M.A. from Johns Hopkins University, Baltimore, and a Ph.D. from the University of Mannheim, Germany. From 1990 to 2001, he was assistant professor at the University of Mannheim; from 1996 to 1997 he was Congressional Fellow of the American Political Science Association. His current research deals with the impact of computer networks on democracy. He has published numerous journal articles and book chapters on this topic and directs a research project on parliaments, representative democracy, and new digital media.

Comparing Political Communication

Theories, Cases, and Challenges

Introduction

Comparing Political Communication

Reorientations in a Changing World

Barbara Pfetsch and Frank Esser

This volume intends to assess the state of the art of comparative research in political communication and to make reference to potential ways in which political communication could and should develop. When Jay Blumler and Michael Gurevitch urged political communication to adapt to the perspective of international comparison more than 25 years ago they were able to refer to only a few studies (Blumler and Gurevitch 1975). At the time, the neglect of comparative work in communication research was even more blatant as this approach had been well established in neighboring social sciences such as political science. However, scholars in comparative politics were never really interested in the mass media and political communication. In communication science on the other hand, political communication has always been a central subject; though it was believed for a long time that it would suffice to describe singular phenomena in the realm of national politics or to subscribe to historical studies. Thus, until the early 1990s communication research lacked an international orientation comparable to that of political science (Kaase 1998; Schoenbach 1998).

From today's point of view it is surprising how long it took for the comparative approach to be acknowledged as a necessary and useful strategy and tool of communication research. Doris Graber (1993, 305) rightly points out that political communication cannot be suitably studied without comparative research "as its form varies between cultures, which makes it necessary and instructive to analyze it from different cultural perspectives." Comparative research in political communication deserves more attention because it enables us to inspect our own findings critically by using the examination of others, and only by doing so enables us to reach conclusions with an extensive claim to validity.

Against this background, it is all the more remarkable that we lack a comprehensive publication in the English-speaking world that brings to the fore and discusses the questions and concepts as well as the applications and problems of comparative political communication research. Such a publication[1] has become all the more important as we can meanwhile document a rapid development of relevant research. During the 1990s, various productive networks of researchers working across national borders were formed that were responsible for a series of prominent and fruitful projects. Moreover, the process of European integration gives the activities on this side of the Atlantic further impetus. Any doubts pertaining to the benefits and the prospect of the comparative approach have been abandoned. Hence, Michael Gurevitch and Jay Blumler (Chapter 14, this volume) note: "Far from being neglected, comparative political research has almost become fashionable." With this in mind, the challenge now is to revisit and systematize the manifold studies into a comprehensive "state-of-the-art" report, which is a suitable document of the advances of comparative research in this subfield of communication science.

Going beyond the sociology of communication science as an academic discipline, this volume also allows for the deeper insight that political communication processes in themselves are by no means to be understood as delimited phenomena. In the twenty-first century we are confronted with developments in the realm of politics and mass communications that rule out the conception of political communication as a phenomenon that could be defined within singular national, cultural, or linguistic boundaries. In fact, the challenge today is to face the developments and consequences arising from the modernization and globalization of political processes. This is not least necessary because we now know that the structures and processes of media development and communications do systematically impact the development of democracy, the legitimization of political power, and the participation in politics (Chapter 6, this volume).

However, studies on the relationship between political communication and the quality of democracy across different countries (Gunther and Mughan 2000; Thomass and Tzankoff 2001) reveal that the role of political communication is by no means consistent. It is far more dependent on whether established "old" democracies or so-called new

---

[1] A German edition of this volume was published by Westdeutscher Verlag, Wiesbaden, 2003, under the title Politische Kommunikation im internationalen Vergleich – Grundlagen, Anwendungen, Perspektiven.

democracies are being considered. While there is evidence that the media in transition countries support the adoption of democratic norms and play a marked constructive role in political consolidation (Schmitt-Beck and Voltmer 2001), their contribution to the democratic process in contemporary Western systems is no more than ambivalent. Thus, the interrelations and consequences of political communication clearly vary according to the duration and the traditions of the development of democracy, whereby the problems and deficits of modernized political communication mainly occur in the Western mass democracies. As a consequence, the contributions to this volume – with the exception of the study by Norris (Chapter 6, this volume), which takes a global perspective – concentrate on the "old," established democracies in Western Europe and the United States.

In view of the significance of communication processes for the development of democracy many mainstream researchers dwelled on the United States as the country in which the modernization of political communication seemed furthest advanced and most apparent. The American "media democracy" appeared for a long time to be *the* role model for the development of political communication in all Western democracies (Blumler and Gurevitch 1995, 77). With the creation of the term *Americanization* the essential paradigm had been set that generated a great deal of dynamics in international research. A boom in comparative political communication studies was the outcome following the criticism of the parochial perspective of many U.S.-centered projects, which tended to neglect institutional arrangements as well as cultural and structural contexts of political communication. Since the 1990s, European and American scholars have been asking themselves whether the American model of media democracy is indeed appropriate for describing generalizable patterns of developments of modern political communication in today's Western democracies (Gurevitch and Blumler 1990; Swanson 1992; Negrine and Papathanassopoulos 1996; Swanson and Mancini 1996). The fundamental transformation of the media systems of the Western world, which was caused by the changes in information technology and communication infrastructure and by the global media economy and diffusion of news, also belongs to the driving forces behind comparative research. A clear sign of the globalization of media is the growth and concentration of internationally active media conglomerates. This development has had significant repercussions for national media systems. In almost all European countries there has been a reorientation of media policy with respect to deregulation and the opening up of media markets. In the case of the United States there has been a further wave of commercialization over the past decade (Underwood 1998; Bogart 2000). While the long-term consequences are still not foreseeable, it was already clear at the beginning of the transformation process that political communication would not go unaffected by the technical development and the increase in competition and commercialization. In view of the development of global communication systems and processes, which no longer stop at national borders, it is obvious that research also cannot be limited to examining particularities that concern one country only. The onus now was on discovering transnational trends, similarities, and deviations from general patterns that only become apparent when a broad – comparative – perspective is taken.

The growth of comparative research has led to a cornucopia of studies. In this situation it is appropriate and necessary to establish paradigmatic paths in the knowledge jungle and to bundle results in order to be able to develop new perspectives. This is the starting point of this volume. In the appraisal of the current research, we follow an outline of three main sections, discussing the fundamentals, applications, and perspectives of comparative political communication research. The first part will access comparative political communication by expounding the basic themes, the problems, and overall developments and by providing an overview of the spectrum of comparative studies. Furthermore, an introduction would be incomplete if it did not address the problems of comparative research designs and its methodological foundations. The essays in the second part of the volume highlight concrete examples of comparative studies in specific subareas of political communication. The focus here is on comparative investigations into the structures, processes, actors, contents, and effects of political communication. These contributions are not just concerned with presenting tangible projects and their results but also with discussing the specific added value of the comparative approach. This added value takes the form on the one hand of a substantial increase in insight regarding the respective research questions and on the other of experience gained regarding the implementation of comparative designs. The contributions in the third part of the volume look to the future and discuss the theoretical and methodological prospects of the comparative approach. The final chapter provides a synthesis of the common theoretical and methodological issues of the studies presented and attempts to integrate the manifold approaches, questions, and concepts.

INTERNATIONAL COMPARISON AS A RESEARCH STRATEGY AND METHODOLOGY

The acknowledgment of the relevance of communication in political processes is of course not synonymous with the successful implementation of comparative studies. A widening of the perspective thus implies research designs in which a variety of exogenous influencing factors that are difficult to control must be considered. As a matter of principle, various methodological conditions are to be set when a comparative perspective is taken.

Comparative research lives up to the rule that "every observation is without significance if it is not compared with other observations." It can be said, arguing theoretically from the point of view of epistemology, that we form our ideas through comparisons. We know that apples are not pears because we have compared them with each other. An object only develops an identity of its own if it is compared with others" (Aarebrot and Bakka 1997, 49). This means that we observe at least two populations when making comparisons. In the field of political communication we usually compare political systems that can be comprehended as nation states, regional entities, political subsystems, or parts of subsystems (e.g., local areas of communication or elite or media cultures). Comparative political communication research is also always a cultural comparison. Even though many studies that compare across countries are based on the assumption that culture and nation overlap, this must not disguise the fact that both parameters are not necessarily congruent. It is often the case that contradictory and discrepant processes and phenomena of political communication appear within one single political system taking the form of a nation state, as is shown by comparing journalistic cultures, for instance, in Francophone and Anglo-American Canada (Pritchard and Sauvageau 1997) or by comparing media effects in Western and Eastern Germany (Chapter 13, this volume). Cultures constitute communities of values in the broadest sense. In comparative political communication research, therefore, it is possible to study specific subcultures and their value structures such as the political communication cultures emerging between journalists and political spokespeople in different political systems (Chapter 15, this volume) or the local communication cultures within their specific media environments across countries (Chapter 7, this volume).

Although the nation-state is by no means the only reference frame for comparative studies, we adhere to the term *comparative* in this volume to signify the comparison across national political systems or societies. We are deliberately not using the terms *interculturally comparative* or *intersystemically comparative*. The pragmatic reason for this convention is that of all conceivable reference frames national political systems are the most clear-cut (Kohn 1989; Chapter 17, this volume). If the terms *interculturally* or *intersystemically* were used we would have to define in every case what is meant by *culture* or *system*. Because the overwhelming majority of studies in this volume is concerned with comparisons between countries it seems justified to speak of comparative research. As we understand it in this volume, comparative political communication research refers to comparison between a minimum of two political systems or cultures (or their subelements) with respect to at least one object of investigation relevant to communication studies. Furthermore, correlations with explanatory variables are considered on the microanalytical actors' level; the meso-analytical organizational and institutional level; and on the macroanalytical system or cultural level.

Moreover, we assume that the specific structures, norms, and values in political systems shape the political communication roles and behaviors. Therefore, comparative research is often designed in such a way that the countries studied are selected with regard to the contextual conditions of the object of research (Chapter 17, this volume). Thus, the crucial questions to be answered are 1) What always applies regardless of the contextual influences? 2) How does the object of investigation "behave" under the influence of different contextual conditions? Michael Gurevitch and Jay Blumler (Chapter 14, this volume) rightly stress that comparative research "should be designed to realize 'double value.' That is, it should aim to shed light not only on the particular phenomena being studied but also on the different systems in which they are being examined. In other words, more mature comparative research will be 'system sensitive.'" The way in which the context shapes the object of investigation and, conversely, any repercussions on the system resulting from the object of investigation, is of central importance in comparative political communication.

Since the early days of comparative studies, enormous progress has been made with respect to the refinement of research designs. In the meantime, the more demanding studies are built on the logic of "quasi-experimental methods." Researchers select their cases or countries in such a way that they correspond with the differing characteristics of the independent, explanatory variables (e.g., suffrage in countries with the majority vote system versus countries with proportional representation) in different system contexts. The groups in field experiments comparing different countries are then compared to see to which degree the systems differ with respect to the dependent variables (e.g., personalization of election campaign reporting). Such quasi-experimental research designs certainly forbid a strongly causal attribution of explanatory factors for the determined variance of the dependent variable. However, "soft control" of the variance can be achieved by describing systematically the institutional and cultural contexts, and thereby fulfill the requirements "to think structurally, to conceptualize in macro terms, to stretch vertically across levels and horizontally across systems" (Blumler et al. 1992, 8). Against the background of these specifications the understanding of the comparative approach underlying this volume can be complemented in the following way: Comparative political communication research refers to a particular strategy to gain insight that allows for general conclusions, the scope of which cover more than one system and more than one cultural context, and that explains differences (or similarities) between objects of investigation within the contextual conditions of the surrounding systems or cultures.

The comparative research strategy in political communication is not only associated with chances but also risks. The fundamental problem of comparative research in the social sciences lies, as Werner Wirth and Steffen Kolb (Chapter 5, this volume) point out, with the establishing of functional equivalence. The authors show in their chapter that the pitfalls of comparability appear on many levels so that researchers have to make a series of far-ranging strategic decisions when conceiving studies. Among these, the selection of countries and the determining of a quasi-experimental design seem to be among the easier ones. The authors rightly refer to the two strategies that are discussed as "most similar" and "most different systems design" in the literature (Przeworski and Teune 1970). Studies that are based on a "most similar design" make it possible to study the cultural differences in most similar systems. Studies that are based on a "most different design" unearth the similarities in the systems that differ the most. It is more difficult, on the other hand, to determine functionally equivalent constructs, indicators, and methods in such a way that it doesn't amount to contortions and the interpretation of measurement artifacts as differences. The chapter by Wirth and Kolb makes us sensitive to the fact that comparative research rests on many prerequisite and implicit conditions. Moreover, the quality of comparative studies regarding their potential to empirically determine and explain interrelationships all the more depends on whether the research is systematically guided by theory.

The range of themes and research questions associated with comparative political communication research is – as Hans Kleinsteuber (Chapter 4, this volume) points out – enormously broad and diverse. In this respect, comparative research goes well beyond determining similarities and differences between different objects studied. Kleinsteuber stresses that comparative designs fit to analyze complex interrelationships and thereby shed light on processes of diffusion, dependence, temporality, or performance. With respect to political communication, Kleinsteuber's overview reminds us that comparative studies are by no means limited to the prominent subject of election campaign communication, as one may believe from glancing through the literature. In fact, comparisons across countries have been applied in many fields of communication studies and media policy. Moreover, concerning the analysis of media systems we are on the way to understanding international processes of modernization and transformation as well as processes and effects of media regulatory policy. However, Kleinsteuber also emphasizes that some political developments, that is the problem of multilevel governance as observed, for instance, with the expanding competences following European Union integration policy, represent a serious challenge for comparative research.

THE QUESTIONS AND THEMES OF COMPARATIVE POLITICAL COMMUNICATION RESEARCH IN THIS STUDY

The demand for comparative research in political communication is consequential because it requires abstracting from the implicit premises and the national idiosyncrasies in both politics and media communications in the search for generalizable communication patterns and their consequences. Considering the substantial driving forces of comparative research two comprehensive themes stand out. On the one hand, fears concerning the homogenization of media, media contents, and political communication processes as a result of technological, social, and political change led to the debate of concepts of convergence such as Americanization, globalization, and modernization. On the other hand, the suspicion that the media would dominate the modern political publicity process with the implication of dysfunctional effects on modern democracies provoked an exhaustive preoccupation with the structures, actors, media contents, and effects of political communication.

METATHEMES OF COMPARATIVE POLITICAL COMMUNICATION
RESEARCH: AMERICANIZATION, GLOBALIZATION,
AND MODERNIZATION

The idea of a convergence of media systems and of a homogenization of media contents has established itself at a relatively early stage as a process of "Americanization" in the literature. As Daniel Hallin and Paolo Mancini (Chapter 2, this volume) write, "in terms of the kinds of media structures and practices that are emerging and the direction of change in the relation of media to other social institutions, it is reasonable to say that homogenization is to a significant degree a convergence of world media toward forms that first evolved in the United States." Americanization accordingly comprises a targeted, uni-linear diffusion of political communication practices from the United States to other countries. Central parameters of behavioral logic converge with those of the corresponding actors in the United States, irrespective of institutional restrictions. The source of innovation is without doubt the United States, the adoption pattern is an imitation of communication practices that are prevalent there. This view, however, remains for the most part superficial, as it refers only to symptoms and practical patterns of political communication, whereas the institutions of the political system or the organizations and roles of media and political actors are neglected.

Daniel Hallin and Paolo Mancini therefore suggest that the changes in political communication are assigned to the broader and more complex concept of "globalization." This perception implies a reciprocal, free, even conflicting exchange of values, norms, and practices between cultures. The far-reaching integration of modern means of communication facilitates that actors in one country orient themselves to the practices of other countries – including those of the United States – and adopt their strategies. In so doing, however, there is no hierarchical subordinance/superiority, as implied by the term *Americanization*. The perspective of globalization points to mutual interaction or transaction processes of communication stemming from various sources. Many of the structures and behavior patterns that characterize an increasingly homogenous global communication system were in fact first of all observed in the United States. "Where European countries have borrowed American innovations, they have done so for reasons rooted in their own economic and political processes, often modifying them in significant ways" (Chapter 2, this volume).

A decisive shift in perspective regarding the changes in political communication was to attribute these to endogenous causes in the respective countries instead of considering them as consequences of exogenous influences. Approaches that follow the notion of "modernization" or "secularization" (Chapter 2, this volume), refer to changes in political communication as a consequence of a prolonged, universal structural change in politics, society, and media systems, which is generally apparent in modern Western democracies. The developments of political communication thus mark the consequences of a fundamental transformation in society, which has changed the three integral coordinates of the communication system – political actors, media, and the public. With respect to the public, processes of individualization have led to a dilution of traditional patterns of identity formation. The result of this was a loosening of ties with political parties and increasingly volatile elections. In the case of the media this amounted to secularization and commercialization. In accordance with the modernization thesis the structural changes of political actors, media, and the public are attributable to the long-term processes of increasing functional differentiation of modern societies. More or less all modern democracies see themselves confronted with this structural transformation and react to it with specific national adaptation strategies. Some elements of this process can be seen more clearly in the particularly advanced media-centered democracy of the United States than elsewhere.

The contribution of David Swanson (Chapter 3, this volume) takes up the discussion on the developments and the consequences of modernized political communication systems and confronts us with "new realities." The most recent political developments in the United States as well as in Islamic countries make us realize that political communication systems and their effects are profoundly dynamic. It is not only the European systems that are in flux but also the American system, the one that has long been seen as a fairly stable role model. This dynamic complicates the generalization and universal validity of developments, which we observe in political communication. For instance, in the United States there has for a long time been consensus that the increase in political cynicism and the decline of trust in government signify long-term trends that are associated with the functions and political contents of television. The "new" political realities since the terror attacks of September 11, 2001 put a question mark over the previous "wisdom" in the field of political communication. David Swanson (Chapter 3, this volume) judges the sizable increase in Americans' trust in government as an indication that the hitherto evident correlations between media contents and political attitudes only apply in times of national consensus and not at all in times of crisis.

THE MODERN POLITICAL PUBLICITY PROCESS IN AN INTERNATIONAL COMPARISON

The second major theme of comparative communication research refers to the emergence of the modern political publicity process (Blumler and Gurevitch 1995, 84). It is the common denominator of many studies that tackle with the cross-national developments of political communication. Irrespective of whether one sees the cause in exogenous factors of cultural diffusion or in endogenous factors of the transformation of modern Western democracies, the thesis is that the mass media are an independent force for the transformation of political communication. Against the background of this presumption, a series of comparative studies on the structures and processes, the actors and contents, and the effects of political communication have emerged and are introduced in the second part of this volume.

STRUCTURES OF POLITICAL COMMUNICATION. Using classical approaches in democratic theory, Pippa Norris (Chapter 6, this volume) argues that democratization processes are conditional on the activities of the mass media. Media systems must indeed meet a series of fundamental conditions so that they can have a positive effect on democratic development: media freedom and freedom of information, availability of uncensored information, public control of the rulers as well as unhindered articulation of different political standpoints can only be carried into effect if the media are accessible and independent. Pippa Norris examines this hypothesis by testing the correlations between different structural conditions of media systems and indicators of good governance and human development in 135 countries across the world. The analyses substantiate that the normatively postulated positive relationship between democratic government and human development and media systems is manifest only in countries, that meet both conditions of an independent free press *and* open pluralistic access for all citizens.

The standards expected from national media systems also apply, as Sabine Lang (Chapter 7, this volume) ascertains, to communications on the local level. Independent and pluralistic media are a particularly important precondition for the complex and multilayered communication processes in the local public sphere. Sabine Lang discusses the structures and developments of local media and emphasizes in terms of transnational developments that the democratic potential of local press, radio, and television are compromised above all by economic competition and horizontal and vertical concentration processes. This causes a change in the culture of local journalism as well as in local media contents, which is not necessarily beneficial to a pluralistic local public sphere. In view of this disillusioning conclusion, Sabine Lang argues that local communication must not be limited to the local mass media. Rather, the public sphere at a local level is decisively shaped through the contacts and communications of groups in civil society, which in particular make use of the new electronic media for forming networks.

PROCESSES OF POLITICAL COMMUNICATION: POLITICAL MOBILIZATION AND ELECTION CAMPAIGNS. Even though free and independent media have to be considered as necessary structural conditions of the modern democratic process, the logic and the mechanisms of media communications in the Western democracies lead to " 'the growing intrusiveness of media' in politics, resulting in a perception, shared by many influence-seeking political actors, of the greater centrality of the mass media to the conduct of political conflict and its outcomes. This has propelled emergence of a 'modern publicity process,' defined as involving 'a competitive struggle to influence and control popular perceptions of key political events and issues through the mass media'" (Seymour-Ure 1987; Blumler and Gurevitch 1995, 84). One of the merits of comparative research is that it presents concepts and findings that describe this modern political publicity process in a cross-national perspective.

Hanspeter Kriesi (Chapter 8, this volume) characterizes the manifestation of this process as "audience democracy." Essentially, political actors, media, and outsiders mobilize public opinion so as to assert their positions in the political decision making. The mass media act as the motor and means of the mobilization of public opinion. Hanspeter Kriesi discusses which political publicity strategies are successful under which conditions, thereby promoting a model that differentiates between top-down strategies, media strategies, and bottom-up strategies of political actors. Different conditions regarding events, actor constellations, and speaker attributes are connected with each strategy, so that audience democracy appears to be a complex set of interrelations, which, on the one hand, is shaped by situational political constellations and on the other by the structural contexts of the political system and of the media system. Hanspeter Kriesi presents a classification of the system contexts and argues that politically top-down strategies ought, above all, to be successful in majority-vote democratic systems.

The most frequent and most conventional form of mobilization of public opinion in modern Western democracies is the election campaign. During this phase, the modern political publicity process comes to a climax in an almost paradigmatic way. Against this background, it is no wonder that comparative research in the field of election campaign communications is at a very advanced stage. Christina Holtz-Bacha (Chapter 9, this volume) discusses the professionalization of election campaign communications as an answer to the challenges of societal change and the development of the media and asks for evidence that speaks for a convergent development. In her summary of the current research, Christina Holtz-Bacha draws a rather sobering conclusion: On the one hand, the search for transnational developments of election campaign communications in Europe has hardly led to results that can be generalized. Instead, the respective European projects can be cited as prime examples of the theoretical, methodological, and practical difficulties of comparative research. On the other hand, the studies that were inspired by the Americanization-thesis show that the developments in the United States must be considered as the exceptional case in election campaign communications. Christina Holtz-Bacha thus shares the view held by Dan Hallin and Paolo Mancini (Chapter 2, this volume), that we are confronted with processes of modernization in election campaign communications that are highly dependent on the political cultures of the respective democracies.

ACTORS OF POLITICAL COMMUNICATION. The design of the modern political publicity process, as we can describe it in a comparative way, is not least the result of adaptation processes owing to a sustained transformation of the media environment. Comparative studies can make a significant contribution here to describing and explaining how these adaptations are pursued by political actors and journalists.

An important element of the change in the communication environment of political actors is the global expansion of network communications. The Internet brings with it a series of hopes with respect to the opening up of new avenues for democratization, the focus of which is the discussion of "electronic democracy." This notion suggests that the increasing potentials of network communication in modern societies promote political participation and direct relations between citizens and political actors. While the initial studies celebrated the "brave new world of a direct internet democracy" (Küchler 2000, 325), the conclusions in the meantime have become rather sobering. More recent research deals with the implementation of network communication in participatory designs and asks how Internet communication influences political representation within the given structures of political institutions. Against this background, Thomas Zittel (Chapter 10, this volume) poses the question whether electronic democracy needs to be understood as an American concept that only enables democracy to be transformed in association with the specific contextual conditions of the American system of government. Thomas Zittel refers in his study to the actor's level of analysis and investigates the extent to which the Internet is used by parliamentarians in the United States, Germany, and Sweden as a decentralized and interactive means of communication with citizens. His findings point out that technically induced electronic democracy needs to be considered as an American exception. In European party democracies, however, the electronic communication of parliamentarians is secondary to the communication activities between party elites. Thomas Zittel gives the institutional contexts of the political process as the reason for the differences in the use of electronic network communication.

Just as the constitutional conditions of the political process influence the behavior of political actors so do the structural conditions of the media system with respect to the behavior of journalists. Wolfgang Donsbach and Thomas Patterson (Chapter 11, this volume) argue in their chapter that the specific conditions of the environment of journalism – aspects relating to occupational socialization, professional norms, and forms of editorial control – shape the behavior of media actors. Wolfgang Donsbach and Thomas Patterson compare the similarities and differences in the professional behavior of journalists in Western European countries and the United States on the basis of data from the comparative "Media and Democracy" project. Their findings suggest that the essential differences with respect to political attitudes and the understanding of professional and political roles are rooted in different media cultures between the United States and Western Europe. The authors assert in particular that there are significantly more similarities than differences across Western European news systems. Finally, the study refers to the existence of an international consensus with respect to the fundamental duties of journalists.

POLITICAL MEDIA CONTENTS AND THEIR EFFECTS. Journalists create a media reality, which, especially in the format of television news, has become a prominent subject of political communication research. National studies concentrate above all (perhaps against the background of the video malaise hypothesis or agenda-setting research) on the effects of television news on public perception of issues and political orientations. In contrast, comparative studies attempt to gain insight into international news flows and, in the truest sense of the word, images and pictures of the world. One of the driving forces behind this research was, not least, the debate in the 1970s about American cultural imperialism, which was associated with the fear that the voices of the Third World were being systematically overruled by the media of the First World (Chapters 2 and 16, this volume).

Patrick Rössler (Chapter 12, this volume) submits a comparative study of television news. Against the background of an appraisal of the relevant concepts in television news research, he investigates the news geography of television news across different countries. Even though the findings highlight a news geography that focuses on the politically dominant news centers and actors, the data reveal considerable variations and no convergent patterns in international news coverage. Even within the countries studied, the share of concurring reporting is incredibly low. This means that comparative communication research has so far hardly managed to supply empirical evidence for a balanced transnational development in political television news. Against this background, Patrick Rössler rightly calls for further studies and in particular for sustainable theoretical concepts, which help to explain the divergent worldviews in television news.

In some countries the features of political news are directly implicated with the "loss of credibility of politicians and ultimately political apathy" (Blumler and Coleman 2001, 4). David Swanson (Chapter 3, this volume) discusses a series of studies, mainly from the United States, that connect the contents of political news with growing cynicism of citizens toward politicians and politics (Patterson 1993, 1996; Capella and Jamieson 1996, 1997). However, with respect to media effects in election campaigns comparative research can, in the meantime, show differentiated findings that point to an American exception. Rüdiger Schmitt-Beck (Chapter 13, this volume) shows in his study that media effects on voting decisions are in no way to be taken for granted nor do they become apparent in all countries in the same way. In the Western European systems, where significant proportions of the electorate still identify with a particular political party, personal communication has a stronger influence on individual voting decision than does the mass media. If, therefore, strong associations between media contents and political orientations are discovered in the United States, this is not least related to preexisting orientations determined by political culture.

PROSPECTS OF INTERNATIONAL COMPARATIVE COMMUNICATION RESEARCH.
The contributions in this volume show that a variety of aspects of the modern political publicity process have been explored based on scenarios of Americanization, modernization, and globalization. In so doing it hardly comes as a surprise that the established Western democracies exhibit very different modernization phenomena in the field of political communication. The conclusion of the research carried out to date also shows that the prospects of comparative political communication research must not lie in the further accumulation of studies on a multitude of objects of comparison. Instead, Gurevitch and Blumler (Chapter 14, this volume) call for an assertive intellectual strategy, which is aimed at developing a general conceptual framework for future research.

A possible starting point for such a prospect is the conclusion that the various phenomena in political communication can only be explained and interpreted in a meaningful way once they are linked with the respective relevant contexts. If this consideration is consistently taken further, political communication in comparative perspective must be conceived as a system that has a structural and a cultural dimension. The structure of political communication implies the institutional and cultural contexts of the political system and the media system on the macro- and mesolevels. The cultural dimension refers to the observation of actors and denotes the interaction processes of political actors and media actors as well as their preconditions, results, and effects. If political communication processes are conceptualized as interplay of actor's behavior and structural contexts then the comparative approach offers considerable potential for insight. Comparing in that case means varying the structural and contextual conditions in terms of quasi-experimental designs and enquiring as to how the orientations and behavior of the actors are laid out in relation to these contexts.

This view is not new to research in political science. It is the view of political culture, which Michael Gurevitch and Jay Blumler (Chapter 14, this volume) suggest as a future trajectory of comparative political communication: "Just as comparative communication research can be regarded as a subset of the comparative study of culture, comparative political communication research should be seen as the examination of political cultures and their impact on political communication in different societies." The main objective of Michael Gurevitch and Jay Blumler is to identify key dimensions, which are applied in various societies to regulate political communication. The desiderata lie, therefore, in the relationships between political culture and political communication, which include the construction and encoding of political messages, their reception by the public, and the changeable relationships between political culture and the culture of journalism, between citizens and political elites and between media and political institutions.

The perspective of this research agenda is consistently taken further in the chapter by Barbara Pfetsch (Chapter 15, this volume). The concept of political communication culture takes center stage here, and enables comparative analysis of the orientations, which forms the basis of the relationship between political spokespeople and journalists. Barbara Pfetsch argues that in modern Western societies a specific environment of interaction has emerged between political spokespeople and journalists where media and politics overlap that determines the patterns and the results of political communication. The respective type of political communication culture depends on the macrostructural constellations of the political system and the media system. Four different forms of political communication cultures are theoretically outlined and put to discussion. Comparative analyses can contribute to clarifying the question of whether the types of political communication culture that are presented are empirically sustainable and under what postulated macroanalytical conditions they occur. The connection of the structural contexts in the realm of the political system and the media system with the emergence of particular types of political communication culture is demonstrated using the cases of the United States, Germany, Switzerland, and Italy.

Robert L. Stevenson (Chapter 16, this volume) puts the argument of the particular significance of culture on a broader basis. He perceives cultures as communities of values promoting a feeling of togetherness that bestows identity, which often, but by no means always, coincide with national boarders. Robert L. Stevenson identifies culture as a key variable of comparative communication studies and complains that too little attention has been paid to it so far, although he says that expressions such as *intercultural* or *trans-cultural* are used by everybody. He encourages a stronger emphasis on cultures instead of nations when conducting comparative work, and for factual differences between cultures to be acknowledged as well as for them to be systematically considered as descriptive variables. Stevenson provides evidence that the differences discovered in international research can best be described with reference to different (cultural) circles. His social science–based viewpoint leads him, however, to reject cultural studies and other culturally critical approaches because these do not use any strict comparative methodology based on quasi-experimental designs. Furthermore, these approaches would not actually test their initial hypothesis against an alternative hypothesis but instead one-sidedly search for evidence for their substantiation. For these reasons, Stevenson encourages cultural comparisons that follow a social sciences–based empirical perspective.

In the final chapter of this study the most important problems and approaches of comparative research are balanced and integrated. We (Chapter 17, this volume) present a synthesis that systematically links the crucial questions relating to comparative designs, theory formation, and methods and discuss the future challenges of the subdiscipline. Using the prospect of comparative political communication research suggested at the beginning, we present a theoretical macroconcept that can constitute a framework spanning disciplines and nations for the questions presented in this volume. This macroconcept of a political (communication) system links the structural and cultural components of political communication as called for by Michael Gurevitch and Jay Blumler (Chapter 14, this volume) as well as Barbara Pfetsch (Chapter 15, this volume). It might be considered as a starting point for future empirical or theoretical studies. We argue that a mandatory methodology is necessary in order to fully exhaust the specific potential of the comparative research. As called for by the authors of this volume, high methodological standards must be applied to sustainable comparative studies. Our chapter discusses and expounds the problems of this intellectual exercise from the exposure of a research question, concept specifications, and operationalizations to the central decisions with respect to the research design. Thus, we take up opportunities for the interweaving of theories, methods, and the national contexts of comparative studies and develop a framework, within which middle-range theories can be contextualized, generalized, or constructed.

In conclusion, we discuss the problems of the new challenges of comparative research. In the light of globalization in politics and media as well as against the background of the discussion on the emergence of world systems, we ask whether comparative research – as discussed in this volume – is still appropriate at all for understanding these developments. This problem is not trivial as transnationalization threatens to undermine the fundamental principle of comparative research, which assumes independent systems that can be delimited. We suggest that the challenges are met by complementing existing research designs and taking new theoretical aspects and variables into consideration. In view of the processes of globalization and integration it appears necessary with respect to theory building and hypotheses to integrate aspects of international communication and to draw on additional external data sources when developing future research designs.

If comparative political communication research reacts to the challenges of globalization by "modernizing" its theories and study designs, then it is well equipped for another markedly pronounced dynamic development: Comparative research might not just be conceived as a self-contained subdiscipline of communication science, but instead as an indispensable cornerstone of the analysis of (post)modern society.

REFERENCES

Aarebrot, Frank H., and Pal H. Bakka. 1997. Die vergleichende Methode in der Politikwissenschaft. In Dirk Berg-Schlosser, and Ferdinand Müller-Rommel, eds. *Vergleichende Politikwissenschaft.* 3rd ed. Opladen, Germany: Leske + Budrich, pp. 49–66.

Blumler, Jay G., and Stephen Coleman. 2001. *Realising Democracy Online. A Civic Commons in Cyberspace.* London: Citizens Online/Institute for Public Policy Research.

Blumler, Jay G., and Michael Gurevitch. 1975. Towards a Comparative Framework for Political Communication Research. In Steven H. Chaffee, ed. *Political Communication. Issues and Strategies for Research.* Beverly Hills, CA: Sage, pp. 165–93.

————. 1995. *The Crisis of Public Communication.* London: Routledge.

Blumler, Jay G., Jack M. McLeod, and Karl Erik Rosengren, eds. 1992. *Comparatively Speaking. Communication and Culture Across Space and Time.* Newbury Park, CA: Sage.

Bogart, Leo. 2000. *Commercial Culture. The Media System and the Public Interest.* New Brunswick, NJ: Transaction Publishers.

Cappella, Joseph, and Kathleen H. Jamieson. 1996. News Frames, Political Cynicism, and Media Cynicism. *Annals of the American Academy of Political and Social Science* 546: 71–84.

————. 1997. *Spiral of Cynicism: The Press and the Public Good.* New York: Oxford University Press.

Graber, Doris. 1993. Political Communication: Scope, Progress, Promise. In Ada W. Finifter, ed. *Political Science: The State of the Discipline. Part II.* Washington: American Political Science Association, pp. 305–32.

Gunther, Richard, and Anthony Mughan. 2000. *Democracy and the Media. A Comparative Perspective.* Cambridge: Cambridge University Press.

Gurevitch, Michael, and Jay G. Blumler. 1990. Comparative Research. The Extending Frontier. In David L. Swanson, and Dan Nimmo, eds. *New Directions in Political Communication. A Resource Book.* Newbury Park, CA: Sage, pp. 305–25.

Kaase, Max. 1998. Politische Kommunikation: Politikwissenschaftliche Perspektiven. In Otfried Jarren, Ulrich Sarcinelli, and Ulrich Saxer, eds. *Politische Kommunikation in der demokratischen Gesellschaft.* Wiesbaden, Germany: Westdeutscher Verlag, pp. 97–113.

Kohn, Melvin L. 1989. Cross-National Research as an Analytic Strategy. In Melvin L. Kohn, ed. *Cross-National Research in Sociology.* Newbury Park, CA: Sage, pp. 77–102.

Küchler, Manfred. 2000. Mehr Demokratie oder mehr Manipulation? Neue Informations- und Kommunikationstechnologien und politische Willensbildung.

In Oskar Niedermayer, and Bettina Westle, eds. *Demokratie und Partizipation*. Wiesbaden, Germany: Westdeutscher Verlag.

Negrine, Ralph, and Stylianos Papathanassopoulos. 1996. The "Americanization" of Political Communication. *Harvard International Journal of Press/Politics* 1 (2): 45–62.

Patterson, Thomas E. 1993. *Out of Order*. New York: Knopf.

———. 1996. Bad News, Bad Governance. *Annals of the American Academy of Political and Social Science* 546: 97–108.

Pritchard, David, and Florian Sauvageau. 1997. Les 2 Solitudes du Journalisme Canadièn. *L'actualité* June 1: 46–7.

Przeworski, Adam, and Henry Teune. 1970. *The Logic of Comparative Social Inquiry*. Malabar, FL: Krieger.

Schmitt-Beck, Rüdiger, and Katrin Voltmer. 2001. *The Mass Media in Third-Wave Democracies: Gravediggers or Seedsmen of Democratic Consolidation?* Paper prepared for the conference of the CNEP2 project, Santiago de Chile, December 10–13, 2001.

Schoenbach, Klaus. 1998. Politische Kommunikation: Publizistik- und kommunikations–wissenschaftliche Perspektiven. In Otfried Jarren, Ulrich Sarcinelli, and Ulrich Saxer, eds. *Politische Kommunikation in der demokratischen Gesellschaft*. Wiesbaden, Germany: Westdeutscher Verlag, pp. 114–37.

Seymour-Ure, Colin. 1987. Leaders. In J. Seaton, B. Pimlott, eds. *The Media in British Politics*. Aldershot: Avebury.

Swanson, David L. 1992. Managing Theoretical Diversity in Cross-National Studies of Political Communication. In Jay G. Blumler, Jack M. McLeod, and Karl Erik Rosengren, eds. *Comparatively Speaking: Communication and Culture Across Space and Time*. Newbury Park, CA: Sage, pp. 19–34.

Swanson, David L., and Paolo Mancini. 1996. Patterns of Modern Election Campaigning and Their Consequences. In David L. Swanson, and Paolo Mancini, eds. *Politics, Media and Modern Democracy. An International Study of Innovations in Electoral Campaigning and Their Consequences*. Westport, CT: Praeger, pp. 247–76.

Thomass, Barbara, and Michaela Tzankoff, eds. 2001. *Medien und Transformation in Osteuropa*. Wiesbaden, Germany: Westdeutscher Verlag.

Underwood, Doug. 1998. Market Research and the Audience for Political News. In Doris Graber, Denis McQuail, and Pippa Norris, eds. *The Politics of News. The News of Politics*. Washington, DC: Congressional Quarterly Press, pp. 171–92.

PART I

Theories and Methods

TWO

Americanization, Globalization, and Secularization

Understanding the Convergence of Media Systems and Political Communication

Daniel C. Hallin and Paolo Mancini

A powerful trend is clearly underway in the direction of greater similarity in the way the public sphere is structured across the world. In their products, in their professional practices and cultures, in their systems of relationships with other political and social institutions, media systems across the world are becoming increasingly alike. Political systems, meanwhile, are becoming increasingly similar in the patterns of communication they incorporate.

We will explore this trend toward global homogenization of media systems and the public sphere, focusing particularly on the relations between media and political systems, and on the industrialized, capitalist democracies of Western Europe and North America. We will organize our discussion of how to account for this trend around two pairs of contrasting perspectives. Much of the literature on homogenization sees it in terms of Americanization or globalization: that is, in terms of forces *external* to the national social and political systems in which media systems previously were rooted. Other explanations focus on changes *internal* to these national systems. An important distinction can also be made between *mediacentric* perspectives, for which changes in media systems are autonomous developments that then influence political and social systems, and those that see social and political changes as causally prior to media system change.

AMERICANIZATION AND GLOBALIZATION

The phenomenon of homogenization in world media systems was first emphasized as a scholarly issue in the cultural imperialism literature of the 1960s and 1970s. Cultural imperialism theory was obviously a theory of external influence (e.g., Schiller 1969, 1976; Boyd-Barret 1977). It saw homogenization as a result of cultural domination. The global expansion of mass media industries based in advanced capitalist countries and particularly in the United States resulted in the destruction of local cultures and their replacement by a single, standardized set of cultural forms tied to consumer capitalism and American political hegemony. Europe occupied an ambiguous middle position in this literature. European media were seen as part of the dominant Western cultural influence on developing countries; at the same time, the early cultural imperialism literature also raised the issue of U.S. influence over European culture.

The idea that media system change can be understood as a process of Americanization is still very much alive, and there is obviously much truth to it. American programming still dominates many media markets, in some industries – film for example – perhaps as much now as ever before. And at a deeper level, in terms of the kinds of media structures and practices that are emerging and the direction of change in the relation of media to other social institutions, it is reasonable to say that homogenization is to a significant degree a convergence of world media toward forms that first evolved in the United States. The United States was once almost alone among industrialized countries in its system of commercial broadcasting; now commercial broadcasting is becoming the norm. The model of information-oriented, politically neutral professionalism that has prevailed in the United States and to a somewhat lesser degree in Britain increasingly dominates the news media worldwide. The personalized, media-centered forms of election campaigning, using techniques similar to consumer-product marketing, which again were pioneered in the United States, similarly are becoming more and more common in European politics (Butler and Ranney 1992; Swanson and Mancini 1996).

It is clear too that direct cultural diffusion from the United States has played a role in these changes. American concepts of journalistic professionalism and press freedom based in privately owned media, for example, were actively spread by the government-sponsored "free press crusade" of the early cold war period (Blanchard 1986), and reinforced in later years by a variety of cultural influences, ranging from professional education and academic research in U.S. universities and private research institutes (Tunstall 1977; Mancini 2000) to internationally circulated media such as the *Herald-Tribune* and CNN and products of popular culture such as the film *All the President's Men*.[1] American campaign consultants are active in Europe (Plasser 2000), as are American firms that advise television companies on the production of commercially successful news broadcasts. One important recent illustration of American influence is the transformation of the Labor party in Britain under Tony Blair, which involved a shift in the party's structure toward one more suitable for a media-based campaign, drawing on Clinton's earlier experience (Butler and Kavanagh 1997; Jones 1997).

Recent scholarship has tended to subsume the kinds of influences originally identified by cultural imperialism theory under the broader and more complex concept of globalization. From this point of view, attention is focused not on a single country to blame for exporting and imposing a single social imagery, but rather on a complex set of interactions and interdependencies among different countries and their systems of communications (Tomlinson 1991; Thompson 1995). The concept of globalization is clearly more adequate in that it makes it possible to integrate the analysis of external sources of influence with the internal processes of social change that, as we shall see, are clearly essential to understanding change in European media and public sphere. It is certainly possible to affirm that many of the structures and routines that dominate an increasingly homogeneous global communication system were tried and tested in the United States. Their diffusion around the world cannot, however, be attributed to the action of a single agent. It has not been a unilateral process: where European countries have borrowed American innovations, they have done so for reasons rooted in their own economic and political processes, often modifying them in significant ways (Negrine and Papathanassopoulos 1996; Farrell and Webb 2000).

Two important elements of globalization clearly rooted within Europe – though also influenced by developments in worldwide political economy – should be noted here. One is European integration. With the Television without Frontiers Directive of 1989, the European Union (EU) embarked deliberately on an attempt to create a common broadcasting market, an objective that required harmonization of regulatory regimes across the continent. This and other elements of European

---

[1] Rieffel (1984) for example, notes the influence of the *Herald-Tribune* on French journalists (114), and recounts that *L'Express* changed its format in 1964 "à l'imitation de périodiques américaines" (33).

law have undercut the earlier multiplicity of communication policies and patterns of relationship between the media and national political systems. Closely related is a strong trend toward internationalization of media ownership. The search for ever greater amounts of capital to invest in new technologies and to compete in liberalized international markets has produced a strong trend toward the development of multinational media corporations (Herman and McChesney 1997). In order to achieve economies of scale and scope and to take advantage of market integration, such corporations tend to internationalize both products and production and distribution processes, contributing further to the homogenization of strategies and professional practices. The extranational circulation of professionals, the integration of company management within the same group and the universal circulation of the same products can only weaken those national characteristics that, at least in part, had made economic and entrepreneurial systems of individual countries different from each other.

MODERNIZATION AND SECULARIZATION

The term *modernization* has often been proposed as an alternative to *Americanization* in an effort to stress that changes in political communication in Europe are not created purely by exogenous forces, but are rooted in a process of social change endogenous to European society. The term *modernization* is problematic. It carries an evolutionist connotation, for one thing, an implicit assumption that change is to be seen as "progress," necessary and unilinear. It also lumps together many dimensions of change – technological, cultural, political, and economic – that need to be distinguished analytically if we are to be clear about the forces at work, even if we conclude in the end that these different dimensions are interrelated.

One important component of the modernization perspective is the idea that the importance of group solidarity and the centrality of organized social groups is giving way to greater individualism. The European political order, according to this view, was at one time organized around social institutions – political parties, trade unions, and churches, among others – rooted in ideological commitments and group loyalties related to broad social divisions, especially those of social class and religion. The ties of individuals to these groups were central both to their identity and to their material well-being, and the institutions connected with these groups were central to the organization of the public sphere. If political communication is being transformed, this cannot be understood without reference to the collapse of this old political order, and its displacement by a more fragmented and individualistic society. Another term that might help to capture the nature of the change is *secularization*. Just as the Church is no longer able to control the socialization or behavior of populations now attracted to values and institutions that transcend the field of faith, so parties, trade unions, and other institutions that structured the political order Lipset and Rokkan (1967) once described as essentially "frozen" now are not able to hegemonize the course of a citizen's community life.

The "depillarization" of Dutch society is perhaps the classic example of this change. So-called pillarization indicated the subdivision of Dutch society into several religious and political subcommunities. The socialization of Dutch citizens was carried out within these communities, and they structured both political life and the mass media. "These pillars have their own institutions: schools, universities, political parties, hospitals, sport clubs and other associations. It goes without saying that these various pillars also wanted to have their own daily newspapers and periodicals (Nieuwenhuis 1992, 197)." "Each member of each minority could operate within the walls of his or her own confessional pillar, which had its own schools, social facilities, unions, political organizations and institutions (McQuail 1993, 76)." By the 1970s, "the average Dutch citizen had become primarily an individual consumer rather than a follower of a particular religious or political sector" (Nieuwenhuis 1992, 207).

Italian society has gone through a similar change, although at a lower level of institutionalization. For years political subcultures had highly developed institutions of socialization, including education, communication, and entertainment. In the Italian case, this mainly applied to the Communist and Catholic subcultures (Bagnasco 1977; Marletti 1999). The first was built on the basis of political and ideological membership, the second on political and religious membership. Both had ramified structures that organized the participation of citizens in community life, often in a clientelist or semiclientelist fashion. The two subcultures had their own organizations for entertainment and sports and were connected with educational structures; many of their structures served as vehicles of communication. Over the years, these subcultures progressively weakened, surrendering most of their functions to other institutions, including the mass media.

European societies differed in the extent to which different social groups developed their own organizations, as well as in the exact form of the social cleavages and their institutional expressions. This was one reason political and media systems differed across the continent. At the same time, most were characterized in one way or another by a rooting of the party and media systems in organized social groups, and this set them apart from the more individualistic, market-oriented American political and media system.

The "secularization" of European society has been accompanied by a transformation of political life, which has been extensively documented by political scientists. This transformation involves the decline of the mass party, ideologically identified and rooted in distinct social groups, and its replacement by the "catch-all" or "electoral-professional party," oriented not primarily toward the representation of a group or ideology but toward the conquest of electoral market share. This is sometimes interpreted as a "decline of party," though some analysts dispute this interpretation, arguing that professional electoral parties are actually more effective than earlier mass parties at conquering and wielding political power. It does seem to be correct, however, that the stable psychological and sociological bonds that once existed between parties and citizens have been weakened in this transformation. Party membership has declined (as have church and trade union membership). So has party loyalty, measured either by identification with political parties or by partisan consistency in electoral behavior, at least in many cases (in the U.S. case, actually, partisan consistency in voting and political attitudes declined from the 1950s to 1970s, and then subsequently strengthened [Jacobson 2001]). Voting turnout has declined in many countries. "When partisanship was closely tied to class and religion, the conjoint of social and political identifications provided a very strong incentive for party identifiers to turn out. These linkages, however, have withered in recent years . . ." (Dalton and Wattenberg 2000, 66). The grassroots political organizations that once tied parties to citizens have atrophied, while professional staffs concerned with media and marketing have grown. Individual leaders have become increasingly important to the appeal of parties, while ideology and group loyalties have become less so. The shift in Italy from the mass politics of the Communist and Christian Democratic parties to Silvio Berlusconi's Forza Italia, a party created essentially as a vehicle for marketing a single political leader, is a particularly striking symbol of this change, but a similar trend toward "presidentialization" can be seen, in differing degrees, in other cases as well – with Blair in Britain, for example, or Schröder in Germany.

A number of social processes, many of them interrelated, have been identified as possible causes of this transformation of political life. In the sphere of economics, the manufacturing industries in which traditional working-class organizations were rooted have declined, displaced by the growing service sector. Perhaps most fundamentally, European economies have expanded, and it seems likely that increased affluence and the growth of the consumer society resulted in an increasing emphasis on individual economic success rather than political defense of group interests. A contrasting, though not necessarily incompatible interpretation of the effect of economic growth is Inglehart's (1977) argument that affluence and the stabilization of liberal democracy led to the rise of postmaterialist values. This change in political culture is seen as undercutting the ideological divisions on which the old party system was based and making individuals increasingly unwilling to defer to the leadership of traditional organizations. It may in turn be related to the rise of new social movements raising issues that cut across traditional party lines.

These same factors cited by Inglehart – affluence and the consolidation of parliamentary democracy within the context of a capitalist economy – may also be responsible for a marked decline in ideological polarization. There is considerable evidence that the ideological differences between political parties have decreased (Mair 1997, 133). This is probably connected with the acceptance of the broad outlines of the welfare state by conservative parties and of capitalism and liberal democracy by the parties of the left; an important symbol of this shift would be the "historic compromise" that incorporated the Communist Party into the division of political power in Italy in the 1970s. The literature on "plural" societies such as the Netherlands, where the various subcultures had separate institutions at the grassroots level, often notes that the leaderships of these communities became accustomed to cooperation and compromise at the level of national state institutions.

Some accounts of change in European political systems also point to increased education, which might result in voters seeking information independently rather than relying on the leadership of political parties. In some accounts this is connected with a shift from voting based on party and group loyalty to issue-based voting. Some also mention that patronage systems have declined, in part because of economic integration and the pressures it puts on government budgets, undercutting the ability of parties to provide material incentives to their active supporters (Kitschelt 2000). Finally, the rise of new demographic groups as a result of immigration may have weakened the old order, both because the new populations are not integrated into traditional group-based structures and because tensions over immigration lead to the defection of traditional adherents.

Whatever the exact connections among these forces, and whatever the exact weights of their importance, these processes of change have taken place to a significant degree in all of Western Europe. To a substantial degree, they probably account for the shift toward catch-all political parties marketing themselves to individual voters without strong ties to collective organizations. In this sense, they probably account to a large extent for the Americanization of European political communication.

THE ROLE OF THE MEDIA

It is clear that the mass media play an important role in this process of political change; indeed, the increasing centrality of the mass media to the process of political communication is central to the very definition of *Americanization* or *modernization* in most discussions of political change. Does media system change play an independent causal role in this process? Or is it simply one effect of the processes of social change previously noted? Most accounts of political change in Europe list media system change as a significant and independent factor:

> ... [N]ew technologies and ... changes in the mass media ... have enabled party leaders to appeal directly to voters and thereby undermined the need for organizational networks ... (Mair 1997, 39).

> Increasingly ... media have taken over [information and oversight functions] because they are considered unbiased providers of information and because electronic media have created more convenient and pervasive delivery systems. ... The growing availability of political information through the media has reduced the costs of making informed decisions (Flanagan and Dalton 1990, 240–2).

The mass media are assuming many of the information functions that political parties once controlled. Instead of learning about an election at a campaign rally or from party canvassers, the mass media have become the primary source of campaign information. Furthermore, the political parties have apparently changed their behavior in response to the expansion of mass media. There has been a tendency for political parties to decrease their investments in neighborhood canvassing, rallies, and other direct contact activities, and devote more attention to campaigning through the media (Dalton and Wattenberg 2000, 11–12).

The growth of electronic media, especially television, has tended to diminish the role of the party. The electronic media also make it easier to communicate events and issues through personalities... (Dalton et al. 2000, 55).

In most cases, however, media system change is not analyzed with the same rigor as other variables, either conceptually or empirically, and we are left with many ambiguities about what exactly has changed in media systems and how those changes are related to the wider historical process.

"EXPANSION OF THE MEDIA"

In what sense has the media system "expanded"? Certainly, it has not done so in a unilinear manner: there are various countertrends during the late twentieth century, the most significant of which is probably the reduction in the number of newspapers that characterizes most countries, resulting in a disappearance of newspaper competition in many markets. Nevertheless, it is accurate in many ways to say that there has been an expansion of media in the post–World War II period. There are fewer newspapers but they are bigger enterprises, with more pages; the number of journalists has increased; and, most dramatically, new forms of media have evolved. The most important form of media expansion is clearly the growth of electronic media. It is very plausible that the unprecedented reach of electronic media, and their ability to carry messages to the entire population simultaneously, across social and political divisions, changed political communication in important ways, encouraging political parties and other organizations to abandon earlier forms of communication in favor of centralized use of mass media as well as to target audiences outside their original social bases. (Other new information technologies may also have encouraged the shift toward more professionalized and individualized patterns of political communication, including the development of polling, direct mail marketing, and eventually the Internet.) It is also very likely that the increased reach of electronic media, combined with the increased assertiveness of journalists and with commercialization – both of which will be discussed in the following text – have made the media an increasingly central social institution, to a significant extent displacing churches, parties, trade unions, and other traditional organizations of "civil society" as the central means by which individuals are connected to the wider social and political world.

One specific version of the argument that expansion of the media leads to political change is the hypothesis that a "growing availability of political information through the media" makes individual citizens less dependent on party and group leadership. This hypothesis involves particularly tricky issues, and only limited empirical evidence is available. That more political information is available in the abstract is certainly true. But how much political information is actually taken in by the "average" citizen is an extremely complex issue. On the one hand, it is certainly plausible that the rise of electronic media increased the flow of political information, both through their wide reach and their relatively accessible forms of presentation. This may have been especially important in Southern Europe where newspaper circulation is limited. On the other hand, many have argued that the commercialization of media – which we will take up in detail in the following text – creates a powerful countertrend, pushing political content out of the media. Empirical evidence on this point is fragmentary and inconclusive.[2] It may be that the flow of political information did increase up to a point – perhaps in the 1980s – and since has diminished; it may also be that the downward tendency is just beginning. A strong emphasis on public affairs content was clearly one of the distinctive characteristics of European public service broadcasting. Its most important manifestation was the placement of substantial news broadcasts in the heart of prime time, often simultaneously on all available channels. Commercialization and the multiplication of channels is clearly eroding this emphasis – though political content does migrate into new, more entertainment-oriented forms (talk shows and the like) – with uncertain consequences for the net flow of political ideas and information.

TELEVISION AND SECULARIZATION

To understand the impact of electronic media, of course, we need to look beyond their mere existence to their social organization. The electronic media were organized originally in Europe under political authority.

---

[2] Some of the – conflicting – evidence on commercialization of broadcasting is summarized in Brants and Siune 1988. Information – again conflicting – on changing political content in the British press can be found in McLachlan and Golding (2000) and Rooney (2000).

The exact form of governance of broadcasting varied considerably from one system to another, but certainly in many systems political parties had considerable influence on broadcasting systems, as did, in certain cases, what German media law (which gives them a particularly important place) refers to as "socially relevant groups." One might, therefore, have expected electronic media to *reinforce* rather than to undercut the traditional role of political parties and organized social groups.

One account of the impact of television is provided by Wigbold (1979), focusing on the particularly interesting Dutch case. Broadcasting was organized in the Netherlands following the pillarized model that applied to the press, education, and other cultural institutions. Each of the different communities of Dutch society had a separate broadcasting organization, just as they had traditionally had separate schools and newspapers. One might have thought that by extending their reach to a powerful new medium, the pillars would have become even more entrenched in Dutch society. Nevertheless, depillarization clearly did coincide historically with the rise of television. And Wigbold makes the argument that Dutch television "destroyed its own foundations, rooted as they were in the society [it] helped to change" (230).

His argument has three parts. First, he argues that despite the existence of separate broadcasting organizations, television broke down the separateness of the pillars:

> Television was bound to have a tremendous influence in a country where not only the doors of the living room were closed to strangers but also the doors of schoolrooms, union meetings, youth hostels, football grounds and dancing schools. . . . It confronted the masses with views, ideas and opinions from which they had been isolated. . . . [T]here was no way out, no hiding place, except by the difficult expedient of switching the set off. Television viewers could not even switch to a second channel, because there wasn't one. . . . Catholics discovered that Socialists were not the dangerous atheists they had been warned about, Liberals had to conclude that orthodox Protestants were not the bigots they were supposed to be (201).

Second, he argues that television journalists shifted substantially in the early 1960s toward a more independent and critical attitude toward the leaders of established institutions, toward whom they had previously deferred.

Third, a new broadcasting organization (Televisie Radio Omroep Stichting [TROS]) was founded at the end of the 1960s that was the broadcasting equivalent of the catch-all party: originating from a pirate broadcaster, it provided light entertainment and "was the very negation of the broadcasting system based . . . on giving broadcast time to groups that had something to say" (225).

The Dutch case is unique in many ways, of course. Still, it seems likely that each of these factors had close parallels across most of Europe: the role of *television as a common ground*, the development of *critical journalism*, not only in television but in the media generally, and *commercialization*.

TELEVISION AS A COMMON GROUND

Across Europe, broadcasting was organized under political authority, and often incorporated principles of proportional representation drawn from the political world. Nevertheless, it is quite plausible that it served as a social and political common ground and had some role in weakening separate ideological subcultures. It was highly centralized, with one to three channels (of television and of radio) in most of the post–World War II period. Most programming was aimed at the entire public, regardless of group boundaries. The production of news was generally bound by the principle of political neutrality, which separated broadcast journalism from the traditions of partisan commentary that often characterized the print press (in the Dutch case, while the pillarized broadcasting organizations produced public affairs broadcasts, news, similar to sports, was produced by the umbrella organization Nederlandse Omroep Stichting [NOS]). Television entertainment, meanwhile, provided a common set of cultural references, whose impact on political culture would be very difficult to document, but certainly might have been quite significant.

THE JOURNALIST AS "CRITICAL EXPERT"

In both Western Europe and the United States, there was a significant shift in the 1960s and 1970s from a form of journalism that was relatively deferential toward established elites and institutions, toward a relatively more active, independent form of journalism that Padioleau (1985), in a comparative study of *Le Monde* and *The Washington Post*, termed "critical expertise." This shift took place both in electronic and print media. In the case of Swedish television, for example, Djerff-Pierre (2000) writes:

> The journalist culture of 1965–1985 embraced a new ideal of news journalism, that of critical scrutiny. The dominant approach was now oriented toward exerting influence, both *vis-à-vis* institutions and the public at large. . . . [J]ournalists sought to bridge information gaps in society and to equip their audiences for active citizenship and democratic participation. . . . Journalists also had the ambition to scrutinize the actions of policy makers and to influence both public debate on social and political issues and the policies made by public institutions (254).

This shift varied in form and extent, but seems to have been quite generalized across national boundaries. It involved the creation of a journalistic discourse that was distinct from the discourse of parties and politicians, and also a conception of the journalist as representative of a generalized public opinion that cuts across the lines of political parties and social groups. Critical professional journalists, as Neveu (2002, 31) puts it, ". . . spot blunders in strategy, mistakes in governing, from an in-depth knowledge of issues. They question politicians in the name of public opinion and its requests – identified 'objectively' by the polls – or in the name of suprapolitical values such as morality, modernity or the European spirit."

Why did this change take place? Surely it was to a significant extent rooted in the broader social and political changes previously discussed. If, for example, affluence, political stability, and increasing educational levels led to a general cultural shift toward postmaterialist values of participation and free expression, the rise of critical expertise in journalism might be seen as one effect of this deeper social change. If catch-all parties were already being formed in the 1950s – Kirchheimer noted their rise in 1966 – the discourse of a general public opinion made up of individualized voters committed to "suprapolitical" values, which would be crucial to the perspective of critical professionalism in journalism, may predate the latter. Even if the rise of critical professionalism in the media was in part an effect or reflection of other social forces, however, it seems likely that at some point it began to accelerate and amplify them. It is also possible that a number of factors internal to the media system contributed to the shift in the political role of journalism. These include:

(1) Increased educational levels of journalists, leading to more sophisticated forms of analysis, in part by the incorporation into

journalism of critical perspectives from the social sciences and humanities;

(2) Increased size of news organizations, leading to greater specialization and greater resources for news gathering and news processing;

(3) Internal development of the growing professional community of journalism, which increasingly develops its own standards of practice; and

(4) Development of new technologies of information processing that increase the power of journalists as information producers. This includes, of course, the visual techniques of television, as well as many developments in printing and in information technology. One interesting example would be polling: Neveu (2002) argues that opinion polling gave journalists increased authority to question public officials, whose claims to represent the public they can now independently assess.

COMMERCIALIZATION

The most powerful force for homogenization and globalization within the media system, we believe, is commercialization. Commercialization has transformed both print and electronic media in Europe, though the change is especially dramatic in the latter case. In the case of print media, the post–World War II period is characterized by a gradual decline of the party press and general separation of newspapers from their earlier rooting in the world of politics. As party papers have declined, commercial newspapers have grown in strength; these newspapers, similar to their American counterparts, tend to be catch-all papers, defining themselves as politically neutral (though generally liberal and centrist in ideological orientation) and committed to an informational model of journalism. As Curran (1991) and Chalaby (1996) have pointed out, the style of neutral professionalism allows commercial media to maximize their audience, and commercialization clearly tends to favor this style. It is an interesting question as to what extent the shift from party to commercial newspapers reflects the social and political secularization previously discussed and to what extent it results from forces internal to the media system. Did the party press decline because readers were less committed politically, or was it destroyed by competition from the expanding electronic media and commercial press – the commercial press being fed by the expanding consumer society and consequent growth of advertising expenditure? No doubt both processes were at work.

The most dramatic change, however, has clearly been the commercialization of European broadcasting. There is no doubt that starting with the end of World War II a process of progressive weakening of the relatively separate national cultures had already commenced, faced with the growing global flow of messages, products, and institutional forms, mainly coming from the United States. An important restraint to this flow, however, and one that also had consequences for other means of communication, was the prevalence of the public service broadcasting across Europe. Public service broadcasting was regulated by norms and values firmly rooted in the distinct cultural and political paradigms that prevailed in the different nation states of Europe. "Sustaining and renewing the society's characteristic cultural capital and cement" was indeed one of the central missions of public service broadcasting (Blumler 1992, 11). In important ways the public service system limited the social and political impact of television, creating continuity between television culture and the established culture of the wider society.

Regarding Italy, Bettetini (1985) used the expression "pedagogizing palimpsest" (*palinsesto pedagogizzante*) to describe how the primary objective of television programming was education and propagation, creating, among other things, a strong link between television language and the language of traditional literature. Therefore, the great television events of that period were mostly television transpositions of the most important works of Italian and foreign literature, preserving continuity with existing traditions. Another equally important example is that of France where the extremely strong "prescriptive" nature of the public television service tended in a similar way to favor the defense of national identity. French cultural and political traditions were in perfect harmony with the ideal of the "grandeur" of General de Gaulle that permeated French society – and no less French broadcasting – of those years (Vedel and Bourdon 1993). In a similar way, each system strongly tied television to established political institutions.

Commercialization is now dramatically undercutting this system, disrupting the connection between broadcasting and national systems, submitting electronic media to globalizing forces similar to those that prevail in other industries, and spreading cultural forms and professional practices, including those of electronic journalism, that developed originally in the United States, though they now evolve in an increasingly global way. Many of the characteristics commonly attributed to television in discussions of the transformation of political communication – personalization, for example, and the tendency to focus on the experience and perspective of the "common citizen" (Neveu 1999) – are characteristics of commercial media, more than of television as a technology, and were developed only to a limited extent under the public service system (Hallin and Mancini 1984).

The commercial "deluge," as many discussions have characterized it, did not come to Europe in full force until the 1980s, and this certainly suggests that we should be careful about exaggerating the social impact of commercial television. Secularization was well underway before commercial television fully emerged. As the case of TROS in the Netherlands suggests, however, commercial forces were beginning to make themselves felt in a variety of ways before the 1980s: through import of American programs and imitation of American practices, through advertising in some European systems, through pirate and transborder broadcasting, including the important case of the *périfériques* in France, and with the breakdown of the public service monopoly in Italy at the end of the 1970s. It is certainly plausible that if Europe was becoming more of an individualist, consumer society in the 1960s, television and radio did play some role, despite the limits imposed by the public service system.

CONCLUSION

One way to synthesize the many influences discussed in this chapter would be to say that it is driven at the deepest level by the growth of a secularized market society. This is the core of what is generally referred to as modernization, and the deeper meaning of Americanization. It is a global process, and certainly does involve diffusion of cultural and social practices from one country to another, and specifically from America to Europe. At the same time it is clearly rooted in forces internal to Europe – including a deliberate effort to make Europe a "common market" integrated with the world economy – and internal to each individual nation state. The mass media play an important role in this process, and one of its principal effects is to shift social and political power to a significant extent from the "aggregating" institutions of an earlier era – political parties, churches, trade unions, and other "peak organizations" – toward the mass media. It involves a shift, in Mazzoleni's (1987) terms, from "political logic" in the process of communication to "media logic," the latter being a complex phenomenon shaped by technical requirements of the media, the evolution of journalistic professionalism and commercial imperatives. At the same time, deeper social forces are clearly at work, and the changing role of the media can only be understood in the context of a broader process of social change.

The global expansion of the market society has clearly diminished the differences between nationally distinct systems of media and political communication. It is hard to say how far this process of convergence might go. It could lead to complete homogenization, to the point that national differences, including differences between the United States and Europe essentially vanish. It also may be that convergence will stop short of complete homogenization. There are, certainly, structural and cultural differences between the United States and Europe that may prove to be of continued relevance. These include parliamentarism and proportional representation in European political systems, the tradition of the welfare state, and differences in traditions on media regulation, which mean, for example, that many European countries still ban paid political advertising in electronic media – not a small difference from the American media environment.

The implications of these changes for democracy and the public sphere are as complex as the process of change. We cannot explore them fully here. One hint at their complexity can be illustrated by a return to the Dutch example, in which the old regime was undermined, in Wigbold's view, simultaneously by the rise of critical professionalism – by an intensified questioning of established authority that was part of the process of secularization and connected to the rise of new social movements – and by "Trossification," that is, by a flight into the privatism of the consumer society, that was in some sense the other face of the same process of social change. The public sphere thus became more open in certain ways – less bound by the limits imposed by the established political subcommunities and their leaderships – and in other ways less so, as commercial imperatives have imposed new constraints.

REFERENCES

Bagnasco, Arnaldo. 1977. *Tre Italie*. Bologna: Il Mulino.

Bettetini, Gianfranco. 1985. Un fare italiano nella televisione. In Fondazione Giovanni Agnelli, ed. *Televisione: la provvisoria identità nazionale*. Torino: Fondazione Giovanni Agnelli.

Blanchard, Margaret A. 1986. *Exporting the First Amendment: The Press-Government Crusade of 1945–1952*. New York: Longman.

Blumler, Jay. 1992. *Television and the Public Interest*. London: Sage.

Boyd-Barrett, Oliver. 1977. Media Imperialism. Towards an International Framework for the Analysis of Media Systems. In James Curran, Michael Gurevitch, and Janet Woolacott, eds. *Mass Communication and Society*. London: Arnold, pp. 116–35.

Brants, Kees, and Karen Siune. 1998. Politicization in Decline? In Denis McQuail and Karen Siune, eds. *Media Policy: Convergence, Concentration and Commerce*. London: Sage, pp. 128–43.

Butler, David, and Dennis Kavanagh. 1997. *The British General Election of 1997*. London: Macmillan.

Butler, David, and Austin Ranney. 1992. *Electioneering*. Oxford: Clarendon.

Chalaby, Jean K. 1996. Journalism as an Anglo-American Invention. A Comparison of the Development of French and Anglo-American Journalism, 1830s–1920s. *European Journal of Communication* 11 (3): 303–26.

Curran, James. 1991. Rethinking the Media as a Public Sphere. In Peter Dahlgren and Colin Sparks, eds. *Communication and Citizenship. Journalism and the Public Sphere in the New Media Age*. London: Routledge, pp. 27–57.

Dalton, Russell J., Ian McAllister, and Martin P. Wattenberg. 2000. The Consequences of Partisan Dealignment. In Russell J. Dalton and Martin P. Wattenberg, eds. *Parties without Partisans: Political Change in Advanced Industrial Democracies*. Oxford: Oxford University Press, pp. 37–63.

Dalton, Russell J., and Martin P. Wattenberg, eds. 2000. *Parties without Partisans. Political Change in Advanced Industrial Democracies*. New York: Oxford University Press.

Djerff-Pierre, Monika. 2000. Squaring the Circle. Public Service and Commercial News on Swedish Television 1956–99. *Journalism Studies* 2 (2): 239–60.

Farrell, David M., and Paul Webb. 2000. Political Parties as Campaign Organizations. In Russell J. Dalton and Martin P. Wattenberg, eds. *Parties without Partisans: Political Change in Advanced Industrial Democracies*. New York: Oxford University Press, pp. 102–12.

Flanagan, Scott, and Russell J. Dalton. 1990. Parties under Stress. In Peter Mair, ed. *The West European Party System*. New York: Oxford University Press, pp. 232–46.

Hallin, Daniel C., and Paolo Mancini. 1984. Speaking of the President: Political Structure and Representational Form in US and Italian TV News. *Theory and Society* 13: 829–50.

Herman, Edward, and Robert McChesney. 1997. *The Global Media. The New Missionaries of Corporate Capitalism*. London: Cassel.

Inglehart, Ronald. 1977. *The Silent Revolution. Changing Values and Political Styles among Western Publics*. Princeton: Princeton University Press.

Jacobson, Gary. 2001. A House and Senate Divided. The Clinton Legacy and the Congressional Elections of 2000. *Political Science Quarterly* 116: 5–27.

Jones, Nicholas. 1997. *Campaign 1997. How the General Election Was Won and Lost*. London: Indigo.

Kirchheimer, Otto. 1966. The Transformation of the West European Party Systems. In Joseph LaPalombara and Myron Weiner, eds. *Political Parties and Political Development*. Princeton: Princeton University Press, pp. 50–60.

Kitschelt, Herbert. 2000. Citizens, Politicians and Party Cartelization. Political Representation and State Failure in Post-Industrial Democracies. *European Journal of Political Research* 37: 149–79.

Lipset, Seymour M., and Stein Rokkan. 1967. *Party Systems and Voter Alignments. Cross-National Perspectives.* New York: Free Press.

Mair, Peter. 1997. *Party System Change. Approaches and Interpretations.* Oxford: Clarendon Press.

Mancini, Paolo. 2000. Political Complexity and Alternative Models of Journalism: The Italian Case. In James Curran and Myung-Jin Park, eds. *De-Westernizing Media Studies.* London: Routledge, pp. 265–78.

Marletti, Carlo, ed. 1999. *Politica e società in Italia.* Milano: Angeli.

Mazzoleni, Gianfaranco. 1987. Media Logic and Party Logic in Campaign Coverage. The Italian General Election of 1983. *European Journal of Communication* 2 (1): 81–103.

McLachlan, Shelly, and Peter Golding. 2000. Tabloidization and the British Press. A Quantitative Investigation into Changes in British Newspapers, 1952–1997. In Colin Sparks and John Tulloch, eds. *Tabloid Tales. Global Debates Over Media Standards.* Oxford: Rowman & Littlefield, pp. 75–90.

McQuail, Denis. 1993. Dutch Public Service Broadcasting. In Robert K. Avery, ed. *Public Service Broadcasting in a Multichannel Environment. The History and Survival of an Ideal.* New York: Longman, pp. 75–92.

Negrine, Ralph, and Stylianos Papathanassopoulos. 1996. The "Americanization" of Political Communication. *Harvard International Journal of Press/Politics* 1 (2): 45–62.

Neveu, Erik. 1999. Politics on French Television. Toward a Renewal of Political Journalism and Debate Frames? *European Journal of Communication* 14 (3): 379–409.

————. 2002. The Four Generations of Political Journalism. In Raymond Kuhn and Erik Neveu, eds. *Political Journalism. New Challenges, New Practices.* London: Routledge, pp. 22–43.

Nieuwenhuis, J. 1992. Media Policy in The Netherlands: Beyond the Market. *European Journal of Communication* 7 (2): 195–218.

Padioleau, Jean G. 1985. *Le Monde et Le Washington Post: Précepteurs et Mousquetaires.* Paris: Presses Universitaires de France.

Plasser, Fritz. 2000. American Campaign Techniques Worldwide. *Harvard International Journal of Press/Politics* 5 (4): 33–54.

Rieffel, Rémy. 1984. *L'Élite des Journalistes: Les Hérauts de L'Information.* Paris: Presses Universitaires de France.

Rooney, Dick. 2000. Thirty Years of Competition in the British Tabloid Press: The Mirror and the Sun 1968–1988. In Colin Sparks and John Tulloch, eds. *Tabloid Tales. Global Debates Over Media Standards.* Oxford: Rowman & Littlefield, pp. 91–109.

Schiller, Herbert I. 1969. *Mass Communications and American Empire.* Boston: Beacon Press.

————. 1976. *Communication and Cultural Domination.* White Plains, NY: International Arts and Sciences Press.

Swanson, David, and Paolo Mancini, eds. 1996. *Politics, Media and Modern Democracy.* Westport, CT: Praeger.

Thompson, John B. 1995. *The Media and Modernity.* Cambridge: Polity.

Tomlinson, John. 1991. *Cultural Imperialism: A Critical Introduction.* Baltimore: Johns Hopkins University Press.

Tunstall, Jeremy. 1977. *The Media Are American.* London: Constable.

Vedel, Thierry, and Jérome Bourdon. 1993. French Public Service Broadcasting. From Monopoly to Marginalization. In Robert K. Avery, ed. *Public Service Broadcasting in a Multichannel Environment. The History and Survival of an Ideal*. New York: Longman, pp. 29–52.

Wigbold, Herman. 1979. Holland: The Shaky Pillars of Hilversum. In Anthony Smith, ed. *Television and Political Life: Studies in Six European Countries*. London: Macmillan, pp. 191–231.

THREE

Transnational Trends in Political Communication

Conventional Views and New Realities

David L. Swanson

Political communication systems are dynamic, constantly evolving, never settled. Just when we think we understand how it all works, things change. Sometimes the changes seem to be evolutionary, steps along a path that leads to a destination we can foresee. At other times, the familiar path turns in new and unexpected directions.

Quite recently, the transnational trends in political communication that have been observed in many countries over the preceding decade have taken some unexpected turns. In some ways, these new turns challenge the conventional wisdom that emerged from many comparative studies. In other ways, the new turns confirm the conventional wisdom. We cannot yet know where the new turns will lead, but we do know that our settled views must be revisited. It is ever thus in the study of political communication. The game is always afoot.

This chapter describes some of the conventional wisdom concerning transnational trends in political communication that has emerged from comparative studies, then identifies recent developments that seem alternately to confirm and challenge the received view. The chapter concludes by considering what we may learn from the new realities and where the new paths may lead.

TRANSNATIONAL TRENDS: THE CONVENTIONAL VIEW

The search for transnational trends in political communication through comparative studies hardly seems old enough to have a history. It was in 1975 that Blumler and Gurevitch (1975, 165) proposed a comparative framework for studies of political communication, noting that "few political communication studies have yet been mounted with a comparative focus" and that "comparative political communication research must be the least advanced topic dealt with in this volume [of approaches to the study of political communication]." By 1992, they were able to survey with some satisfaction the accomplishments of a growing number of comparative studies, even as they still felt it necessary to argue to researchers that comparative studies were needed and could produce results that are uniquely interesting and valuable (Blumler and Gurevitch 1992).

Throughout the 1990s, the number of explicitly comparative studies and nationally focused studies with comparative dimensions grew steadily (e.g., Semetko et al. 1991; Butler and Ranney 1992; Kaid and Holtz-Bacha 1995; Maarek 1995; Scammell 1995; LeDuc et al. 1996; Negrine 1996; Swanson and Mancini 1996b; Åsard and Bennett 1997; Mayhew 1997; Swanson 1999). There began to emerge from many of these studies something similar to a conventional *fin de siècle* view of transnational trends in political communication. Not all scholars of political communication accept this view, of course, but many do, and even the dissenters use the conventional view as a starting point for their own analyses (e.g., Negrine and Papathanassopoulos 1996).

According to the conventional view, modern political communication is shaped by some transnational trends that have led to structurally similar but by no means identical consequences in each country, and especially in countries that have advanced media systems. The underlying process is one of adaptation, where national institutions and practices shape in locally appropriate ways the manner in which transnational trends become manifest in each country. National studies reveal, among other things, how the practices of political communication always reflect particular political cultures, institutions, actors, histories, and circumstances. The contribution of comparative studies is to reveal transnational trends and similarities that become evident when we step back from the uniqueness of political communication in each country in order to take a broader view.

SECULAR POLITICS

One of the trends that comparative studies have noted in many democracies is the secularization of politics. Across many of the older democracies and for various reasons that are well documented in both national and comparative studies, the relationship between voters and political parties over the last few decades has become less a relationship based on identity and long-term commitment and more a relationship based on persuasion in which voters, lacking enduring political convictions, are induced to support a particular candidate or party at election time. It may be helpful to understand this change as a transition from a sacred politics to a secular politics. Politics takes on some elements of the "sacred" when it is an expression of community, with political leaders and parties arising as expressions of the particular collective identity and aspirations of their followers. Traditional political cleavages based on class or region long found expression in political parties, as did great mobilizing ideals such as social justice and individual freedom. When citizens found their identity in collectives and regarded political parties as vehicles for expressing the collectives' values, claims, and aspirations, party campaigns mobilized masses of voters in great crusades.

In the postindustrial era, sweeping social and economic changes have eroded the traditional bases of support for political parties. In the twenty-first century, the fault lines that divide voters are more personal than collective, constantly shifting and intersecting, giving rise to identities that are unstable, complex, and fragmented. Voters are less likely to see their identities as contained within and expressed through membership in a collectivity, and the political parties' appeals to traditional economic and social interests and ideals do not resonate with citizens' new concerns about matters such as lifestyle issues and the environment that have not been part of the political parties' traditional portfolios of issues. In the face of such issues, political institutions may seem less effective than new power centers that have emerged outside the political system.

One such power center reflects corporate globalization. The integration of capital, information, and technology across national borders is creating international corporate institutions and alliances that wield economic, political, and cultural power beyond the control of national institutions. Public protests directed against meetings of the World Trade Organization (WTO), for example, make it clear that citizens in many countries understand the growing strength and apparent autonomy of these power centers.

A second power center consists of the growing number of nongovernmental organizations, both national and international, that offer citizens vehicles for action on issues they care about and increasingly are given voice in national and transnational policy forums.

A third power center consists of proliferating single-issue groups, protest movements, and voluntary associations of all kinds that are found in the advanced democracies. The United Kingdom, for example, is described by Alderman (1999, 128) as having become "two nations politically: . . . that of [the] two parties which continue to monopolize power at the parliamentary and governmental level and . . . that of the single issue groups and protest movements, whose membership has long since outstripped the active grassroots support the parties can call upon." Alderman's point applies equally well to a number of countries, and especially to the United States where the political influence of powerful lobbying groups of all kinds is widely discussed and fully appreciated by citizens.

The changing political landscape has rendered the old discourse of politics quaint rather than compelling and engendered a fundamental change in how political communication is practiced and received by citizens. As Waisbord (1996, 220–1) observed about politics in Argentina,

> The aura of ideological faiths has disappeared and ancient idols have fallen. Argentine political culture has been secularized. Pragmatism has diluted the magic of discourses that impregnated party life and political debates . . . [with] sublime aspirations [for] national sovereignty, liberty, and social justice. . . . In recent elections, voters have demanded less celestial and more terrestrial goods: economic stability . . . better education, and safer cities. The vanishing of the charm and romanticism of old rallying cries looms behind the transformations in electioneering. Formerly strong identities have become thinner, and ideological convictions that dominated policymakers have receded in favor of pragmatic solutions. This cultural transformation has undermined the bases upon which the old campaigning order was grounded.

Argentina is an especially clear case of the clash between the old politics of faith and redemption and the new politics of opinion and pragmatism, but the same sort of change has been noted generally across the older democracies (see Mayobre 1996; Mazzoleni 1996; Dogan 1997; Giddens 1999; Mazzoleni and Schulz 1999). Everywhere, it seemed, political parties found themselves no longer able to command so fully the loyalties of their traditional partisans by repeating old political rituals and the timeworn themes of their traditional political rhetoric. The crisis of political parties was the growing perception that they were not relevant to contemporary voters' interests and concerns. Thus, parties faced the need to find new bases for appealing to voters in the increasingly volatile electoral environment.

Political Marketing

To adapt to their altered circumstances and remain viable, the major parties in many countries turned to experts in marketing and public relations, opinion polling, and other techniques to discover how they could effectively appeal to citizens. In place of or in addition to traditional campaign practices such as rallies of the party faithful, they relied on the sophisticated use of the mass media to persuade voters – the "consumers" of political communication – to support them at election time, and they offered campaigns that featured the appealing personalities of party leaders (e.g., Franklin 1994; Kavanagh 1995; Maarek 1995, 1997; Scammell 1995, 1999; Blumler et al. 1996; Negrine 1996). Some of the best studies that revealed these phenomena to be emerging in many democracies were explicitly comparative (e.g., Butler and Ranney 1992; Kaid and Holtz-Bacha 1995; Swanson and Mancini 1996b; Holtz-Bacha 1999; Mancini 1999; Mazzoleni and Schulz 1999).

In older democracies, the transition from traditional methods of political electioneering to media campaigns based on political marketing was incremental, taking place in steps over a period of years. In newer democracies such as Spain and Russia, for example, the media-intensive "modern model of political campaigning" (Swanson and Mancini 1996a, 249–52) was well developed when the transition to democracy began and was adopted more or less intact as the model for how democratic electioneering would be done.

However quickly or fully it has been adopted, the modern model of campaigning has been identified with some important and fundamental changes in political parties and their relationship to voters. The media-intensive modern model has brought the professionalization of political campaigning, as technical experts in using mass media, opinion polling, and marketing techniques have been brought into political parties – sometimes as consultants, sometimes as party employees or officials – and been given voice in party decision making (one difference in how the modern model has been adopted in different countries concerns the degree of authority given to the professional experts).

As political campaigning has been professionalized, the content of campaigns – and the nature of the political parties that are most successful – also has changed. The modern model is, above all, a model for how to win elections. It leads to catch-all political parties and catch-all political campaigns, in which the parties try to appeal to the broadest range of political opinions and, thereby, the greatest number of voters. In consequence, parties driven by the modern model tend to seek broad,

centrist positions that shift with changes in voters' opinions in preference to defined programs and sustained ideological commitments. At the
core of the modern, catch-all political campaign is, often, the personality
of the party leader, whose appealing qualities are featured to catch the
attention and support of voters.

The modern model of campaigning has also become the modern
model of political communication in governing more generally, as so
many have observed. With political power resting on the transitory opinions of voters whose support must be cultivated continuously through
communication, the culture of image management and perpetual spin
has come to dominate the discourse of political leaders and government
officials. Political marketing has thus become a critical part of what are
considered the primary functions of government.

POLITICAL NEWS AS EXPOSÉ

One of the transnational trends that led to development of the modern
model of political communication is the proliferation of mass media
driven by commercial values. The expansion of privately owned media
to compete with public broadcasters has created in nearly every country
an intensely competitive media environment. There is greater pressure
than ever before on news media to compete for audiences in a market in
which it is increasingly difficult to do so. This competitive pressure has
been identified as one of the causes of particular changes in the content
and character of news, especially news about politics (e.g., Hvitfelt 1994;
McManus 1994; Underwood 1995; Pfetsch 1996).

In general, intensified competition and growing commercialization
of the media sphere are thought to have led to greater infusion of entertainment values into editorial decisions and political reporting, covering
politics "only in the ways and to the extent that it is good business to
do" in order to attract and hold the audience (Swanson 1997, 1269). The
competitive pressures driving construction of political news have been
linked to, among other things, "sound bite" coverage in which political actors have little opportunity to express their thoughts in their own
words (e.g., Hallin 1992), and coverage of politics that centers always
on conflict, such as "horse race" news that covers election campaigns
as suspenseful contests more than policy disagreements (e.g., Patterson
1993, 1996; Cappella and Jamieson 1996, 1997).

With mass media becoming the arena in which so much of politics
and government is conducted and presented to the public, news coverage of politics and government has assumed greater importance to

political actors than ever before. As a result, politicians and officials have become more sophisticated and effective at manipulating news coverage by such means as staging events that are guaranteed to satisfy journalists' commercial need for interesting video pictures, timing statements and actions to meet news deadlines, staying "on message" to attract coverage to well-chosen campaign themes, and the omnipresent "spin" by which political actors try to shape journalists' reports to partisan advantage. Not surprisingly, journalists in many countries have sought to resist politicians' manipulation and assert their own independence. This growing adversarialism between journalists and politicians has been noted in a number of studies (e.g., Blumler and Gurevitch 1995; Bennett 1996; Fallows 1997; Blumler and Coleman 2001). One consequence of growing adversarialism is an increasingly negative view of politics and politicians offered in political news stories, which seek to expose political actors' statements and actions as public relations ploys and which have become less documentary and more heavily interpretive, emphasizing the journalists' own views (e.g., Patterson 1993, 1996; Barnhurst and Steele 1997; Blumler and Kavanagh 1999; Mancini 1999).

In a number of important studies, these attributes of political news have been linked to citizens' growing cynicism about politics and politicians (e.g., Patterson 1993, 1996; Cappella and Jamieson 1996, 1997). As Blumler and Coleman observe, "A seemingly unbreakable chain links the centrality of the media in modern politics with politicians' adaptations to news imperatives, the emergence of 'spin politics,' journalists' frequent and aggressive disclosure of such politics, politicians' loss of credibility, and finally public apathy" (4).

THE CONVENTIONAL VIEW: AN ASSESSMENT

As the modern model of campaigning became the model of political communication – in governing as well as at election time – in more countries, researchers became more convinced that it is corrosive to the health of democracy. The forces that drove the emergence of the modern model – the rise of the postindustrial economy, the decline of the influence of traditional institutions, the weakening of bonds to class and region, the expansion of commercial mass media, growing public concern about issues and topics that were not in the political parties' traditional portfolios, the growing feeling that centers of economic power and influence were becoming transnational and beyond the control of any government, and so on – seemed to be inexorable. The consequences of the modern political communication model seemed to be public apathy and cynicism about politics and government, a style of journalism that was more entertaining but less informative, and an approach to governing that was closely bound with public relations. Realistically, the prospects for reversing the trend were not encouraging. Blumler and Coleman summarized the British experience in this way: "communications as presently organized is sucking both the substance and the spirit out of the politics it projects. This is naturally mistrusted and spurned by many of the independent-minded and wary electors who form its intended audience. Yet their chances of enjoying a more nourishing or engaging supply of messages from a public service broadcasting system in crisis, or from a press system embroiled in circulation wars must be rated as no better than slim" (2001, 4).

This brief summary of the conventional view is, of course, an overly simplified portrait. It stresses the common themes that have emerged from transnational studies but gives insufficient attention to the complex influences that shape the specific forms those themes take in each country. Those influences – such as the role played by different electoral systems, approaches to regulating political communication, different structures of political competition, different national political cultures – are discussed at length elsewhere (e.g., Swanson and Mancini 1996a). It is to these influences we must look to explain the particular forms that modern political communication takes in each country, and the rich variety of practices we see – where sophisticated media campaigns sometimes exist side by side with traditional customs and at other times overwhelm traditional communications altogether. Overly simplified as it is, however, this summary of the traditional view serves well enough to set the stage for understanding how the "new realities" discussed in the following text raise such questions about whether the forces that shaped political communication in so many countries in the 1980s and 1990s really are inexorable, and whether the conventional view grants too much power and autonomy to political communication.

TRANSNATIONAL TRENDS: SOME NEW REALITIES

Two recent developments give reason to question some of researchers' settled views about the evolving models of political communication and their inevitable consequences. One development concerns whether public cynicism about politicians and government is in fact the inescapable result of modern political communication. A second development concerns whether the coalescence of transnational broadcast journalism necessarily undermines local viewpoints and political cultures, and thus leads to acceptance everywhere of a recognizable modern model of political communication. These developments and their implications for how we understand political communication are discussed in the following text.

Seasons of Trust, Seasons of Cynicism

As noted, some common forces have been discovered to be acting on media institutions and systems in most nations. These forces include intensified competition for audiences in an arena in which more television viewers, especially, have ready access to more choices than ever before, including in many countries choices of broadcasts that originate in other countries or are offered by transnational services. The need to compete for audiences has been cited as leading both private and public broadcasters to adopt approaches to journalism that are more commercial, infusing news decisions and the content of news stories with entertainment values to a greater extent than before. In this way, broadcast journalists endeavor to increase the audiences for their newscasts to include more viewers who lack an abiding interest in public affairs and current events but may be attracted to stories that are entertaining in their own right. This development has been documented extensively in television news coverage of politics and government in many countries (e.g., Franklin 1997; Mazzoleni and Schulz 1999; Neveu 1999).

At the same time, other broad forces have been thought to be shaping institutions of politics and government in many countries. As we have seen, these forces have been thought to undermine citizens' traditional loyalties and sense of identification with political parties. In turn, political parties have turned to marketing approaches to win the support of voters at election time and to maintain the approval of citizens when the parties are in government. One element of the marketing approach is use of strategies to manipulate journalists to give to politicians the frequent and favorable coverage that is thought to be essential to political success. As politicians' efforts to orchestrate news coverage have become more sophisticated and successful, journalists have struggled to assert their independence in a style of political news that is more adversarial and disdainful of politicians. The result has been a trend in numerous countries toward political journalism that is less concerned with reporting politicians' actions and statements but more concerned with exposing the political motives behind what politicians do and say. In this way, many believe, news about politicians has become more negative in its tone, more skeptical of leaders' motives, and more centered on the journalists as independent actors and adversaries of politicians (e.g., Semetko et al. 1991; Franklin 1994; Bennett 1996; Steele and Barnhurst 1996; Barnhurst and Steele 1997; Fallows 1997; Patterson 2000).

These trends produce a style of political journalism that portrays politics and politicians in terms that are most unflattering, as actors who are concerned primarily with their own power and influence and whose words cannot be taken at face value. It is not surprising that such journalism has been cited as a cause of growing public cynicism and mistrust of political actors and institutions. High levels of cyncism about politics have been noted in all the Western democracies, accompanied by doubts about the political system's effectiveness, responsiveness, and especially, relevance. Some of the blame for voters' mistrust has been placed on these transnational trends in political journalism (e.g., Patterson 1993, 1996; Cappella and Jamieson 1996, 1997).

Cynicism has been documented extensively in the United States. In a 2000 national survey in the United States, 87 percent of respondents agreed that "most politicians are willing to say whatever it takes to get elected," and 71 percent agreed that "politics in America is pretty disgusting" (Patterson 2002). Such cynicism has been rising for a number of years. Around 1960, about 75 percent of the American public believed that they could trust "the people in Washington to do what is right" always or most of the time, but only 25 percent held this belief by 1995. Cappella has noted that "Although these changes in trust in governmental institutions are not uniform over time, they do exhibit a consistent pattern of declining trust, and that decline applies to every agency at every level of government" (2002, 231).

As disenchantment with democratic politics and institutions, along with low rates of citizen participation in traditional forms of political expression, were noted in both older, established democracies as well as some of the new democracies (e.g., Dogan 1997; Giddens 1999; Norris 1999), it came to seem that growing skepticism about traditional political institutions was an unavoidable consequence of the modern model of political communication. The marketing strategies used by catch-all political parties and the negative news coverage of politics, together, appeared to lead inexorably to erosion of the public's confidence in government. Thus, a key question facing those who were concerned about the health and future of democracy concerned how to reverse the steadily growing cynicism that publics everywhere felt toward democratic politics.

In the United States, the seeming irreversibility of public cynicism was called into question in the aftermath of the September 11, 2001 terrorist attacks on the World Trade Center in New York City and the Pentagon in Washington, DC. Within a matter of days, the American public evinced a striking reversal of its attitudes toward politics and government. Confidence in government, in governmental leaders, and especially in the military rose dramatically. A study among university students conducted by Harvard University's Institute of Politics in mid-October, 2001 – historically members of the cohort of young voters who feel most alienated from traditional politics – found that 75 percent trusted the military to do the right thing, 69 percent trusted the president, and 62 percent trusted the Congress. Fully 77 percent said that politics is relevant to their lives, compared to 68 percent who gave the same response a year earlier. And 60 percent trusted the federal government to do the right thing all or most of the time, compared to only 36 percent who trusted the federal government in the 2000 survey.

Elevated levels of trust and confidence in government may reflect only a momentary response to a national crisis. We are not yet far enough removed from the September 11 attacks to know whether the long-term trend toward rising cynicism will be affected. And, the example of the short-term U.S. response to terrorist attacks does not make a compelling case for a more general proposition about whether or not high levels of cynicism are irreversible. Speaking to the more general question, Karol Jakubowicz observed during Poland's transition to democracy that "the media's influence on election results is in inverse proportion to the gravity of issues facing the voters, the stakes involved for them personally in the election" (1996, 135).

The issue raised by these developments is this: Perhaps it is the case that, in times of broad national consensus over goals and aspirations, when there are no internal or external crises, the marketing strategies that mass parties use to attempt to create political interest and the disdainful practices by which journalists cover these strategies fuel public cynicism and skepticism. These are also times during which most members of the public have little interest in politics and follow the actions of government and leaders with only casual interest except when those actions affect individual citizens directly. But maybe things change when a genuine crisis presents itself, or when the national consensus breaks down and real, substantive disagreements polarize the public. At such times, perhaps the trends in political communication that have seemed irreversible do indeed reverse themselves, at least for a time. Put another way, perhaps the trends we have been observing reflect the fact that, in the countries most studied, a broad national consensus has been in place for a number of years, so our conventional view of seemingly permanent transnational trends is, in fact, a snapshot of what happens during times of broad consensus but not at other times.

This question challenges us to step back from the conventional wisdom and look again, across a broader horizon, to see if there are limitations to the conventional view that have not so far been acknowledged. Is it possible that we have overestimated the autonomy of political communication and underestimated the importance of the social, economic, and political context in which citizens receive and understand messages about politics?

THE EFFECT OF GLOBALIZED TELEVISION NEWS PRACTICES

The conventional view rightly stresses the many ways in which political journalism shapes political communication. In country after country, many of the same themes and practices have come to dominate political journalism. Although there remain important national differences, of course, the similarities are striking. With ample evidence that modern political communication is, in part, a reaction to modern political journalism, it is easy to imagine that the spread of the modern model of political communication is fueled particularly by the convergence of political journalism on a common set of professional practices.

"Globalization" in news is more than just the newest phase in a process that began with development of the news wire services. Rather, the proliferation of formal and informal links binding national, regional, and international news broadcasters is thought by many to have created a new phenomenon. Increasingly, television news services around the world have become interconnected within a global system. The proliferation of communication satellites, expansion of international news video services, organization of regional television news exchanges, and growth of international satellite-delivered news services are key elements of this global system. The system not only provides alternative news sources through transnational satellite services but also penetrates national systems as coverage of events beyond national borders is routinely acquired from interconnected regional and global production and distribution systems.

An impressive number of studies have documented similarities in the practices of television news around the world (e.g., Cohen et al. 1990; Straubhaar et al. 1992; Cohen et al. 1996). In most cases, the similarities have been attributed to Western practices coming to serve as a professional model for the rest of the world (Nasser 1983; Straubhaar et al. 1992). As a result, scholars have speculated about a "transnational news-value culture" (Cohen et al. 1990, 44) in which, regardless of their location, television journalists share a common professional culture, one that reflects a Western view of what counts as news and how it should be reported (Swanson and Smith 1993).

Recently, this settled view of the Western-oriented, transnational news-value culture has been questioned by the success of the Al-Jazeera Satellite Channel, a television news broadcaster based in Qatar. Al-Jazeera received worldwide attention as a result of its extensive and sometimes exclusive coverage of the Israeli-Palestinian conflict and the Afghan war, especially when it was the only broadcaster allowed to remain in Afghanistan during the early stages of the war and was also the only broadcaster to receive and televise videotapes of Osama bin Laden. Al-Jazeera was established in 1996 with a subsidy from the emir of Qatar, who planned for it to be "an independent and nonpartisan satellite TV network free from government scrutiny, control, and manipulation" (El-Nawawy and Iskandar 2002, 33). Al-Jazeera receives a large annual subsidy from the emir (although it hopes to become self-supporting soon through growing advertising revenue) and has a staff of 350 journalists and fifty foreign correspondents working in thirty-one countries around the world. The core of this staff consists of journalists who were hired when the BBC Arabic TV Service was closed in 1996, so that Al-Jazeera began with an editorial staff that was thoroughly trained in the Western news tradition but also, unlike Western media, was deeply knowledgeable about Arab politics (El-Nawawy and Iskandar 2002).

Al-Jazeera broadcasts in Arabic twenty-four hours a day with a mix of Western-style news programs, political talk, and call-in shows. Its editorial independence sets it apart sharply from other Arab broadcasters, who work mostly in government-controlled media and are constrained to support the views of their national governments and not to give voice to opposition spokespersons. In contrast, the journalistic models employed on Al-Jazeera are distinctly Western. Hosts of Al-Jazeera's talk shows invite guests of opposing views to challenge each other and respond to telephone callers, a distinct rarity in Arab broadcasting. Its popular program, "The Opposite Direction," is modeled directly on CNN's *Crossfire*. "Secularists debate fundamentalists, Israelis debate Palestinians, Iraqis debate Kuwaitis" (El-Nawawy and Iskander 2002, 51). Guests have included Tony Blair, Ehud Barak, Shimon Peres, Condoleeza Rice, and Donald Rumsfeld.

Al-Jazeera's Western-style approach to news and political discussion programs is controversial in the Arab world, particularly with Arab governments, where the tradition of spirited debate is a private affair not conducted in public media. Charges of bias have been made frequently against Al-Jazeera, often from opposing sides of the same issue. Recently, the Australian Broadcasting Corporation quoted Israeli Foreign Minister Shimon Peres complaining that Al-Jazeera incites hatred against Israel (Australian Broadcasting Corporation 2002), while only a month earlier the government of Bahrain banned the broadcaster from covering Bahrain's elections because Al-Jazeera is pro-Israel and "penetrated by Zionists" (BBC News 2002). A former spokesperson for the President of Egypt said on the U.S. television program, *60 Minutes*, in late 2001: "They are undermining us. They are undermining Egypt, undermining Saudi Arabia, undermining all the Arab countries. They are separating the Arab world. It's no good" (*60 Minutes* 2001).

In a region of the world where media are government controlled and do not give voice to opposition and criticism, Al-Jazeera's Western-style news has won a large following. Largely because of its editorial independence, the broadcaster has attracted an audience estimated at thirty-five million viewers in many countries and has come to be regarded by many as the CNN of the Arab world. Whereas Arab audiences once turned to sources such as the BBC and VOA for credible reporting, now many Arabs turn to Al-Jazeera. El-Nawawy and Iskander claim that "in some respects, many feel the network ended the Western monopoly of global dissemination of information" (2002, 197).

Al-Jazeera raises several issues concerning the conventional view of political communication. One issue concerns whether, as has been alleged, the spread of transnational broadcasting necessarily undermines local cultures and viewpoints, particularly in non-Western countries. Al-Jazeera seems to be a clear counterexample to that general trend. It presents a vigorous clash of opposing views on a wide range of issues but framed within the Arab perspective. To be sure, some traditional views are challenged in ways that Arab viewers may find shocking. But the Arab perspective is reinforced, not undermined. The success of Al-Jazeera and the political importance is has come to enjoy despite its relatively small scale and audience suggest that international television news broadcasting in the future may not be the monolithic force driving worldwide adoption of the modern model of political communication that it has been claimed to be.

At the same time, the experience of Al-Jazeera suggests that the practices of Western-style journalism – editorial independence, freedom from close government supervision and censorship, and the like – create credibility for newscasters everywhere. Al-Jazeera has built credibility with the Arab audience just by adhering to these practices. And in the Arab world, as elsewhere, adherence to these practices allows the media to assume the role of a political actor, wielding considerable influence in shaping public debate and perceptions. Such power, in turn, leads politicians to seek to influence the content of Al-Jazeera, as a host of Arab and Western governments have attempted to do both overtly by offering their officials for interviews and covertly by trying to exert pressure through governmental and other channels. It seems that the spread of transnational broadcasting with Western journalistic news values need not undermine local viewpoints and cultures, but it does produce the same attempts to manipulate the content of news that have been seen in the United States and Europe.

CONCLUSION

The comparative study of political communication is an essential supplement to the nationally focused studies on which most of our knowledge of the subject has been built. They have brought to light transnational trends that otherwise would be difficult to notice, and these trends have greatly advanced our appreciation of how the relationship between political institutions and media institutions shapes political communication everywhere.

The recent developments concerning the temporality of political cynicism and the success of an influential non-Western television news service employing Western journalistic models may point to some new directions for comparative research. Diachronic comparative studies that compare developments across time can reveal whether, as in the case of cycles of political cynicism, what seem to be irreversible trends are in fact inexorable or merely prolonged periods at the apogee or perigee of a repeating cycle. Synchronic comparative studies of expanded scope that range beyond American, European, and more generally Western developments can reveal whether what appear to be universal phenomena are in fact more limited in their scope.

As Livingstone recently observed, "It seems that without deliberate strategies for comparison, it is difficult to recognize how taken-for-granted aspects of everyday life may be distinctive while features considered nationally significant may in fact be shared with other countries. Thus comparative research aims to enhance understanding by improving an understanding of one's own country, gaining knowledge of other countries and, perhaps most valuable, examining how common, or transnational, processes operate in specific conditions in different national contexts" (2001, 1).

REFERENCES

60 Minutes. 2001. *Inside Al Jazeera* (online). CBSnews.com (cited October, 10 2001). Available from the World Wide Web at http://www.cbsnews.com/now/story/0,1597,314278–412,00.shtml.

Alderman, Keith. 1999. Parties and Movements. *Parliamentary Affairs* 52: 128–30.

Åsard, Eric, and W. Lance Bennett. 1997. *Democracy and the Marketplace of Ideas*. Cambridge: Cambridge University Press.

Australian Broadcasting Corporation. 2002. *Al-Jazeera Incites Hatred: Israel* (online). ABC online (cited June, 1 2002). Available from the World Wide Web at http://abc.net.au/news/mewsitems/s570664.html.

Barhnurst, Kevin G., and Catherine A. Steele. 1997. Image-Bite News. The Visual Coverage of Elections on U.S. Television 1968–1992. *Harvard International Journal of Press/Politics* 2 (1): 40–58.

BBC News. 2002. *Bahrain bans Al Jazeera TV* (online). BBC News, Middle East (cited May, 10 2002). Available from the World Wide Web at http://news.bbc.co.uk/hi/english/world/middle_east/newsid_1980000/ 1980191.stm.

Bennett, W. Lance. 1996. *New: The Politics of Illusion*. White Plains, NY: Longman.

Blumler, Jay G., and Stephen Coleman. 2001. *Realising Democracy Online. A Civic Commons in Cyberspace*. Swindon, UK: Citizens Online; London: Institute for Public Policy Research.

Blumler, Jay G., and Michael Gurevitch. 1975. Towards a Comparative Framework for Political Communication Research. In Steven H. Chaffee, ed. *Political Communication. Issues and Strategies for Research*. Beverly Hills, CA: Sage, pp. 165–93.

———. 1992. Comparative Research. The Extending Frontier. In David L. Swanson and Dan Nimmo, eds. *New Directions in Political Communication*. Newbury Park, CA: Sage, pp. 305–25.

———. 1995. *The Crisis of Public Communication*. London: Routledge.

Blumler, Jay G., and Dennis Kavanagh. 1999. The Third Age of Political Communication: Influences and Features. *Political Communication* 16: 209–30.

Blumler, Jay. G., Dennis Kavanagh, and Thomas J. Nossiter. 1996. Modern Communications Versus Traditional Politics in Britain. Unstable Marriage of Convenience. In David L. Swanson and Paolo Mancini, eds. *Politics, media, and modern democracy*. Westport, CT: Praeger, pp. 49–72.

Butler, David, and Austin Ranney, eds. 1992. *Electioneering. A Comparative Study of Continuity and Change.* Oxford: Clarendon Press.

Cappella, Joseph N. 2002. Cynicism and Social Trust in the New Media Environment. *Journal of Communication* 52 (1): 229–41.

Cappella, Joseph N., and Kathleen H. Jamieson. 1996. News Frames, Political Cynicism, and Media Cynicism. *Annals of the American Academy of Political and Social Science* 546: 71–84.

———. 1997. *Spiral of Cynicism. The Press and the Public Good.* New York: Oxford University Press.

Cohen, Akiba A., Hanna Adoni, and Charles R. Bantz. 1990. *Social Conflict and Television News.* Newbury Park, CA: Sage.

Cohen, Akiba A., Mark R. Levy, Itzhak Roeh, and Michael Gurevitch. 1996. *Global Newsrooms, Local Audiences. A Study of the Eurovision News Exchange.* London: John Libbey.

Dogan, Mattei. 1997. Erosion of Confidence in Advanced Democracies. *Studies in Comparative International Development* 32 (3): 3–29.

El-Nawawy, Mohammed, and Adel Iskandar. 2002. *Al-Jazeera: How the Free Arab News Network Scooped the World and Changed the Middle East.* Boulder, CO: Westview.

Fallows, James. 1997. *Breaking the News. How the Media Undermine American Democracy.* New York: Vintage Books.

Franklin, Bob. 1994. *Packaging Politics. Political Communications in Britain's Media Democracy.* London: Edward Arnold.

———. 1997. *Newszak and the News Media.* London: Edward Arnold.

Giddens, Anthony (1999, May 5). *Democracy.* London: BBC Reith Lectures.

Hallin, Daniel C. 1992. Sound Bite News. Television Coverage of Elections, 1968–1988. *Journal of Communication* 42 (2): 5–24.

Holtz-Bacha, Christina. 1999. The American Presidential Election in International Perspective. Europeanization of the U.S. Electoral Advertising Through Free-Time Segments. In Lynda L. Kaid and Diane G. Bystrom, eds. *The Electronic Election: Perspectives on the 1996 Campaign Communication.* Mahwah, NJ: Erlbaum, pp. 349–61.

Hvitfelt, Håkan. 1994. The Commercialization of the Evening News. Changes in Narrative Technique in Swedish TV News. *The Nordicom Review* (2): 33–41.

Jakubowicz, Karol. 1996. Television and Elections in Post-1989 Poland. How Powerful is the Medium? In David L. Swanson and Paolo Mancini, eds. *Politics, Media, and Modern Democracy. An International Study of Innovations in Electoral Campaigning and Their Consequences.* Westport, CT: Prager, pp. 129–54.

Kaid, Lynda L., and Christina Holtz-Bacha, eds. 1995. *Political Advertising in Western Democracies.* Thousand Oaks, CA: Sage.

Kavanagh, Dennis. 1995. *Election Campaigning. The New Marketing of Politics.* Oxford: Blackwell.

LeDuc, Lawrence, Richard G. Niemi, and Pippa Norris, eds. 1996. *Comparing Democracies. Elections and Voting in Global Perspective.* Thousand Oaks, CA: Sage.

Livingstone, Sonia (2001, May 14). *Media. The Missing Comparative Dimension.* Paper presented at a seminar on "Media Research. New Agendas, New Priorities?" at the London School of Economics and Political Science.

Mancini, Paolo. 1999. New Frontiers in Political Professionalism. *Political Communication* 16: 231–45.

Maarek, Philipe J. 1995. *Communication and Political Marketing.* London: John Libbey.

———. 1997. New Trends in French Political Communication. The 1995 Presidential Elections. *Media, Culture & Society* 19: 357–68.

Mayhew, Leon H. 1997. *The New Public. Professional Communication and the Means of Social Influence.* Cambridge: Cambridge University Press.

Mayobre, José Antonio. 1996. Politics, Media, and Modern Democracy. The Case of Venezuela. In David L. Swanson and Paolo Mancini, eds. *Politics, Media, and Modern Democracy.* Westport, CT: Praeger, pp. 227–45.

Mazzoleni, Gianpietro. 1996. Patterns and Effects of Recent Changes in Electoral Campaigning in Italy. In David L. Swanson and Paolo Mancini, eds. *Politics, Media, and Modern Democracy.* Westport, CT: Praeger, pp. 192–206.

Mazzoleni, Gianpietro, and Winfried Schulz. 1999. "Mediatization" of Politics. A Challenge for Democracy? *Political Communication* 16: 247–61.

McManus, John H. 1994. *Market Driven Journalism.* London: Sage.

Nasser, Munir K. 1983. News Values Versus Ideology. A Third World Perspective. In L. John Martin and Anju Grover Chaudhary, eds. *Comparative Mass Media Systems.* New York: Longman, pp. 44–66.

Negrine, Ralph. 1996. *The Communication of Politics.* London: Sage.

Negrine, Ralph, and Stylianos Papathanassopoulos. 1996. The Americanization of Political Communication. A Critique. *Harvard International Journal of Press/Politics* 1 (2): 45–63.

Neveu, Erik. 1999. Politics on French Television. Towards a Renewal of Political Journalism and Debate Frames? *European Journal of Communication* 14 (3): 379–409.

Norris, Pippa. 1999. *Critical Citizens.* Oxford: Oxford University Press.

Patterson, Thomas E. 1993. *Out of Order.* New York: Knopf.

———. 1996. Bad News, Bad Governance. *Annals of the American Academy of Political and Social Science* 546: 97–108.

———. 2000. *Doing Well and Doing Good. How Soft News and Critical Journalism are Shrinking the News Audience and Weakening Democracy – And What News Outlets Can Do About It.* Cambridge, MA: Joan Shorenstein Center on the Press, Politics, and Public Policy, Harvard University.

———. 2002. *The Vanishing Voter. Public Involvement in an Age of Uncertainty.* New York: Knopf.

Pfetsch, Barbara. 1996. Convergence Through Privatization? Changing Media Environments and Televised Politics in Germany. *European Journal of Communication* 11: 427–51.

Scammell, Margaret. 1995. *Designer Politics. How Elections Are Won.* Basingstoke, UK: Macmillan.

———. 1999. Political Marketing. Lessons for Political Science. *Political Studies* 47 (4): 718–39.

Semetko, Holli A., Jay G. Blumler, Michael Gurevitch, and David Weaver. 1991. *The Formation of Campaign Agendas. A Comparative Analysis of Party and Media Roles in Recent American and British Elections.* Hillsdale, NJ: Erlbaum.

Steele, Catherine A., and Kevin G. Barnhurst. 1996. The Journalism of Opinion. Network News Coverage of U.S. Presidential Campaigns, 1968–1988. *Critical Studies in Mass Communication* 13: 187–209.

Straubhaar, Joseph D., Carrie Heeter, Bradley S. Greenberg, Leonardo Ferreira, Robert H. Wicks, and Tuen-Yu Lau. 1992. What Makes News. Western, Socialist and Third World Television Newscasts Compared in Eight Countries. In Felipe Korzenny and Stella Ting-Toomey, eds. *Mass Media Effects Across Cultures*. Newbury Park, CA: Sage.

Swanson, David L. 1997. The Political-Media Complex at 50. Putting the 1996 Presidential Campaign in Context. *American Behavioral Scientist* 40: 1264–82.

Swanson, David L., ed. 1999. Symposium. A Third Age of Political Communication? Special Issue. *Political Communication* 16 (3): 203–84.

Swanson, David L., and Paolo Mancini. 1996a. Patterns of Modern Electoral Campaigning and Their Consequences. In David L. Swanson and Paolo Mancini, eds. *Politics, Media, and Modern Democracy. An International Study of Innovations in Electoral Campaigning and Their Consequences*. Westport, CT: Praeger, pp. 247–76.

Swanson, David L., and Paolo Mancini, eds. 1996b. *Politics, Media, and Modern Democracy. An International Study of Innovations in Electoral Campaigning and Their Consequences*. Westport, CT: Praeger.

Swanson, David L., and Larry David Smith. 1993. War in the Global Village. A Seven-Country Comparison of Television News Coverage of the Beginning of the Gulf War. In Robert E. Denton, ed. *The Media and the Persian Gulf War*. Westport, CT: Praeger, pp. 165–96.

Underwood, Doug. 1995. *When MBAs Rule the Newsroom*. New York: Columbia University Press.

Vanishing Voter Project (March 13, 2000). Americans "disgusted" with politics. Available at http://www.vanishingvoter.org.

Waisbord, Silvio. 1996. Secular Politics. The Modernization of Argentine Electioneering. In David L. Swanson and Paolo Mancini, eds. *Politics, Media, and Modern Democracy. An International Study of Innovations in Electoral Campaigning and Their Consequences*. Westport, CT: Praeger, pp. 207–25.

FOUR

Comparing Mass Communication Systems

Media Formats, Media Contents, and Media Processes

Hans J. Kleinsteuber

For a long time comparative media research led nothing more than a shadowy existence in international communication. This corresponded to a generally low interest in activities in other parts of the world. If at all, it was above all American developments that were included in the analysis. However, even descriptions of the United States remained rather superficial – this country often served the purpose of being either a dream or a nightmare vision, that is, a projection of one's own thoughts, while at the same time its existing contradictions remained unperceived. In a globalizing world, cross-national developments have more immediate and weighty results at home: Satellites allow an insight into programs from other continents, the Internet provides access to information from every corner of the world. More directly than ever before, we are confronted with other cultures and their media products. The incomprehensible must be understood and translated into the language of our particular experience. Comparative research is deeply involved in trying to gain an understanding of a politically and culturally fragmented world, which, of course, also shares common features. Both the common features and the differences are at the core of every comparative approach.

THE BASICS OF COMPARISON AND THE GENERATION OF COMPARATIVE THEORY

Comparison can be seen as a universal category of human behavior in everyday life ("comparing prices") just as in the structured, methodological procedures of science (e.g., legal and linguistic comparative studies). Because people have been thinking about themselves and others, the familiar and the "foreign," cross-national comparisons have been made.

From the first reporter who returned with tidings of foreign lands and foreign peoples, impressions of things that are apparently completely different have been emphasized, thus often reconstructing the world with an exotic touch. Herodot, the Greek, returned from his long voyages and "reported" back on what he had noticed out there and thought worth reporting. The first essays that comprise a scientifically founded comparison date back to antiquity: Aristotle sent his students out to describe Greece's state systems. In his comparative evaluations he found the "good" constitution of great interest. He was already working with terms such as *democracy* and *oligarchy*, which could thus be regarded as a result of the creation of comparable types.

The comparison, as an instrument of systematic research, was first developed by the British philosopher John Stuart Mill (1806–73), who, as could be expected, was also a utilitarian. He described two basically different but at the same time complementary procedures. He designed a "method of agreement," which states the question about similarities, separating it clearly from the "method of difference" (Mill 1872, 648–50). Up to the present day, these are still the central aspects of every comparison that leads to two central consequences:

- The objects to be compared must be neither identical nor completely lacking common features.
- Every comparison has to ask the two-sided question as to the similarities and differences. A focus on only one of these two components is incomplete and can therefore lay no claim to science.

In most western languages, the term *comparison* is derived from the Latin word *comparatio* (which actually means *with same*), which nowadays is used for describing a neutral method (*comparative media systems*). Indeed, a comparison must – from a methodological point of view – incorporate more than the search for similarity.

The comparative method is closely intertwined with the procedures, in which abstract and generalizing statements and ultimately theories can be generated from single observations. When a typology is developed, groups with different characteristics are created as a result of the comparison. Groups possessing similar characteristics can form the basis of a typology, which is concerned with the systematic order of phenomena. Characteristic typologies emphasize, for example, the differences between independent and state-controlled media structures, or between public and commercial broadcasting systems. Theories involve a higher degree of abstraction. They can be seen as a generalization generated from the empirical, in which a complex reality is reduced to a limited number of variables.

The formulation of theories, in which the overall common features are emphasized – despite differences in detail – nearly always presupposes the comparison of various single examples. Many of these comparisons work cross-nationally, which means that countless theories possess a comparative core. To keep to the preceding example: Theories describe the relationship between politics and the media in various (e.g., open or closed) societies. Probably the best-known typology of "global media philosophies" (Siebert et al. 1956) is based on the evaluation of past and present experience and identifies the following four types: "authoritarian," "libertarian," "communist," and "social responsibility." Other approaches of the latter years of the east-west divide have formed the following categories: "market (first world)," "Marxist (second world)," and "advancing (third world)" (Lambeth 1995).

Generally speaking, it is true that many theoretical concepts have stemmed from a comparative perspective: for instance "information society," "knowledge gap," or "digital divide." Also the various (often ethnographical) views of cultural studies point in this direction. This approach claims quite appropriately to keep an eye on the diversity of cultures and to gain access by, for example, ethnographical methods and sensitive analyses of ethnicity, which all work in a comparative manner (Hepp 1999).

COMPARISON AS A METHOD

THE UNITS OF ANALYSIS

The usual definition of comparative research mostly starts with national systems, which are then compared with other systems. Thus, crossing national borders becomes a criterion of the definition. Although this may apply to a large number of the scenarios for comparison, it forces them into an unnecessary corset in two respects:

- Elements within the national system, such as specific markets, actors, or products, can also form "units of analysis." Here it is useful to divide the field of research into three spatially different variants: the macro level (e.g., national media), the intermediate level (e.g., market shares, organizations), and the micro level (e.g., communicators). The latter is not of interest here, as the subject matter of interest is media systems.

- The units of analysis can occasionally neglect national borders, such as in comparisons of cross-border regions (e.g., Euro regions), differently defined spaces (e.g., Bavaria with Belgium, as they are about the same size and have similar population numbers), or even a functional equivalent (e.g., the national broadcasting authorities in other countries with the regional broadcasting authorities of the German federal states).

In all the examples mentioned so far, the central point of research has been objects that were physically separated from each other. We are talking about a "horizontal" form of comparison. It is also usually accepted that a comparison does not have to be synchronized, that is, not referring to the same time slot, for instance when the beginnings of television or a certain phase of transformation is the subject in question there can be a difference of many years. Here horizontal elements are tied up with "vertical" ones. It is disputed whether purely vertical comparisons are of any value, in which, for example, various epochs of the same country are compared. As this process requires completely different, that is, historical, methods, it is usually excluded from the context described here (although other views exist on this subject – see Chapter 14, this volume). The historically oriented comparison is certainly useful. However, because it goes beyond the subject to be dealt with here it will have to be left aside.

The comparative method is hard to apply to modern multilevel structures, as the integral parts and the entirety are increasingly interwoven. This problem is found, for example, in the case of the European Union (EU), whose politics (at least up to this point) must be seen above all as an aggregate of national politics. A comparison of European developments with those of single countries within the EU harbors the danger of comparing something with itself. This is true as far as a comparison between the media politics of Germany and the EU is concerned. A comparative analysis of developments in member states, which is followed by a second part of comparative evaluation, is methodically clearer in this case. A considerable part of research on Europe is indeed set up in such a way.

The dividing line between comparative analysis and area studies is not always easy to define. Many studies do in fact present an extensive description of large regions of the world or representative systems of them, while the explicit comparison is either left out completely or is only mentioned briefly (e.g., Merrill 1995). Therefore, it is important to differentiate between two levels: It is certainly useful to present the world in its diversity under the title of a "Comparison of Systems" (e.g., in teaching), however the true core of comparative research is defined by the application of comparative methods. Such studies were in most cases designed for states within the western, industrialized region of the world, or for a comparison between them and other regions of the world. So far, predominantly studies with a transatlantic logic have been presented, comparing America with Europe (or specific European states), or between or within large geographical regions (Europe – Western/Eastern, North America with the interesting and unusual case of Canada, Latin America, Asia, Africa, etc.) (Corner et al. 1997, 4–5).

An important aspect of every comparison is that not only the situation of different regions is portrayed, but that one's own system gains new and clearer contours through the comparison with others. Only through such comparisons does the broadcasting federalism characterizing Germany reveal its uniqueness.

METHODS OF COMPARATIVE RESEARCH

In principle, all media systems, or research objects concerning political communication, can be compared. The first distinction that should be noted is that the comparative approach also exists within one country (e.g., a comparison between the political communications of two parties). This kind of approach is not included in this analysis, even if some of the following methodological hints can also be of use for this kind of comparison. Furthermore, it is a fact that the primary gathering of cross-national data requires enormous effort. This is why most comparative studies rely on a secondary evaluation of existing material that has already been produced in the country in question and is evaluated according to comparative criteria (meta-analyses).

Some of the methods used in comparative contexts are:

- Analysis of Documents and Academic Literature: Constitutions and legal texts, government reports, and party programs are relatively easy to compare. In addition, there are scientific studies, written in the country in question. Nevertheless, mistakes in translation or transcultural misunderstandings often occur. This highlights the need of knowing the languages of the country studied in comparative research – if this is at all possible. All comparative studies begin with an evaluation of the literature of the country to be examined.
- Content Analysis: The systematic comparison of contents (in the form of texts, pictures, symbols, etc.) is appropriate for the description of similarities and differences in press coverage (a classical

study, researching into political symbols used in the prestige press, proceeds in this way [de Sola Pool 1970]). Here it is particularly important to be sensitive to differences in language and meaning (e.g., the word *government* in some countries has a broader meaning than in others; correct translations have to relate to the specific context). Furthermore, important features may be missing altogether in other countries. For example, those who want to include the yellow press in their comparison of contents will find that in some countries it is nonexistent or leads only a rudimentary existence.

- Evaluation of Statistical Data: In a national context, comprehensive sets of data are usually provided, containing similar terminology that gives the impression that a comparison is an easy task. However, the figures have arisen under completely different conditions and are only valid in context. An example: Figures on the use of computers and the Internet are usually based on statistics of the number of households equipped with these facilities. This makes sense in industrialized countries where individual use dominates. However, in other parts of the world, computers are often used collectively (e.g., in Internet cafés). According to study and to point of view, the number of Internet users in Latin America, for example, varies by a factor of 3 (2.6 to 6.8 percent for 2001).

- Audience Ratings and Readership Figures: This kind of material is often available in great quantity, but applies to national systems with different starting points. In the United States, for example, regional TV ratings are researched in metropolitan areas; in Germany they are mostly researched based on the area of the federal states.

- Evaluation of Opinion Polls: Survey results are easy to compare, but here too, particular conditions should be taken into consideration. Inquiries into matters that can not be experienced in one's own country, can only be of limited value (e.g., to ask about majority representation in a country that has proportional representation in election laws).

- Expert Interviews and Participant Observation: The systematic inquiry of people in positions of responsibility – for example, in media or politics, and participant observation in decision-making processes, in, for example, an editor's office or a political party's campaign team – are often very valid and explicit sources of information that are hard to gain access to. Foreigners to a country are often met with mistrust and experience problems in their research process.

- A Combination of Various Methods: Using a combination of procedures, classifications can be developed that lead to value judgments (in the tradition of Aristotle). This applies, for example, to studies on the degree of freedom of the press in different countries, based on the evaluation of various indices on human rights and the state of the press. The organization Freedom House sorts the regimes of the world into three categories: free, partly free, and not free (Stevenson 1995).

Generally speaking, the methods of comparative research are relatively refined and can be found in textbooks, yet this field has remained relatively undeveloped in communication studies (Edelstein 1982). Within the realms of social science, comparative research is best established in political science and textbooks on this subject can be recommended (e.g., Landman 2000).

With regards to intercultural and transcultural irritations, one is usually referred to literature on intercultural communication. In any case, it is necessary to be cautious about the universal plausibility of statements: All too often unfounded statements are made about another country that prove to be untenable when examined more closely. There are countless traps: in a study on communication in politics the author expressed his surprise over the absence of reports on the sessions of government commissions in Germany, as opposed to the United States. The explanation for this, which is not included, is simple: Only in the United States are such sessions public and therefore open to journalists (Negrine 1996, 54). In addition, the fundamental database and the comparative research often rely on unscientific criteria, such as economic or political motives, and therefore do not give an accurate picture of the situation.

Strategies of Comparative Procedures

Comparative studies follow various strategies or patterns that each lead to different research questions and results. The most frequently used are presented in the following text:

- Concordance: The similarity of the objects compared is central to the analysis and common characteristics are primarily sought. For instance, theoretical perspectives of an emerging information society follow this principle, which assumes that societies pass through similar stages of development (agricultural society → industrial society → information society). Perspectives of a modernization by communication or the universality of human rights assume the emphasis of concordant research questions.

- Difference: Methodologically the focus is on the identification of differences. For instance, ideas of a "clash of Civilizations" (Samuel Huntington) point in this direction when they argue that irreconcilable differences exist between the cultures of the world that are supposed to have emerged over long periods of time and cause cultures (to want) to separate from each other.

These two procedures are obviously linked to the research methods described previously (originally Mill's) that focus on the similarity (common features) or differences. When a study focuses on one of these two approaches, it should be insured that the other perspective is not left out as this would endanger the study's scientific character.

Scientific approaches are always of a procedural nature; step by step one approaches one's own questions so that one can finally present answers. Regarding complex hypotheses, the simple contrast of two elements is often insufficient as scientific findings only come to light through a series of dynamic processes. In addition, there is the intention behind the scientific procedure: Is it simply a question of understanding and explaining the context? Or is it about a practical matter, for instance, to find out how ideas are passed on or to learn from global experiences? This leads us in the direction of further comparative approaches. Some typical approaches will be mentioned at this point:

- Diffusion: New ideas (business concepts, etc.) originate in one country but, due to their success, penetrate other regions of the world; they disseminate. For example, the principle of commercial broadcasting originated in the United States and from there spread to nearly all regions of the world. In Europe, Great Britain proved to be the region with the strongest links to the United States (Tunstall 1999). The BBC developed the principle of public service that was later introduced throughout Europe and the Commonwealth. Diffusion describes processes of the voluntary adoption of ideas and innovations.
- Dependency: The world does not just consist of horizontal communication with the chance to learn from each other, it also contains massive vertical dependencies. Former colonies were forced to take over elements of their respective mother country's media systems, which they could only develop further after independence. In Nigeria, the British left behind the Nigerian Broadcasting

Corporation, which had been modeled on the BBC. In the previously Soviet camp, a largely similar understanding of the media as a "collective agitator and propagandist" had been established. This led to structurally similar media that were under the direction of the respective Marxist-Leninist parties.

- Temporality: A fundamental aspect of global modernization is that processes do not take place simultaneously. The United States has been a forerunner in many areas of the media in the past decades (television, cable, computer, Internet, etc.). An analysis of the developments in this country therefore allows a kind of insight into one's own foreseeable media future. In many fields the word *Americanization* is used in this context (see the following text), which can be seen as a scientific concept and be tested. Other regions play the role of forerunner for other areas, for example in mobile communication this role goes to Northern Europe or Japan. Temporality means – colloquially speaking – that you don't always have to go back to reinvent the wheel.

- Performance: If another country, which is more advanced as far as certain developments are concerned, is systematically observed with the intention of preparing for political (or commercial, etc.) innovations at home, the concept of performance emerges. In Germany, for example, since the year 2000 legislation on "Freedom of Information," which orients itself toward American, British, and Scandinavian models, is being worked on. This is a sort of global benchmarking for the best solution (performance). In this respect, the world appears to be a global political laboratory. The observation of the world has the purpose of political consultancy and the implementation of the internationally most-promising specifications and is thus limited to concrete goals.

Portraying the comparison of media systems can only be conducted by way of examples. The emphasis lies on media systems and political communication in this chapter. A systematic view is the focus here, that is, the macro and, to an extent, the intermediate levels of the systems are at the forefront. Individual actors on the micro level, for example journalists, are dealt with in a different chapter (see Chapter 11, this volume). The following sections are concerned with some examples of comparative perspectives in various subdivisions: the theory of communication and political communication; media systems and media politics; and media transformation and media technology.

EXAMPLES OF COMPARATIVE PERSPECTIVES
IN AREAS OF COMMUNICATIONS THEORY AND
POLITICAL COMMUNICATION

THEORIES OF COMMUNICATION

It has already been described how theories can stand at the end of a process of comparative research. This leads to the question of whether theories can be compared, in particular concerning transcultural differences. Although they receive little attention from the Western academic community, new culture-bound schools of thought do emerge, which, time and again, include a reaction to regional experience. The relatively well-equipped Latin American science of communications, for example, has concerned itself with the potential for political reform in the media for many years (Fox 1997). In Asia, Western perspectives had been accepted rather uncritically for decades before attempts were made to combine local traditions in thinking with these imports. By now, characteristic perspectives on communications theory have been developed in Asia, in which, for example, peculiarities of the Indian language, the symbolic system of I Ching in China, or impulses of Islam or Taoism have been incorporated (Dissanayake 1993).

This example underscores that theories wander over cultural boundaries in the form of ideas and make productive suggestions, thereby changing and expanding their content. This is illustrated in the famous approach "Structural Transformation of the Public Sphere" (Habermas 1962; 1989). The study, which dates from 1962 – based, at the time of its publication, on a comparison between France, the United Kingdom, and Germany – was not translated into English until over a quarter of a century later. The German key term *Öffentlichkeit* was translated into the artificial term *public sphere*. This was necessary as there is no equivalent to the word *Öffentlichkeit* in many languages (which throws some light on German particularities). Obviously, *Öffentlichkeit* stems from a different context than *public sphere*, illustrated by the fact that this theory has meanwhile often been used to defend the public broadcasting service, as it is closely related to the term *public service* (see previous). In processes involving the transcultural passing on of theories, certain ideas embedded in these theories are lost and others are newly created. A comparison of Habermas's original (1962) with today's non-German Habermas adaptations shows how this kind of transcultural diffusion works (Kleinsteuber 2001b).

POLITICAL CULTURE AND POLITICAL COMMUNICATION

A classical object of comparative research is the analysis of political culture, meaning studies on informal forms of behavior of the citizen vis-à-vis the political system and their (historically grown) differences. The classic work "Civic Culture" compared specially obtained questionnaire results in five countries (the United States, the United Kingdom, Germany, Italy, and Mexico) for this purpose. Its priorities lay on how citizens see the state and how they communicate with it. It showed that in the late 1950s Germany's citizens were comparatively well-informed yet not very politically active; in the United States it was the other way around (Almond and Verba 1963). In more recent studies the whole range of the variations of political communication is revealed, such as when different authors of a book (Paletz 1996) describe the parallel positions of the media elite cross-nationally, as well as the greatly differing local characteristics: for instance how ethnic, tribal, and regional elements influence Nigeria's political communication (Olayiwola 1996); how the effects of terror and political violence shape communication in Peru, India, or South Africa; or how massively the mass media in South Korea is still subject to manipulative political pressure (Kim and Lee 1996).

One study approaches the subject in a completely different manner, by focusing on a comparison of political communication cultures. The author provides an analysis of the "norms and communication roles that govern the interaction between political spokespeople and journalists" (Pfetsch 2001, 47). To gather data, the author carried out semistructured interviews with journalists and politicans' spokespeople from the United States and Germany. The results showed clear differences: American actors take on a much stronger professional role as journalists who determine the interaction between the two sides, while in Germany social norms dominate the situation, such as ethical and appropriate behavior, openness, or dignity. In the United States the behavior of the actors is more media-oriented and aims at a strategic orchestration of communication, while in Germany the strong position of the political parties (which are protected by the constitution) allows other priorities to emerge.

POLITICAL ADVERTISING, COMMUNICATION IN ELECTION CAMPAIGNS, AND THE HYPOTHESIS OF AMERICANIZATION

A common subject of comparative analysis is communication in election campaigns. It seems sensible to study comparable objects in the countries examined, for example television advertisement spots by political parties, which appeared sufficiently similar for their verbal and nonverbal messages to be evaluated and their contents analyzed. The result reads as follows: Although the political systems researched (the United States, France, Italy, and Germany) appear to be relatively different (party system, election rights), an amazing similarity was recognizable in the political party broadcasts. The comparison "of the content, style, and effects of exposure to televised political advertising show some striking similarities across cultures." The corresponding results showed, among others, that the spots concentrated on issues, that messages are usually positively formulated and emotional arguments are put before logical ones (Kaid and Holtz-Bacha 1995, 221–2).

Another comparative analysis concentrates on the formulation of campaign agendas. It compares the roles of parties and the media (television and press) in the United Kingdom and the United States. As a common feature, the release "of an implacably competitive struggle to control the mass media agenda" is described. The media replies with their own defense strategy of not permitting the politicians to have a "free ride." On the other hand, it notes that differences should be observed, some of which are the strength of party systems, public service versus commerce in the television networks, the method of courting media consumers, varying degrees of election campaign professionalization, and cultural differences, for instance, the public's esteem of politicians (Semetko et al. 1991, 175–8). Along with the more obvious comparative content analysis of the campaign media and reporting, primarily participant observations at newsrooms and at competing parties' press conferences were carried out and evaluated. Yet another approach was used in a cross-country study that compared the influence of interpersonal and mass communication on voting decisions in the United States, the United Kingdom, Spain, and East and West Germany (see Chapter 13, this volume).

Some of the above-mentioned studies have also addressed the question of whether a kind of Americanization might have taken place in the procedure of election campaigns in western countries. In this context Americanization means strategies that are successful in the United States are carefully observed and consequently copied in other countries. While the studies previously cited emphasize the visible closeness of campaign strategies, other analyses, which concentrate on political structures and institutions, come to somewhat different conclusions. Here it is emphasized that the context is very different, for example election campaigns in Germany, as opposed to in the United States, are above all organized by the party organization; the candidate is of secondary importance (Kamps 2000). The term *Americanization* proves to be primarily used by the media as a catchword to avoid complicated comparisons. Despite all the differences in the concrete campaign procedures, similarities are also observed, especially in visual strategies or the intentional influencing of reporting.

It is indisputable that European politicians observe U.S. election campaigns closely. A leading politician of the German Liberal Party, Guido Westerwelle, when questioned as an observer at an American National Convention in 2000, said: "Don't copy, just understand." All in all, the Americanization hypothesis falls into the temperance and the performance categories, because the situation in an "advanced" country is being examined and evaluated with a concrete aim.

POLITICAL REPORTING

While media structures clearly differ from a global perspective, media contents are frequently relatively similar – not least because they often originate from a limited number of news agencies. This makes a comparison easier – even more so when similar kinds of media (e.g., the "quality" press) or similar subjects (e.g., events of global significance) are compared. The comparative analysis of contents looks back on a considerable history: Back in the early fifties, "political symbols" were sought for in the quality press (de Sola Pool 1970). In this context, the analyses of world news trends prepared in the 1970s, which reveal a great amount of one-way movement and are interpreted as "one-way streets," are also important: The United States and also Western Europe are major producers, while regions of the Third World are merely recipients and have no chance of making their issues heard. They have been the subject of many lengthy and difficult controversies in the United Nations Educational, Scientific, and Cultural Organization (UNESCO).

In international cooperation, reporting on the Gulf War has been studied in depth (Nohrstedt and Ottosen 2000). Based on a pattern of double framework of comparison, using multiple forms of media (television news, tabloids, quality press) and various countries (the United States, Denmark, Norway, and others), in the final analysis the U.S. reporting during the events of the war was found to have been very hegemonic, while the United Nation's (UN's) role was almost negligible. Among the national media of Europe common features could be discovered, for example that militaristic logic played only a small part, as opposed to in the United States. While in Germany the war events were simultaneously sold with controversial positions as well as propaganda in favor of military intervention, the coverage in Norway was much more distanced (Kempf 2000). It is part of the nature of these kind of analyses that it can only be used for meaningful topics of common interest, as only then does the material basis needed for comparison exist.

EXEMPLARY COMPARATIVE PERSPECTIVES IN THE AREA OF MEDIA SYSTEMS AND MEDIA POLITICS

MEDIA SYSTEMS AND MEDIA POLITICS

A field that has recently become popular is the complete presentation of media systems. There is a wide range of handbooks in which single systems are described according to a fixed scheme. In the German-speaking world, the most reliable source is the *Hans-Bredow-Yearbook* published every other year (Hans-Bredow-Institute 2002). Many, above all Anglo-American textbooks, either present single national media systems, which are supposed to be representative of certain world regions (Head 1985), or else analyze the situation in world regions, for example Latin America, where a considerable level of comparability is assumed (Fox 1997). A different perspective emerges when the author does not come from the country examined, and his or her angle is more or less detached from the research object. The British writer Peter J. Humphreys has written an overview of the German media system that unmistakably focuses on the interests of the British observer, for instance on German federalism or the powerful assertiveness of parties in media politics (which are both unknown in the United Kingdom) (Humphreys 1994, 315–20). In turn, Germans occupy themselves with the situation abroad, above all in the United States, in which the question of Americanization is almost always involved and transposed into questions such as: "What will happen to us in the future?" or "What can we copy?" (Bachem 1995; Kleinsteuber 2001a).

The founding of the EU provided comparative research with far-reaching impulses. Processes of political integration, in which units that were previously separate have now gained in similarity, show an elective affinity to the process of generation of comparative theory previously outlined. The gathering of data and consequent comparison of conditions within member states constitutes a fixed repertoire of the formulation phase of EU politics. For example, this is what happened in the

1989 case of the media directive "Television without Borders." In the green book with the same title, the commission researched the situation in every country in the EU in order to make decisions about further procedure (European Commission 1984).

As another result of intensified European research, cooperation studies that follow one of the following three patterns have become widespread:

- The situation in member states is systematically presented, for example in the handbooks of the Euromedia Research Group in which national media systems are dealt with according to fixed criteria and figures are provided for orientation (ERG 1997). The systemization provided simplifies the comparison, which, however, must be performed by the user.
- In a two-step procedure, the national situation is first researched using case studies, after that trends within Europe are presented. In studies that originated in Catalonia/Barcelona for example, the focus is on local/regional television. In their evaluation, it is possible to identify various types of "decentralized TV." Then, just to name two poles, the situation in states with centralized authorities and power structures (such as Greece and Portugal) falls into the category of "regional delegated production centers," while Germany, with its large proportion of regionally produced broadcasting, comes under the heading "federated television" (de Moragas Spá et al. 1999, 9–12).
- The varying situations in different parts of the EU form the basis for cross-national studies, in order to locate Europe-wide trends or contradictions. For example, commercialization and the introduction of the dual system happened relatively simultaneously in the EU; the use of cable TV, pay TV, and the Internet, however, is quite unevenly distributed (McQuail and Siune 1998).

Studies on the European subject matter underline that something approaching a "European Model" has not developed beyond its rudiments (Corner et al. 1997, 5). Therefore it seems even more surprising that the promotion of the process toward European unity for some time used a media-centered strategy, where deregulation and privatization have always constituted a part of their repeatedly proclaimed goals. This strategy with the aim of attaining unity based on common media and telecommunications politics was above all attempted in the 1980s and the early 1990s, albeit with little success (Burgelman 1997, 142–5).

MEDIA SURVEILLANCE AND MEDIA REGULATION

Comparison of media surveillance and regulation presents itself as a standard area of comparative research. A similar functional necessity, regarding the tendencies toward liberalization and the opening of the market exists in all countries: the construction of effective supervision structures. A comparative study on regulating the media examines licensing and regulation in six countries (the United States, the United Kingdom, Germany, France, Canada, and Australia): national regulation structures and their context are researched according to a partly unified scheme. In a second step, common features are sought for, according to the principle of "method of agreement." The author stresses that a change of paradigm can be observed in all of the states examined, which can be described as "from the trustee model to the market model" or "from cultural to economic legitimization" (Hoffmann-Riem 1996, 340–1). Attention is paid to differences as well: two groups of countries are formed. Three countries with a long-standing privately owned media sector (the United States, Canada, and Australia) are compared with three countries in the public service tradition (the United Kingdom, Germany, and France). The two categories differ clearly in their results, simultaneously describing the difference between developments within and outside Europe while using area studies. The result is a classical type formation, taking into account the concepts of agreement and difference.

Questions about regulation become apparent in the case of the Internet as well, albeit in a different way. The Bertelsmann Foundation has presented a study on this subject, which primarily pleas for self-regulation (Waltermann and Machill 2000). One part of the study comprises an opinion poll of Internet users in three countries (Australia, Germany, and the United States). It was based on identical questions so that results could be compared. The results show that, despite "extreme national differences" in the diffusion of Internet use (at least at the time of the research in mid-1999), respondents gave similar answers. Particularly control over abuse was seen as an important task in every country and self-control was favored. State control was, as was to be expected, especially unpopular in the United States, while in Germany the ban of extreme right-wing or extreme left-wing opinions was favored more than anywhere else (Germany: 58 percent, the United States: 28 percent) (Köcher 2000). These kinds of questionnaires with an explicitly comparative focus remain somewhat rare as they are very expensive.

It is generally true that the politics of regulation are a good example of diffusion because of their great international significance – the first government institution responsible for communication was founded in the United States in 1934. Today there is (at least) one in almost every developed political system. The fact that problems have similar origins in many countries motivates us to study the experiences of others or also (e.g., on regulating the Internet) work together on common applicable solutions; temperance and performance accompany international regulation research.

PUBLIC SERVICE AND COMMERCIAL BROADCASTING

Two types of organization are known in the international development of broadcasting: the original European public service and the private commercial broadcasting, which had its beginnings in the United States. When they coexist, we speak of a dual system. The complete field of research is characterized by processes that can be described with comparative methods, as the European commercial suppliers applied many concepts and specialist terminology from the United States (soap opera, format radio, etc.). The term *dual system* came into existence in the United Kingdom. Diffusion, temperance, and performance are related catchwords.

Public service is a generic concept and is such as a result of comparative processes. It describes systems in which broadcasting is produced in a kind of public trusteeship. The German *Öffentlich-Rechtliche Anstalten* (literally *public institutions governed by law*) appear to be a subcategory – in some ways a very special one. The legal construction is only referred to in Germany and the form of organization, *Anstalt* (*institution*), is unique – and defies any meaningful translation. Public service first became a scientific object in the United Kingdom (the first attempt at a definition was by the Broadcasting Research Unit in 1985). Comparative analyses show that *the public service* should not just be seen as a descriptive concept, it always has a normative element to it in the countries concerned (e.g., as far as the strengthening of public discourse through public institutions is concerned) (Raboy 1996).

Dual systems can also be the object of comparative analysis. In a study of the Bertelsmann Foundation, dual systems came under scrutiny. In order to attain any comparability at all in this study of six countries (the United Kingdom, France, Australia, New Zealand, the United States, and Germany), so-called public interest programs were defined as the starting point. In the United States public broadcasting was included, although it only resembles public service in name (there is no public sector in the United States). In fact, *public* in the United States means something similar to programming in the interest of the general public, which is, however, above all carried out by private organizations and financing (Hamm 1998). Studies of this kind underline how difficult it often is to create terminological unity and conceptional bases of comparison.

EXAMPLES OF COMPARATIVE METHODS IN THE AREAS OF MEDIA TRANSFORMATION AND MEDIA TECHNOLOGY

MEDIA TRANSFORMATION

Media systems develop a natural capacity for self-preservation, even if they find themselves in a state of complete reorganization in certain phases of their development. The last large region that found itself in such a process largely simultaneously (and partially still ongoing) is the group of countries whose systems used to be called *real socialism*. The Soviet Union, as a center of power, had forced its dependent states to adopt its concept of the media by using its dominant status. With the end of communism, media systems set out on the road to transformation, which can be seen as modernization according to a conscious, planned, catching-up process. Actually transformation is a comparative theoretical concept, which came into existence during the analysis of earlier processes of democratization in Latin America and Southern Europe (Thomass and Tzankoff 2001). Apart from parallel processes, media transformation in (Central and) Eastern Europe also clearly differs: Poland now has a largely westernized system; in Russia, the state and oligarchies have created new dependencies (Trautmann 2002). Differently again, the media in (former) Yugoslavia have become a great source of ethnic defamation and the construction of enemy images with well-known destructive consequences.

STATE SYSTEMS AND ECONOMIC ACTORS

A reduction in importance of individual nation-states in favor of the world economy, especially the increasingly powerful transnational companies of the media and communications industry, can be observed internationally. The strategies of the large, globally active media actors are perfect for comparative analyses: AOL Time Warner for instance was aiming at convergence and the synergetic combination of old and new forms of media; Murdoch's News Corporation was aiming at worldwide digital pay TV and satellite distribution, and Bertelsmann (the world's biggest publishers) at the production of content. For example, the Bertelsmann Group, actually based in the small German town of

Gütersloh, has settled parts of its top management in New York and obtains its highest turnover in the United States. It is a good example of how a global structure dissolves national boundaries and enterprises are becoming transnational actors.

In international research, controversial positions are developed on this point: a rather affirmative view stresses the chances offered by global media, for instance the capacity to break up the traditional authorities internationally and promote social change (Demers 1999). The critical analysis focuses on terms such as *transnational corporate capitalism*; describes the destruction of local traditions, primarily in the South through the North (*Hollywoodization*); and the activities of the largest media players, which remain unhindered by democratic control (Sussman and Lent 1991). These theoretical perspectives see, for example, the construction of global "Electronic Empires" as central and are often linked to political economy approaches, a direction of thought that is strong in the international context, but almost forgotten in Germany (Thussu 1998).

In this context, two aspects are usually dealt with: The question of how existing communication cultures react to threats from the outside and develop their own adaptation and countering strategies. Another direction stresses the necessity to react to tendencies to globalization with demands for democratization, which corresponds with the general tendency in the direction of more democracy in the world. "Democratizing Communication" is thereby used as a concept to oppose the media-industrial imperative, evaluating the manifold experiences of the world with comparative methods (Bailie and Winseck 1997).

The Technical Future of Communication

Media and communications technologies always originate in one corner of the world: telegraphy and the computer in the United States, broadcasting technologies in Europe. They then spread to the rest of the world. Technologies represent an aspect of universal similarity as they tend toward global resemblance in their technical construction, while, in comparison, cultures seem to have many facets and to be inconsistent. The former produce conformity, the latter favor difference. In reality the situation is more complex, because, for instance, the same technologies can be used in different ways. Technologies developed in the Western world (such as the Internet) and designed for individual use (in households) are in other places used much more collectively (e.g., Internet cafes). Illiterate oral cultures conquer radio technologies in a completely new way as they discover it as an opportunity for sharing traditional stories. It is fascinating to see how differently our familiar technologies are used in the geographical and cultural periphery (e.g., by Inuits in the arctic region [Greenland, Canada, Alaska]) (Perrot 1986).

Even within the Western world, the interpretations and metaphors of new technologies differ considerably. The idea of establishing an Information Superhighway in the form of a national and digital information infrastructure, as it was proclaimed in American politics in 1993, has wandered through many states and has been furnished with completely different accents. In the United States, the term metaphorically transported a claim of state regulation of private investors, parallel to the construction of the real highway that is regimented by the police; the Canadians were above all careful to add their "Canadian content" to the infrastructure; and Australians hoped to reduce the geographical distance between their country and the world markets (Kleinsteuber 1996). In Europe, the picture of the Autobahn (in German) or Autostrada (in Italian) for data was above all filled with economic meaning, the chances offered by e-commerce were praised highly and emphasis was laid on the creation of new jobs in a Europe expected to grow together in electronic networks (Kubicek et al. 1997).

CONCLUSION

Apart from the individual aspects of comparative procedure described here, this field in general has a particular task in the scientific analysis of the media and communication. It is about – generally speaking – processing world knowledge, the insight into foreign cultures, discovering different approaches to different subjects and gaining a different kind of experience of similar objects in distinct cultures. Without exception, the relationship between the familiar and the foreign lies behind the comparative analysis. This underlines that sound comparative research can only be achieved with great multicultural sensitivity. It is a question of scientifically corroborating "Border Crossing" (Dallmayr 1999). Stereotyping therefore is an archenemy of any comparative procedure; even worse is the construction of prejudices. It is neither true that the United States is the land of neoliberalism, that the Japanese are copycats, nor that the Germans are perfectionists. Comparative research attributes great importance to avoiding stereotyped simplifications and the fabrication of clichés, which often suit political purposes nicely.

An overwhelming trend can be subsumed under the term *globalization*. When this catchword is examined more thoroughly, very different forms of reaction to the internationalization of communication in technology, organization, program, and so forth come to light. It is often possible to identify confusing developments along with global transcultural communication – often interacting with it, which only reveal their secret when subjected to comparative research. Without a clear improvement and intensification of comparative research the future will be unmanageable.

REFERENCES

Almond, Gabriel, and Sidney Verba. 1963. *Civic Culture*. Princeton: Princeton University Press.

Bachem, Christian. 1995. *Fernsehen in den USA. Neuere Entwicklungen von Fernsehmarkt und Fernsehwerbung*. Opladen, Germany: Westdeutscher Verlag.

Bailie, Mashoed, and Dwayne Winseck, eds. 1997. *Democratizing Communication? Comparative Perspectives onf Information and Power*. Cresskill, NJ: Hampton Press.

Blumler, Jay G., Jack M. McLeod, and Karl Erik Rosengren, eds. 1992. *Comparatively Speaking: Communication and Culture Across Space and Time*. Newbury Park, CA: Sage.

Broadcasting Research Unit. 1985. *The Public Service Idea in British Broadcasting*. London.

Burgelman, Jean-Claude. 1997. Communication Policy in Western Europe. In John Corner, Philip Schlesinger, and Roger Silverstone, eds. *International Media Research. A Critical Survey*. London: Routledge, pp. 123–53.

Corner, John, Philip Schlesinger, and Roger Silverstone, eds. 1997. *International Media Research. A Critical Survey*. London: Routledge.

Dallmayr, Fred, ed. 1999. *Border Crossing*. Lanham, MD: Lexington Books.

Demers, David. 1999. *Global Media. Menace or Messiah?* Cresskill, NJ: Hampton Press.

de Moragas Spá, Miquel, Carmelito Garitaonandía, and Bernat López, eds. 1999. *Television at Your Doorstep. Decentralization Experiences in the European Union*. Luton, UK: Luton Press.

de Sola Pool, Ithiel. 1970. *The Prestige Press. A Comparative Study of Political Symbols*. Cambridge, MA: M.I.T. Press (in collaboration with Harold D. Lasswell and Daniel Lerner, original studies from 1951–52).

Dissanayake, Wimal. 1993. *Communication Theory. The Asian Perspective*. Singapore: AMIC.

European Commission. 1984. *Television Without Frontiers*. Brussels: Commission of the European Communities.

Edelstein, Alex S. 1982. *Comparative Communication Research*. Beverly Hills, CA: Sage.

ERG – Euromedia Research Group. 1997. *The Media in Western Europe. The Euromedia Handbook*. London: Sage.

Fox, Elizabeth. 1997. Media and Culture in Latin America. In John Corner, Philip Schlesinger, and Roger Silverstone, eds. 1997. *International Media Research. A Critical Survey*. London: Routledge, pp. 184–205.

Habermas, Jürgen. 1989. *Structural Transformation of the Public Sphere*. Cambridge: Polity (German edition: Habermas, Jürgen. 1962. *Strukturwandel der Öffentlichkeit*. Neuwied: Luchterhand).

Hamm, Ingrid, ed. 1998. *Fernsehen auf dem Prüfstand. Aufgaben des dualen Systems.* Gütersloh, Germany: Bertelsmann.

Hans-Bredow-Institute, ed. 2002. *International Handbook for Radio and Television 2002/2003.* Baden-Baden: Nomos (published every two years).

Head, Sydney W. 1985. *World Broadcasting Systems. A Comparative Analysis.* Belmont, CA: Wadsworth Publishing.

Hepp, Andreas. 1999. *Cultural Studies und Medienanalyse.* Opladen, Germany: Westdeutscher Verlag.

Hoffmann-Riem, Wolfang. 1996. *Regulating Media. The Licensing and Supervision of Broadcasters in Six Countries.* New York: Guilford Press.

Humphreys, Peter J. 1994. *Mass Media and Media Policy in Western Europe.* Oxford: Berg Publisher.

Huntington, Samuel P. 1996. *The Clash of Civilizations and the Remaking of World Order.* New York: Simon & Schuster.

Kaid, Lynda Lee, and Christina Holtz-Bacha, eds. 1995. *Political Advertising in Western Democracies. Parties & Candidates on Television.* Thousand Oaks, CA: Sage.

Kamps, Klaus, ed. 2000. *Trans-Atlantik – Trans-Portabel? Die Amerikanisierungsthese in der politischen Kommunikation.* Wiesbaden, Germany: Westdeutscher Verlag.

Kempf, Wilhelm. 2000. News Media and Conflict Resolution. A Comparative Study of Gulf War Coverage in U.S. and European Media. In Stig A. Nohrstedt and Rune Ottosen, eds. *Journalism and the World Order. Gulf War, National News Discourses and Globalization.* Göteborg, Germany: Nordicom, pp. 149–74.

Kim, Chie-Woon, and Hyo-Seong Lee. 1996. Political Power and Mass Manipulation in South Korea. In David L. Paletz, ed. *Political Communication in Action. States, Institutions, Movements, Audiences.* Cresskill, NJ: Hampton Press, pp. 97–116.

Kleinsteuber, Hans J., ed. 1996. *Der 'Information Superhighway.' Amerikanische Visionen und Erfahrungen.* Opladen, Germany: Westdeutscher Verlag.

———. ed. 2001a. *Aktuelle Medientrends in den USA.* Wiesbaden, Germany: Westdeutscher Verlag.

———. 2001b. Habermas and the Public Sphere. From a German to a European Perspective. *Javnost – The Public* (8) 1: 95–108.

Köcher, Renate. 2000. Repräsentativbefragung von Internet-Nutzern in Australien, Deutschland und den Vereinigten Staaten von Amerika. In Jens Waltermann, and Marcell Machill, eds. *Verantwortung im Internet. Selbstregulierung und Jugendschutz.* Gütersloh, Germany: Bertelsmann, pp. 433–87.

Kubicek, Herbert, William H. Dutton, and Robin Williams, eds. 1997. *The Social Shaping of Information Highways.* Frankfurt, Germany: Campus.

Lambeth, Edmund B. 1995. Global Media Philosophies. In John C. Merrill, ed. *Global Journalism. Survey of International Communication.* White Plains, NY: Longman, pp. 3–18.

Landman, Todd. 2000. *Issues and Methods in Comparative Politics. An Introduction.* London: Routledge.

McQuail, Denis, and Karen Siune, eds. for the Euromedia Research Group. 1998. *Media Policy: Convergence, Concentration and Commerce.* London: Sage.

Merrill, John C., ed. 1995. *Global Journalism. Survey of International Communication.* White Plains, NY: Longman.

Mill, John Stuart. 1872. *A System of Logic.* London (1973; reprint, London: Routledge).

Negrine, Ralph. 1996. *The Communication of Politics*. London/Thousand Oaks, CA: Sage.

Nohrstedt, Stig A., and Rune Ottosen, eds. 2000. *Journalism and the World Order. Gulf War, National News Discourses and Globalization*. Göteborg, Germany: Nordicom.

Olayiwola, Abdur-Rahman Olalekan. 1996. Political Communication In Nigeria. In David L. Paletz, ed. *Political Communication in Action. States, Institutions, Movements, Audiences*. Cresskill, NJ: Hampton Press, pp. 55–72.

Paletz, David L., ed. 1996. *Political Communication in Action. States, Institutions, Movements, Audiences*. Cresskill, NJ: Hampton Press.

Perrot, Michel. 1986. *Les moyens de communication publique chez les Inuit*. Lille, France: Thèses de l'Université.

Pfetsch, Barbara. 2001. Political Communication Culture. *Harvard International Journal of Press/Politics* 6 (1): 46–67.

Raboy, Marc, ed. 1996. *Public Broadcasting for the 21st Century*. Luton, UK: Luton Press.

Schmitt-Beck, Rüdiger. 2000. *Politische Kommunikation und Wahlverhalten*. Wiesbaden, Germany: Westdeutscher Verlag.

Semetko, Holli A. 1991. *The Formation of Campaign Agendas. A Comparative Analysis of Party and Media Roles in Recent American and British Elections*. Hillsdale, NJ: Erlbaum.

Siebert, Fred S., Theodore Peterson, and Wilbur Schramm. 1956. *Four Theories of the Press*. Urbana: University of Illinois Press.

Stevenson, Robert L. 1995. Freedom of the Press Around the World. In John C. Merrill, ed. *Global Journalism. Survey of International Communication*. White Plains, NY: Longman, pp. 63–76.

Sussman, Gerald, and John A. Lent, eds. 1991. *Transnational Communications. Wiring the Third World*. Newbury Park, CA: Sage.

Thomas, Barbara, and Michaela Tzankoff, eds. 2001. *Medien und Transformation in Osteuropa*. Wiesbaden, Germany: Westdeutscher Verlag.

Thussu, Daya Kishan, ed. 1998. *Electronic Empires. Global Media and Local Resistance*. London: Arnold.

Trautmann, Ljuba. 2002. *Die Medien im russischen Transformationsprozess*. Frankfurt, Germany: Lang.

Tunstall, Jeremy. 1999. *The Anglo-American Media Connection*. Oxford: Oxford University Press.

Waltermann, Jens, and Marcell Machill, eds. 2000. *Verantwortung im Internet. Selbstregulierung und Jugendschutz*. Gütersloh, Germany: Bertelsmann.

FIVE

Designs and Methods of Comparative Political Communication Research

Werner Wirth and Steffen Kolb

Some "25 years after 'Extending the Frontier'" (Gurevitch and Blumler 1990), a sophisticated discussion about designs and methods in comparative communication research has not even begun.[1] This delay is rather astonishing if one takes into account the huge number of publications on this topic in other social sciences – especially in political science, psychology, and sociology. Surprisingly, most of the literature does not take into account the research done in neighboring disciplines. Przeworski's and Teune's publication of 1970 is one of the few exceptions: their research approach is known across disciplines, even though there are some studies that replicate their ideas (Rosengren et al. 1992, 275).

The lack of shared knowledge across disciplines is all the more suprising if one considers the similarities in making international comparisons in the social sciences. In the field of communication research, Gurevitch (1989); Blumler, McLeod, and Rosengren (1992); and Schmitt-Beck (1998) have published seminal works on this subject. In political science, Hartmann (1995), van Deth (1998), and Przeworski and Teune (1970, especially 3–16) have also made important contributions. In psychology, van de Vijver and Leung (1997; 2000) and the cross-cultural research methods series (edited by John W. Berry and Walter J. Lonner since 1975) offer interesting insights. Nowak (1989) and Kohn (1989a; 1989b) have produced well-known sociological works in this field.

Obviously, the approaches of the social sciences differ, because they focus on the problems particular to each discipline. This chapter tries to

---

[1] We will not enter into the discussions on different meanings of the terms *international, intercultural, cross-national, cross-cultural, multinational,* or *multicultural* comparisons, all of which will be used synonymously.

integrate these different ways of dealing with comparative research problems and to make them appropriate for use in the field of communication research.

First, it introduces the general problem of comparability and of the equivalence of comparisons. It then presents a number of approaches to international comparisons, based on existing studies. This is followed by a review of how studies are conceptualized, how cultures are selected, how data is analyzed, and how results are interpreted. There is then a detailed discussion about different kinds and levels of equivalence, as well as cultural bias due to a lack of equivalence. Finally, a five-step guideline for planning and carrying out intercultural studies is suggested.

COMPARABILITY AND EQUIVALENCE: THE MAIN PROBLEM
OF COMPARATIVE RESEARCH

Comparability and the maintenance of equivalence can be seen as the major problems of comparative research, as the objects to compare usually belong to different system contexts (Luhmann 1970; Nowak 1989; Niedermayer 1997). To make the term *equivalence* accessible for the social sciences, it is often "operationalized" as functional equivalence: the functionality of the research objects within the different system contexts must be equivalent. On the item level, equivalence occurs whenever the same subdimensions or issues can be used to explain theoretical constructs in every country or culture. If the constructs can be integrated into theories equivalently, one would assume construct equivalence.

The implications of this concept should not be underestimated. When comparing political institutions, for example, these must be embedded equivalently into the higher system level. However, they do not have to be equal, as the comparison of equal or identical elements would offer little results other than the equality of these elements (van Deth 1998). The Anglo-American metaphor of comparing apples and oranges is as misleading as the common use of the term *comparable* for describing two or more similar objects. Apples and oranges are, in fact, quite comparable, due to their common functional integration into the "concept" fruit (Aarebrodt and Bakka 1997).

In brief, neither equivalence nor its absence can ever be presumed. Equivalence has to be analyzed and tested for on all the different levels of research, that is, on the level of indicators, constructs, theories, and for the entire research process.

THEORETICAL DIVERSITY AND ORIENTATION IN RELATION TO CONTEXTUAL FACTORS: EIGHT GENERAL TYPES OF INTERNATIONAL RESEARCH

Theoretical Diversity

Theory should play a major role when looking for a research strategy. One important advantage of international research is the possibility of integrating a variety of (national) concepts or theories (e.g., Swanson 1992). This can be a fruitful basis for interdisciplinary and "intertheoretical" analyses (Kleiner and Okeke 1991; Swanson 1992; Berg-Schlosser and Müller-Rommel 1997, 19–22). Swanson (1992) distinguishes between three principal strategies for dealing with theoretical diversity:

(1) The simplest possibility is called *avoidance strategy*. Most international comparisons are made by teams that come from only one culture or nation. Usually, their research interests are restricted to their own (scientific) socialization. Within this mono-cultural context, broad approaches cannot be applied and intertheoretical questions cannot be answered (Swanson 1992, 26).

(2) The *pretheoretical strategy* tries to avoid cultural and theoretical differences in another way: studies are undertaken without a strict theoretical framework until results are ready to be interpreted. The advantage of this strategy lies in the exploration, that is, in developing new theories. Following the strict principles of critical rationalism, however, the testing of hypotheses is not possible (Popper 1994, 198–9). Most of the results remain on a descriptive level and never reach theoretical diversity. The instruments for pretheoretical studies are necessarily "holistic," in order to integrate every theoretical construct conceivable for the interpretation. As a result, these studies can be rather extensive (Swanson 1992, 26).

(3) When a research team develops a *metatheoretical approach* to building a framework for the basic theories and research questions, the data can be analyzed using different theoretical backgrounds. This metatheoretical strategy allows the extensive use of all data. It produces, however, quite a variety of very different results, which are not easily summarized in one report (Swanson 1992, 28–9).

The decision for or against the use of theoretical diversity should always be based on research aims as well as time and financial costs. Niedermayer

(1997, 90–1) emphasizes the frictional losses in internationally cooperating research teams: the higher the necessary level of integration, the higher the cost of establishing consensus. These problems may possibly be overcome by a culture-specific training of the researchers (Bhawuk 1998).

CONTEXT FACTORS AND THEORETICAL ORIENTATION

Van de Vijver and Leung (1996, 287–9; 1997, 20–6; 2000, 34) propose another typology of theoretical orientation and the use of context factors. These authors differentiate between theory-driven and exploratory studies. In both, however, the researchers can use context factors to improve the results. For example, in a comparative content analysis of television news, the context factors "historical development," "competition on the television market," and "media systems characteristics" can be applied (Ragin 1989; Abell 1990). Combining these two dimensions of theory and context, van de Vijver and Leung (1997, 20–6) present four types of studies:

(1) *Generalizability studies* test nationally developed theories and hypotheses on an international level. Such studies can usually be described as theory oriented without taking alternative explanations into account.

(2) *Theory-driven studies* are those in which collection of data is hypothesis driven and the analysis remains open for alternative explanations, by measuring context factors. These are anchored in a theoretical framework that can be overruled if the hypothesis fails to be verified. Analysis of the context factors can even lead to theoretical advances, due to the open study design.

(3) *Difference studies*: If the researchers focus on the production of data without any theoretical orientation and without considering context factors, they will usually be limited to describing (similarities and) differences of the countries involved. Any interpretation or explanation must remain on a very superficial level and can only be made post hoc.

(4) *External validation studies* are those that use context factors without a theoretical framework. The descriptive results are at least clarified by the presentation of context variables, such as national statistics.

Integration of the Two Typologies: Eight Research Strategies

Rosengren, McLeod, and Blumler (1992, 274–5) recognize two dimensions in the typology of Swanson (1992): the degree of *theoretical diversity* and *theoretical drivenness*. According to these authors, a theory-driven study will test a hypothesis, whereas a study without theoretical drivenness will be descriptive, open, and/or exploratory. The integration of both approaches leads to eight research strategies for international projects presented in Table 5.1 and described in the following text.

(1) *Metatheoretical research strategy with context factors:* Potentially every cultural and theoretical background can be used. The researchers form a metatheoretical guideline from different theories that are attached to their cultural backgrounds. Theories and hypotheses to be tested are deduced from this metatheory. Integrating context factors into the operationalization and data analysis process even allows unexpected results to be interpreted appropriately.

(2) *Metatheoretical research strategy without context factors:* In contrast to the first strategy, the lack of contextual variables makes this approach strictly deductive in the sense of critical rationalism. This strategy facilitates the optimal adaptation of research questions to the theoretical background. However, questions that come up during the research process cannot be sufficiently answered.

(3) *Unitheoretical research strategy with context factors:* If a single national theory is tested in an international context, the creation of a metatheoretical framework through international cooperation is no longer possible. Studies with this strategy are usually undertaken by a national researcher or research team who take their own specific theoretical ideas as a starting point. The general research aim is to test the applicability of their theory on other countries, that is, the generalizability of their theory. The inclusion of context factors assures a minimal level of open-mindedness.

(4) *Unitheoretical research strategy without context factors:* The same procedure as described under point 3, without an open perspective on the generalization. The results will state either the generalizability of the theory or describe the theory as a national phenomenon.

Table 5.1 Eight Research Strategies for Comparative Studies

		Theoretical Diversity			
		Yes		No	
		Contextualization	No Contextualization	Contextualization	No Contextualization
Theoretical Drivenness	High	1. metatheoretical, contextualized	2. metatheoretical, not contextualized	3. unitheoretical, contextualized (generalization)	4. unitheoretical, not contextualized (generalization)
	Low	5. pretheoretical, contextualized (exploration)	6. pretheoretical, not contextualized (exploration)	7. atheoretical, contextualized (description)	8. atheoretical, not contextualized (description)

Source: Adapted from Rosengren, McLeod, and Blumler (1992, 275); Vijver and Leung (1997).

(5) *Pretheoretical research strategy with context factors:* This strategy identifies a rather loose and minor theoretical guideline due to its focus on descriptive and exploratory research questions. In general, it is imperative that the focus integrates a huge number of context factors in order to allow the researchers to create broad-based results. During data analysis and interpretation, the inductive approach is a means to theory development and/or the connection to previously existing theories. While the advantage of this research strategy is its substantial open-mindedness, there is a reasonable risk of implicitly sliding into an atheoretical description (cf. type 7 and 8).

(6) *Pretheoretical research strategy without context factors:* If the integration of context factors is abandoned in a pretheoretical strategy, the openness will be reduced to an absolute minimum.

(7/8) Completely *atheoretical research* can only lead to trivial conclusions – with or without contextual factors. The results will likely be limited by the description of empirical similarities and/or differences between the cultures or nations under examination.

THE RESEARCH DESIGN OF INTERNATIONAL COMPARISONS

LEVEL- AND STRUCTURE-ORIENTED QUESTIONS

In conceiving an internationally comparative study, research questions must be examined in light of the implications they have for methodology. Van de Vijver and Leung (1996; 1997) distinguish between two types of questions: *structure-oriented* questions, which are mostly interested in the relationship between certain variables, and *level-oriented* questions, which focus on the parameter values. If, for example, a knowledge-gap study analyzes the relationship between the knowledge gained from television news by high and low socioeconomic status (SES) in the United Kingdom and the United States, the question is structure oriented, because the focus is on a national *relationship* (of knowledge indices) and the average gain of knowledge is not taken into account. Usually, structure-oriented data require analyses of correlation or regression. If the main interest of the study is a comparison of the average gain of knowledge of low SES in the United Kingdom and the United States, the research question is level oriented, because the knowledge indices of the two nations are to be compared. In this case, one would most probably use analyses of variance.

Structure-oriented questions will generally call for relatively simple research designs, as the *relationship* of variables is in question. Level-oriented questions need more complex designs and a higher level of equivalence. In addition, they require more data that may have an effect on the structure or the single values (van de Vijver and Leung 1996, 269–71; 1997, 21–3).

EMIC AND ETIC STRATEGY OF OPERATIONALIZATION

Before the operationalizing of an international comparison, the research team has to analyze construct equivalence to prove comparability. If an equivalent structure of subdimensions can be found in every country in question, construct equivalence is well established. Do the different national contexts really allow for the assumption that, for example, the "ritual" of watching television news has an equal function in the countries under examination? To be sure, the researchers have to demonstrate that the construct (e.g., ritual of television news watching) consists of the same dimensions, perhaps with different characteristics. Whenever they fail to do so, the construct cannot be measured equivalently in every country. It is important to state that the decision of whether or not to use the same instruments in every country does not have any impact on the problem of a lack of construct equivalence.

When construct equivalence is missing, the researchers can undertake their study following an *emic* approach: The operationalization for the measurement of the construct(s) is developed nationally, to provide for a highly adequate, culturally specific national instrument. The idea behind this procedure is to measure, for example, the ritual of watching television news correctly, in other words, culture-specifically. The comparison on the construct level remains possible, even though the instruments vary culturally, because functional equivalence has been established on the construct level by the culture-specific measurement. The ritual exists in every country examined in the study, but it cannot be measured using the same instrument. In general, this procedure will also be possible if one or more national instruments already exist and the instruments for the other countries have to be developed seperately (van de Vijver and Leung 1996, 271).

As measurement differs from culture to culture, the integration of the national results can be very difficult. Strictly speaking, this disadvantage of emic studies results in the interpretation of a structure-oriented outcome with a thorny validation process. Measurements with different indicators on different scales do lead to data on equivalent constructs.

By using external reference data from every culture, complex weighting and standardization procedures can possibly lead to valid equalization of levels and variance (more detailed in van de Vijver and Leung 1997). In research practice, emic measuring and data analysis are used to highlight cultural *differences* (Hui and Triandis 1985; Greenfield 1996, 306; Piedmont and Chae 1997, 132–3).

If construct equivalence can be assumed after an in-depth analysis, the research team should prefer an *etic* modus operandi. Here, approaching the different cultures with the same instrument[2] is valid because the constructs function equally in every culture. Consequently, an emic procedure should probably come to similar instruments in every culture (Hui and Triandis 1985; Helfrich 1993; Piedmont and Chae 1997, 132–4; van de Vijver and Tanzer 1997, 265–6). Reciprocally, an etic approach must lead to bias and measurement artifacts, when applied under the circumstances of missing construct equivalence.

The advantages of emic proceedings are not only the adequate measurement of culture specificity but also the possible inclusion of idiographic elements of each culture. Thus, this approach can be seen as a compromise of qualitative and quantitative methodologies. The psychologist Greenfield (1996, 307–9) and – in political science – Hartmann (1995, 25–30) suggest analyzing cultural processes in a holistic way without crushing them into variables; psychometric, quantitative data collection would only be suitable for similar cultures. As an objection to this simplification, one should remember the emic approach's potential to provide the researchers with comparable data, as previously described. In contrast, holistic analyses produce culture-specific outcomes that will not be comparable.

The etic and emic approaches both have advantages and disadvantages, so that the aim must be to determine a fitting compromise between "purely" etic and "purely" emic procedures for a well-founded research project (e.g., Triandis et al. 1993; Piedmont and Chae 1997).

Linguistic Adaptation of the Instruments

Difficulties in establishing equivalence are regularly linked to linguistic problems: How can a researcher try to establish functional equivalence without the knowledge of every language of the cultures under examination? Cultural differences *between* states or countries can

---

[2] The instruments used in an etic study do not have to be absolutely identical, but can be adapted, culture-specifically.

be rather small, while cultural or ethnic differences among groups *within* some specific states or countries can be substantial. Nevertheless, the (methodologically) typical case for a comparison between countries is a comparison between different cultures and language areas.

Cooperation among researchers with different cultural research backgrounds (usually publishing in different languages) poses specific problems (van Deth 1998). For a linguistic adaptation of the theoretical background as well as for the instruments, one can discriminate between "more etic" and "more emic" approaches, too:

(1) *Translation-oriented approaches:* Most of the translation-based procedures produce two translated versions of the text: one in the "foreign" language and one after translation back into the original language. The latter version can be compared to the original version to evaluate the translation. In general, this is repeated until a complete match of the two versions is obtained (Sperber et al. 1994, 503; van de Vijver and Tanzer 1997, 267; Erkut et al. 1999, 208–10 – all based on Werner and Campbell 1970). Sperber, Devellis, and Boehlecke (1994) even introduce bilingual specialists to validate the instrument. Lauf and Peter (2001) discuss these problems with a special focus on reliability of multilingual codebooks for content analyses.

This method produces eticly formed instruments due to the focus on "linguistic equivalence," which can only work as a criterion of evaluation whenever functional equivalence has been established on every superior level. The constructs have to be measurable by the same wording in all the countries. Van de Vijver and Tanzer (1997, 267) call this procedure the *application* of an instrument in another language. However, there are "more emic" orientations based on translation (e.g., Usunier 1999). In a *cultural adaptation*, cultural singularities can be included if, for example, culture-specific connotations are counterbalanced by a different item-formulation. Purely emic approaches develop entirely culture-specific instruments. Consequently, these instruments cannot be produced by translation. This alternative, called *assembly* (van de Vijver and Tanzer 1997, 267), is seen as a "silver bullet," for example, by Greenfield (1996, 311–17), as the process of communication during the complete phase of data collection could be culturally adapted. However, the problems concerning the comparability of results from emic studies have already been mentioned.

(2) *Committee approach:* Van de Vijver and Tanzer (1997, 266–7) recommend an international interdisciplinary group of experts of the cultures, languages, and research field in question. This committee decides whether the instruments are to be formed culture-specifically or whether a cultural adaptation will be sufficient.

(3) *Dual-focus approach:* This approach tries to find a compromise between literal, grammatical, syntactical, and construct equivalence. Native speakers and/or bilinguals should arrange the different language versions together with the research team in a complex five-step procedure (Erkut et al. 1999, 210–15). This seems to be the ideal, yet labor intensive way to an etic-emic set of instruments that combines the highest levels of literal similarity and culture-specific adaptation (Erkut et al. 1999, 216; Niedermayer 1997, 93–7).

SAMPLING OF CULTURES OR COUNTRIES

In many international comparisons, the sampling of countries does not follow any theoretical idea or criterion. Usually, the researchers use personal preference and accessibility of data to select the countries to study (Greenfield 1996, 309; similarly Kohn 1989a; Ragin 1989). This kind of sample avoids many problems, but at the same time it ignores theoretical advantages or representative sampling. In most cases, these studies are pre- or atheoretical, because the research interest is not a theoretical one.

If you want to select the countries or cultures in a systematic and theory-driven way, Przeworski and Teune (1970, 32–43) suggest two opposing approaches:

(1) The quasi-experimental *most similar systems design* tries to stress cultural differences. To minimize the possible causes for the differences, one should choose countries that are the "most similar," so that the few dissimilarities between these countries are most likely to be the reason for the different outcomes. For example, the differences between political participation in Sweden and Denmark are surely less numerous and less severe than those between political participation in Sweden and Japan.

(2) Whenever the hypotheses highlight intercultural similarities, the authors propose to select the *most different systems design*. In a kind

of turned-around quasi-experimental logic, studies following this design focus on similarities between cultures, even though these differ in the greatest possible way. One example might be the search for correspondence in the yellow press in many different countries.

The *most different systems design* has often been favored due to the higher number of possible cases (i.e., "most different" countries) and due to overly specialized research on single phenomena (similarly van de Vijver and Leung 1997, 29–30). Hartmann (1995, 31–3) has pointed out that, for the sake of a higher number of cases, the impact of context variables has been underestimated. Intercultural comparisons that value their data profiles higher than history, religion, tradition, and so forth, risk ending up with trivial results. Berg-Schlosser (1997) suggests a *parallel* analysis of the *most different systems with the same outcome* (MDSO) and the *most similar systems with different outcomes* (MSDO) to improve the results. Ragin (1989) prefers a medium number of cases to combine intensive and extensive research strategies. The intensive strategy will produce in-depth knowledge of the research objects, but it is only suitable for a small number of cases due to the effort involved. For a large number of cases, the extensive strategy would be preferable, but it remains a superficial way to analyze cultures. In addition to these approaches, there are several criteria for the selection of countries or cultures. For example, the research objects could be chosen following a theoretically built factor matrix or following some previously fixed guidelines for decision making. In most cases, "modified most similar systems designs" seem to be "seen as the optimum" (Niedermayer 1997, 97).

Whenever any kind of representativity is needed, random selection will be advantageous. Random samples of countries, however, are rather problematic from a statistical point of view, because the number of states in the world is limited. Thus, a normal distribution for the social factors under examination, that is, the precondition of random sampling, cannot be assumed, and some parametric analytic methods may hereby be rendered inapplicable. Moreover, many statistical methods face problems when applied under the condition of a low number of cases (Ragin 1989; Hartmann 1995, 34; Aarebrot and Bakka 1997; Widmaier 1997). These problems of low numbers of cases are, of course, irrelevant for studies that are measuring on an individual level, that is, analyzing cultural groups by survey or experimental research or examining international media products. Random sampling is applied frequently in psychological research, whereas random selections are inapplicable to political comparisons of systems. Nevertheless, psychological studies, too, meet severe problems of cost and availability of data when using random sampling (van de Vijver and Leung 1997, 28–32).

To summarize, systematic or even theoretically driven sampling should produce the best results. The researcher is provided with the opportunity to interpret results causally, especially when following the quasi-experimental research strategy. In order to optimize this procedure, the researcher could form quasi-experimental factors with more than two values, overcoming the dichotomy of "most similar" and "most different." The basis for the selection of cultures, for example, could be an independent variable with five possible values. For a quasi-experimental analysis, at least one country is chosen for each given value (see the individualism-collectivism studies of Phalet and Claeys 1993, 320–5; Triandis et al. 1998).

Data Analysis and Interpretation of Results

Given the conceptual and methodological problems of international research, special care must be taken over data analysis and the interpretation of results. As the implementation of every single variable of relevance is impossible, the documentation of methods, work process, and data analysis is even more important than in single-culture studies. The evaluation of the results must continue in additional studies. An intensive use of different statistical analyses beyond the general comparison of arithmetic means can lead to further validation of the results and the interpretation (Abell 1990). Van de Vijver and Leung (1997, 88–130) present a widespread summary of data analysis procedures, including structure- and level-oriented approaches, examples of Statistical Program for the Social Sciences (SPSS) syntax, and references.

Following Przeworski's and Teune's research strategies (1970; more explicitly Berg-Schlosser 1997), results of comparative research can be classified into *differences* and *similarities* between the research objects. For both types, Kohn (1989b) introduces separate ways of interpretation. Intercultural similarities seem to be easier to interpret, at first glance. The difficulties emerge when regarding equivalence on the one hand (i.e., there may be covert cultural differences within culturally biased similarities), and the causes of similarities on the other. The causes will be especially hard to determine in the case of "most different" countries, as different combinations of different indicators can theoretically produce the same results. Esser (2000, 144) refers to diverse theoretical backgrounds that will lead either to differences (e.g., action theoretically based microresearch) or to similarities (e.g., system theoretically oriented macroapproaches). In general, the starting point of Przeworski and Teune (1970) seems to be the easier way to come to interesting results and interpretations, using the quasi-experimental approach for "most similar systems with different outcome" (Berg-Schlosser 1997, 77). In addition to the advantages of causal interpretation, the "most similar" systems are likely to be equivalent from the top level of the construct to the bottom level of indicators and items. "Controlling" for most of the variables of possible impact can thus minimize methodological problems, which makes analysis and interpretation more valid.

To clarify what is meant by careful data analysis and interpretation: the level of equivalence determines the extent to which data can be compared. If equivalence is guaranteed, structure-oriented and level-oriented questions can be answered. If functional equivalence has been established (e.g., by using an emic strategy), the interpretation of level-oriented variables and results is impossible, due to the lack of intercultural standardization of instruments and data. Sometimes it makes sense to think about the relevance of the differences between the instruments, because *complete* equivalence can rarely be obtained. At least on the level of theoretical constructs, the research strategy should be an etic one, allowing for a minimum of comparability. Hui and Triandis (1985, 144) suggest omitting the application of the "functional equivalence" approach to completely emic measurement due to the loss of comparability. Such studies should be seen as measurements of two or more constructs rather than the measurement of one construct (using one adapted instrument).

EQUIVALENCE AND BIAS

Equivalence has to be analyzed and – if necessary – established on at least three levels: on the levels of the construct, the item, and the method. Following van de Vijver and Leung (1996; 1997) we label these types of equivalence *construct equivalence*, *item equivalence*, and *method equivalence*. Whenever a test on any of these levels shows negative results, cultural bias can be assumed. Thus, bias on these three levels can be described as the opposite of equivalence.

Van de Vijver and Leung define bias as the variance within certain variables or indicators that can only be caused by culturally unspecific measurement. For example, a media content analysis could examine the amount of foreign affairs coverage in one variable, by measuring the length of newspaper articles. If, however, newspaper articles in country A are generally longer than they are in country B, irrespective of their topic, the result of a sum or mean index of *foreign affairs coverage* would almost inevitably lead to the conclusion that the amount of foreign affairs coverage in country A is higher than in country B. This outcome would hardly be surprising and would fail to answer the research question, because the countries' average amount of foreign affairs coverage is not related to the national average length of articles. To get comparable results, that is, to avoid cultural bias, the results must be standardized or weighted, for example, by the mean article length. Analogous to this standardization and weighting of the article length, Kolb et al. (2001) propose the weighting of newspaper articles using the estimated amount of recipients, which may improve inference of "public opinion" from the articles' contents. In the following three sections of the chapter, we will illustrate different sources of bias on the three levels and try to show ways of avoiding the trap of cultural bias.

CONSTRUCT EQUIVALENCE AND CONSTRUCT BIAS

Construct bias (van de Vijver and Tanzer 1997, 264) can be found whenever the construct of interest is not equivalent in all the cultures included in the study. To find out whether the construct is equivalent in every country in question, the researcher will generally require external data and rather complex procedures of culture-specific construct validation(s). Ideally, this includes analyses of the *external structure*, that is, theoretical references to other constructs, as well as an examination of the latent or *internal structure*. The internal structure consists of the relationships between the construct's subdimensions. It can be tested using confirmatory factor analyses, multidimensional scaling, or item analyses (Hui and Triandis 1985, 141–3; Bentler 1990; Pedhazur and Schmelkin 1991, 60; Byrne and Campbell 1999; Caprara et al. 2000). Equivalence can be assumed if the construct validation for every culture has been successful and if the internal and external structures are identical in every country. As a less complicated but expensive alternative, one could use triangulation, that is, a combination of different methods or methodologies to measure the construct in each country (Denzin 1978; Abell 1990). To reduce cost and complexity, the researchers could undertake a survey of local experts or conduct focus-group discussions before embarking on the main part of the study. It is obvious that a very good knowledge of every country or culture included in the study is absolutely indispensable, especially if the research team is nationally based and is not cooperating with international partners.

It is extremely difficult to prove construct equivalence beyond any doubt. Construct validation is a difficult task in one country alone, so that the international perspective only complicates the situation further. Besides, an identical state of internal and external structures might even be the result of cultural bias and/or occur at random. The probability of a *random* state of "sameness" decreases with the number of countries included in the study. Moreover, this probability can be calculated statistically and published in the findings. Most procedures of construct validation require multidimensional or item-battery measurement, because the internal structure cannot be tested when measured in just one variable (van de Vijver and Leung 1996, 273; 1997, 17; van Deth 1998). In the face of these problems, one might ask whether the effort undertaken to achieve construct validation is worthwhile. Yet, only the procedures we have presented will lead to a *well-founded* decision, irrespective of the preferred approach to be undertaken for the enquiry, be it etic, emic, or etic-emic (van de Vijver and Leung 1997, 12–15).

ITEM EQUIVALENCE AND ITEM BIAS

Even with a given construct equivalence, bias can still occur on the item level. The verbalization of items in surveys (and of definitions and categories in content analyses) can cause bias due to culture-specific connotations. Item bias is mostly evoked by bad, in the sense of nonequivalent, translation or by culture-specific questions and categories (van de Vijver and Leung 1997, 17). Psychological inventories and item batteries in particular can be tested for item equivalence, using several procedures derived from the "item response theory" (e.g., Lienert and Raatz 1994; van de Vijver and Leung 1997, 62–88). Compared to the complex procedures discussed in the case of construct equivalence, the testing for item bias is rather simple (once construct equivalence has been established): Persons from different cultures, who take the same positions or ranks on an imaginary construct scale, must show the same attitude toward every item that measures the construct. Statistically, the correlation of the single items with the total (sum) score have to be identical in every culture, as the test theory generally uses the total score to estimate the position of any individual on the construct scale. Hui and Triandis (1985, 135) add *scalar equivalence* to the list. This tests whether the construct is measured on the same scale. In general, different wordings of questions or categories have to be well-founded and published in the research report. The best way to avoid item bias seems to be pretesting, which can help to detect bias and control it within the main study (Greenfield 1996; Niedermayer 1997, 95).

METHOD EQUIVALENCE AND METHOD BIAS

When the instruments are ready for application, three other levels of equivalence must be taken into account: sample equivalence, instrument equivalence, and administration equivalence. These three levels can be summed up in the term *method equivalence.* Van de Vijver and Tanzer (1997, 264) call a violation of equivalence on this level *method bias.*

Sample equivalence and sample bias: Sample equivalence refers to an equivalent selection of subjects, interviewees, or units of analysis (for content analyses). Identical sampling procedures for every country in question do not suffice to guarantee equivalence, because different cultures can have different distributions, for example, concerning levels of education. Thus to avoid sample bias, a culture-specific sampling regarding the (main) dependent and independent variables is required (Niedermayer 1997, 93, 96–7).[3] Analogically, when undertaking a press content analysis, for example, the distribution of different types of newspapers has to be taken into account. Sample bias can only be detected and avoided by cultural expertise and the use of external data (van de Vijver and Tanzer 1997, 264).

Instrument equivalence and instrument bias: Instrument equivalence can be seen as independent of the specific research project. One has to examine whether there is equivalence in terms of the people in each culture who agree to take part in the study, as well as whether participants are familiar with the instruments (e.g., paper and pencil, telephone, or online surveys) (van de Vijver and Tanzer 1997, 264; "stimulus equivalence" in Niedermayer 1997). At first sight, content analyses seem to be rather resistant to instrument bias, however, the risk of bias here lies on the side of the coders and the codebook. Within an international coding team, different understanding of the codebook and possibly different tendencies toward extremes in coding may occur (Lauf and Peter 2001; more general Wirth 2001). This kind of problem can be found analogically in surveys, where culture-specific attitudes to social desirability, acquiescence, extremes in answering, and so forth, can cause cultural

---

[3] For different ways of sampling see the overview of Niedermayer (1997, 97–100) or any basic references for methodology of the social sciences (e.g., Schnell et al. 1999). For an in-depth presentation of sampling procedures see, for example, Cochran (1972).

bias (see Hui and Triandis 1989; Cheung and Rensvold 2000; Little 2000 for publications on "response sets"; Bortz and Döring 2002, 215).

Adminstration equivalence and administration bias: Bias on the administration level can occur due to culture-specific attitudes of the interviewers that might produce culture-specific answers. Another source of administration bias could be found in sociodemographic differences between the various national interviewer teams (van de Vijver and Tanzer 1997, 264).

It is noteworthy that the functional equivalence approach to international research overrides the inaccurate belief that identical instruments automatically measure in an identical or equivalent way. For example, Greenfield (1996, 330) emphasizes the great potential of using video recording in process-oriented research on cultural differences without expounding on the problems caused by the culture-specific reaction of being recorded. Such a reaction would most probably vary between cultures in the field of participant-observation studies, too. A Caucasian observer would not be the cause of any bias in Europe, but might cause a sensation in rural parts of Africa or Asia (Niedermayer 1997, 93–7).

Method bias is especially treacherous, because it will appear as "cultural differences" in the results when analyses of variance are undertaken. These differences are bound to run directly into misinterpretation due to their source of inadequate measurement. Moreover, significant cultural differences could be lost in a mixture of method bias and "real" results, so that the entire interpretation would be useless (van de Vijver and Leung 1997, 15–17).

TESTING FOR AND ESTABLISHING EQUIVALENCE: A GUIDELINE

As shown previously, equivalence can be seen as the major problem of comparative research. For data to be adequate and interpretable, the researcher requires the highest possible level of equivalence. A hierarchical step-by-step procedure can help to test for and establish equivalence on every level of the research process. The following guideline will describe the most important steps in the establishment of equivalence.[4]

---

[4] See van de Vijver and Leung (1997, 42–51) and van Deth (1998, 9) for other guidelines.

(1) *Bring all the elements of the wider description of the research issue into a hierarchical scheme.*

Following Patzelt (1997, 40–5) and Esser (2000, 131), it can be helpful to locate the research issue in a hierarchical model of social reality. Patzelt (1997) starts from the level of structure of perception and information processing. The second level consists of culture-specific knowledge such as norms, values, and positions. A third level finds the single acting individual and his or her personality. Having presented several levels, from small groups to social organizations or institutions and states, the scheme ends on an international or transnational level. It is obvious that this sophisticated model is related to the micro-, meso-, and macrologic. These different levels are subject to change, according to specific research interests. For every study there must be a specific definition of where the research issue is located, and of what belongs to which level in general. After the research issue has been clearly determined, the surrounding levels can be analyzed, in order to find social phenomena or constructs strongly related to the research objects. A standard context factor that should not be ignored is the dimension of history, which can bring valuable insight on many levels (Greenfield 1996, and applied in Rosengren 1992).

> *Example:* In a content analysis of soft journalism in different types of daily press, the culture-specific press systems, press markets, legal aspects of press, and so forth, should be located on the *macro level*. The political system, historical development, economic system, functions of the press, general legal and ethic framework, and so forth could be used as *context-constructs*. On a *meso level*, the characteristics of the single newspapers, such as periodicity of publication, area of circulation, political position, structure of recipients, type of editorial system, and distribution channel could be of interest. The *micro level* includes single editions of the papers and characteristics such as layout, mean length of articles, and so forth. The focus varies depending upon the research questions.

(2) *Define the focus: What is important and what can be treated as less important context factors?*

To be clear, the establishment of total equivalence between different states or cultures is impossible. One should define the *basic* and the *context* social phenomena or scientific constructs of the scheme in the first step. Equivalence in the basic part could be given higher priority than that in the context constructs. We cannot give any general suggestion as to where an acceptable limit would be found, because this decision highly depends on the research question.

(3) *Test for construct equivalence.*
By now, we have formed a hierarchical scheme of social phenomena or scientific constructs, with a basic part and a context part. Starting with the *basic part,* equivalence on the construct level has to be discussed, tested for, and established. This can be done by pretesting, focus-group discussions, or at least by analyzing strategies to control possible sources of bias. For the less important *context area,* a discussion of equivalence and a test for plausibility should be sufficient. The current theoretical discussion in each country and the empirical "state of the art" should be taken into account, in order to avoid construct bias in the optimal way. Possibly some *peripheral* context constructs can be left out completely if the expenses for the basic part have already been very high.

(4) *Test for item equivalence.*
Whenever the measurement of the construct is to be undertaken eticly, the linguistic adaptation of the instrument to each culture must be tested. Once again, tests for item equivalence can be applied either before the study (i.e., by pretests or by group discussions with linguists and communication researchers on culture-specific connotations) or when analyzing the data (i.e., by calculating the item-total-correlation for every item used in an item battery). For content analyses, analogical tests can be carried out depending on the scale of the variables.

(5) *Test for method equivalence.*
Usually, external statistical data on the structure of a country's population is easily available, so that sample bias can easily be avoided. The structure of different media systems is not too difficult to analyze, either. Stacked sampling before gathering the data or weighting procedures afterward can help to establish equivalence on the sample level.

To test instrument equivalence, additional data on culture-specific response sets (such as social desirability or acquiescence for surveys and culture-specific coding for content analyses) are necessary. In the case of surveys, different response rates, as well as the culture-specific habituation to different survey modes (i.e., mail, telephone, or personal interviews, CATI, CAPI, etc.), should be taken into account.

Administration equivalence can be tested but can hardly be established. For international studies, the variety of possible scientific and commercial cooperation partners is limited. If cultural differences concerning the organization of research are detected in the process, one can describe these problems in the resulting report. It is nearly impossible to rectify administration bias.

CONCLUSION

The methodology of cultural comparisons in the social sciences has been developed by several disciplines at the same time. Astonishingly, the communication of findings across disciplines has been very limited. But research into political communication could benefit from these efforts of the other disciplines, due to its interdisciplinary orientation. The aim of this chapter has been to compile, systemize, and combine some of the methodological approaches to international comparative work.

It should be made clear, how difficult it is to establish validity in international comparisons. Even in *unicultural* research, establishing validity can be seen as one of the major problems, but when "extending the frontier" these problems increase significantly. As possible research topics are integrated into culture-specific social, political, economic, legal, and media contexts, the research team has to ask whether they can be treated as equivalent and, consequently, as comparable. Given at least functional equivalence, a comparison of cultures can be undertaken and will provide some valid insight. But does this need for equivalence automatically imply that the researcher has to know every similarity and difference in advance?

The procedures presented demand considerable effort, but in-depth analysis shows that there is light at the end of the tunnel. For example, peripheral constructs may be omitted when testing for equivalence. Nevertheless, the research report should include a detailed explanation why these constructs are more or less irrelevant to the research question. When the relevance of a construct is merely moderate, some plausibility checks may suffice, that is, some culture-specific references should be integrated without undertaking preliminary empirical research. However, comparative researchers should be very cautious when limiting themselves to small numbers of basic factors, so as not to risk excessively curbing the explanatory power of their study. Instead, the integration of a set of context factors can notably improve the scientific worthiness of a study.

REFERENCES

Aarebrot, Frank H., and Pal H. Bakka. 1997. Die vergleichende Methode in der Politikwissenschaft. In Dirk Berg-Schlosser and Ferdinand Müller-Rommel, eds. *Vergleichende Politikwissenschaft*. Opladen, Germany: Leske + Budrich, pp. 49–66.

Abell, Peter. 1990. Methodological Achievements in Sociology over the Past Few Decades with Special Reference to the Interplay of Quantitative and Qualitative Methods. In Christopher G. A Bryant and Henk A. Becker, eds. *What Has Sociology Achieved?* London: Macmillan, pp. 94–116.

Bentler, Peter M. 1990. Comparative Fit Indexes in Structural Models. *Psychological Bulletin* 107 (2): 238–46.

Berg-Schlosser, Dirk. 1997. Makro-qualitative vergleichende Methoden. In Dirk Berg-Schlosser and Ferdinand Müller-Rommel, eds. *Vergleichende Politikwissenschaft*. Opladen, Germany: Leske + Budrich, pp. 67–88.

Berg-Schlosser, Dirk, and Ferdinand Müller-Rommel, eds. 1997. *Vergleichende Politikwissenschaft*. Opladen, Germany: Leske + Budrich.

Berry, John W., Ype H. Poortinga, and Janak Pandey, eds. 1996. *Handbook of Cross-Cultural Research*. Boston: Allyn and Bacon.

Bhawuk, Dharm P. S. 1998. The Role of Culture Theory in Cross-Cultural Training. A Multimethod Study of Culture-Specific. Culture-General, and Culture Theory-Based Assimilators. *Journal of Cross-Cultural Psychology* 29 (5): 630–55.

Blumler, Jay G., Jack M. McLeod, and Karl Erik Rosengren, eds. 1992. *Comparatively Speaking: Communication and Culture Across Space and Time*. Newbury Park, CA: Sage.

Bortz, Jürgen, and Nicola Döring. 2002. *Forschungsmethoden und Evaluation für Sozialwissenschaftler*. Berlin: Springer.

Byrne, Barbara M., and T. Leanne Campbell. 1999. Cross-Cultural Comparisons and the Presumption of Equivalent Measurement and Theoretical Structure. *Journal of Cross-Cultural Psychology* 30 (5): 555–74.

Caprara, Gian V., Claudio Barbaranelli, José Bermúdez, Christina Maslach, and Willibald Ruch. 2000. Multivariate Methods for the Comparisons of Factor Structures in Cross-Cultural Research. *Journal of Cross-Cultural Psychology* 31 (4): 437–64.

Cheung, Gordon W., and Roger B. Rensvold. 2000. Assessing Extreme and Acquiescence Response Sets in Cross-Cultural Research Using Structural Equitations Modeling. *Journal of Cross-Cultural Psychology* 31 (2): 187–212.

Cochran, William G. 1972. *Stichprobenverfahren*. Berlin: de Gruyter.

Denzin, Norbert K. 1978. *The Research Act. A Theoretical Introduction to Sociological Methods*. New York: McGraw-Hill.

Deth, Jan W. van 1998. Equivalence in Comparative Research. In Jan W. van Deth, ed. *Comparative Politics: The Problem of Equivalence*. New York: Routledge, pp. 1–19.

Erkut, Sumru, Odette Alarcón, Cynthia García Coll, Linda R. Tropp, and Heidie A. Vázquez García. 1999. The Dual-Focus Approach to Creating Bilingual Measures. *Journal of Cross-Cultural Psychology* 30 (2): 206–18.

Esser, Frank. 2000. Journalismus vergleichen. Journalismustheorie und komparative Forschung. In Martin Löffelholz, ed. *Theorien des Journalismus. Ein diskursives Handbuch*. Wiesbaden, Germany: Westdeutscher Verlag, pp. 123–46.

Greenfield, Patricia M. 1996. Culture as Process: Empirical Methods for Cultural Psychology. In John W. Berry, Ype H. Poortinga, and Janak Pandey, eds. *Handbook of Cross-Cultural Psychology. Theory and Methods.* Vol. 2. Boston: Allyn and Bacon, pp. 301–46.

Gurevitch, Michael. 1989. Comparative Research on Television News. *American Behavioral Scientist* 33: 221–9.

Gurevitch, Michael, and Jay G. Blumler. 1990. Comparative Research: The Extending Frontier. In David L. Swanson and Dan Nimmo, eds. *New Directions in Political Communication: A Resource Book.* Newbury Park, CA: Sage, pp. 305–25.

Hartmann, Jürgen. 1995. *Vergleichende Politikwissenschaft. Ein Lehrbuch.* Frankfurt/ Main, Germany: Campus.

Helfrich, Hede. 1993. Methodologie kulturvergleichender psychologischer Forschung. In Alexander Thomas, ed. *Kulturvergleichende Psychologie. Eine Einführung.* Göttingen, Germany: Hogrefe, pp. 81–102.

Hui, C. Harry, and Harry C. Triandis. 1985. Measurement in Cross-Cultural Psychology: A Review and Comparison of Strategies. *Journal of Cross-Cultural Psychology* 16 (2): 131–52.

Hui, C. Harry, and Harry C. Triandis. 1989. Effects of Culture and Response Format on Extreme Response Style. *Journal of Cross-Cultural Psychology* 20 (3): 296–309.

Kleiner, Robert, J., and Barnabas I. Okeke. 1991. Advances in Field Theory. New Approaches and Methods in Cross-Cultural Research. *Journal of Cross-Cultural Psychology* 22 (4): 509–24.

Kohn, Melvin L. 1989a. Introduction. In Melvin L. Kohn, ed. *Cross-National Research in Sociology.* Newbury Park, CA: Sage, pp. 17–31.

Kohn, Melvin L. 1989b. Cross-National Research as an Analytic Strategy. In Melvin L. Kohn, ed. *Cross-National Research in Sociology.* Newbury Park, CA: Sage, pp. 77–102.

Kolb, Steffen, Rainer Mathes, and Christoph Kochhan. 2001. Von der kommunikatzentrierten Auswertung von Medieninhaltsanalysen zur Schätzung von Rezeptionswahrscheinlichkeiten? – Wahrnehmungschancen als Ansatz für eine Weiterentwicklung der Inhaltsanalyse. In Edmund Lauf and Werner Wirth, eds. *Inhaltsanalysen. Perspektiven, Probleme, Potentiale.* Cologne, Germany: Halem Verlag. pp. 244–61.

Lauf, Edmund, and Jochen Peter. 2001. Die Codierung verschiedensprachiger Inhalte: Erhebungskonzepte und Gütemaße. In Edmund Lauf and Werner Wirth, eds. *Inhaltsanalysen. Perspektiven, Probleme, Potentiale.* Cologne, Germany: Halem Verlag, pp. 199–217.

Lienert, Gustav A., and Ulrich Raatz. 1994. *Testaufbau und Testanalyse.* Weinheim, Germany: Beltz, PVU.

Little, Todd D. 2000. On the Comparability of Constructs in Cross-Cultural Research. *Journal of Cross-Cultural Psychology* 31 (2): 213–19.

Luhmann, Niklas. 1970. *Soziologische Aufklärung. Aufsätze zur Theorie Sozialer Systeme.* Opladen, Germany: Westdeutscher Verlag.

Niedermayer, Oskar. 1997. Vergleichende Umfrageforschung. In Dirk Berg-Schlosser and Ferdinand Müller-Rommel, eds. *Vergleichende Politikwissenschaft.* Opladen, Germany: Leske + Budrich, pp. 89–102.

Nowak, Stefan. 1989. Comparative Studies and Social Theory. In Melvin L. Kohn, ed. *Cross-National Research in Sociology*. Newbury Park, CA: Sage, pp. 34–56.

Patzelt, Werner J. 1997. *Einführung in die Politikwissenschaft. Grundriß des Faches und studiumbegleitende Orientierung*. Passau, Germany: Richard Rothe.

Pedhazur, Elazar J., and Liora Pedhazur Schmelkin. 1991. *Measurement, Design, and Analysis: An Integrated Approach*. Hillsdale, NJ: Erlbaum.

Phalet, Karen, and Willem Claeys. 1993. A Comparative Study of Turkish and Belgian Youth. *Journal of Cross-Cultural Psychology* 24 (3): 366–83.

Piedmont, Ralph L., and Joon-Ho Chae. 1997. Cross-Cultural Generalizability of the Five-Factor Model of Personality. Development and Validation of the NEO PI-R for Koreans. *Journal of Cross-Cultural Psychology* 28 (2): 131–55.

Popper, Karl R. 1994. *Logik der Forschung*. Tübingen, Germany: Mohr.

Przeworski, Adam, and Henry Teune. 1970. *The Logic of Comparative Social Inquiry*. Malabar, FL: Krieger.

Ragin, Charles. 1989. New Directions in Comparative Research. In Melvin L. Kohn, ed. *Cross-National Research in Sociology*. Newbury Park, CA: Sage, pp. 57–76.

Rosengren, Karl Erik. 1992. The Structural Invariance of Change: Comparative Studies of Media Use (Some Results from a Swedish Research Program). In Jay G. Blumler, Jack M. McLeod, and Karl Erik Rosengren, eds. *Comparatively Speaking: Communication and Culture Across Space and Time*. Newbury Park, CA: Sage, pp. 140–78.

Rosengren, Karl Erik, Jack M. McLeod, and Jay G. Blumler. 1992. Comparative Communication Research: From Exploration to Consolidation. In Jay G. Blumler, Jack M. McLeod, and Karl Erik Rosengren, eds. *Comparatively Speaking: Communication and Culture Across Space and Time*. Newbury Park, CA: Sage, pp. 271–98.

Schmitt-Beck, Rüdiger. 1998. Of Readers, Viewers, and Cat-Dogs. In Jan W. van Deth, ed. *Comparative Politics: The Problem of Equivalence*. New York: Routledge, pp. 222–46.

Schnell, Rainer, Paul B. Hill, and Elke Esser. 1999. *Methoden der empirischen Sozialforschung*. Munich, Germany: Oldenbourg.

Sperber, Ami D., Robert F. Devellis, and Brian Boehlecke. 1994. Cross-Cultural Translation – Methodology and Validation. *Journal of Cross-Cultural Psychology* 25 (4): 501–24.

Swanson, David L. 1992. Managing Theoretical Diversity in Cross-National Studies of Political Communication. In Jay G. Blumler, Jack M. McLeod, and Karl Erik Rosengren, eds. *Comparatively Speaking: Communication and Culture Across Space and Time*. Newbury Park, CA: Sage, pp. 19–34.

Triandis, Harry C., Xiao P. Chen, and Darius K.-C. Chan. 1998. Scenarios for the Measurement of Collectivism and Individualism. *Journal of Cross-Cultural Psychology* 29 (2): 275–89.

Triandis, Harry C., Christopher McCusker, Hector Betancourt, Sumiko Iwao, Kwok Leung, Jose Miguel Salazar, Bernadette Setiadi, Jai B. P. Sinha, Hubert Touzard, and Zbignew Zaleski. 1993. An Etic-Emic Analysis of Individualism and Collectivism. *Journal of Cross-Cultural Psychology* 24 (3): 366–83.

Usunier, Jean-Claude. 1999. *The Use of Language in Investigating Conceptual Equivalence in Cross-Cultural Research*. Paper presented at the 7ᵗʰ Cross-Cultural Consumer and Business Studies Research Conference in Cancun, Mexico, December 12–15, 1999.

Vijver, Fons van de, and Kwok Leung. 1996. Methods and Data Analysis of Comparative Research. In John W. Berry, Ype H. Poortinga, and Janak Pandey, eds. *Handbook of Cross-Cultural Psychology. Theory and Methods*. Vol. 2. Boston: Allyn and Bacon, pp. 257–300.

Vijver, Fons van de, and Kwok Leung. 1997. *Methods and Data Analysis of Cross-Cultural Research*. Thousand Oaks, CA: Sage.

Vijver, Fons van de, and Kwok Leung. 2000. Methodological Issues in Psychological Research on Culture. *Journal of Cross-Cultural Psychology* 31 (1): 33–51.

Vjiver, Fons van de, and Norbert K. Tanzer. 1997. Bias and Equivalence in Cross-Cultural Assessment: An Overview. *European Journal of Applied Psychology* 47 (4): 263–79.

Werner, Oswald, and Donald T. Campbell. 1970. Translating, Working Through Interpreters, and the Problem of Decentering. In Raoul Naroll and Ronald Cohen, eds. *A Handbook of Method in Cultural Anthropology*. New York: The National History Press, pp. 398–420.

Widmaier, Ulrich. 1997. Vergleichende Aggregatdatenanalyse. In Dirk Berg-Schlosser and Ferdinand Müller-Rommel, eds. *Vergleichende Politikwissenschaft*. Opladen, Germany: Leske + Budrich, pp. 49–66.

Wirth, Werner. 2001. Der Codierprozeß als gelenkte Rezeption. Bausteine für eine Theorie des Codierens. In Edmund Lauf and Werner Wirth, eds. *Inhaltsanalysen. Perspektiven, Probleme, Potentiale*. Cologne, Germany: Halem Verlag, pp. 157–82.

PART II

Cases

SIX

Global Political Communication

*Good Governance, Human Development,
and Mass Communication*

Pippa Norris

The growth in electoral democracies presents many potential opportunities for human development. The last quarter of the twentieth century witnessed a dramatic expansion in political rights and civil liberties worldwide. Since the start of the "third wave" of democratization, in 1974, the proportion of states that are electoral democracies has more than doubled, and the number of democratic governments in the world has tripled (Diamond 2001).[1] Countries as diverse as the Czech Republic, Mexico, and South Africa have experienced a radical transformation of their political systems through the establishment of more effective party competition, free and fair elections, and a more independent and pluralistic press. Many hoped that these developments would expand the voice of the disadvantaged and the accountability of governments, so that policy makers would become more responsive to human needs, and governments could be removed from power through the ballot box if citizens became dissatisfied by their performance.

Yet in practice, after the initial surge in the early 1990s, many electoral democracies in Latin America, Central Europe, and Sub-Saharan Africa remain fragile and only poorly consolidated, often divided by ethnic conflict and plagued by a faltering economic performance, with excessive executive power in the hands of one predominant party and a fragmented opposition (Linz and Stephan 1996). The central danger, illustrated by the nations of the Andean region, lies in disillusionment with democracy, and even occasional reversals (Norris 1999; Pharr and Putnam 2000; Lagos 2001; Plattner and Diamond 2001). Achieving their full democratic

---

[1] Freedom House estimates that in 2000–1 there were 120 electoral democracies around the world, and the highest proportion of people (40.7 percent) living under freedom since the survey started in 1980. See *Freedom Around the World, 2000–2001* at www.freedomhouse.org.

potential depends on widening and deepening the institutions of voice and accountability, which commonly remain deeply flawed. The key issue examined here is whether there is systematic evidence that channels of mass communications play a vital role in strengthening good governance and human development, as liberal theorists have long claimed.

The first section of this chapter theorizes that the mass media will have a positive impact on democratization and human development if they function effectively as a watchdog holding the powerful to account and as a civic forum facilitating a diversity of voices in public debate. Yet in practice the press is often limited in these roles, and in many authoritarian regimes, far from serving the needs of the public, the channels of communication reinforce state control and the power of established interests. Liberal theories stress the importance of an independent fourth estate as a check on the abuse of power. The study suggests that this is necessary but not sufficient; in particular, media systems strengthen good governance and promote positive development outcomes most effectively under two conditions: (1) where channels of mass communications are free and independent of established interests, and in addition (2) where there is widespread diffusion and public access to these media. Both independence *and* access are required. Freedom of the press by itself is insufficient to guarantee development outcomes if poor people are excluded from media markets and the information resources provided by newspapers, radios, television, and now Internet technologies. Moreover media access is insufficient, if the press is subservient to established interests, uncritical of government failures, and unable to hold the powerful to account for their actions.

The second section of this chapter outlines the comparative methodology, adopting the "most different" research strategy, and operationalizes this typology to classify and compare media systems in 135 nations around the world. The third section examines the cross-national evidence for the impact of these patterns. The study confirms that countries with media systems characterized by widespread mass access *and* by an independent free press experience less corruption, greater administrative efficiency, higher political stability, and more effective rule of law, as well as better social outcomes such as higher per capita income, greater literacy, lower economic inequality, lower infant mortality rates, and greater public spending on health.

The *conclusion* considers the implications of the results and the advantages of a broad cross-national approach in understanding political communications.

THEORIES OF THE ROLE OF MASS COMMUNICATIONS

What is the role of the mass media in strengthening voice and account-ability in good governance and human development (Shah 1996; Asante 1997; McQuail 2001)? Liberal theorists from Milton through Locke and Madison to John Stuart Mill have argued that a free and independent press within each nation can play a vital role in the process of democ-ratization by contributing toward the right of freedom of expression, thought, and conscience, strengthening the responsiveness of govern-ments to all citizens, and providing a pluralist platform of political ex-pression for a multiplicity of groups (Sen 1999). Recent years have seen growing recognition that this process is not just valuable in itself, but that it is also vital to human development. This perspective is exem-plified by Amartya Sen's argument that political freedoms are linked to improved economic development outcomes and good governance in low-income countries, through their intrinsic value, their instrumental role in enhancing the voice of poor people, and their impact on gen-erating informed choices about economic needs (Sen 1999; Besley and Burgess 2001, 629–40). The guarantee of freedom of expression and in-formation is regarded as a basic human right in the Universal Declaration of Human Rights adopted by the United Nations in 1948, the European Convention on Human Rights, the American Convention on Human Rights, and the African Charter on Human and Peoples' Rights. In the words of the president of the World Bank, James D. Wolfensen, "A free press is not a luxury. A free press is at the absolute core of equitable development, because if you cannot enfranchise poor people, if they do not have a right to expression, if there is no searchlight on corruption and inequitable practices, you cannot build the public consensus needed to bring about change" (1999).

In modern societies, the availability of information is critical to the quality of decision making by citizens and policy makers. In economic markets, consumers need accurate and reliable information to compare and evaluate products and services. In political markets, electors need information to judge the record of government and to select among al-ternative candidates and parties. If citizens are poorly informed, if they lack practical knowledge, they may cast ballots that fail to reflect their real interests (Lupia and McCubbins 1998). Moreover policy makers need accurate information about citizens, to respond to public con-cerns, to deliver effective services meeting real human needs, and also, in democracies, to maximize popular electoral support to be returned to office. Information in the political marketplace comes from two primary sources. Personal interactions commonly include informal face-to-face political conversations with friends, family, and colleagues; traditional campaign rallies; community forums; and grassroots meetings. These information resources remain important, especially for election campaigns in poorer democracies, and the growth of e-mail and online discussion groups may revive the importance of personal political communications (Norris 2000). But these channels have been supplemented in modern campaigns by the mass media, including the printed press (newspapers and magazines), electronic broadcasts (radio and television news), and also more recently the bundle of technologies associated with the Internet (including political Web sites). The rise of the Internet may be a particularly important development for the process of democratization, due to its potential for interactive, horizontal linkages breaking down the traditional boundaries of space and time, and facilitating oppositional voices, new social movements, and transnational advocacy networks, despite the highly uneven distribution of these technologies around the globe (Norris 2001, ch. 1).

Classical liberal theories suggest that the free press serves to strengthen the process of democratization and human development in their *watchdog* role, where the channels of mass communications function to promote government transparency and public scrutiny of those in authority, highlighting policy failures, maladministration by public officials, corruption in the judiciary, and scandals in the corporate sector (Donohue and Tichenor 1995). Ever since Edmund Burke, the "fourth estate" has traditionally been regarded as one of the classic checks and balances in the division of powers (Köcher 1986). Investigative journalism can open the government's record to external scrutiny and critical evaluation, and hold authorities accountable for their actions, whether public sector institutions, nonprofit organizations, or private companies.

Equally vital, in their *civic forum* role, liberal theories argue that the free press can provide a public sphere, mediating between citizens and the state, facilitating informed debate about the major issues of the day (Dahlgren 1995; Dahlgren and Sparks 1995). If the channels of communication reflect the social and cultural diversity within each society, in a fair and impartial balance, then multiple interests and voices are heard in public deliberation. This role is particularly important during political campaigns. Fair access to the airwaves by opposition parties, candidates, and groups is critical for competitive, free, and fair elections.

It is particularly important that state-owned or public television stations should be open to a plurality of political viewpoints and viewpoints during campaigns, without favoring the government. This principle has been recognized in jurisprudence from countries as varied as Ghana, Sri Lanka, Belize, India, Trinidad and Tobago, and Zambia (Administration and Cost of Elections [ACE] Project).

What empirical evidence supports the claims made in liberal theories? Early accounts assumed a fairly simple and straightforward relationship between the spread of modern forms of mass communications, socio-economic development, and the process of democratization. Early studies in the late 1950s and early 1960s by Lerner, Lipset, Pye, and Cutright, among others, suggested that the diffusion of mass communications represented one sequential step in the development process. In this perspective, urbanization and the spread of literacy led to growing use of modern technologies such as telephones, newspapers, radios, and television, and the diffusion of the mass media laid the basis for an informed citizenry able to participate in democratic life (Lerner 1958; Lipset 1959; Pye 1963; McCrone and Cnudde 1967). Based on simple correlation analysis, showing a strong connection between the spread of communications and political development, Daniel Lerner theorized: "The capacity to read, at first acquired by relatively few people, equips them to perform the varied tasks required in the modernizing society. Not until the third stage, when the elaborate technology of industrial development is fairly well advanced, does a society begin to produce newspapers, radio networks, and motion pictures on a massive scale. This, in turn, accelerates the spread of literacy. Out of this interaction develop those institutions of participation (e.g., voting) which we find in all advanced modern societies" (Lerner 1958, 60). Yet in the late 1960s and early 1970s the assumption that the modernization process involved a series of sequential steps gradually fell out of fashion. Factors contributing to a more skeptical view of the promises of modernization included (1) the complexities of human development evident in different parts of the world, (2) major setbacks for democracy with the "second reverse wave" experienced in Latin America, Sub-Saharan Africa, and Asia, and (3) growing recognition that control of newspapers and television broadcasting could be used effectively to prop up authoritarian regimes and reinforce the power of multinational corporations, as much as to advance human rights and provide a voice for the disadvantaged (Hur 1984, 365–78; Sreberny-Mohammadi et al. 1984; Stevenson and Shaw 1984; Mowlana 1985; Preston et al. 1989; Huntington 1993).

LIMITS ON THE FREE PRESS

Despite liberal ideals, in practice channels of communication can and often do fail to strengther democracy, for many reasons. Limitations on the role of the press include explicit attempts at government propaganda; official censorship; legal restrictions on freedom of expression and publication – like stringent libel laws and official secrecy acts; partisan bias in campaign coverage; oligopolies in commercial ownership; and more subtle unfairness in the balance of interests and those whose voices are commonly heard in the public sphere (Sussman 2001). There are multiple examples.

- State control of information, particularly through state regulation and ownership of radio and television broadcasting, can reinforce ideological hegemony for autocratic regimes, and this may have negative consequences for social development (Djankov et al. 2001). In Malaysia and Singapore, for example, regimes have used the press to stifle internal dissent and forced journalists employed by the international press to modify or suppress news stories unflattering to the regime (Rodan 1998, 125–54).
- Governments in Myanmar, Sri Lanka, Iraq, and Saudi Arabia, among others, commonly place serious restrictions on press freedom through official regulations, legal restrictions, and censorship (e.g., Index on Censorship; The World Press Freedom Council; International Press Institute; Inglehart 1998). This practice remains more difficult in cyberspace, but nevertheless state-controlled monopolies exert control over access and content through providing the only Internet service in some nations (Sussman 2000; Kalathil and Boas 2001).
- During elections progovernment bias on television and radio has failed to provide a level playing field for all parties in many countries, exemplified by recent campaigns in Russia, Belarus, Ukraine, and Mozambique (e.g., OSCE 2000).
- Statistics collected by media freedom organizations show that each year dozens of media professionals are killed or injured in the course of their work. In many parts of the world, journalists face the daily threat of personal danger from wars, internal conflict, coups, terrorism, and vendettas (e.g., International Federation of Journalists). In Colombia, Sierra Leone, Liberia, Zimbabwe, and Egypt there are many cases of journalists, broadcasters, and editors experiencing

intimidation, harassment, and imprisonment by the police and military.

- Some express concern about concentration of ownership in the hands of major multinational corporations with multimedia empires around the globe. Well-known examples include AOL Time Warner and the Walt Disney Corporation in the United States; News International in Australia; Bertelsmann in Germany; Thomson in Canada; and Fininvest in Italy (Tunstall and Palmer 1991; Sanchez-Tabanero 1993). It is feared that media mergers may have concentrated excessive control in the hands of a few multinational corporations, which remain unaccountable to the public, reducing media pluralism (Bogart 1995; Bagdikian 1997; Picard 1988; McChesney 1999).

Therefore in practice, far from strengthening the voice of marginalized and disadvantaged groups, and bolstering government accountability to citizens, the mass media may instead serve to reinforce the control of powerful interests and governing authorities. The long-term dangers of these practices are that electoral democracies experience ineffective governance and growing disillusionment with representative institutions, hindering the process of democratization and human development, while communication channels strengthen the control of governing parties and established elites in nondemocratic states.

COMPARING MEDIA SYSTEMS

This study seeks to understand the role of media systems in development by comparing many countries around the globe. As discussed elsewhere in this volume, much existing research on political communications is based upon studies of the United States, as well as paired cross-national comparisons, for example between Britain and Germany. But there are major problems in attempts to generalize from one or two countries to map out broader relationships. As Lipset has long stressed, the United States, in particular, is so "exceptional" in its political system that it is atypical of many other nations (Lipset 1990; Lipset 1996). The individualistic values and particular constitutional structures created at the founding of the United States sets a specific cultural milieu. Particular circumstances, particular historical legacies, and particular institutional structures may well structure the American media system. For example, the predominance of the commercial broadcasting channels mean that tendencies in American network news may well prove different to media systems where public service broadcasting has a long tradition. The United States is also distinctive from equivalent established democracies in Europe for many other reasons, such as the marathon length and sheer frequency of American elections, the role of private funding in campaigns, the importance of entrepreneurial candidates over parties, the lack of a significant national newspaper sector, the complexity and fragmentation of the policy-making process, and the culture and traditions of journalism.

Another body of research, exemplified by the Euromedia group, has compared political communications within established West European democracies, while others have compared media systems in affluent postindustrial states (e.g., Østergaard 1992; Norris 2000). Yet it is not clear how far we can generalize more widely from these particular contexts to middle- and low-income countries around the globe. West European media systems that gradually evolved in the mid-nineteenth and early twentieth century, following the long-term process of industrialization, are unlikely to be similar to those found in Latin American, African, Middle Eastern, or Central European states. Where distinctive historical experiences stamp their cultural mark on different global regions, they may continue to influence patterns of political coverage today, in a path-dependent pattern. Another common approach is that many edited collections consist primarily of country-by-country case studies, from established and consolidating democracies, within a loose theoretical framework. This is a step in the right direction, for example when comparing changes in campaign communications, but nevertheless it still remains difficult to develop and test more systematic comparisons from separate studies of particular nations (e.g., Swanson and Mancini 1996; Gunter and Mughan 2000). Unlike some other fields of comparative politics, such as the study of parties, electoral systems, and voting behavior, or constitutions, political communications lacks strong and well-established conceptual typologies. The best known classification of media systems, Siebert, Peterson, and Schramm's *Four Theories of the Press*, developed at the height of the Cold War era, is now so dated as to provide little contemporary value (Siebert 1984). As a result of all these problems, older comparative politics textbooks commonly relegated the mass media to a minor player as an agent of political socialization, or a channel of interest group demands, at most, rather than as an institution and political actor in its own right (e.g., Almond and Powell 1992).

Given these considerations, this study follows the well-known conceptualization of Prezeworski and Teune in adopting the "most different systems" research design, seeking to maximize contrasts among societies worldwide to distinguish systematic clusters of characteristics associated with different dimensions of the mass media (Przeworski and Teune 1970). The comparison includes some of the most affluent countries in the world such as Sweden, Germany, and the United States; those characterized by middle-level human development; and transitional economies typified by nations such as Taiwan, Brazil, and South Africa, as well as poorer rural societies, such as India and China. Some states under comparison are governed by authoritarian regimes while others have experienced a rapid consolidation of democracy within the last decade. Today the Czech Republic, Latvia, and Argentina are ranked as equally "free" as West European nations with a long tradition of democracy, such as Belgium, France, and the Netherlands (Freedom House 2000). Clearly there are some important trade-offs involved in this approach, notably the loss of the richness and depth that can come from case-study comparison of a few similar countries within relatively homogeneous regions. A broader canvass increases the complexity of comparing societies that vary widely in terms of cultural legacies, political systems, and democratic traditions. There are major limitations in understanding the processes at work behind any patterns we establish at one point in time. Ideally, temporal as well as cross-national comparisons should be integrated. Aggregate data collected for other purposes, such as the circulation of newspapers or the distribution of television sets, provides only approximate proxy indicators for the matters we wish to investigate, such as actual readership or viewership patterns. The series of Eurobarometer surveys provide thirty years of trends in media use within Europaen Union (EU) member states, but we are only starting to get equivalent measures in reliable cross-national surveys elsewhere, and media items are still not standard even in the International Social Survey Programme and national election studies. In short, our hands are tied. Despite these well-known limitations, the strategy of attempting a global comparison, where data is available, has multiple advantages for sharpening our conceptual frameworks, broadening our understanding, and establishing reliable cross-national generalizations.

Liberal theories have long stressed the importance of an independent journalism as a check on the abuse of power. The study theorizes that this is necessary but not sufficient, in particular media systems strengthen good governance and promote positive development outcomes most

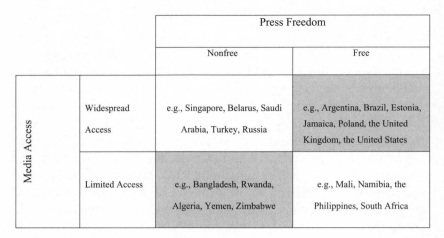

Figure 6.1 Typology of Media Systems. *Note:* Measures of media access and press freedom. See technical appendix for details.

effectively under two conditions: In societies where channels of mass communications are free and independent of established interests; *and* in addition where there is widespread public access to these media. The reason is that freedom of the press by itself is insufficient to guarantee positive development outcomes if disadvantaged groups and marginalized communities are excluded from the information resources provided by the mass media. For example, the potential impact of the Internet on democracy and social progress will continue to be limited if there is no closure of the digital divide, and if online political resources, as well as access to basic information about jobs, educational opportunities, news, and social networks, are unavailable to many poorer populations in large swathes of Sub-Saharan Africa, South-East Asia, and Latin America (Norris 2001). Yet access to communications is insufficient by itself, if the printed press remain subservient to established interests, if television news fails to report government policy failures, if radio broadcasters are unable to hold the powerful to account for their actions, and if there are relatively few Web sites reflecting the concerns of local groups and minority languages in poorer societies. For communication channels to function effectively in accordance with the hopes of liberal theory we can theorize that access and independence are required (see Figure 6.1).

Levels of *access* influence the scope and reach of mediated channels of communication, how widely politicians can reach the public through the press, as well as how far citizens can use these channels to learn about public affairs. The wider the level of access to news from daily papers, radio, television, and the Internet then, *ceteris paribus*, the greater the potential for media impact. Access to the mass communications most commonly includes the printed press (newspapers and magazines), the traditional electronic broadcast media (radio and television), and the new technologies associated with the Internet (including e-mail and the World Wide Web). *Media access* can be measured by World Development Indicators monitoring the circulation of daily newspapers, and the distribution of radio receivers and television sets per 1,000 population in 135 nations, the proportion of the population online population and the weighted distribution of Internet hosts (see Table 6.A1).[2] These indicators of media diffusion are strongly interrelated (all correlations are strong and significant: R = 0.55 and above Sig.01), although there are some societies that rely more heavily than average upon the printed press, such as South Korea, Norway, Romania, and Israel, while other countries are more reliant upon television in patterns of media use, such as the United States, Portugal, and El Salvador (see Appendix Figure 6.1). Given the strong correlations, access to all mass media were combined into a single scale and standardized to 100-points, including the per capita circulation of daily newspapers, the availability of radio receivers and television sets, and the proportion of the population that used the Internet and the distribution of Internet hosts. As the scale was heavily skewed toward richer nations, using a logged scale normalized the distribution.

Press freedom can be expected to influence whether the impact of the news media promotes pluralistic voice and government accountability, or how far it serves to reinforce the power of established interests and state control. Press freedom is far more complex and difficult to assess in any comprehensive fashion but the annual Freedom House Press Freedom Survey (2000) can be used as the standard cross-national indicator. Press freedom is measured by how much the diversity of news content is influenced by the structure of the news industry; legal and administrative decisions; the degree of political influence or control; the economic influences exerted by the government or private entrepreneurs; and actual incidents violating press autonomy, including censorship, harassment and physical threats to journalists. The assessment of press freedom distinguishes between the broadcast and print media, and the resulting

---

[2] The data for daily newspapers and radios are originally derived from UNESCO, and the information about television sets, personal computers, and Internet hosts from the International Telecommunications Union (ITU).

ratings are expressed as a 100-point scale for each country under comparison. Evaluations of press freedom in 186 nations were available in the 2000 Freedom House survey.

THE MAP OF MEDIA SYSTEMS

Figure 6.2 shows the distribution of 135 nations across these dimensions. The scatter of societies in the top right-hand corner shows that in many older democracies, as well as some newer democracies such as the Czech Republic, Thailand, the Republic of Korea, Jamaica, and Venezuela, liberal patterns of press freedom are strongly related to widespread media access. Some of these societies are among the most affluent around the globe, yet only moderate levels of human development characterize others such as South Africa, El Salvador, and Poland. In contrast, in societies located in the top left-hand corner of the map, exemplified by Singapore, Belarus, Saudi Arabia, Turkey, and Russia, there is relatively widespread access to most modern forms of mass media such as television and yet limited freedom of the press, suggesting the greatest potential for domestic news channels to be used by government, official agencies, and established interests as an agency of partisan bias, or even state propaganda, with a scope that reaches large sectors of the population (Hachten 1989, 822–7).

Media systems in countries such as India, Botswana, Namibia, and the Philippines, located in the bottom right-hand corner of the scatter plot, are characterized by a flourishing independent press and yet limited public access to newspapers, television, and the Internet, due to problems of literacy and poverty. In these countries, the media can be expected to have a positive impact on pluralism and government accountability, especially through competition among elites in civil society, but to exert only limited influence on the general population because of its limited reach. Lastly, most low-income nations are scattered in the bottom left-hand corner, such as Angola, Rwanda, Cambodia, and Bangladesh, where there are major restrictions on the freedom of the press as a force capable of challenging government authorities, and yet the role of the media is also limited as a channel of state propaganda because of restricted levels of mass access to newspapers, television, and the Internet. In these nations, traditional forms of campaign communication such as local rallies, posters, and community meetings, and grassroots party organizations, are likely to be more important in mobilizing political support than mediated channels.

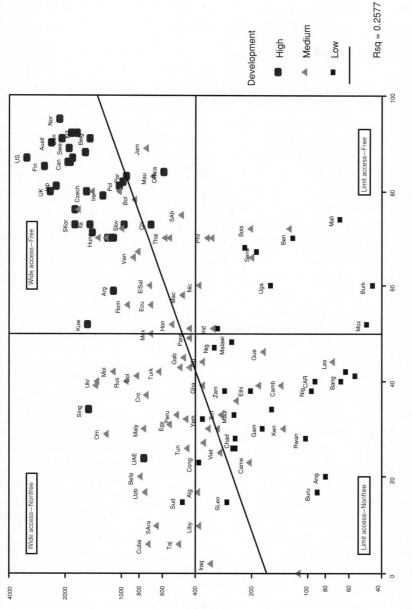

Press Freedom (Freedom House 2000)

Figure 6.2 Types of Media Systems

127

PIPPA NORRIS

THE IMPACT OF MEDIA SYSTEMS ON GOOD GOVERNANCE
AND HUMAN DEVELOPMENT

What is the impact of this pattern on good governance and human development? Recent years have seen growing attempts to gauge and measure systematic, valid, and reliable indicators of political development and the quality of democracy in a wide range of countries worldwide. We can draw on a recent study for the World Bank (Kaufman et al. 1999) that developed subjective perceptions of indicators of good governance, drawing on multiple surveys of experts, that assessed four dimensions based on the criteria of political stability, the rule of law, government efficiency and levels of corruption (see the Technical Appendix for details). Political stability is important as this reflects the regular rotation of government office, consolidation of the "rules of the game," continuity in constitutional practices, and lack of political violence due to acts of terrorism. The rule of law concerns the independence and effectiveness of the judiciary and courts, perceptions of violent or nonviolent crime, and the enforceability of contracts. Government efficiency is gauged by perceptions of the quality of the public service and the independence of the civic service from political pressures. Lastly, perceptions of corruption reflect the success of a society in developing fair, transparent, and predictable rules for social and economic interactions. Subjective judgments may prove unreliable for several reasons, including reliance upon a small number of national "experts," the use of business leaders and academic scholars as the basis of the judgments, variations in country coverage by different indices, and possible bias toward more favorable evaluations of countries with good economic outcomes. Nevertheless in the absence of other reliable indicators covering a wide range of nations, such as surveys of public opinion, these measures provide one of the best available gauges of good governance.[3] If widespread access to the free press plays an important role in promoting government accountability, then this should be evident in these indicators. Table 6.1 and Figure 6.3 show the simple correlations among these indicators without any controls. The results confirm that the indicators of media access, press freedom, and the combined communications index were all strongly and significantly related to good governance. Countries where much of the public has access to the free press have the greater political stability, rule of law, government efficiency in the policy process, and least corruption.

[3] It should be noted that none of the indicators that were selected included measures of freedom of the press or media access.

Table 6.1 Correlations Between Media and Indicators of Good Governance

		Press Freedom (2000)	Media Access (Logged % Papers + % TVs + % Radio + % Online) (1997–9)	Communication Index
Political Stability/ Violence	R	.633	.633	.727
	Sig.	.000	.000	.000
	N	140	119	120
Rule of Law	R	.644	.682	.763
	Sig.	.000	.000	.000
	N	151	124	125
Government Efficiency	R	.688	.649	.771
	Sig.	.000	.000	.000
	N	141	120	121
Corruption	R	.674	.652	.788
	Sig.	.000	.000	.000
	N	140	119	120

Note: See technical appendix for details.

Liberal theories claim that in addition to promoting a more efficient public-policy process, by publicizing social problems and articulating public concerns, mass communications also function to make the authorities more responsive to basic human needs. Table 6.2 and Figure 6.4 examine the correlations between communication measures and several common indicators of human development. The results confirm that press freedom, access to the mass media, and the combined Communication Index are all strongly related to positive development outcomes, measured by the Human Development Index (HDI), income, economic equality, lower infant mortality, longer life expectancy, higher spending on public health, and greater adult literacy. These coefficients need to be interpreted with caution, as no controls are included, and the causal interpretation of these relationships is not unambiguous.[4] In particular it could well be argued that greater levels of economic prosperity produced

---

[4] Multivariate Ordinary Least Square (OLS) regression models were tested, including the communications index and logged per capita Gross Domestic Product (GDP) regressed on the indicators of good governance and human development, but the multicollinearity statistics (measured by Tolerance and the Variance Inflation Factor) suggest that the results have to be treated with caution, as there is a strong linear relationship among the independent variables.

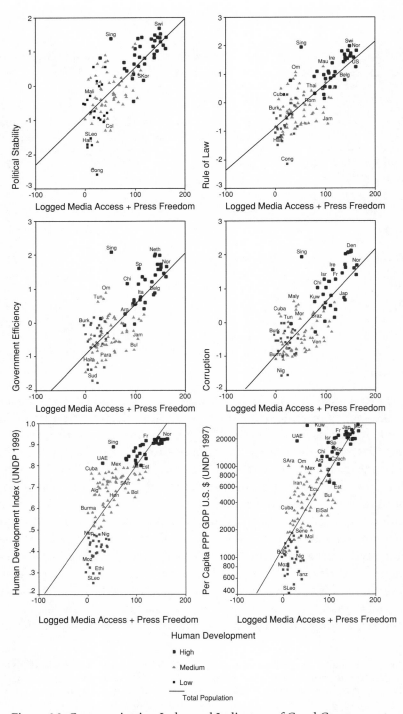

Figure 6.3 Communication Index and Indicators of Good Government.
Note: See technical appendix for details.

Table 6.2 Correlations Between Media and Human Development Indicators

		Press Freedom (2000)	Media Access (Logged % Papers + % TVs + % Radio + % Online) (1997–9)	Communication Index
Human Development	R	.519	.879	.801
Index	Sig.	.000	.000	.000
1999 UNDP	N	167	127	128
Income (Per Capita GDP	R	.508	.752	.793
in PPP U.S. $ 1997)	Sig.	.000	.000	.000
	N	167	127	128
Economic Equality	R	.246	.401	.403
(Reversed Gini Index)	Sig.	.009	.000	.000
	N	113	101	101
Lower Infant Mortality	R	.405	.813	.670
	Sig.	.000	.000	.000
	N	142	129	130
Public Expenditure on	R	.475	.604	.659
Health (% of GDP)	Sig.	.000	.000	.000
	N	140	127	128
Life Expectancy (years)	R	.464	.803	.700
1999 UNDP	Sig.	.000	.000	.000
	N	168	127	128
Adult Literacy Rate %	R	.404	.776	.673
1997 UNDP	Sig.	.000	.000	.000
	N	167	127	128
% With secondary	R	.459	.766	.731
education	Sig.	.000	.000	.000
1999 UNDP	N	125	100	101

Note: See technical appendix for details.

by development generate the underlying conditions for the purchase of household consumer durables such as televisions, radios, and personal computers. The expansion of the middle-class service sector in more developed economies is associated with greater affluence and growing leisure time, which are both strongly linked to use of the mass media. Use of newspapers and the Internet, in particular, require cognitive skills and knowledge that are strongly related to levels of education and literacy. Nevertheless, despite a process of interaction, the consistent and strong

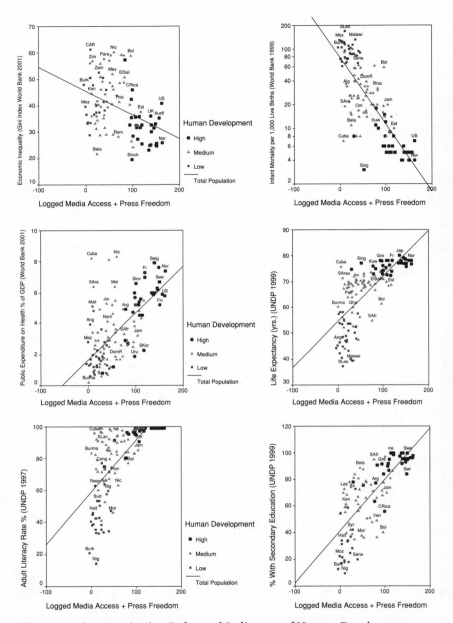

Figure 6.4 Communication Index and Indicators of Human Development;
Note: See technical appendix for details.

Table 6.3 Mean Scores on Good Governance Indicators by Type of Media System

Type of Media System	N.	Political Stability	Rule of Law	Government Efficiency	Corruption
Limited access to nonfree press	59	−.65	−.63	−.65	−.60
Limited access to free press	22	−.28	−.16	−.22	−.34
Wide access to nonfree press	17	−.09	.02	−.11	−.22
Wide access to free press	*53*	*.74*	*.80*	*.73*	*.80*

Note: See technical appendix for details.

relationship across all the different indicators of human development and good governance is striking.

The relationship between the typology of media systems and these indicators are illustrated in Tables 6.3 and 6.4. The results confirm that the fifty-two societies with widespread access to the free press consistently scored far higher than all other media systems across all the indicators of good governance and human development: people living in these nations have more stable political systems, more efficient government processes, and less corruption, as well as living longer, with greater affluence, and more economic equality. In sharp contrast, countries lacking an independent press and public access to mass communications scored consistently worst across all these indicators. Media matters, both for its own sake, and for development.

CONCLUSIONS: STRENGTHENING CHANNELS OF VOICE AND ACCOUNTABILITY

The lessons from this analysis suggest that strengthening the channels of communication is vital for development, particularly for electoral democracies that are in the process of establishing more effective political and economic institutions. It is widely assumed that a free press is necessary for social and political development, although this proposition is rarely tested in any systematic fashion. Because many studies are conducted within affluent societies, where newspapers and television are widely available, the basic issue of access to the mass media is rarely linked explicitly to issues of how the press functions within a democracy. The results indicate that those societies characterized by both press freedom and widespread access to the mass media are characterized by many indicators of good governance and human development. The reason, it

Table 6.4 Mean Scores on Human Development Indicators by Type of Media System

Type of Media System	N.	Human Development Index 1999	Per Capita PPP GDP U.S. $ 1997	Gini Index 2001	Infant Mortality per 1,000 Live Births 1999	Public Expenditure on Health % of GDP	Adult Literacy Rate % 1997	% With Secondary Education 1999
Limited access to nonfree press	68	.560	3208	42.1	67.5	2.1	66.3	52.2
Limited access to free press	31	.619	3621	47.0	64.6	2.9	71.0	53.1
Wide access to nonfree press	17	.759	7919	40.2	16.2	4.1	89.3	70.3
Wide access to free press	*52*	*.843*	*14,278*	*34.8*	*11.7*	*4.8*	*95.7*	*83.2*
Total	167	.678	7183	39.7	42.1	3.4	78.5	65.6

Note: See technical appendix for details.

134

is suggested, is that the free press plays an important role in promoting the voice of disadvantaged groups in the policy-making process and strengthening the accountability of governments to citizens. Liberal theories, which focus only on the conditions of independent journalism without taking account of the problems of restricted access, tell only one half of the story.

More generally, the global comparative approach adopted by this study suggests that we can go beyond more limited case studies of particular countries, or research that contrasts media systems among a few countries within a particular region or continent. Clearly there is a need for complementary multimethod research designs, which benefit from combining the strengths and weaknesses of any single approach. For example, it is difficult to go beyond the simple correlations examined here to establish patterns of causality that could be explored by detailed historical case studies. Other approaches such as interviews with media and policy elites would provide alternative insights into this process, such as how far journalists see their role as watchdogs. Systematic content analysis could reveal patterns of news coverage, for example reporting incidents of abuse of government power or cases of corruption. Surveys could shed light on audience patterns of use and the impact of news coverage on political attitudes and values. No single method is wholly satisfactory. Nevertheless the end of the Cold War and dramatic changes in human development in recent decades have broken down the old tripartite distinctions between postindustrial, postcommunist, and developing societies, as well as between established democracies, consolidating democracies, and nondemocracies. The process of globalization and the rise of new information technologies have similarly transformed the subject. We are commonly still stuck in the rut of studying the mass media within particular nation-states, when some of the most electric transformative movements fall outside these boundaries (Norris 2002). Studies of political communication need to revise and retool our conceptual frameworks to reflect these developments. A broad-brush comparative framework utilizing aggregate data in many different nations around the world, mapping media systems, is one more research strategy that should be added to our comparative toolbox.

Table 6.A1 Measures of Press Freedom, Media Access and the Communication Index

	Nation	Press Freedom 2000 (i)	Newspapers per 1,000 1996 (ii)	Radios per 1,000 1997 (iii)	TV Sets per 1,000 1999 (iv)	% Of Population Online 2000 (v)	Media Access (ii to v)	Communication Index (Freedom + Access)
1	Afghanistan	10	–	–	–	–	–	–
2	Albania	44	36	217	113	.0	7	37.8
3	Algeria	17	38	241	107	.0	8	15.1
4	Angola	20	11	54	15	.1	2	4.1
5	Antigua and Barbuda	54	–	–	–	4.3	–	–
6	Argentina	59	123	681	293	1.0	22	79.4
7	Armenia	43	23	224	238	.1	9	41.7
8	Australia	90	293	1376	706	37.4	55	156.5
9	Austria	88	296	753	516	5.5	33	133.7
10	Azerbaijan	30	27	23	254	.0	6	23.5
11	Bahrain	25	–	–	–	5.4	–	–
12	Bangladesh	40	9	50	7	.0	1	4.6
13	Barbados	84	–	–	–	1.9	–	–
14	Belarus	20	174	296	322	.1	16	23.9
15	Belgium	91	160	793	523	19.8	34	139.2
16	Belize	75	–	–	–	4.3	–	–
17	Benin	70	2	108	11	.1	2	26.9
18	Bhutan	24	–	–	–	–	–	–
19	Bolivia	78	55	675	118	.1	17	95.9

20	Bosnia and Herzegovina	44	152	248	112	.0	9	**41.6**
21	Botswana	72	27	156	20	.2	4	**44.3**
22	Brazil	67	40	444	333	4.1	17	**82.2**
23	Brunei	26	–	–	–	3.1	–	**–**
24	Bulgaria	70	257	543	408	1.8	24	**97.0**
25	Burkina Faso	60	1	33	11	.0	1	**−3.8**
26	Burundi	17	3	71	15	.0	2	**3.3**
27	Cambodia	39	2	127	9	.0	5	**27.4**
28	Cameroon	23	7	163	34	.0	4	**14.0**
29	Canada	86	159	1077	715	41.9	49	**145.0**
30	Cape Verde	68	–	–	–	.0	–	**–**
31	Central African Rep.	40	2	83	6	.0	2	**10.2**
32	Chad	28	0	242	1	.0	5	**19.2**
33	Chile	73	98	354	240	1.0	14	**83.5**
34	China	20	–	333	292	.7	–	**–**
35	Colombia	41	46	581	199	.9	17	**50.5**
36	Comoros	60	–	–	–	.1	–	**–**
37	Congo, Dem. Rep.	23	8	375	2	.1	10	**23.4**
38	Costa Rica	84	94	271	229	.8	15	**99.4**
39	Côte d'Ivoire	26	17	164	70	.04	5	**18.2**
40	Croatia	37	115	336	279	2.22	15	**43.5**
41	Cuba	6	118	353	246	.22	14	**6.9**
42	Cyprus	84	–	–	–	4.35	–	**–**
43	Czech Republic	80	254	803	487	2.83	31	**119.2**

(continued)

Table 6.A1 (continued)

	Nation	Press Freedom 2000 (i)	Newspapers per 1,000 1996 (ii)	Radios per 1,000 1997 (iii)	TV Sets per 1,000 1999 (iv)	% Of Population Online 2000 (v)	Media Access (ii to v)	Communication Index (Freedom + Access)
44	Denmark	91	309	1141	621	20.75	46	**151.4**
45	Djibouti	37	–	–	–	.15	–	–
46	Dominica	84	–	–	–	.31	–	–
47	Dominican Republic	70	52	178	96	.24	7	**57.2**
48	Ecuador	56	70	419	205	.04	16	**66.9**
49	Egypt	31	40	324	183	.62	10	**30.8**
50	El Salvador	60	48	464	191	.50	24	**82.6**
51	Equatorial Guinea	22	–	–	–	.01	–	–
52	Eritrea	32	–	91	16	.03	–	–
53	Estonia	80	174	693	555	10.86	30	**117.6**
54	Ethiopia	38	1	195	6	.01	4	**23.0**
55	Fiji	42	–	–	–	.63	–	–
56	Finland	85	455	1496	643	28.04	60	**151.1**
57	France	76	218	937	623	10.60	38	**119.6**
58	Gabon	45	29	183	251	.27	5	**32.9**
59	Gambia	30	2	169	3	.04	4	**16.3**
60	Georgia	53	–	555	474	.09	–	–
61	Germany	87	311	948	580	14.97	40	**139.6**
62	Ghana	39	13	238	115	.08	7	**33.0**

63	Greece	70	153	477	480	1.05	22	94.3
64	Grenada	80	–	–	–	2.00	–	–
65	Guatemala	46	33	79	61	.46	5	31.6
66	Guinea	29	–	47	44	.22	–	–
67	Guinea-Bissau	44	5	44	–	.04	–	–
68	Haiti	42	3	55	5	.03	1	4.3
69	Honduras	52	55	386	95	.27	11	53.5
70	Hungary	70	186	689	448	4.96	27	100.7
71	Iceland	88	–	–	–	40.36	–	–
72	India	58	–	121	75	.08	–	–
73	Indonesia	51	24	156	143	.04	6	40.9
74	Iran	32	28	265	157	.15	9	30.6
75	Iraq	2	19	229	83	–	–	–
76	Ireland	79	150	699	406	12.00	28	114.0
77	Israel	70	290	520	328	10.17	25	97.5
78	Italy	73	104	878	488	15.68	33	110.6
79	Jamaica	89	62	480	189	1.97	15	104.4
80	Japan	81	578	955	719	15.48	48	136.4
81	Jordon	43	58	287	83	.82	8	39.1
82	Kazakhstan	32	–	384	238	.12	–	–
83	Kenya	30	9	104	22	.16	3	13.0
84	Kiribati	83	–	–	–	.38	–	–
85	Korea, Republic of	73	393	1033	361	21.88	40	116.9
86	Kuwait	52	374	660	480	3.69	31	77.6

(continued)

139

Table 6.A1 (continued)

	Nation	Press Freedom 2000 (i)	Newspapers per 1,000 1996 (ii)	Radios per 1,000 1997 (iii)	TV Sets per 1,000 1999 (iv)	% Of Population Online 2000 (v)	Media Access (ii to v)	Communication Index (Freedom + Access)
87	Kyrgyzstan	39	15	112	57	.05	3	21.0
88	Laos	34	4	143	10	–	–	–
89	Latvia	76	247	710	741	4.07	30	112.2
90	Lebanon	39	107	906	351	4.26	28	56.5
91	Lesotho	44	8	49	16	.03	2	9.5
92	Liberia	33	–	–	–	.01	–	–
93	Libya Arab Jamahiriy	10	14	233	136	–	–	–
94	Lithuania	80	93	513	420	2.16	22	107.1
95	Luxembourg	90	–	–	–	11.90	–	–
96	Macedonia	58	21	200	250	1.00	10	57.1
97	Madagascar	68	5	192	22	.03	4	43.5
98	Malawi	48	3	249	3	.06	5	33.9
99	Malaysia	30	158	420	174	2.86	15	35.7
100	Maldives	35	–	–	–	.54	–	–
101	Mali	74	1	54	12	.01	1	9.5
102	Malta	83	–	–	–	5.26	–	–
103	Marshall Islands	92	–	–	–	–	–	–
104	Mauritania	33	0	151	96	.01	5	22.6
105	Mauritius	83	75	368	230	3.55	14	95.4

140

106	Mexico	50	97	325	267	.95	14	**57.2**
107	Micronesia, Fed. State	76	–	–	–	.91	–	**–**
108	Moldova	42	60	740	297	.08	22	**56.3**
109	Mongolia	71	27	151	61	.05	5	**48.6**
110	Morocco	51	26	241	165	.45	9	**47.7**
111	Mozambique	52	3	40	5	.07	1	**–.6**
112	Myanmar	0	10	95	7	–	–	**.0**
113	Namibia	66	19	144	38	.56	4	**40.7**
114	Nepal	41	11	38	7	.06	1	**1.9**
115	Netherlands	86	306	978	600	24.36	42	**139.9**
116	New Zealand	92	216	990	518	14.77	39	**146.0**
117	Nicaragua	60	30	285	69	.34	10	**60.4**
118	Niger	38	0	69	27	.01	2	**10.8**
119	Nigeria	47	24	223	68	.01	6	**37.4**
120	Norway	95	588	915	648	41.59	52	**162.8**
121	Oman	29	29	598	575	1.74	25	**40.4**
122	Pakistan	36	23	98	119	.04	4	**22.4**
123	Panama Canal Zone	70	62	299	192	1.08	11	**73.4**
124	Papua New Guinea	72	15	97	13	.00	3	**31.3**
125	Paraguay	49	43	182	205	.02	7	**39.9**
126	Peru	33	84	273	147	.08	10	**33.1**
127	Philippines	70	79	159	110	.45	7	**59.2**
128	Poland	81	113	523	387	5.17	22	**108.9**
129	Portugal	83	75	304	560	2.02	19	**106.2**

(continued)

Table 6.A1 (continued)

	Nation	Press Freedom 2000 (i)	Newspapers per 1,000 1996 (ii)	Radios per 1,000 1997 (iii)	TV Sets per 1,000 1999 (iv)	% Of Population Online 2000 (v)	Media Access (ii to v)	Communication Index (Freedom + Access)
130	Qatar	38	–	–	–	4.58	–	–
131	Romania	56	300	319	312	.67	17	69.2
132	Russian Federation	40	105	418	421	3.66	20	51.7
133	Rwanda	28	0	102	0	.01	2	8.7
134	Saint Lucia	87	–	–	–	1.33	–	–
135	Sao Tome and Principe	73	–	–	–	.29	–	–
136	Saudi Arabia	10	57	321	263	.58	13	11.1
137	Senegal	67	5	142	41	.09	4	38.7
138	Seychelles	50	–	–	–	3.00	–	–
139	Sierra Leone	15	4	253	13	.01	5	11.0
140	Singapore	34	360	822	308	14.71	34	52.2
141	Slovakia	70	185	580	417	9.44	25	98.2
142	Slovenia	73	199	406	356	23.00	24	100.8
143	Solomon Islands	82	–	–	–	.48	–	–
144	Somalia	12	–	–	–	–	–	–
145	South Africa	75	32	317	129	4.18	10	76.0
146	Spain	82	100	333	547	7.85	21	107.7
147	Sri Lanka	30	29	209	102	.08	7	24.6
148	St. Kitts and Nevis	82	–	–	–	3.75	–	–

149	St. Vincent and Grenadine	84	–	–	–	1.82	–	–
150	Sudan	15	27	271	173	.00	8	13.3
151	Suriname	69	–	–	–	1.64	–	–
152	Swaziland	23	–	–	–	.30	–	–
153	Sweden	89	445	932	531	44.38	48	149.9
154	Switzerland	92	337	1000	518	16.44	42	148.9
155	Syrian Arab Republic	27	20	278	66	.07	7	23.4
156	Taiwan	79	–	–	–	21.84	–	–
157	Tajikstan	6	20	142	328	–	–	–
158	Tanzania	51	4	279	21	.02	6	40.0
159	Thailand	70	63	232	289	.22	11	72.0
160	Togo	26	4	218	22	.12	5	17.8
161	Trinidad and Tobago	72	123	534	337	1.56	20	93.9
162	Tunisia	26	31	223	190	.52	9	25.0
163	Turkey	42	111	180	332	.95	12	45.0
164	Turkmenistan	14	–	276	201	–	–	–
165	Uganda	60	2	128	28	.05	3	29.9
166	Ukraine	40	54	884	413	.29	29	58.3
167	United Arab Emirates	24	156	345	252	8.88	18	30.0
168	United Kingdom	80	329	1436	652	23.90	54	138.4
169	United States	87	215	2146	844	39.11	73	161.9
170	Uruguay	71	293	607	531	2.73	24	97.4
171	Uzbekistan	17	3	465	276	.04	15	19.9
172	Vanuatu	56	–	–	–	.06	–	–

(continued)

Table 6.A1 (continued)

	Nation	Press Freedom 2000 (i)	Newspapers per 1,000 1996 (ii)	Radios per 1,000 1997 (iii)	TV Sets per 1,000 1999 (iv)	% Of Population Online 2000 (v)	Media Access (ii to v)	Communication Index (Freedom + Access)
173	Venezuela	66	206	468	185	.35	17	**81.6**
174	Viet Nam	25	4	107	184	.02	3	**12.5**
175	Western Samoa	66	–	–	–	.24	–	–
176	Yemen	32	15	64	286	.04	2	**10.8**
177	Yugoslavia	19	107	297	273	.94	13	**21.5**
178	Zambia	38	12	121	145	.10	5	**27.9**
179	Zimbabwe	33	19	93	180	.27	3	**15.2**
Total	**179**	**179**	**136**	**143**	**142**	**169**	**130**	**131**

Note: See technical appendix for details.

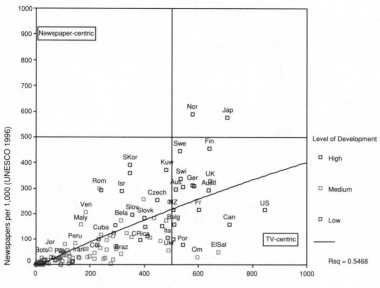

Appendix Figure 6.1 Correlations between Access to Newspapers and Television

TECHNICAL APPENDIX

Variable	Definition and Source
Media Access	
Newspapers	Daily newspaper circulation (published at least four times a week) per 1,000 people (1996). UNESCO Statistical Yearbook 1999.
Television Sets	Television sets in use per 1,000 people, 1999. International Telecommunications Union World Telecommunications Indicators Database 2000.
Radio Receivers	Radio receivers in use per 1,000 people, 1997. International Telecommunications Union World Telecommunications Indicators Database 2000.
Online Users	The percentage of online users in the adult population derived from national surveys asking respondents whether they use e-mail or the World Wide Web. The figures represent the latest survey available in fall 2000. Available from the World Wide Web at www.NUA.ie.
Hosts	Computers with active Internet Protocol (IP) addresses connected to the Internet, per 100 people, July 2000. Available from the World Wide Web at www.Netcraft.com. Hosts without a country code identification were weighted and relocated (Pippa Norris 2001).
Press Freedom Scale	Diversity of news content is measured in the 2000 Freedom House annual survey of Press Freedom according to the structure of the news industry; legal and administrative decisions, the degree of political influence or control; the economic influences exerted by the government or private entrepreneurs; and actual incidents violating press autonomy, including censorship, harassment, and physical threats to journalists. The 100-point scale combines the broadcasting and newspaper scores and the scale is reversed so that a higher score represents greater press freedom. Available from the World Wide Web at www.FreedomHouse.org.
Media Access	A summary-logged standardized scale of the proportion of newspapers, television sets, radio receivers, online users, and Internet hosts.
Communication Index	This combines the Logged Media Access Scale and the Press Freedom Scale.

Variable	Definition and Source
Human Development Indicators	
Human Development	The Human Development Index (1998) is based on longevity, as measured by life expectancy at birth; educational achievement; and standard of living, as measured by per capita GDP (PPP U.S. $) (UNDP Human Development Report 2000).
Per Capita GDP	Measured in U.S. $ in Purchasing Power Parity, 1998 (UNDP Human Development Report 2000).
Economic Equality	The Gini Index measures the extent to which the distribution of income within an economy deviates from a perfectly equal distribution. The index has been reversed so that the number one represents perfect equality (World Development Indicators 2001 World Bank).
Lower Infant Mortality	The number of infants dying before the age of one year, per 1,000 live births, 1999. The indicator has been reversed so that a higher figure represents lower infant mortality (World Development Indicators 2001 World Bank).
Public Health Expenditure	Public health expenditure consists of recurrent and capital spending from government budgets, external borrowings, and grants as a percentage of GDP, 1997–9 (World Development Indicators 2001 World Bank).
Life Expectancy	Life expectancy at birth (years) 1995–2000 (UNDP Human Development Report 2000).
Adult Literacy Rate	Literacy as a percentage of adults (15 and above) 1998 (UNDP Human Development Report 2000).
% Secondary Education	Secondary age group enrollment as a percentage of the relevant age group, 1997 (UNDP Human Development Report 2000).
Governance Indicators	
Political Stability	An aggregated measure of political stability and violence based on expert assessments (Kaufman, Kraay, and Zoido-Lobaton, 1999).
Rule of Law	An aggregated measure of rule of law based on expert assessments (Kaufman, Kraay, and Zoido-Lobaton 1999).
Government Efficiency	An aggregated measure of government efficiency based on expert assessments (Kaufman, Kraay, and Zoido-Lobaton 1999).
Corruption	An aggregated measure of corruption based on expert assessments (Kaufman, Kraay, and Zoido-Lobaton 1999).

REFERENCES

ACE Project. Available from the World Wide Web at http://www.aceproject.org/main/english/me/mea01b.htm.

Almond, Gabriel A., and G. Bingham Powell, Jr. 1992. *Comparative Politics Today: A World View*. New York: Harper Collins Publishers.

Asante, Clement E. 1997. *Press Freedom and Development: A Research Guide and Selected Bibliography*. Westport, CT: Greenwood Press.

Bagdikian, Ben. 1997. *The Media Monopoly*. Boston: Beacon Press.

Besley, T., and R. Burgess. 2001. Political Agency, Government Responsiveness and the Role of the Media. *European Economic Review* 45 (4–6): 629–40.

Bogart, Leo. 1995. *Commercial Culture. The Media System and the Public Interest*. New York: Transaction.

Dahlgren, Peter. 1995. *Television and the Public Sphere*. London: Sage.

Dahlgren, Peter, and Colin Sparks. 1995. *Communication and Citizenship*. London: Routledge.

Diamond, Larry. 2001. Consolidating Democracies. In Lawrence LeDuc, Richard G. Niemi, and Pippa Norris, eds. *Comparing Democracies 2: Elections and Voting in Global Perspective*. London: Sage.

Djankov, Simeon, Caralee McLiesh, Tatiana Nenova, and Andrei Shleifer. 2001. Who Owns the Media? Paper presented at the World Bank meeting "The Role of the Media in Development."

Donohue, George A., and Philip Tichenor. 1995. A Guard Dog Perspective on the Role of the Media. *Journal of Communication* 45 (2): 115–28.

Freedom House. 2000. *Freedom in the World 2000–2001* (online). Available from World Wide Web at http://www.freedomhouse.org.

Gunter, Richard, and Anthony Mughan. 2000. *Democracy and the Media: A Comparative Perspective*. New York: Cambridge University Press.

Hachten, W. A. 1989. Media Development without Press Freedom – Lee Kuan Yew's Singapore. *Journalism Quarterly* 66 (4): 822–7.

Human Rights Watch. Available from the World Wide Web at http://www.hrw.org/.

Huntington, Samuel. 1993. *The Third Wave*. Norman: The University of Oklahoma Press.

Hur, K. Kyloon. 1984. A Critical Analysis of International News Flow Research. *Critical Studies in Mass Communication* 1: 365–78.

Index on Censorship. Available from the World Wide Web at http://www.indexoncensorship.org.

Inglehart, Louis Edward. 1998. *Press and Speech Freedoms in the World, from Antiquity until 1998: A Chronology*. Westport, CT: Greenwood Press.

International Federation of Journalists. Available from the World Wide Web at http://www.ifj.org.

International Press Institute. Available from the World Wide Web at http://www.freemedia.at.

Kalathil, Shanthi, and Taylor C. Boas. 2001. *The Internet and State Control in Authoritarian Regimes: China, Cuba and the Counterrevolution. Global Policy Program No 21*. Washington, DC: Carnegie Endowment for International Peace.

Kaufman, Daniel, Aaart Kraay, and Pablo Zoido-Lobaton. 1999. *Governance Matters. World Bank Policy Research Paper 2196.* Washington, DC: World Bank. Available from the World Wide Web at www.worldbank.org.

Köcher, Renate. 1986. Bloodhounds or Missionaries: Role Definitions of German and British Journalists. *European Journal of Communication* 1: 43–64.

Lagos, Marta. 2001. Between Stability and Crisis in Latin America. *Journal of Democracy* 12 (1): 137–45.

Lerner, Daniel. 1958. *The Passing of Traditional Society.* Glencoe, IL: The Free Press.

Linz, Juan, and Alfred Stephan. 1996. *Problems of Democratic Transition and Consolidation.* Washington, DC: Johns Hopkins Press.

Lipset, Seymour Martin. 1959. Some Social Prerequisites of Democracy: Economic Development and Political Legitimacy. *American Political Science Review* 53: 69–105.

———. 1990. *Continental Divide: The Values and Institutions of Canada and the United States.* New York: Routledge.

———. 1996. *American Exceptionalism: A Double Edged Sword.* New York: W. W. Norton.

Lupia, Arthur, and Mathew D. McCubbins. 1998. *The Democratic Dilemma.* Cambridge: Cambridge University Press.

McChesney, Robert. 1999. *Rich Media, Poor Democracy: Communication Politics in Dubious Times.* Urbana: University of Illinois Press.

McCrone, Donald J., and Charles F. Cnudde. 1967. Toward a Communication Theory of Democratic Political Development: A Causal Model. *American Political Science Review* 61 (1): 72–9.

McQuail, Denis. 2000. *Mass Communication Theory.* London: Sage.

Mowlana, Hamid. 1985. *International Flow of Information: A Global Report and Analysis.* Paris: UNESCO.

Norris, Pippa, ed. 1999. *Critical Citizens: Global Support for Democratic Governance.* Oxford: Oxford University Press.

———. 2000. *A Virtuous Circle: Political Communications in Post-Industrial Societies.* New York: Cambridge University Press.

———. 2001. *Digital Divide: Civic Engagement, Information Poverty and the Internet Worldwide.* New York: Cambridge University Press.

———. 2002. *Democratic Phoenix: Political Activism Worldwide.* Cambridge: Cambridge University Press.

OSCE. *Report by the Organization for Security and Cooperation in Europe on the October 2000 Parliamentary Elections in Belarus* (online). Available from World Wide Web at http://www.osce.org/odihr/documents/reports/election_reports/by/bel200fin.pdf.

Østergaard, Bernt Stubbe, ed. 1992. *The Media in Western Europe.* London: Sage.

Pharr, Susan, and Robert Putnam, eds. 2000. *Disaffected Democracies: What's Troubling the Trilateral Countries?* Princeton: Princeton University Press.

Picard, Robert G. 1988. *Press Concentration and Monopoly: New Perspectives on Newspaper Ownership and Operation.* Norwood, NJ: Ablex Publishing Corp.

Plattner, Marc, and Larry Diamond. 2001. High Anxiety in the Andes. *Journal of Democracy* 12 (2): 59–73

Preston, William, Edwards S. Herman, and Herbert I. Schiller. 1989. *Hope and Folly: The United States and UNESCO 1945–1985.* Minneapolis: University of Minnesota Press.

Przeworski, Adam, and Henry Teune. 1970. *The Logic of Comparative Social Inquiry*. New York: Wiley-Interscience.

Pye, Lucian W. 1963. *Communications and Political Development*. Princeton: Princeton University Press.

Rodan, Garry. 1998. Asia and the International Press: The Political Significance of Expanding Markets. *Democratization* 5: 125–54.

Sanchez-Tabernero, Alfonso. 1993. *Media Concentration in Europe: Commercial Enterprises and the Public Interest*. London: John Libbey.

Sen, Amartya. 1999. *Development as Freedom*. New York: Anchor Books.

Shah, H. 1996. Modernization, Marginalization and Emancipation: Toward a Normative Model of Journalism and National Development. *Communication Theory* 6 (2): 143–66.

Siebert, Fred S., Theodore Peterson, and Wilbur Schramm. 1984. *Four Theories of the Press*. Urbana: University of Illinois Press.

Smith, Anthony. 1991. *The Age of Behemoths: The Globalization of Mass Media Firms*. New York: Priority Press.

Sreberny-Mohammadi, Annabelle et al. 1984. *Foreign News in the Media: International Reporting in Twenty-Nine Countries*. Reports and Papers on Mass Communication 93. Paris: UNESCO.

Stevenson, Robert L., and Donald Lewis Shaw, eds. 1984. *Foreign News and the New World Information Order*. Ames: Iowa State University Press.

Sussman, Leonard R. 2000. Censor Dot Gov: The Internet and Press Freedom. In Freedom House, ed. *Press Freedom Survey 2000*. Washington DC: Freedom House. Available from the World Wide Web at http://www.freedomhouse.com.

————. 2001. *Press Freedom in Our Genes*. Reston, VA: World Press Freedom Committee.

Swanson, David L., and Paolo Mancini, eds. 1996. *Politics, Media and Modern Democracy*. Westport, CT: Praeger.

Tunstall, Jeremy, and Michael Palmer. 1991. *Media Moguls*. London: Routledge.

Wolfenson, James D. 1999. Voices of the Poor. *Washington Post*, November 10, 1999, p. A39.

World Press Freedom Council. Available from the World Wide Web at http://www.wpfc.org.

SEVEN

Local Political Communication

Media and Local Publics in the Age of Globalization

Sabine Lang

Local publics are neglected entities within the broad scope of communication studies. Our knowledge of how people communicate politically in their local communities is limited. This is a fact not only in regard to underresearched peripheral societies, but also in relation to the developed publics of Western democracies. Daily newspapers have long had a reputation of parochialism, local television news shows are associated with low standards and obsession with crime and scandals, and local radio has abandoned news in favor of music or talk show formulas.

Even though *globalization* has advanced to become a catchword in analyses of urban economies and politics, communication studies seem reluctant to confront the interdependence between local and global media markets, local and global communication practices (i.e., local groups sustaining global movements) and local and global tools to gain political voice (i.e., the impact of the Internet on local communication). This chapter aims at diffusing notions of the local as being provincial or too small a unit for the analysis of public life. It intends to stimulate discussion about the relevance of local political communication arenas as unique public spaces as well as signifiers of national and global communication trends.

It is common knowledge that social and political capital is acquired primarily through socialization processes in the immediate life world (Bourdieu 1982; Putnam 2000). Theories of democracy have argued that local political communication and participation options are a prerequisite for sustained civic engagement and that the spatial radius of the local provides initiation into democratic practices and accountabilities (see Barber 1984; Phillips 1996). Numerous studies claim that, even though participation in local elections is often lower than on the national level, the majority of participatory and politically communicative activities of citizens take place on the local level (see for Great Britain, Parry et al. 1992; for the United States, Berry et al. 1993; for Germany, Roth 1994). For many citizens localities provide the most accessible and organized political arena in which opinions can be transformed into political action, such as participation in political organizations, issue-specific networks or neighborhood initiatives.

Yet despite the evident relevance of the local, political communication studies have been hesitant to feature it prominently on the research agenda – a reluctance that is underlined by two barriers that have traditionally defined the field. The first barrier marks the overall importance granted to opinion formation through the *national* media. The second obstacle is the *dominant role* in political communication research of media variables. The focus on media obfuscates a perspective on interpersonal political communication as one of the distinguishing features of local political publics. Several reasons come into play for this prohibitive downsizing of analytic curiosity.[1] Jarren (1994) cites the disillusionment following the high expectations being placed on local counterpublics in the 1970s and early 1980s that generated the idea of "grassroots politics" or "politics from below." Another factor contributing to the perception of local publics as too parochial for theoretically useful research is the visible lack of autonomy of local media due to mergers and concentration processes. As much as the media industry has paid lip service to keeping a strong independent profile of local media, the reality of mergers speaks to the contrary. Local profile has been lost, cutbacks in staff result in less capacity to focus on local affairs, and local audiences tend to identify less with "their" local newspaper or television newscast. Yet there are also numerous indicators that the local as a communicative arena is being revitalized in late modern societies. In the countries of the European Union (EU), cities and communities have learned that funding from Brussels often is attached to active improvement of communication between local governments and citizens. Political institutions and organizations make

---

[1] Public sector and urban politics analyses reach the same conclusion. For Germany, Ruediger Voigt argues in favor of the necessity for a "cross country analysis of local communication processes and their ramifications for the political identity and the level of action of citizens in their local communities" and he suggests that "comparative public policy science which already deals with comparative aspects of local political structures and decision making processes should expand their focus to include communication processes" (Voigt 1989, 4 [transl. S. L.]).

use of interactive communication technologies (ICT) for engagement processes on the local level. And in developing countries, resources are allocated to the mobilization of rural areas and to the idea of offering local communication infrastructure. Thus, local publics provide the ground for much of today's civic engagement and political activism.

The assessment of research on local political publics in this chapter follows three main lines of inquiry. One theme addresses the question of whether local publics expose specific cross-cultural traits that identify them as relatively autonomous units of analysis and independent variables within their respective larger communication ecologies. Second, local media development is traced by focusing on how globalization puts its imprint on local communication processes, possibly leading from path-dependent to transnational synchronized local media structures. Because the scope of existing research is limited, results from this inquiry are at best preliminary. And third, I investigate how traditional local media are embedded in the larger interpersonal and organizational communication arenas of localities and how alternative media, supported by new technologies, may help to develop sustainable counterpublics on the local level. The final part of the chapter will develop a comparative set of research questions that draw on the voids of existing studies. The conclusion maintains that while local publics exhibit fragmentation and diversification similar to national publics in late modern societies, they are undergoing transformations aimed at innovating governance and citizen engagement.

WHAT IS A LOCAL PUBLIC SPHERE?

Defining local publics is as much of a challenge as defining national or global publics, as their scope and form varies historically, across cultures and across political systems. Besides the tangible variations, what seems to be equally in flux is our individual understanding of belonging to one or several local publics. Historically, the assumption that local communication (up until the mid-nineteenth century) ended "in principle at the city boundaries or on the village road" (Kieslich 1972, 96) has proven to be misleading. As empirical historical research has revealed, local communication was never confined to those issues that made up the microcosm of the village commons (Lang 2001). Instead, local publics always harbored a mix and interplay of information originating on the local level with news that traveled from other informational hubs into the local scene. This traffic between local, regional, and international news flows has increased greatly with the advent of globalized information systems. The local today is infused more than ever with translocal issues, with ideas that are conceived and decisions that are taken elsewhere. Therefore, we can describe the local political public – in contrast to a geographically defined and closed unit of analysis – as a relatively open space in which information flows of local origins intersect with translocally important news, and together create a common discursive space of political activity.

How can we systematically distinguish the local communication sphere from national and global publics? My claim is that there are four aspects of local communication practices that identify it as a specific unit of analysis, entailing a cognitive, a symbolic, an interactive, and a democratic dimension (Lang 2003a). The cognitive dimension refers to shared knowledge about the history and facets of the common public space. The symbolic dimension points to the experience of being part of a locality in which people share specific cultural, social, and political practices. The interactive aspect alludes to the local as providing relatively more "face-to-face" interactions and interpersonal communications than larger publics. And the fourth dimension addresses the inherent democratic potential of local publics by way of providing easy access to political communication and participation forums. The narrow spatial dimension of local publics encourages the exercise of deliberative and participatory citizenship in addition to representative decision making. Taken together, these four key elements make up a soft frame for the local public sphere. Some citizens identify more with some parts of urban public cultures than with others. Some don't have a sense of belonging to a local communication system at all. In urban spaces, most visibly, local publics are made up of dominant, sub- and counterpublics. Yet the majority of citizens draw their sense of belonging to a public sphere at least in part from the above-mentioned notions.

Assessing existing studies on local political communication, we can roughly distinguish three research eras, each informed by respective developments in media systems as well as by general trends in the social sciences (Lang 2003a).[2] In a first phase from the 1950s to the 1960s, local

---

[2] I include studies that are not explicitly part of the relatively new field of political communication research, yet have analyzed communication processes from the perspective of political science and sociology as well as urban studies.

communication processes were primarily conceived in terms of their relevance for political participation (Janowitz 1952; Wood 1959). This research, originating mostly in the United States, was being placed within the discourses on "small town community" and "participatory democracy." A second research phase in the 1970s and 1980s focused more specifically on the effects of emerging local mass-media cultures and analyzed the role of print media, radio, and television for local communication (Haenisch and Schroeter 1971; Cox and Morgan 1973; Dorsch 1978; Schoenbach 1978; Heyn 1979; Rager and Schibriani 1981; Jarren 1984). A third research frame, developed in the late 1980s, tried to critically assess the diversification processes in local media by reconnecting media development once again to issues of democratic accountability (Jarren 1991; Dubois 1993; Kurp 1994; Valle 1995; Salvador and Sias 1998). On a parallel note, for the first time since the 1980s we see some case studies emerging that aim at a more detailed assessment of local communication spaces (Kaniss 1991, 1995; Brettschneider and Neller 1997; Neller 1999).[3] In general, though, the number of case studies of local public spheres is limited. Moreover, the field is marked by a strong bias toward Western Europe and the United States. African, Latin American, and Asian local publics have in some instances been researched in the context of how to use mass media to educate and politicize local publics (see Okunna 1995). However, the primary sources of knowledge about local publics limit this comparison for the most part to the United States, Great Britain, France, and the German-speaking countries.

LOCAL MEDIA DEVELOPMENT

THE LOCAL PRESS

Until the early 1970s, local media was a synonym for the print media, or – more specifically – for the local daily paper (for Great Britain, Franklin and Murphy 1998, 7; for Germany, Jonscher 1991, 74; Lang 2001; for the United States, Schudson 1978; Kaniss 1991). The press had become the catalyst and focus of local political life. It framed local policy processes, it commented on political decision making, it reflected local controversies and helped to organize political participation.[4]

---

[3] Neller (1999) provides the most detailed overview of the state of the arts in local communication studies for the German-speaking countries. To my knowledge and reception capabilities, there seem to be no comparable assessments for other countries.

[4] Whether this early political catalyst function of the local press is also a feature of the local publics in less economically developed countries will have to be addressed in

Historically, this growth of the local press can be traced back to industrialization and urbanization, yet so far this "link between newspapers and the growth and development of cities" (Kaniss 1991, 13) has not been established systematically and across cultures. Conversely, the rapid trend toward suburbanization after the 1950s in Western urban centers and the "urban plight" of big cities exposed how much the local press depended on a readership that identified with their urban public space. Newspaper companies reacted by refocusing their agenda toward more regional and less purely local news. Yet the more regionalized the local press of bigger cities became, the less attractive it seemed to its core urban constituencies.

Today, the daily print press navigates between the demands of economic concentration in the industry and the spatial as well as social differentiation of its clientele. Increasingly diverse, partly regionally oriented and partly sublocal print media arrange themselves under what James A. Rosse calls an "umbrella competition pattern" (Kaniss 1991, 43; also Graber 1997). Under this umbrella competition pattern, different print-press models operate and circulate on four levels. On the top level we find the large metropolitan dailies that integrate international, national, and regional with local reporting, but have a stronger stake in the former. Underneath this level operate so-called satellite dailies that cover some regional pieces, but focus more on the local news in their suburban community. On the next level down are strictly suburban papers, serving localities beyond the reach of satellite dailies. The fourth level consists of free media. Even though some form of this umbrella competition pattern seems to emerge in all urban public spaces, we know too little about its arrangements and effects – in particular about how it plays out in specific national cultures, how it affects the quality of the news, the working conditions of journalists, and the consumption patterns of local readers.

In general, the local press has developed the dubious reputation of being provincial, parochial, fixated on easy entertainment, and under too much influence from the local power elites. Schoenbach assesses for Germany that until the 1970s, 90 percent of all news in the local papers was presented as mere local or community-related problems

future research. In India, for example, we know that after the end of British rule there already existed a lively print culture of over 4,000 newspapers in seventeen languages and dialects (see Kishan Thussu 1998, 274). But it might well be that in societies with low rates of literacy, not the print media but the new electronic media take over this traditional catalyst function.

(Schoenbach 1978, 263). Only a small fraction of local news consisted of frames in which locality was placed within the context of regional and national, or even global forces. About two-thirds of all political news was mentioned in the papers only once (Schoenbach 1978, 264), and about 50 percent of all news concerned "internal security" and "entertainment" issues (Rager and Schibriani 1981, 499). While such parochialism has changed specifically in urban settings where the effects of nonlocal developments leave substantial imprints on the local commons day-by-day, other features of local newspapers seem to have stayed virtually untouched. A number of studies provide evidence that political agenda setting was historically and still is dominated by local elites (for France, Neveu 1998, 452; for the United States, Kaniss 1991, 91; Graber 1997, 317; for Germany, Rager and Schibrani 1981, 498; for Great Britain, Franklin and Murphy 1991, 63–4). As Kaniss argues "while there is much in the news and editorial columns that is critical of local officials, this criticism is limited when compared with the amount of information that is taken directly, and almost unquestioningly, from official bureaucratic sources" (Kaniss 1991, 91). Journalistic independence and investigating initiative have come to take backstage to reactive news reporting. It remains to be seen whether such a downsized understanding of journalism is being challenged by the reshaping of local governance structures in the 1990s, namely by a substantial number of new actors from civic political associations entering the local public stage and becoming credible spokespersons in fields such as housing, the environment, or transportation.

A number of studies indicate that local politicians traditionally prioritized local politics primarily through the print-media news flow. While these officials now monitor local evening newscasts with similar scrutiny, print coverage remains paramount (Kaniss 1991, 164). Politicians get most of their contextual information about local issues from the local print media, thus endowing the press with more power and framing capacity than for example local radio or television (Dunn 1969; Jarren 1984; Kurp 1994, 49). The most ambiguous effect of such prioritizing is "reification" of the very ideas that local officials deem central to their work in the community: Local elites "take . . . the local press reports as an indicator for the social problems and processes within their city. If they find there (in the paper) the majority of news bites that they themselves have generated, this will reinforce their initial – and maybe less than adequate or even false – perceptions of the problems within their county" (Murck 1983, 373). In the minds of consumers, the local press still has the reputation as being the trustworthiest source of political news. Even though the local daily today is not reaching as many readers, and its readers spend less time reading the paper than watching television or listening to the radio,[5] reception studies still give the press highest marks in terms of informational density and competence (see for Germany, Jonscher 1991, 26; for Great Britain, similar results in Franklin and Murphy 1991, 6–7). A number of studies about news origins support this view and claim that the local daily remains the source for about 50 to 60 percent of all local news (for Great Britain, Franklin and Murphy 1991, 7; for Switzerland, Saxer 1986, 329; for Germany, Schwiderowski 1989, 158). Yet even though we can see some similar trends in the local press of Western European countries and the United States, we still lack a more substantial and comparatively tested understanding of the arrangements between the press and the electronic media in generating and indexing news flows in the local public sphere.

Local Radio

With the rise of radio in the 1920s, the local daily press confronted an increasingly strong competitor for audiences and advertising revenues. Depending on national regulation standards and economic interests, local radio expansion did not happen in a uniform way, but with different models marked by top-down or bottom-up regulatory systems. Great Britain and the United States have provided ideal types for the initial bipolar radio politics that persisted until the late 1950s and still leave imprints today. In Great Britain, the new electronic medium was developed nationally and top down since the 1930s and, as a consequence, "local radio virtually disappeared. What persisted was regional variation within what was in essence a network service controlled, if not originated, from London" (Crisell 1998, 25). In the United States, on the contrary, strong local diversification of radio stations and limited national regulation resulted quite early in cooperation among local stations in order to remain economically viable (Kleinsteuber 1992, 552). The stations within those networks remained largely independent in their political orientation and news delivery; state regulation was basically limited to protection of small providers from takeovers by larger conglomerates. Network providers could, for example, only purchase a percentage of affiliated stations and had to guarantee the journalistic independence

---

[5] In Germany, 1970 marked the year when for the first time audiences for television were bigger than those for the daily press. In 1985, radio surmounted the dailies as second in the battle over audiences (see Kurp 1994, 139).

of the small providers, while the latter could gain a share in the advertisement revenue of the whole network. Thus, a number of factors related to technology, state regulation, and economic interests have produced nationally unique infrastructures of local radio culture that in the beginning – as in the case of Britain – left little, or – as in the case of the United States – much space for journalistic reporting that originated within the local public sphere.

The Scandinavian countries were historically most concerned about the autonomy of local radio stations. Scandinavia has therefore gained the reputation of being a "model for non-commercial local radio with a focus on the activation of its listeners, on citizen representation and neighborhood assistance" (Koschnick 1995, 785). But even Scandinavia was not exempt from the repercussions of the trends toward mixed public/private systems in all Western European countries – albeit the differentiation and commercialization of local stations came later and was less severe. Today, Denmark is seen internationally as the country with the strongest localization in radio, hosting about 300 local stations of which about 60 to 70 percent are financed through advertisements (Koschnick 1995). Finland (with fifty-eight local stations), Norway (with 350 to 400 local stations), and Sweden have also continued to put emphasis on making radio stations the public signatures of cities and communities.[6]

Besides the Scandinavian countries, Great Britain can be singled out as having counteracted the global trend toward privatization in the radio segment most creatively and successfully. Today, the nationwide ratio between public and private radio stations is stable at around 40 to 60 percent. While the national government has given licenses to private providers since the 1960s – initially trying to counteract the steep rise of local pirate stations – it has also managed to balance out the prevailing orientation toward easy-listening formats through an extension of attractive local BBC programming (Berrigan 1977, 195). Today, thirty-nine local BBC stations operate in England and additional ones in Scotland, North Ireland, and Wales in competition with about 180 independent stations (Crisell 1998). Since the early 1990s, the BBC has aimed at strengthening and reinventing its news-based identity in the local radio markets. More specifically, a focus on ethnic minorities and on

---

[6] See the country-specific case studies on local radio and television in Western Europe in Jankowski et al. 1992.

local culture is intended to create a new listener segment among young people. The BBC is holding about 15 percent audience ratings in this program segment and about 20 percent of adults in Great Britain listen to its local stations regularly. Yet in recent years the BBC has embarked also on quite expansive technological improvement projects such as digitalization, which put the company in financial difficulties. Predictable results were cuts on the journalistic side as well as concentration processes, shifting the focus from local autonomous productions to more regional co-operation of its channels. Nevertheless, the BBC has so far made the most successful attempt to creatively use the potential of public local radio to combine dense local information with diverse, multicultural-oriented entertainment segments. The BBC has also introduced formats such as "talk shows" and "studio debates" that engage citizens in meaningful and complex political discussions about their communities. These formats are models for devising community-oriented participation venues with less inflammatory content than found on American talk radio.

All in all, there were 7,934 radio stations in Western Europe in 1992, of which 90 percent were local or regional providers (Koschnick 1995, 781). Eastern European countries have also seen the establishment of a large number of local radio stations since their transformation in the early 1990s (Thomass and Tzankoff 2001). In Hungary, today there are about 80 local radio stations (Bajomi-Lázár 2001, 198). In Poland, estimates run up to several hundred stations (see Hadamik 2001, 159). Similar localization and regionalization trends are visible in Russia where the BBC Fund has invested considerably in the stabilization of local radio markets by training journalists and technicians as well as providing infrastructure and technology. However, foreign media companies have invested less in the Eastern European radio markets than for example in the print market, because state regulation for foreign investments are generally tighter in the former segment and advertisement revenues are harder to anticipate and so far less optimistic.

In sum, global radio trends on the local level point toward more privatized and larger units of cooperation, thus privileging regional over merely local issues, easy-listening formats over political programming, younger over generationally mixed audiences, and advertising revenue over editorial risks. Program segments addressing neighborhood, ethnic, social, and political issues are on the decline, and so is the idea of local radio as a citizen-driven technology. The only contradictory evidence can be found in countries with a strong tradition of public radio such as Great Britain, the Scandinavian countries, and Germany. Some German state-regulation authorities, for example, tried to mediate the effects of commercial network radio at the height of privatization efforts by licensing a number of subregional and local radio stations,[7] but most of these small community radio stations turned out to be rather unattractive for audiences, lacking professional production and trained staff. Conversely, they were not able to attract a steady flow of advertisement clients due to their narrow reach. Moreover, what had been hailed in the 1970s in Western Europe and the United States as the dawn of a "community radio movement" seems today like a marginal facet of local radio markets. The principles of community radio, namely democratically organized access for citizens, joint use of all media resources, a focus on local and neighborhood issues, and participatory structures do not succeed in highly competitive media markets. Without steady and financially strong sponsorship from engaged citizens, foundations, universities, or public agencies, community radio never leaves the precarious state of producing under highly adversarial conditions (for Great Britain and Canada, Berrigan 1977; for the United States, Widlok 1992). The alternative between "amateur-driven radio-club models" and "recipient-driven public-service models" has been almost unequivocally settled in favor of the latter. Thus we can predict that only in local radio markets where the public sector sponsors a professionalized public-service model will community radio in the future become a viable third column next to existing public and private radio stations.

LOCAL TELEVISION

The strongest competitor for the local press and radio is local television. Whereas local television did not seem to have much economic drive and attraction in the beginning, this changed rapidly with the advent in the United States of cable broadcast networks consisting largely of independent local affiliate stations. In most Western European countries, local television got to a bumpy start on the community level in the mid-1980s. Likewise, as a commercial enterprise it has not lived up to the expectations it produced. In Germany today, there are thirty commercial local television stations – if we include regional channels that offer substantial local programming windows. All of these produce deficits and can only survive by operating under the umbrella of larger media conglomerates.

---

[7] This happened in Baden-Wuerttemberg, Bavaria, Hamburg, and Northrhine-Westphalia (see Jarren 1994, 303).

The "success story" that is written by commercial local television in the United States remains unique. Today in the United States there are about 740 commercial local stations on air that use about 40 percent of their own, that is, non-network programming, airtime for local news (Klite et al. 1997, 102). Local news time has far surpassed national newscasts on network outlets. While 67 percent of adults watch local news daily, only 49 percent follow the national network news (Graber 1997, 326). Even the distinction between local and national programs is blurring as new video technologies and new transmission options have empowered local networks to offer national news scaled down to local size and to effectively localize national topics. The political establishment in Washington, in response, has made use of the localized news markets by providing sound bites for their respective local electorate on a regular basis. Preproduction of important policy events for local television, which are often able to stress specific local angles of a topic, is now a routine for the White House and for members of Congress (Kiolbassa 1997).

At the same time as this localization of political news frames takes place, we see a downsizing of political news production. A comparison between national and local newscasts in the United States in 1995 showed that "political news" in its narrow sense, defined as government affairs, the economy, and social issues, accounted for only 62 to 69 percent of local news, but accounted for 85 to 93 percent of national news (Graber 1997, 327). Sports, entertainment, and other nonstrictly political news have gained much higher relevance in local television in recent years. This tendency also translates into specific formats and styles. Commercial local television in the United States communicates its agenda with emphasis on sensationalism and negativity, thereby contributing to its image as less professional and an even more marketing and profit-driven news delivery system than the national news (Kaniss 1991, 113–14; Kiolbassa 1997). "The need to appeal to a mass audience, the cult of personality, the limited number of reporters and their reliance on routine channels of information, the importance of dramatic video and sound bites, and the element of timeliness, all lead to a distinctive definition of what is 'local news'" (Kaniss 1991, 113). Most importantly, the news is a substantial source of income for local stations in the United States, generating on average about 40 percent of a stations' profit (Graber 1997, 326). The dependence on advertising revenue increases the pressure on local stations to keep up high viewer ratings and to generate as little controversial political substance as possible in the local public sphere. Investigative reporting and longer news stories in particular fall by the wayside. Television newscasts get their political substance primarily out of newspapers and press releases from public officials and agencies. A recent study of three local, economically vulnerable stations that were part of national networks concludes that 75 percent of local news were direct offshoots of press releases by local actors or newspaper reports. The stations investigated 20 percent independently, but on the basis of press declarations and newspaper reports. And only 5 percent of the information conveyed came through a television reporter's initiative (Graber 1997, 332).

Yet there is also increasing evidence that points to the shortsightedness of such downsized and undercomplex news production. The Project for Excellence in Journalism has recently studied nineteen local television markets and came to the conclusion that the stations that emphasized quality production, defined as less crime coverage, fewer gimmicks, and more focus on local issues, actually built solid ratings (Rosenstiel et al. 2000; Lipschultz and Hilt 2002, 147). But it also costs more to produce quality news. The study concludes that "a newscast should reflect its entire community, cover a broad range of topics, focus on the significant aspects of stories, be locally relevant, balance stories with multiple points of view, and use authoritative sources (Rosenstiel et al. 2000, 87). Lipschultz and Hilt argue in a 2002 study of crime and local television news in the United States that this "lack of creativity on the part of many newsrooms across the country, ironically, may be based on a false sense of security – a sense that the safest path is keeping the status quo model developed during the 1970s" (Lipschultz and Hilt 2002, 147).

Keeping these contested features of local political television news in mind, we can somewhat modify its success story in the United States: What we see on the local television market since the 1970s is an increasing interest in framing news locally – an interest that also is fueled by the "distance-from-Washington-syndrome" that is engrained in American political culture. Local television provides representation and recognition of such localized identities. However, it also seems as though local commercial television in its persistent fight for audience quotas has for the most part disengaged from complex portrayals of local politics and from conveying to its audience a sense of place that goes far beyond constructions of fear and fun. While public criticism of local television news is on the rise, only a few bold stations are trying to recast their identities. As a result, a grassroots movement is reclaiming the idea of community television of the 1970s and demanding a larger share of public access television in local communities.

In Europe, local community television movements reached their first peak with the citizen-driven television broadcasting experiments of the 1970s. Great Britain, Belgium, and the Netherlands were at the forefront in experimenting with community television (Hollander 1992, 11). So-called public access channels were aimed at providing alternative news production and neighborhood-oriented agenda setting to enable and facilitate civic engagement on the local public stage. In Germany, the first open channel was established relatively late in 1984 within the framework of a temporarily and spatially limited pilot project.[8] In 1994, eight German states altogether housed twenty-seven open channels with a weekly airtime between two and fifty-six hours. In 2003, that number slightly increased to seventy-nine channels, reflecting the tendency in Western European metropolitan communities to invest in government-sponsored public-access channels (http://www.openchannel.se/cat/overview/htm). The Open Channel Organization in 2003 provided links to about 6,000 open-access television stations worldwide – the United States with an estimated 1,800 channels again being at the forefront. A study by the California Center for Civic Renewal analyzing the California public-access market between 1993 and 2000 came to the conclusion that government-sponsored public-access television "has been the single greatest contributor to positively increasing public participation in local government decision-making in the last decade" (Conklin 2000). In 1989, local governments in California spent about $3.9 million to support government-access channels; in 2000, these investments had increased to about $15 million (Conklin 2000).

In Europe, local governments are not quite as willing to support expensive communication technologies. Deregulation and the fiscal strains of local states in the 1980s slowed down public discourse regarding participatory media (Prehn 1992, 256; Jankowski and Prehn 2002). However, studies of community programming still conclude that the globalized

[8] Widlok and Jarren claim that the reason for Germany's late investment in public-access channels is a result of the monopoly of public networks that did not want to compete with other providers. Newspaper companies that showed interest in diversifying by building radio and television presence in joint ventures with public-access initatives were strongly discouraged by public networks. When the privatization of radio started after the end of the social-liberal coalition in 1982, public access projects in radio as well as television segments were crushed by private competitors or had to adopt more easy-listening formats (see Widlok and Jarren 1992, 133).

societies of the twenty-first century should not easily give up on this specific means of political communication: "The need for locally oriented media to confront oligopolistic and transnational cultural industries will become more urgent in the coming years. Non-commercial and locally oriented media as social and cultural tools – and not as mass media in local disguise – can play an important role in strengthening local identity and self-respect. In the dialectic nexus of internationalization and localization, local media with a community orientation along with a trans-local perspective supported with international program exchange networks can contribute to both local self-awareness and international understanding" (Prehn 1992, 266).

LOCAL MEDIA IN THE 1990S

Local media publics in Western democracies have undergone substantial changes in the 1990s, primarily induced by economic restructuring and forces of social change that hit cities and regions. We witnessed the attraction of transnational corporations into the local media sector, leading to concentration processes not just in large metropolitan markets but also far beyond them. Second, not just vertical but also horizontal concentration processes took place in which the traditional division of labor between different kinds of electronic and print media increasingly gave way to more cost-effective forms of cooperation among these media. At the same time, the local media spectrum widened, with new Internet-based media being introduced into the local public and movement actors producing alternative community media sources. In the absence of comparative analyses, the developments that are outlined in this chapter are based on available case studies and remain somewhat sketchy.

MEDIA CONCENTRATION

Economic concentration processes are most noticeable on the print media market. The trend toward single-market newspapers is increasing in all Western democracies. In the Netherlands, most cities today have only one daily newspaper (Denters 2000, 83). In Great Britain, competition among urban evening dailies ended as early as 1964 with the monopolization of the last competitive market in Manchester (Franklin and Murphy 1998, 7).[9] By contrast the German daily newspaper market seems still rather diversified. In 2001, 58 percent of the readers of local dailies still had competitive papers to choose from (Schuetz 2001, 620). Concentration processes, however, are on the rise in Germany, too. Looking at the eighty-three German cities with a population of more than 100,000, thirty of them now only have one daily newspaper. Seventeen cities have two dailies that belong to the same publishing company (Schuetz 2001, 622). In the United States, 98 percent of cities and communities have only one newspaper. A huge concentration and conglomerization wave spilled over the country during the 1990s. Between 1994 and 2000, 47 percent of all local papers changed ownership, mostly joining conglomerates of several dailies. At present, of the 1,500 dailies in the United States, only about 300 remain independent (Yudken and Owens 2002). Analyzing these trends, Thomas Kunkel and Gene Roberts note:

"Unlike other realms of business, in the newspaper industry, consolidation – in tandem with the chains' desperation to maintain unrealistic profit levels (most of these companies are now being publicly traded) – is actually reducing the amount of real news being gathered and disseminated, most conspicuously at the local and state levels, where consumers need it the most. This is because consolidation has resulted in far fewer news outlets, and the economic pressures have resulted in fewer reporters with fewer inches in the paper to say anything" (Kunkel and Roberts 2001).

Globalization processes in the media sector accelerate this increase in local concentration. Best cases in point are Eastern European media, which since the early 1990s have been subject to intensive acquisition efforts by West European and American media conglomerates. In Poland today, 50 percent of the forty-four regional dailies are owned completely or in part by foreign media companies (Hadamik 2001, 154). The whole country has only fifteen local daily papers (Hadamik 2001, 155). In Bulgaria, the German publishing group Westdeutsche Allgemeine Zeitung established a majority owner position in 1996, then later a complete ownership of the so-called 168 press group, consisting of prominent weekly and

---

[9] The *Manchester Evening Chronicle* was dismantled despite daily sales of a quarter million papers (Franklin and Murphy 1998, 7), thus pointing to the fact that the reason for shutting down a paper in many cases is not low readership, but lack of advertisement revenue for competing publications on a single print media market.

daily newspapers (Tzankoff 2001, 85). When the WAZ group bought the Media Holding AG in 1997, it owned 80 percent of the Bulgarian daily paper market (Tzankoff 2001, 85).[10] In the Czech Republic as well, the local print media market is dominated by German publishing houses (Lambrecht and Schroeter 2001, 174). Papers that under the communist regime were published by the local authorities were converted into regional dailies with diversified local sections (Lambrecht and Schroeter 2001, 177). In Hungary, the German Axel Springer media company has a monopoly on dailies in nine of the nineteen regions and publishes them with diversified local inserts, thus forming what some critics term grand "regional power centers" (Bajomi-Lázár 2001, 195). At present, we still lack empirical studies as to how these ownership transferals have influenced profiles, news content, and working conditions of these local papers.

Economic concentration processes, however, do not only take place between formerly independent print media, but also take the shape of cooperation and mergers between different media in local publics. Publishing houses attempt to diversify and at the same time consolidate their operations by investing not just in the print media market, but also buying local radio and television stations. The underlying intention is to foster cost-effective cooperation and promote synergies in the daily operative business. At present, the Federal Communications Commission (FCC) in the United States is about to abandon a provision that had been established in 1975, banning cross-ownership of television and print media outlets in the United States. Increasing multimedia concentration will produce radically different working conditions for journalists. The ideal media workforce of the future is made up of "allrounders" who have knowledge and experience in all stages of media-related production processes and are flexible enough to be put onto any job, be it investigation, writing, presentation, and technical production. The imagined journalist is able to develop, write, and present stories for the print media as well as radio and TV (Franklin and Murphy 1998, 17). But even without further mergers the homogenization of local news content is in full swing: Radio and television in particular have drastically decreased resources to develop their own news stories, and compensate by buying or simply reproducing news stories from the press. In Great Britain, the Broadcasting Act of 1990 states it bluntly: "There is no requirement for (independent) local

---

[10] After intervention of the Bulgarian government the WAZ group agreed to sell 40 percent of its shares in the Media Holding AG to Austrian and Swiss investors.

radio to carry local news and insofar as it does so there is nothing to prevent that local news being bought in from the local newspaper" (British Radio Authority, op.cit. Crisell 1998, 28).

Outsourcing in the Local Media Sector

Outsourcing refers to a process by which parts of production or services that were formerly provided by the newspaper company or the station are now contracted out to independent service providers. Traditionally, outsourcing was practiced in fields such as advertisement acquisition or distribution. More recently, however, it has spilled over into the core tasks of journalistic production, thus adding to the already precarious state of journalists' working conditions and producing an increasing number of independent news bureaus with a set of freelance writers. From the point of view of editors, publishers, and CEOs of media corporations, the intentions of outsourcing are efficiency, flexibility of the workforce, as well as increases in cost effectiveness and profits. The effects of outsourcing are especially severe in countries with a traditionally heavily unionized workforce such as the Scandinavian countries, Great Britain, Austria, and Germany (Schaffelt [BDZ] 1999). German journalists who work in outsourced enterprises lack substantial protections in terms of labor rights, insurance, and organizational powers granted under the German Industrial Relations Act. As a result of this lack of organized bargaining power and deregulation we see wage dumping and the lowering of vocational training standards that affect the journalistic profession as a whole.

New Media Formats

Established local print media find themselves increasingly in competitive struggles with new media formats. At present, commercial dailies in larger urban markets are challenged on two fronts: On one front, they compete with alternative weeklies or monthlies that are mostly free and financed by advertisement and that often display an impressive journalistic depth and skill in framing complex local issues. Franklin and Murphy estimate for Western Europe in the mid-1990s approximately 4,000 of these papers with a distribution of about 200 million copies per week (Franklin and Murphy 1991, 10). On the other front, transnationally operating companies aggressively push into the daily "free media" sector of Europe. In 2001, free dailies operated in fifty-two European cities, altogether amounting to a daily circulation of 6.4 million copies and rightly being heralded as the new "shooting stars" of local media (Vogel 2001, 576). The first free daily called *Metro* was published in Stockholm in 1995; after a few months it ran a profit. *Metro* has since expanded internationally and is serving, among others, the markets of Helsinki, Basel, Bern, Lucerne, Rome, Barcelona, Madrid, Prague, and Budapest. The format of these free media is news-clip oriented. Content is mostly drawn from the big news agencies. Local angles are interspersed infrequently and without much research. The staff of papers such as *Metro* writes little themselves, and editorials and commentary sections are generally missing, thus making the news operation slim and profitable. The size of these free media is calculated to serve the average commuter on his/her way to work with about twenty minutes reading time (Vogel 2001, 583). Free papers such as *Metro* exhibit a professional layout and are easy reading with a strong focus on light news and human-interest stories. Their slim and flexible distribution systems rest on three pillars: One, they are being delivered to commercial sites, ranging from shopping malls to small neighborhood businesses. Second, they are being delivered to news boxes in high-frequency public spaces such as subway and train stations. Third, companies in some cities hire traditional "newspaper men" who distribute the paper on behalf of the company on city squares, at subway entrances or even to the doorsteps of apartment buildings. The audience that free dailies cater to is young, time-constrained, and female, and generally not invested with one of the established paid print media in town. Female consumers frequently experience time constraints that disrupt solid attachment to established news sources. Yet they are major targets of advertising and the "twenty-minute" format makes them the ideal type target audience of free dailies.

Paid media in several urban markets have decided to employ drastic measures to fight off competition by free media. In Cologne, Germany, the editorial board of the established Koelner Stadtanzeiger decided to publish its own version of a free daily and successfully forced the free media competitor out of the market – predictably shutting down its own free operation a few weeks later. Others have put pressure onto the distributive side by forcing local shop owners to either get rid of the free paper or face a delivery stop of the established daily. How this new competitive local print media market will ultimately affect paid media is not clear. Potential scenarios point in opposite directions. In a more optimistic version, paid print media might face up to the existing challenge by investing more in the strengths that they have: building closer ties with their established readers, investing more resources into reporting on community issues and raising the quality of production on the whole. Yet what seems somewhat more likely is a "race-to-the-bottom." The fact that local media depend heavily on advertising revenues gives free media with broad distributive networks a strong leverage that might force paid dailies into down-scaling that most likely will have negative affects on journalistic production quality.

LOCAL MEDIA AND DEMOCRATIZATION IN LESS DEVELOPED COUNTRIES

We know little about local media in less developed countries and, more specifically, about its function in organizing democratic processes and providing voice for nongovernmental groups. While local media in the metropolitan centers of less developed countries often follow the familiar path of economic concentration, umbrella diversification, and government-oriented reporting, there is also evidence of media giving voice to oppositional politics and marginalized actors. The most cited historic example is the establishment of local radio stations by Bolivian mineworkers, starting in 1952. Over the course of twelve years, twenty-seven stations were established and financed by unionized mine laborers (Valle 1995, 210). In Latin America and Africa, local stations are increasingly taken as a means to protect cultural and linguistic diversity of ethnic or regional groups. Video communication is employed to bridge the communication void due to illiteracy, enabling citizens to communicate with regional and national officials in the absence of written testimony. One example for such functional use of video is the "Association for Video Use by Popular Organizations" in several Latin American countries, that uses video communication as an empowerment strategy and has trained rural workers in Chile and Peru to document and relate their problems to a wider audience and to government (Valle 1995, 211; also Media Development issue 1989/4). In India and Nepal we have similar evidence of popular use of video communication to counteract illiteracy (Okunna 1995, 618–19; Stuart 1989). In Nepal, illiterate village women have produced "'video letters,' aimed at improving communication with development organizations and the central government, and developing educational materials for village use, with the women recording their problems, sending the tapes

170

to the capital city and receiving taped solutions to these problems" (Ogan 1989, 4). Comparative studies of such media initiatives would help us understand the political and cultural contexts in which such initiatives rise, the determinants for sustaining them, and what could be considered best-practice models of local communication development in less developed countries.

LOCAL GOVERNANCE AND THE PUBLIC SPHERE. While media are a central part of local communication, local publics echo numerous voices that primarily communicate aside from the media. Interpersonal and organizational communication patterns created within and between neighborhoods, associations, nongovernmental organizations (NGOs), parties, and activists serve to create and sustain public discourse and to offer venues for opinion formation about local affairs. But few studies define spaces of communication broadly enough to include media-induced as well as organizational and interpersonal communication. Fuchs and Schenk found in an empirical survey of Germany in the mid-1980s that 49 percent of local citizens used the daily paper as their primary source of information about local and regional issues. Thirty-two percent, however, extracted their political information out of interpersonal communication (Fuchs and Schenk 1984, 214–15). While undoubtedly today these figures would be more strongly favoring the local media, it would be a mistake to continue to neglect other communication venues that help to channel news gathering and transform news processing into political activity. Civic networks and NGOs help create local publics by relying on less institutionalized, open, and flexible routes of communication (Lang 2003a).

Since the late 1980s, we have witnessed in Western European societies and the United States an increasing commitment to local neighborhood or issue-oriented organizations with fluid and open participatory structures. The 1990s turned former social movement actors into professionalized NGO members. Short-term issue-centered alliances were created that invigorate local publics and challenge traditionally tight communication among elites on the local level (Lang 2000). The local neighborhood alliance today brings a different set of voices to the public than the established Chamber of Commerce or local party or union chapters. Urban environmental activists might politicize different topics and might employ a different set of communication strategies than the Sierra Club. Thus, the information and activist networks of local NGOs transform the local publics of which they are part. Their organized public mobilization campaigns, acts of civil disobedience, or the staging of protest events should be as much taken into account in conceptualizing local publics as the media. NGOs and activists offer new venues for political communication, and they challenge the traditional leverage of established elites as being the primary, sometimes the only "legitimate" voices on local issues. The shift in late modern societies from local government to governance therefore marks a shift from the "government of communication" through the local state, corporatist elites, and the media to the "networked governance of communication" with a wider array of engaged voices and communication practices appearing on the public stage.

GOVERNMENT COMMUNICATION AND E-DEMOCRACY

Government, however, remains central to communication arrangements in local publics. Government agencies, as we have argued, are still the largest providers of political communication content, and they have an interest in framing limits and substance of legitimate public discourse. Moreover, the local state plays a pivotal role as developer and facilitator of citizen participation and mediation processes. In the United States, high fragmentation in local governance authorities, the emphasis on "freedom of information," and strong interest groups are contributing factors to governments' investment in expanding public communication resources. But while democratization of procedural communication and some creative experiments with civic engagement are well under way in a number of communities, technical achievements and innovation often lack perspective.

Cable and Web-based information and communication systems are heralded as the main imprints of the future of local communication. Empirical studies, however, ask for a more cautious evaluation. Aside from the rhetoric of "electronic democratization" we see little actual evidence either in Europe or in the United States that these new media have indeed contributed substantially to the thickening of democratic practices or the establishment of new participatory cultures (Vedel 2003). In the United States, cable and Web-based systems are employed mostly to professionalize and facilitate the transfer of information in local community. In California, in 1996, 112 out of 460 cities had their own Internet presence; this ratio doubled in 1997 (Weare et al. 2000). Yet the quality of Internet platforms is inconsistent and it is impossible to establish a direct correlation between a Web-based presence and transparency or informational density of local government. Effects of these new technologies depend on the innovative capacity and the eagerness of the city agencies that deploy them. E-government is supposed to provide, first of all, better access to documents and materials of local governments. A best-practice setting can be visited on the government Web site of the city of Seattle, that has posted so far about 36,000 pages of searchable informational resources on the Web (Lang 2003). Seattle's Web presence empowers citizens to follow policy processes through different agencies and thereby introduces a fair level of transparency in regard to policy formulation and implementation. Allowing this, e-government has the potential to make government more accountable as well as reciprocal. If government Web sites have workable and professionally managed interactive features, citizens can get in touch with government employees directly using e-mail and thus communicate about work in progress. Chances are that these interactions will bear some positive result for both sides: They might increase the possibility for citizens to hold government agencies accountable, but they also might introduce new communication venues that, if handled responsibly, could reinstitute more reciprocity in communication. Third, video streaming using cable has been put to use by some communities to transmit City Council meetings, committee meetings, and hearings in real time. Government decision making is awarded potentially more legitimacy with this increase of transparency. And fourth, new media can be employed on the local level to organize participatory communication processes such as "electronic town halls," which again can be used to deliberate or to foster deliberatively based decision-making processes (Grosswiler 1998; Weare et al. 2000). But even though there have been a few interesting experiments here, the vast majority of local communities makes use of new technologies simply to expand the flow of informational output and to communicate its image as an investment-friendly and livable community. Dialogical settings are only rarely established, and if so, often not adequately managed. Fears that e-government on the local stays at the level of symbolic use of politics have yet to be disseminated. Yet local e-governance holds promises to reinvigorate the interactive and participatory potential of local publics, and we might see some surprising experiments here in the near future.[11]

---

[11] In Germany, at present the Bertelsmann Foundation is working with several cities to develop more participation-driven e-governance experiments. In the United States, the Santa Monica PEN-network has been heralded as offering a viable technological solution to foster civic engagement and responsive government.

CONCLUSION: MEDIA, DEMOCRACY, AND LOCAL PUBLICS – PUTTING RESEARCH IN COMPARATIVE PERSPECTIVE

The local public spheres of late modern societies are strange hybrids. Depending on perspective, they seem to be under siege by commercial media and public relations–fixated local elites that make them not very different from the worlds of national public spheres. Yet from another view, localities appear to harbor the exciting prospect of invigorating participatory governance and citizen activism from below. Local publics today expose some of the worst of globally mediated culture while producing some of the best ideas about how to strengthen public life and small democracy. This tension, I claim, informs all four of the initially presented distinctive features of the spatial communication arena of the local – that is, its cognitive, symbolic, interactive, and participatory uniqueness, and it makes these features points of continuous contestation.

The cognitive challenge that local publics face can be attributed to two factors: First, we witness a shrinking media commitment to the delivery of shared knowledge about the local. Second, continuous urban segmentation and segregation processes encourage the formation of local subpublics – often with little cognitive awareness of or connection among each other. Across societies, we have established that audiences consider local news to be pivotal for their sense of place and citizenship, and that they tend to respond positively to comprehensive and in-depth political, social, and cultural news delivery. Glocalization leaves citizens in dear need of the interpretive power of the media and the processing of national and global news through the prism of the local. Yet commercial or free media often do not provide adequate information flows and interpretive schemes, and in many metropolitan areas they are being challenged by alternative free media sources that often employ in-depth investigative reporting on local issues with relatively few resources. Cognition about local publics, while being high in demand, lacks commitment and investment on the providers' end. Conversely, neighborhoods, ethnic, or cultural minorities in larger urban spaces have tended to form their own public arenas under the umbrella of the local public – sometimes making a deliberate effort to enhance cognitive awareness in their city of specific aspects of their space or cultures, but sometimes being just as content to provide niches for identity production that do not aim at a larger audience. As a result, the identity of local publics as a relatively unified cognitive arena is constantly in flux.

Second, many local publics experience contestation in regard to their strength in providing spaces for symbolic integration, most prominently visible in the metropolitan spaces of large international cities. Here, the attachment to the city as a whole is often minimal, while attachment to diversified cultural groups or neighborhoods is stable or on the rise. Local governments, quite aware of the need for citywide symbolic integration, try to foster attachments through symbolic event politics such as sports attractions and festivals, or reinvent the identities of their municipalities in glossy brochures and with the help of public relations agencies. Yet in larger urban areas, we can see more symbolic integration in diversified subpublics of the local, as in neighborhood associations or historical societies that make it a point to reconnect citizens to their sublocality by cognitive as well as symbolic means. Often it is unforeseen events such as the opening of the wall in Berlin or 9/11 for New York that ignite symbolic identification of citizens with their public spaces.

Third, local publics face contestation as prime providers for interactive, face-to-face and interpersonal communication, this mostly due to the new interactive and interpersonal options that Web-based communication offers. Today, participating in issue-driven international e-mail list communication might offer as much interpersonal contact and interactive components as the local Greenpeace network or the urban housing coalition. People do not necessarily need to put a face on face-to-face communication in order to feel connected – for some it seems as personal to engage with the imagined face behind the e-mail nickname. Those "imagined communities" can acquire more reality in some people's lives than can local neighborhood councils and coalitions.

The fourth contested dimension of local publics is their capacity to become testing grounds for experiments in participatory democracy. Local governments have as of yet made little use of these assets. The prospects for development seem vast, yet suffer from latent neglect or even deliberate underutilizing of the potential that is inherent in local communication processes.

What follows from these four dynamics of contestation for the study of local publics? In conclusion, I will identify several areas of research that would need to be addressed in order to assess these dynamics more in depth and fill existing research voids. Once again, the argument here is based on a comparative reading of a small number of existing case studies, thus leaving some issues underrepresented and others unaddressed. Moreover, the bias toward West European and North American developments surely taints the picture, while at the same time providing a framework against which to measure constellations and developments in other world regions.

Media Globalization

The structural transformation of local media publics exhibits several similarities, the most noteworthy being

- vertical and horizontal concentration of media markets,
- functional differentiation of specific media segments, and
- easy-listening and consumer-oriented formats.

Underlying these broad tendencies we see specific national, regional, and local marks that reflect frameworks set by law and politics as well as by social and cultural identities. While globalization puts its imprint on the local media publics of Europe and the United States, it does so through specific venues, reproducing and sustaining remarkably different local communication cultures. Here are three examples:

- In December 2002, the German anticartel agency has nullified a co-operation contract for production between two of the major dailies in Germany's capital Berlin. In the United States, such cooperation on the production front, often turning at some point into the demise of one of the papers, is a publicly unquestioned part of local media politics and considered free market self-regulation. In Germany, the ruling of the anticartel agency argued that with the fusion of the two production units one publishing house, the Stuttgart-based Holtzbrinck-Group, would hold more than 50 percent of circulation, and this is considered to be a threat to market competition by the anticartelization agency.
- A second, quite different example of such cultural embeddedness is the discrepancy between large portions of the British daily newspaper market and German dailies. Whereas the British local press seems to be highly entertainment oriented and in its format inspired by tabloid culture, the German daily newspapers are comparatively more information-driven and conservative in style, with hardly any color and much less photography. How is it that British consumers are considered to be so much more prone toward easy-reading formats than Germans? How did these respective media cultures develop historically? One hypothesis is that competition among British local media is much stiffer, due to a more diverse

electronic media market, and that local papers therefore rely more on attention-catching formats than in Germany. Yet again, informative studies are lacking on this topic.

- A third example for underresearched areas of locally specific media is the new wave of "community media" generated by Internet-based technology. We have indicators that Internet-based local communication initiatives not only flourish in many communities but that, albeit depending on the broader political and social environment, some of these initiatives also explore new participatory venues and generate activist politics in these communities (Lang 2003b). Local political communication research needs to investigate which environments are most conducive to such initiatives, how they relate to established media, and what their effects are in terms of a more participatory local political culture. We can suspect that local governance regimes with a longer tradition of experimenting with alternative participation venues are more prone to embrace those initiatives than governance regimes of a more closed or corporatist type.

In sum, only a comparative perspective highlights the characteristics of local media publics and displays their embeddedness in political and cultural environments.

MEDIATIZATION OF LOCAL POLITICS – REPOLITICIZATION OF LOCAL MEDIA?

Beyond the obvious trend toward professionalization of political and public communication there looms the larger issue of how specific governance regimes utilize these resources. Does local government make efforts to use public communication techniques to foster better information and more engagement, or do we see glossy brochures and Web sites with little content and minimal intervention options for citizens? What kind of relationships do specific governance regimes establish with the local media? Do the two work hand in hand or do we see a more neutral or even confrontational arrangement in which the local media have kept independent research angles and framing capacities? And what strategies emerge from the media side as organizations are confronted increasingly with demands to become more active players in the local public, and help stimulate civic engagement and deliberative processes within the community (Rosen 1994; Merritt 1998, 3–4)? In the United States, over the past decade, 200 local communities have experimented with civic or public journalism initiatives, aimed at a more engaging and activating media culture that presents options for citizens to get involved. These initiatives rely in part on older ideas about community journalism, but they also bear some resemblance to media activation initiatives in less developed countries. If these experiments seem to be a passing trend, what other formats may be rising to fill this need for more active community reporting? Again, we need comparative research that addresses the conditions for success and the sustainability of such initiatives in different societal settings.

Strengthening Local Publics

What are the conditions for strengthening local publics, which in some ways seem as media-driven and fractured as national publics? Are strong media systems, media competition, media differentiation, access to information from the local government, and participatory venues sufficiently encompassing variables to assess the viability of local publics across cultures and political systems? Some researchers argue that the sublocalization of publics does not harbor positive effects as much as it appears to be a surrogate for "the lacking orientation function of the media" (Jonscher 1995, 51 [transl. S. L.]). Whereas these new subpublics enable communication and exchange among the diverse partial worlds of the locals, critics argue that they destroy the "integrity of the local public sphere by segmenting it and ultimately result in the dualization of society into groups that are oriented towards the larger issues and those that form in partial life worlds such as self help groups and neighborhood initiatives" (Jonscher 1995, 52 [transl. S. L.]). As a result, such being the critique, the segmented local public could hardly offer "a base for joint discussion and opinion formation" (Jonscher 1995, 52 [transl. S. L.]). We need to ask empirically and comparatively, therefore, whether the sublocalization of publics, that is, using alternative neighborhood media or multiculturally oriented programming, results in weakening the local public or whether it contributes to its strengthening.

The integration of local publics is ultimately a governance process. Studies are needed to show how specific regime types allow various civic actors such as NGOs into the public, how much credibility and acceptance they are being awarded, and whether they take part in confrontational or – to the other extreme – in rather co-opted settings. We need research on who is being portrayed as being a legitimate actor within the local governance regime, who is linked to the official Web sites – and who is being excluded from the network of local initiatives. Because the most notable problem to opinion formation on the local level is the lack of "competing information sources for local politics" (Graber 1997, 333), competent civic actors and groups might contribute indeed to a broader and more diverse news culture within local publics. We have to analyze, therefore, how local governance processes have to be constituted in order to open up ground for the participation of alternative political actors such as NGOs in the area of housing, city development, homelessness, and environmental or women's issues.

STATE DEVOLUTION AND LOCAL PUBLICS

The local communication arena "provides a framework for the exercise of individual and group participation, but it can do so only if significant decisions are taken at the local level (Hill 1994, 238). Therefore we need to connect communicative arenas to questions of power and resource allocation in the local community. How is the institutional place of the local government within the broader national and transnational governance structure affecting the scope and intensity of local publics? Can we assume that in governance systems where more legal and decision-making power rests with the local state we can count on higher levels of public communication and interaction? Or do recent trends of neoliberal devolution policies turn public communication practices into mere legitimizing exercises – depriving communities of the resources to engage in more elaborate communication processes? Again, comparative studies might be instructive. For the United Kingdom, we can establish a direct link between the massive abolishment of local governance units under Heath and Thatcher and the decrease in local newspapers (Franklin and Murphy 1991, 193). On the contrary, we might expect that the revitalization of regional and local authorities in France in recent years – largely due to meeting EU objectives – might result in more complex and lively local publics.

REFERENCES

Bajomi-Lázár, Péter. 2001. Medien und Medienpolitik in Ungarn. In Barbara Thomass and Michaela Tzankoff, eds. *Medien und Transformation in Osteuropa.* Opladen, Germany: Westdeutscher Verlag, pp. 187–202.

Barber, Benjamin. 1984. *Strong Democracy. Participatory Politics for a New Age.* Berkeley: University of California Press.

Berrigan, Frances J. 1977. Access and the Media: New Models in Europe. In Frances J. Berrigan, ed. *Access: Some Western Models of Community Media.* Paris: Unesco, pp. 145–212.

Berry, Jeffrey M., Kent E. Portney, and Kent Thomson. 1993. *The Rebirth of Urban Democracy*. Washington, DC: Brookings Institution.

Bourdieu, Pierre. 1982. *Die feinen Unterschiede. Kritik der gesellschaftlichen Urteilskraft*. Frankfurt/Main, Germany: Suhrkamp.

Brettschneider, Frank, and Katja Neller. 1997. Lokale Kommunikation: Die Perspektive der Zeitungsleser. In Oscar W. Gabriel, Frank Brettschneider, Angelika Vetter, eds. *Politische Kultur und Wahlverhalten in der Grossstadt*. Opladen, Germany: Westdeutscher Verlag, pp. 69–92.

Conklin, Hal. 2000. *Access Television and the Future of Public Participation*. A Study of Government Access Channels in 226 Cities by The California Center for Civic Renewal. Available from the World Wide Web at http://www.westerncity.com/AccTelSept00.htm.

Cox, Harvey, and David Morgan. 1973. *City Politics and the Press. Journalists and the Governing of Merseyside*. Cambridge: University of Cambridge Press.

Crisell, Andrew. 1998. Local Radio: Attuned to the Times or Filling Time With Tunes? In Bob Franklin, and David Murphy, eds. *Making Local News. Local Journalism in Context*. London: Routledge, pp. 24–35.

Denters, Bas A. H. 2000. Urban Democracies in the Netherlands: Social and Political Change, Institutional Continuities? In Oscar W. Gabriel and Vincent Savitch Hoffman-Martinot. *Urban Democracy*. Opladen, Germany: Leske + Budrich, pp. 73–126.

Dorsch, Petra E. 1978. Lokalkommunikation. Ergebnisse und Defizite der Forschung. *Publizistik* 23: 189–99.

Dubois, D. 1993. *Les Politiques de Communiation des Collectivités Territoriales*. Université d'Amiens.

Dunn, Delmar. 1969. *Public Officials and the Press*. Reading, MA: Addison-Wesley.

Franklin, Bob, and David Murphy. 1991. *What News? The Market, Politics, and the Local Press*. London: Routledge.

Franklin, Bob, and David Murphy, eds. 1998. *Making Local News. Local Journalism in Context*. London: Routledge.

Fuchs, Wolfgang, and Michael Schenk. 1984. Der Rezipient im lokalen Kommunikationsraum. *Media Perspektiven* 3: 211–18.

Graber, Doris A. 1997. *Mass Media and American Politics*. 5th ed. Washington: Congressional Quarterly Press.

Grosswiler, Paul. 1998. Historical Hopes, Media Fears, and the Electronic Town Meeting Concept: Where Technology Meets Democracy or Demagogy? *Journal of Communication Inquiry* 22 (2): 133–50.

Hadamik, Katharina. 2001. Medien in Polen. In Barbara Thomass and Michalea Tzankoff, eds. *Medien und Transformation in Osteuropa*. Opladen, Germany: Westdeutscher Verlag, pp. 145–66.

Haenisch, Horst, and Klaus Schroeter. 1971. Zum politischen Potential der Lokalpresse. In Ralf Zoll, ed. *Manipulation der Meinungsbildung. Zum Problem hergestellter Öffentlichkeit*. Opladen, Germany: Westdeutscher Verlag, pp. 242–79.

Heyn, Juergen. 1979. *Partizipation und Lokalkommunikation in Grossbritannien. Video, Fernsehen, Hoerfunk und das Problem der Demokratisierung kommunaler Kommunikation*. Munich: Minerva.

Hill, Dilys M. 1994. *Citizens and Cities: Urban Policy in the 1990s*. Hemel Hampstead, U.K.: Harvester Wheatsheaf.

Hollander, Ed. 1992. The Emergence of Small Scale Media. In Nick Jankowski, Ole Prehn, and James Stappers, eds. *The People's Voice. Local Radio and Television in Europe*. London: John Libbey, pp. 7–15.

Jankowski, Nick, and Ole Prehn, eds. 2002. *Community Media in the Information Age. Perspectives and Prospects*. Cresskill, NJ: Hampton.

Jankowski, Nick, Ole Prehn, and James Stappers, eds. 1992. *The People's Voice. Local Radio and Television in Europe*. London: John Libbey.

Janowitz, Morris. 1952. *The Community Press in an Urban Setting: The Social Elements of Urbanism*. Chicago: Chicago University Press.

Jarren, Otfried. 1984. *Kommunale Kommunikation*. Munich: Minerva.

———.1991. Neue Politik durch Neue Medien? Zur Bedeutung lokaler elektronischer Medien fuer die politische Kultur in der Kommune – Ergebnisse einer Feldstudie. In Bernhard Blanke, ed. *Staat und Stadt*. PVS special issue 22 (32): 422–39.

———.1994. Lokale Medien und lokale Politik. In Roland Roth and Hellmut Wollmann, eds. *Kommunalpolitik. Politisches Handeln in den Gemeinden*. Opladen, Germany: Leske + Budrich, pp. 296–305.

Jonscher, Norbert. 1991. *Einfuehrung in die lokale Publizistik*. Opladen, Germany : Westdeutscher Verlag.

———.1995. *Lokale Publizistik. Theorie und Praxis der oertlichen Berichterstattung. Ein Lehrbuch*. Opladen, Germany: Westdeutscher Verlag.

Kaniss, Phyllis. 1991. *Making Local News*. Chicago: University of Chicago Press.

———.1995. *The Media and the Mayor's Race. The Failure of Urban Political Reporting*. Bloomington: Indiana University Press.

Kieslich, Guenter. 1972. Lokale Kommunikation. Ihr Stellenwert im Zeitgespraech der Gesellschaft. *Publizistik* 17: 95–101.

Kiolbassa, Jolene. 1997. Is Local TV News Still Local? Coverage of Presidential and Senate Races in Los Angeles. *Press/Politics* 2 (1): 79–95.

Kishan Thussu, Daya. 1998. Localizing the Global. Zee TV in India. In Daya Kishan Thussu, ed. *Electronic Empires. Global Media and Local Resistance*. New York: Oxford University Press, pp. 273–94.

Kleinsteuber, Hans J. 1992. Medien und oeffentliche Meinung. In Willi Paul Adams, et al., eds. *Laenderbericht USA*, vol. 1. Bonn: Bundeszentrale fuer Politische Bildung, pp. 546–62.

Klite, Paul, Robert A. Bardwell, and Jason Salzman, 1997. Local TV News: Getting Away with Murder. *Press/Politics* 2 (2): 102–12.

Koschnick, Wolfgang J. 1995. *Standard-Lexikon fuer Mediaplanung und Mediaforschung in Deutschland*. 2nd ed. Munich: K. G. Saur.

Kunkel, Thomas, and Gene Roberts. 2001. Leaving Readers Behind. The Age of Corporate Newspapering. *American Journalism Review* 23 (4): 32–42.

Kurp, Matthias. 1994. *Lokale Medien und kommunale Eliten. Partizipatorische Potentiale des Lokaljournalismus bei Printmedien und Hoerfunk in Nordrhein-Westfalen*. Opladen, Germany: Westdeutscher Verlag.

Lambrecht, Oda, and Katharina Schroeter. 2001. Transformation der Medien in der Tschechischen Republik. In Barbara Thomass and Michaela Tzankoff, eds. *Medien und Transformation in Osteuropa*. Opladen, Germany: Westdeutscher Verlag, pp. 167–81.

Lang, Sabine. 2000. NGOs, Local Governance and Political Communication Processes in Germany. *Political Communication* 17 (4): 383–8.

————.2001. *Politische Öffentlichkeit im modernen Staat*. Baden-Baden: Nomos.

————.2003a. Local Political Communication and Citizen Participation. In Philippe Maarek and Gadi Wolfsfeld, eds. *Political Communication in a New Era: A Cross-National Perspective*. London: Routledge, pp. 171–92.

————.2003b. Die Foerderung von buergerschaftlichem Engagement in US-Amerikanischen Staedten und Kommunen. In Deutscher Bundestag, Enquetekommission 'Zukunft des buergerschaftlichen Engagements,' (German Parliament, Expert Commission on the Future of Civic Engagement). *Die Zukunft des buergerschaftlichen Engagements*. Opladen, Germany: Leske + Budrich.

Lipschultz, Jeremy H., and Michael L. Hilt. 2002. *Crime and Local Television News*. Mahwah, NJ: Lawrence Erlbaum.

Merritt, Davis 'Buzz.' 1998. *Public Journalism and Public Life. Why Telling the News in Not Enough*. Mahwah, NJ: Lawrence Erlbaum.

Murck, Manfred. 1983. Macht und Medien in den Kommunen. *Rundfunk und Fernsehen* 31: 370–80.

Neller, Katja. 1999. *Lokale Kommunikation. Politikberichterstattung in Tageszeitungen*. Wiesbaden, Germany: Deutscher Universitaetsverlag.

Neveu, Erik. 1998. Media and Politics in French Political Science. *The European Journal of Political Research* 33: 439–58.

Ogan, Christine. 1989. Video's Great Advantage: Decentralized Control of Technology. *Media Development* 36: 2–5.

Okunna, Chinyere Stella. 1995. Small Participatory Media Technology as an Agent of Social Change in Nigeria: A Non-Existent Option? *Media, Culture & Society* 17: 615–27.

Parry, Geraint, George Moyser, and Neil Day. 1992. *Political Participation and Democracy in Britain*. Cambridge: Cambridge University Press.

Phillips, Anne. 1996. Why Does Local Democracy Matter? In Lawrence Pratchett and David Wilson, eds. *Local Democracy and Local Government*. New York: St. Martin's Press, pp. 20–37.

Prehn, Ole. 1992. From Small Scale Utopianism to Large Scale Pragmatism. In Nick Jankowski, Ole Prehn, and James Stappers, eds. *The People's Voice. Local Radio and Television in Europe*. London: John Libbey, pp. 247–68.

Putnam, Robert. 2000. *Bowling Alone. The Collapse and Revival of American Community*. New York: Simon & Schuster.

Rager, Guenther, Harald Schibrani. 1981. Das Lokale als Gegenstand der Kommunikationsforschung. Bericht ueber den Stand der Forschung in der Bundesrepublik. *Rundfunk und Fernsehen* 29 (4): 498–508.

Rosen, Jay. 1994. Making Things More Public: On the Political Responsibility of the Media Intellectual. *Critical Studies in Mass Communication* 11: 362–88.

Rosenstiel, Tom, Carl Gottlieb, and Lee Ann Brady. 2000. Time of Peril for TV News. *Columbia Journalism Review* 6: 84–9.

Roth, Roland. 1994. Lokale Demokratie 'von unten.' In Roland Ruth and Hellmut Wollmann, eds. *Kommunalpolitik. Politisches Handeln in den Gemeinden*. Opladen, Germany: Leske + Budrich, pp. 228–44.

Salvador, Michael, and Patricia M. Sias, eds. 1998. *The Public Voice in a Democracy at Risk*. Westport, CIN: Praeger Publishers.

Saxer, Ulrich. 1986. Strukturen und Resultate der schweizerischen Lokalradio-Begleitforschung. *Media Perspektiven* 5: 367–79.

Schaffelt, Burkhard (Bundesverband Deutscher Zeitungsverleger; BDZ). 1999. Stellungnahme: Ein Mittel gegen Verkrustung und Redaktionsbeamtentum. In Frank Meik, ed. *Redaktionen Outsourcen? Die outgesourcte Lokalredaktionen der Tageszeitung*. Marburger Medientag. Marburg, Germany: Hitzroth, pp. 19–22.

Schoenbach, Klaus. 1978. Die isolierte Welt des Lokalen. Tageszeitungen und ihre Berichterstattung ueber Mannheim. *Rundfunk und Fernsehen* 26 (3): 260–77.

Schudson, Michael. 1978. *Discovering the News. A Social History of American Newspapers*. New York: Basic Books.

Schuetz, Walter J. 2001. Deutsche Tagespresse 2001. *Media Perspektiven* 12: 602–32.

Schwiderowski, Peter. 1989. *Entscheidungsprozesse und Öffentlichkeit auf der kommunalen Ebene*. Munich: Minerva.

Stuart, S. 1989. Access to Media: Placing Video in the Hands of the People. *Media Development* 36: 8–11.

Thomass, Barbara, and Michaela Tzankoff, eds. 2001. *Medien und Transformation in Osteuropa*. Opladen, Germany: Westdeutscher Verlag.

Tzankoff, Michaela. 2001. Der Transformationsprozess in Bulgarien und die Entwicklung der postsozialistischen Medienlandschaft. In Barbara Thomass and Michaela Tzankoff, eds. *Medien und Transformation in Osteuropa*. Opladen, Germany: Westdeutscher Verlag, pp. 65–94.

Valle, Carlos A. 1995. Communication: International Debate and Community-Based Initiatives. In Philip Lee, ed. *The Democratization of Communication*. Cardiff: University of Wales Press, pp. 199–216.

Vedel, Thierry. 2003. Political Communication and the Internet. In Philippe Maarek and Gadi Wolfsfeld, eds. *Political Communication in a New Era: A Cross-National Perspective*. London: Routledge, pp. 41–59.

Vogel, Andreas. 2001. Die taegliche Gratispresse. Ein neues Geschaeftsmodell fuer Zeitungen in Europa. *Media Perspektiven* 11: 576–84.

Voigt, Ruediger. 1986. Kommunalpolitik im laendlichen Raum. Plaedoyer fuer die Wiederbelebung lokaler Politik. *Aus Politik und Zeitgeschichte* 46/47: 3–19.

Weare, Chris, Juliet Musso, and Matthew L. Hale. 2000. *The Design of Electronic Democratic Forms: A Comparison of Alternative Theories*. Unpublished manuscript. Los Angeles.

Widlok, Peter. 1992. *Der andere Hoerfunk. Community Radios in den USA*. Berlin: Vistas Publishers.

Widlok, Peter, and Otfried Jarren. 1992. Germany: From Pilot Projects to Commercial Local Radio. In Nick Jankowski, Ole Prehn, and James Stappers, eds. *The People's Voice. Local Radio and Television in Europe*. London: John Libbey, pp. 123–36.

Wood, Robert C. 1959. *Suburbia: Its People and Their Politics*. Boston: Houghton Mifflin.

Yudken, Joel, and Christine Owens. 2002. *Press Release of the AFL-CIO at the Newspaper Guild Reporter* (online) (cited January 18, 2002). Available from World Wide Web at http://www.newsguild.org/gr/gr_display.php?storyID=617.

EIGHT

Strategic Political Communication

Mobilizing Public Opinion in "Audience Democracies"

Hanspeter Kriesi

The democratic systems of government are changing profoundly because the form of representation is fundamentally changing. This is the position defended by Bernard Manin (1995, 247–303) in his influential book on the principles of *representative government*, the term he uses for the form of government of Western liberal democracies. After the classical parliamentarianism of the nineteenth century and the party democracy that was established at the beginning of the twentieth century, according to Manin, representative government currently takes the form of an *"audience democracy."*[1] The characteristics of this new form of government include personalization of elections and the rise of experts in political communication, increasing importance of political offers formulated so vaguely that the governing elites possess a large maneuvering space, the omnipresence of public opinion, and the transfer of the political debate from the backrooms of parliamentary committees and the central offices of parties and associations to the public sphere.

Manin has formulated concisely what party and media experts have observed for quite a while. *Party researchers* point to the decline of the ideologically oriented and structurally rooted mass party and the rise of the "electoral professional party" (Panebianco 1988) or the "cartel party" (Mair 1997). This transformation has led, on the one hand, to the declining importance of the traditional party apparatus and of party militants, and, on the other hand, it has reinforced the importance of the party leaders and of the much more independent electoral audience. *Media researchers* note that political communication is no longer focused on parties but on the media (Swanson and Mancini 1996). They observe the increasing independence of the mass media from the political parties.

---

[1] Manin (1995, 279) uses the term *démocratie du public* in French.

Finally, they begin to speculate about the arrival of a third age of political communication (Blumler and Kavanagh 1999), where the public
possesses greater autonomy with regard to the media. Characteristics of
this new style of political communication include the multiplication of
the means of communication, an affluence of communication channels,
increasing commercialization, the omnipresence of the media, and further acceleration of the speed with which political information becomes
accessible for a significant part of the public.

In the ideal audience democracy, a much larger part of political action becomes public action. If the political actors are more frequently
going public, they are also much more frequently challenged by the public. Today, as Kitschelt (2000, 164) has observed, parties are, much more
than they were some years ago, confronted with political preferences that
are exogenously determined by spontaneous developments in the electorate or by independent media and political entrepreneurs who operate
outside of the parliamentary arena. In this new form of representative
government, public support becomes volatile and unpredictable, but at
the same time crucial for political success. Political communication and
political mobilization are now indispensable components of governing,
"because the substantive action space of politics is diminishing and the
need for legitimacy is rising in a context of intense political competition"
(Pfetsch 1998, 249).

The idea that the public sphere and public opinion become increasingly important for policy-making today is met with some skepticism on
the part of public-policy analysts. Thus, von Beyme (1994, 332) suggests
that we should not overrate the relevance of media-oriented strategies
of political actors for the policy-making process. The routine political
process remains, as far as he is concerned, largely separate from the
public sphere. As Kingdon (1984, 69–70) had already noted many years
ago, "there are . . . severe limits on the ability of general public opinion
to affect policy formation. Many important spheres for one thing, are
nearly invisible to the general public." Habermas (1992, 432–3) concedes
empirically and normatively that routine decision making is a matter to
be dealt with by the central decision makers without public participation. By contrast, he argues that questions of great importance or with
strong normative implications should be dealt with by an "extraordinary
problem-solving procedure" that also includes actors of the periphery –
social movements, citizens' initiatives, and the like.

Public-policy analysts remind us that the audience democracy may
largely consist of "symbolic politics" – events carefully staged by political

actors to legitimate policy decisions taken in the rather inaccessible arenas of policy making, which contribute little to the problem-solving activity that takes place in those arenas. The current trend toward *"governance by networks"* usually leads to less formal modes of decision making within structures that are hardly visible for most of the public and remain independent from the official institutions of representative democracy. This trend, which brings policy making in large, majoritarian countries closer to the policy style that has always dominated in small, consensus-oriented democracies, is quite compatible with the weakening of the political parties and of parliament as an arena of policy making. But contrary to what Manin's vision of an audience democracy implies, this trend leads to a system of "post-parliamentary governance" that increasingly tends to institute expert sovereignty at the expense of popular sovereignty.

Both visions of the trends in contemporary forms of representative government – audience democracy and network governance – share the notion of a declining functional relevance of the political parties and of the parliamentary arena. But they differ fundamentally with respect to the role of the public, that is, the citizens. In the audience democracy the public is called upon to control and to influence the policy-making process, while in the network governance the public is largely irrelevant for the political process.

Given the crucial importance of the public sphere[2] and of public opinion today, it is surprising that the reciprocal topics of the impact of political communication and mobilization on public opinion on the one hand, and the impact exerted by public opinion on the political process on the other hand, have so far not been studied more systematically. Thus, analyses of political decision and implementation processes by political scientists hardly take the public sphere into account, and focus instead on bargaining and debates in the parliamentary or administrative arenas. By contrast, analysts of social movements are primarily interested in the movements' mobilization of the public, but hardly ever pay attention to their impact on bargaining inside the political system. Finally, practitioners from the communication sciences concentrate on how the opinions and electoral decisions of citizens are influenced by the media. As far as they are concerned with the role of the media in the political decision processes, they usually narrowly focus on the specific

---

[2] The public sphere is defined as the arena where the political communication between the political actors and the citizens takes place (Neidhardt 1994).

interactions between journalists and politicians or the latter's public relations specialists, on politicians' perceptions of one another or on the media use of political decision makers.[3]

Against the background of the fundamental transformation described at the outset, the goal of this chapter is to clarify the role of the public sphere in the political process of modern democracies in an internationally comparative perspective. To do so, I choose an actor-centered approach that asks (a) under which conditions actors choose strategies to influence public opinion, and (b) under which conditions such strategies succeed in influencing the political decision-making process. By focusing on political decision making, I explicitly omit elections from the subsequent considerations. I start out with the assumption that the fundamental change in representative government not only concerns periodically recurring elections, but especially the long periods between these special occasions – periods during which the electoral public has been attributed only a marginal role in the party democracies.

In the first part of the chapter, I present a simple heuristic framework for the analysis of the mobilization of public opinion. In a second step, the strategies that the different types of actors use to influence public opinion are discussed. In an internationally comparative perspective it becomes clear that the type of strategies and their success is to an important extent determined by the institutional conditions of different national contexts. Therefore, in the third part, an attempt is made to systematize the political and media-related context conditions in Western liberal democracies, which are likely to influence the public strategies of political actors. Finally, some ideas are presented about how this approach could be implemented in an internationally comparative research design.

A FRAMEWORK FOR THE ANALYSIS OF THE PUBLIC SPHERE'S ROLE IN THE POLITICAL DECISION-MAKING PROCESS

Politics take place in various arenas. Simplifying greatly, I will only distinguish between the public sphere and the arena of decision making. The

---

[3] Exceptions from this general assessment are, in political science, the studies by Page et al. (1987), Baumgartner and Jones (1993), and Stimson et al. (1995), as well as the sociological or communications' studies by Linsky (1986), Pfetsch (1993), Burstein (1998), Gerhards et al. (1998), Koopmans and Statham (1999, 2000), and Ferree et al. (2002).

latter includes all venues (parliamentarian and extraparliamentarian) where political bargaining takes place and political decisions are made. This arena is only partly visible to the public (e.g., plenary parliamentary debates). The public sphere includes all venues visible to a large audience, where political communication among organized political actors and between them and the citizens takes place. Political communication in the public sphere can be understood as a process of agenda building (McCombs and Shaw 1972; Lang and Lang 1983) in which the political actors, the media and the audience of citizens mutually influence each other by presenting information, demands, appeals, and arguments.

Political actors produce *events* and *campaigns*, which the media report and comment upon. Some of these events are explicitly staged (so-called pseudoevents) for the purpose of attracting the public's attention and eventually influencing political decision making. The media play a crucial role in this process not only because of their reach but also because of their *limited carrying capacity* (Hilgartner and Bosk 1988) and their tendency to impose their *own logic of selecting and presenting information*. The public sphere can be conceived as a loosely bound communicative space in which a variety of individual and collective actors compete for public attention and support. Given the restricted communicative space, the public will pay attention to only a small proportion of all the messages that are available for inclusion in the public discourse every day, and it will debate, let alone support, an even smaller proportion of these messages.

Public opinion is the outcome of the process of political communication in the public sphere. Following Neidhardt (1994) and Converse (1987), we can distinguish between two views on public opinion that do not necessarily coincide – the notion of survey analysis and the notion of the sociology of the public sphere. According to the survey analysts' conception, public opinion corresponds to the "opinion of the mass public" or "the opinion of the population" as it is measured by opinion surveys. According to the sociology of the public sphere, by contrast, public opinion corresponds to the totality of the opinions, which is expressed in the public sphere with regard to a specific theme. I will adopt the sociologists' conception. The public opinion in this sense can be more or less consonant, depending on the degree to which the public expression of opinion about a given theme converges. It is an empirical question as to what extent public opinion as publicized opinion is consonant and to what extent it corresponds to the opinion of the population as measured by opinion surveys.

The actors who appear in the public sphere are first of all individual persons – members of the political elites in parties and associations, and journalists and movement activists. These persons, however, typically do not act as individuals, but as representatives of political organizations, which can be classified into three categories:

- *Decision makers*: the dominant coalitions and oppositional minorities in the arenas of decision making – the executive, parliament, and the judiciary
- *Media*: the press – individual newspapers; radio; television – individual channels
- *Challengers*: oppositional actors among insiders – political parties and interest associations; and outsiders – social movement organizations

Decision makers may be grouped into *dominant coalitions* that determine the decisions in the parliamentary and administrative arenas and *oppositional minorities* that do not get their way. These coalitions constitute both "advocacy coalitions" (Sabatier 1993; 1998) and "discourse coalitions" (Hajer 1995). Among the challengers, we can distinguish between *outsiders* (social movement organizations) and more *oppositional actors among insiders* (parties and interest associations). Contrary to insiders, outsiders do not have institutionalized access to the arenas of political negotiation. In reality, this distinction is a gradual one and may vary from one issue to the other. With respect to the media, we note that as the importance of the public sphere increases for politics and as political communication becomes increasingly media centered, the media themselves become producers of events – contradicting the traditional labor division between media and politics.

Depending on the type of actors involved, we can distinguish between three types of *public strategies*, that is, political strategies centered on influencing public opinion:

- The strategies of decision makers (top-down strategies)
- The strategies of challengers (bottom-up strategies)
- The strategies of the media, which become actors in their own right (media-centered strategies)

Arenas, actors, their strategies, and the events they produce constitute the key conceptual elements for the analysis of the "politics of public sphere" that I propose here. Figure 8.1 summarizes the heuristic framework that illustrates how the relationship of these elements can be perceived. In

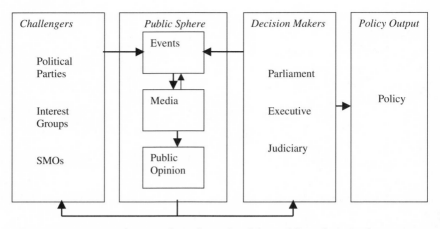

Figure 8.1 Framework to Analyze the Role of the Public Sphere in the Process of Political Decision Making. *Note:* Social Movement Organizations (SMOs).

order to influence the processes taking place in the decision-making arena, public authorities and other political actors produce, among other things, events that the media report on for their audience. Simplifying greatly, the model assumes a media-centered public sphere and does not provide for direct external (e.g., through public assemblies) or internal (e.g., through internal communications in political organizations) links between the collective political actors and the political authorities on the one hand, and the public on the other hand. Although the model focuses on the "production" of public events, it does not exclude that political actors directly access the media without creating public events (e.g., in informal luncheons with journalists). The reciprocal arrows that link media and events indicate that the media not only report and comment upon events, but that they contribute to their production, too. Finally, the events reported on in the media determine public opinion, which in turn exerts an impact on the decision makers and on the positions and strategies adopted by the collective actors in subsequent rounds of decision making.

STRATEGIES FOR MOBILIZING PUBLIC OPINION

Let us now look more closely at the three types of strategies. The interaction among them leads to a complex system of interaction in the public sphere that cannot simply be instrumentalized by one of the political actors, and which is not simply determined by the conditions of political communication imposed by the media (Schmitt-Beck and Pfetsch 1994, 115). Instead, one should presuppose a "symbiotic constellation of mutual dependence," where all the participants are trying to optimize their control over the events. The extent to which the different actors arrive at controlling what is happening depends on the respective contexts.

All three types of strategies focus on the actors' efforts to put their interests on the public agenda and to win the public's support for their own positions. In all three strategies, the media play a central role. On the one hand, under the conditions of a transformed public sphere, formation of public opinion is largely led by professional communicators who speak to each other and to the public through the media. On the other hand, under such conditions the political elite no longer receives a direct feedback from the citizens it represents, but also depends on the professional communicators – media and public opinion researchers – for finding out what is on the citizens' minds. While citizens now tend to perceive politics exclusively through the media, politicians also tend to rely exclusively on the media for their perception of the citizens' concerns.

DECISION MAKERS' TOP-DOWN STRATEGIES

Decision makers habitually address the public. They not only produce institutionalized events on which the media report in a routine fashion, they also stage pseudoevents, which are routinely reported on by the media, too. In this domain, the "principle of cumulative inequality" holds sway (Wolfsfeld 1997, 24): he who has shall be given. According to the "beat system," journalists are assigned to a given institution or policy area in order to routinely collect information from the participants in the political process and from public authorities in general. At the same time, the established political actors have important resources for professional public relations and political marketing at their disposal. This provides them with important advantages in dealing with the media, as is shown by the studies of the German debates about abortion (Gerhards et al. 1998, 113) and about political refugees (Koopmans 1996, 176): The debates about these issues were dominated by the political elites.

Against the background of the increasing importance of the public sphere for the political process, political actors now generally try to reinforce their position in the decision-making arena by directly addressing the public to get its attention and support. The top-down strategies of "going public" have first been observed with U.S. presidents (Kernell 1988). The successful use of such strategies generally depends on very restrictive conditions: The public's attention and support are only forthcoming when the established political actors who use this strategy are highly prominent and very prestigious.

Under current conditions, the strategy of going public can be used in a more focused way and as early as the early stages of the decision-making process. The point of departure for such a strategy is the systematic observation of public opinion through surveys and focus groups. The answers that the political actors receive for their policy-specific questions allow them to formulate a political offer that can count on the citizens' support. For such a strategy to be successful, it is important that the answers are not made public, but are exclusively used by the actors concerned with elaborating their political offer. Only once the offer is carefully engineered based on the indications of citizens' demands, the political actors communicate it to the media which then report on it to the public. The presentation of the political offer in the media, in turn, is professionally prepared by "spin doctors" or public relations specialists who place it in the right media at the right time (Esser 2000, 22). Based on the public's reaction, which is commented on and interpreted by the media, political actors expect to reinforce their position in the political process.

This strategy has two versions: a proactive and a reactive one. The *proactive* version is described by Morris (1999), who advertises its advantages for the American government. In his view, the art of governing does not consist of slavishly following public opinion, but of controlling public events by carefully packaging one's preferred public policy so as not to lose public support. The *reactive* version consists of adapting the policy pragmatically to public opinion as measured by surveys in order to avoid errors. This version does not allow for innovative programs and reinforces the trend toward incrementalism (Neveu 1998).

Of course, political actors cannot count on being able to simply instrumentalize the media. Journalists do not necessarily concentrate on the substantive part of the messages supplied by political actors, but they try to demonstrate their independence by focusing on the social and personal aspects of the political contest and on the strategic intentions of the political actors' campaigns. Blumler and Kavanagh (1999) note an increasingly critical relationship between journalists and political actors.

Journalists react to attempts of instrumentalization by declaring war. Political communication constitutes, as Neveu (1998, 450) has observed, an ideal example of the reflexivity of social actors. The increasing rationalization of communication by political actors – in the sense of a "scientific" anticipation of the media logic by spin doctors – creates its reflexive resistance; the journalists acquire new competences allowing them, in turn, to anticipate and understand the communication strategies of the political actors.

But even if the public receives and supports the message of the political actors, there is no guarantee that the political opponents in the bargaining arena will be impressed by public opinion. Thus, the strategy of going public by certain political actors may be interpreted as breaking traditional political rules and may have results that are counterproductive for the actors adopting such a strategy. As Kernell (1988, 3–4) has pointed out, going public violates the traditional bargaining rules in two respects: actors who go public fix their position publicly, which makes searching for compromise solutions more difficult. At the same time, such actors undermine the legitimacy of other political actors, because they implicitly question their democratic mandate as representatives of the citizens. Given these difficulties and given the restrictive conditions for such a strategy, we may expect that it is only available for a select group of political actors.

However, to the extent that some actors successfully apply such a strategy, it will be copied by other actors. Thus, following the success of the "media-centered personality party" of Berlusconi in the 1994 Italian elections, the challenger Ulivo copied this strategy in 1996 (Seisselberg 1996). The enormous attention that politicians generally pay to the public sphere finally implies that the strategy of going public will also be adopted by established interest associations that have concentrated their activities on the bargaining arena in the past. This kind of "outside lobbying" (Kollman 1998) will be treated in more detail in the section on bottom-up strategies. As a result of the increasing use of such strategies, contemporary politics becomes increasingly "populist" in character and more focused on key leaders (Mény and Surel 2000). Moreover, charisma increasingly becomes a crucial resource in the political process. Grande (2000), for example, notes a search for a charismatic solution on behalf of the citizenry, strengthened by the media that attempt to personalize politics for their own commercial reasons. It appears that nontransparent forms of policy making are increasingly challenged by actors appealing to the public and urging that such forms are put under public scrutiny.

MEDIA-CENTERED STRATEGIES

The media increasingly constitute the crucial channel for conveying politics. In the process, they not only provide information, but they also *become actors of their own in the political process.* As a result of their selection function in the production of events, they can assume a leading role. First of all, the media decide whether they want to report on a subject at all. Their targeted, active selection of events plays, above all, a role in areas in which political actors explicitly try to avoid the public. Where the media try to attract the attention of the public to specific issues against the resistance of at least some political actors, the reporting becomes an event. In such instances, the mobilization of public attention serves to exert pressure on political actors, and the media fulfill a *controlling function,* which corresponds to the traditional role of the opposition.

In addition, the media also have a crucial *structuring and orientation function.* Media commentaries are of particular importance in this context. Commentaries serve to define and interpret political problems, they provide analyses of their causes ("diagnostic framing") and formulate solutions ("prognostic framing"). In the context of their structuring contributions, the media mobilize consensus for their issue- and actor-specific interpretations. As Neidhardt et al. (1998, 2) point out, only few issues become the object of commentaries, and we can assume that those are the issues and problems the editorial staff considers important and in need of some sort of action. As a result of the mechanism of intermedia agenda setting, the commentaries of a few quality papers play a particularly important role. At least for the United States, it was possible to show that news commentaries (and experts) on television (Page et al. 1987) and in the press (Dalton et al. 1998) have strong agenda-setting effects.

The impact of commentaries in the media is, according to Neidhardt et al. (1998), particularly strong if all the media focus on the same issues (congruence of the media agenda) and all adopt the same opinion (consonance and consensus). Page et al. (1987) suspect that commentaries have a strong effect when presidents are weak, and that commentators can under such circumstances serve as substitutes for respected leaders. More generally, we could expect media commentators to become particularly important when the public *distrusts the political elites*. At the same time, they probably are more influential, the more the public trusts the media. In addition, the impact of the media depends on the extent to which the issue in question is *sponsored* by established political actors, who bring it into the public arena (Gamson and Modigliani 1989, 5–9). Finally, and above all, the impact of consensus mobilization by the media depends on the *resonance* they obtain in the public (Gamson and Modigliani 1989, 5–9). In order to obtain such resonance, the media make use of the strategies that have been described by the "framing approach."[4]

By organizing surveys and by publishing their results, the media also fulfill a *control and evaluation function* with regard to politics, which goes beyond the task of commenting and interpreting. This is done in a routine fashion today. With the surveys they organize and the results they stage as public events, the media routinely put established political actors under public pressure. Political actors and the media increasingly disregard formal power and orient themselves exclusively at the capacity of elected political actors to command the support of the citizens on a day-by-day basis. This support is measured by regularly conducted surveys. As a consequence, as Morris observes, each day is election day in the United States today, and in order to govern, an elected official needs a daily majority.

Using polls and presenting them as media events, the media are also able to create specific political facts. An illustrative example is provided by the 1995 French presidential election. In this case, the survey results published by the media had important effects on the candidates that were running (Maarek 1997). First of all, Jacques Delors became a candidate for the Left because of his popularity in early surveys, even though he was not prepared to become one. He had to explicitly distance himself from such media insinuations. Then, the official candidate of the Left, Henry Emmanuelli, the secretary general of the Socialist party at the time, lost the support of party activists because surveys showed that Lionel Jospin had a greater chance to be elected. Finally, the candidate of the Radical party, Jean-François Hory, withdrew early in the race after surveys had shown that he had only little support.

Finally, under special circumstances, the media can even directly mobilize for specific actions ("motivational framing").[5] Above all, action

---

[4] Compare Snow and Benford (1988) and Snow et al. (1986) as well as Kliment (1998).
[5] For the distinction between consensus mobilization and action mobilization, see Klandermans (1984, 586–7).

mobilization is presumably undertaken by alternative or avant-gardist media, which fulfill the function of communication forums for social movements and which at the same time provide a link between these movements and the established media (Pfetsch 1986; Schmitt-Beck 1990). Under certain conditions, however, even established media can call upon their audience to take action. An example of this is the Belgian White March in October 1996. Based on this example, Walgrave und Manssens (2000, 235–7) generalize the necessary conditions for such events to occur. These conditions include a crisis situation with regard to a relatively simple, politically neutral, highly emotional issue about which the population's opinion is homogeneous; a deep general distrust of the political elite and great trust in the media.

CHALLENGERS BOTTOM-UP STRATEGIES

The bottom-up strategies closely resemble the media-centered strategies. The only difference is that the initiative for this kind of action does not come from the media, but from challengers, in other words from actors who do not have routine access to the decision-making arena or to the established media. In order to gain access to these sites, outside challengers may choose between two basic strategies: protest politics and information politics: *protest politics* concerns the mobilization for protest events; *information politics* refers to the collection of credible information and to its introduction at strategically selected points (Keck and Sikkink 1998, 228). Early on, protest politics, that is, the staging of protest events, is likely to constitute the dominant strategy for challengers, because they first need to attract attention to their concerns. One should note that the distinction between challengers and decision makers (insiders) is not a hard and fast one in everyday politics. As has been pointed out by McCarthy, Smith, and Zald (1996, 305) and Gais and Walker (1991), organizational resources constitute a crucial factor in this context: The more such resources a social movement organization has at its disposal, the more it will rely on insider tactics (such as lobbying, litigating, or electioneering). Nevertheless, it is still possible that even established collective actors take the initiative to organize protest events.

Sometimes, for example in a strike, the actions of outsiders are immediately directed against their adversaries and do not take the detour through the media. Very often, however, they try to attract the media's attention for a specific issue. The reports in the media about the protest events should unleash a public debate and strengthen the minority actors' position in the decision-making arena (Gamson 1988, 228; Gamson et al. 1992, 383; Hamdan 2000, 72). By creating controversy where there was none before, speakers of a protest movement and allied sponsors are granted access to and legitimacy among journalists (Gamson and Meyer 1996, 288). Indirectly, protest always creates political opportunities for established political actors as well. This holds in the negative sense – protest may serve as a pretext for repression, as it does in a positive sense – the cause may be adopted by some elite actors (Tarrow 1994, 98). In the final analysis, the goal of creating public attention is to divide the elite and to strengthen the opposition among the decision makers (Wolfsfeld 1997, 27). As Tarrow observes, protests are most successful when they provide a political incentive for elites within the decision-making arena to advance their own policies and careers.

Protest politics and information politics mutually reinforce one another. On the one hand, protests create an opportunity for information politics: once a movement has obtained a certain amount of public visibility, it can successfully deploy its information strategy. Meyer and Tarrow (1998, 18) point out that today the organizational and technical preconditions for the information strategy are less restrictive and that already relatively undeveloped organizations can pursue an efficient information strategy. Given the selection bias of the media in favor of controversy and conflict, providing controversial information about a given issue constitutes a promising strategy complementing the mobilizing for protest events. Conversely, in order to be successful, protests also presuppose a credible information policy. Thus, Greenpeace carefully researches and collects required information and then works on coming up with alternative solutions before it launches its protest campaigns. During the campaigns, this background information is then offered to journalists (Hamdan 2000, 71).

In order to get the media's attention, challengers need to be able to produce events with a certain news value. The news value of a protest event, in turn, is above all a function of the originality of an event (its surprise effect), of the number of participants and of their radicalism (Rochon 1990, 108; Koopmans 1995, 149–52). In addition, embedding the protest event into a more general *political attention cycle* plays a key role. Thus, McCarthy, McPhail, and Smith (1996, 494) have shown in a detailed analysis of the demonstrations in Washington, DC that in addition to the size of the demonstrations, their timing ("being in the right place at the right time in a media attention cycle") is crucial for the reporting on the event. This means peaks in the media attention cycles create windows of opportunity for the challengers, which allow them to get access to the media. The escalation of the reporting on the Gulf War in 1991, for example, allowed for even small demonstrations to get media attention. The media attention cycle may even trigger protests, as Koopmans (1996) has shown in his study on the question of political refugees in Germany.

Media attention, however, is not sufficient. Challengers also need to obtain supportive resonance in the media. According to Wolfsfeld's (1997, 45–9) "principle of resonance," challengers who are able to produce events that resonate in the professional and political culture of important news media will be able to compete with more powerful adversaries. The difficulty for the social movements in this context is that the factors that allow them to gain access to the media do not necessarily contribute to their credibility and, consequentially, to public support. The dramatization of their concerns in protest events necessarily implies a simplification of their message, which parallels the "sound bites" uttered by decision makers. Contrary to the expectations by Habermas (1992), the reasoning of challengers is not characterized by a particularly high level of rationality. In fact, in their analysis of the German abortion debate, Gerhards et al. (1998, 149–52) showed that challengers are "specialized in one-sidedness."

COUNTERSTRATEGIES OF DECISION MAKERS

To meet the challenge of media-centered and challengers' strategies the decision makers react with counterstrategies designed to drive actors and issues out of the public sphere. Among these *techniques of symbolic politics* (Sarcinelli 1989) we can distinguish between issue- and actor-centered strategies. The *issue-centered strategies* include displacing problems, shifting debates to secondary arenas, and transforming substantive conflicts into moral ones. Decision makers generally react to the strategies of the media and challengers by trying to avoid hot issues in the public sphere. Instead, they produce "campaign issues" that allow them to detract attention from the hot issues, minimize the differences between the actors, or, alternatively, gloss over the fact that the real differences between them are actually negligible. The issue of prisoners' furloughs in the presidential campaign between Bush and Dukakis in 1988 illustrates this strategy. According to a study by Kahn and Kenney (1999), candidates for the American Senate generally try to avoid debates about political issues. Only a third of their advertisements address issues at all, and even in issue-specific advertisements the candidates mention their own position in only half of the cases. Moreover, they only rarely address really hot issues.

Such strategies are not limited to electoral campaigns. In addition to the basic repertoire ("stone walling," "half-answering," "not remembering," "disclosing drop by drop," or "suddenly and overwhelmingly"), the strategy of displacing problems includes also more targeted strategies attempting to undermine exclusive reports by unfriendly papers or to dilute the effect of investigative journalists' research. Direct intimidations of such journalists and complaints about them, lodged with their superiors, are part of such strategies as is targeted discrediting (Esser 2000, 22).

Among the techniques of symbolic politics we also find *actor-centered strategies*, especially personalizing and negative publicity ("negative campaigning"). *Personalizing strategies* can be used to distract attention from political issues. Conversely, it is also possible to focus on an issue in order to distract attention from personal questions (e.g., personnel problems within the governing coalition). Pfetsch (1993, 100) suggests that personalizing strategies used by opponents are quite apt to thwart the intended communication effects of political actors, because such strategies correspond to the selection criteria of the media and are readily picked up. In reaction to negative publicity in the media, political actors learn how to deal with the media in an ever more sophisticated way. They try to find ways to reach the public directly without passing through the media (Swanson and Mancini 1996, 252). One possibility to do so is "the news news" – popular interview programs or the use of unorthodox television channels such as the appearance in music channels on cable television. Another possibility is *political marketing* – paid political advertising. Morris (1999, 206–7) believes that citizens like this kind of advertising: citizens distrust both journalists and advertisements, but they use both sources to be able to check the bias in the respective other source. Paid advertisements are the best way, according to Morris, to get positive reporting. It allows political actors to influence the public which then influences the media, because the media have to take into account what the public wishes to see and hear.[6] A final possibility to circumvent the media is political communication using the Internet.

---

[6] Newton (2000) is considerably less sanguine about the success of this kind of political marketing. Although Margret Thatcher had the huge advantage in Great Britain in that she faced a national press that largely supported her and her policy, and although she had a highly effective public relations secretary at her side who had enormous power and resources (in 1989–1990 the government was next to Unilever, the second largest

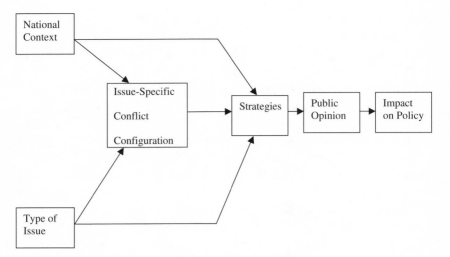

Figure 8.2 Causal Framework for Determining the Strategies of Mobilizing Public Opinion and Their Impact

NATIONAL CONTEXT CONDITIONS

Except for the studies by Ferree et al. (2002) and Koopmans and Statham (1999; 2000) previous studies on the role of the public sphere for political decision making did not proceed comparatively. Although a trend toward an audience democracy is noticeable in all liberal democracies, it is still reasonable to assume that the *institutional context conditions* decisively shape the way this trend is expressing itself in a given country. In addition, the *issue-specific context* is also very likely to have a decisive impact on the kinds of strategies that will be used in the public sphere – independently of the institutional context. Together, the institutional context and the issue-specific context shape the structure of *issue-specific conflict configurations*, which, in turn, will determine the type of strategies chosen by the relevant actors.

Figure 8.2 illustrates the general relationship between the three sets of factors. The basic assumption is that even if we focus on countries that share similar cultural, economic, and politico-institutional characteristics ("most similar systems design") and even if we select the same issues, we will find a great variation in the range of actors and their respective strategies in trying to shape public opinion.

advertisement client of the country), she achieved amazingly little with her public relations-campaigns.

Here, I will deal only with the structure of the national context. Recent work on political mobilization has emphasized that levels and forms of mobilization by social movements, interest groups, and citizens' action groups are strongly influenced by so-called *political opportunity structures* – the set of opportunities and constraints given by the institutional structure and political culture of the political system in which mobilization takes place (e.g., McAdam 1982; Kitschelt 1986; Kriesi et al. 1995; McAdam et al. 1996; Tarrow 1998). We can assume that these findings not only apply to political mobilization, but also to political communication and to public strategies more generally. This assumption is substantiated by more recent efforts to introduce the concept of discursive opportunities (Koopmans and Statham 1999). Although quite a number of specific aspects of national settings are potentially of interest for the selection of the countries to be included in a comparative study, we will have to ignore this complexity for practical reasons by focusing on a limited number of structural features that are likely to have a major impact on whether or not the political actors will choose a strategy of mobilizing public opinion. For the characterization of the political context at the national level, I propose the following two criteria:

- The *concentration of power in parliament and government* (majoritarian versus consensus democracy): This criterion corresponds to Lijphart's (1999) "executives-parties"– dimension, which ranges from democratic systems of government that highly concentrate power in parliament and government (majoritarian democracies) to those that highly fragment power between and within these arenas (consensus democracies).
- The *institutional accessibility of the state actors* (low versus high accessibility): This criterion resembles Lijphart's second dimension, but is not quite equivalent. It also resembles various other veto-player indices of democratic regimes (see Fuchs 2000). In constructing this index, we assume that the accessibility of the state actors increases with the number of institutional access points.[7]

---

[7] Our index of institutional accessibility of state actors has four components: (1) bicameralism; (2) decentralization (= federalism); (3) direct-democracy (= factual use); and (4) openness of civil service career system (= lack of professionalization of civil service). Every component is scaled 0 (low), 1 (medium), or 2 (high accessibility). Components 1 and 2 come from Colomer (1996); component 3 from the Research and Documentation Center on Direct Democracy at the University of Geneva (www.unige.ch/c2d) and component 4 from Schnapp (2000, 38; Table 4).

	Low Accessibility of State Actors			
Majoritarian **Democracy**	France, Ireland, Greece	Austria, Portugal	Belgium, Denmark, Finland, Norway, Sweden	**Consensus** **Democracy**
	United Kingdom, Spain	Germany	Netherlands	
	Italy (since change in electoral system)		Switzerland	
	High Accessibility of State Actors			

Figure 8.3 A Typology of National Political Contexts for Western European Countries

Combining the two dimensions we arrive at four theoretical combinations. Majoritarian democracies of low and high accessibility versus consensus democracies of low and high accessibility. Any specific case resembles more or less one of these ideal types. Figure 8.3 presents the distribution of the Western European countries on these two dimensions: We can assume that the public sphere in general and top-down strategies of going public in particular will be more important in majoritarian democracies than in consensus democracies. The concentration of power in the hands of a few individual actors at the top of the respective institutions creates the necessary preconditions (prominence and prestige of individual personalities). It is hardly an accident that the public sphere plays a particularly important role and that the strategies of going public are particularly well developed in the United States, which, according to this classification, is a majoritarian democracy. By contrast, such strategies remain the exception in Switzerland, the paradigmatic case of a consensus democracy. In the Swiss case, the direct-democratic institutions impose additional constraints on such strategies. The direct-democratic procedures are issue specific, which prevents a far-reaching personalization. Moreover, they allow for a quasi-institutionalized going public, which limits the incentives to use such strategies outside of direct-democratic campaigns. In a country such as Switzerland, members of government who go public over the heads of their colleagues are violating the rules of the game and will most likely obtain counterproductive results.

Media-centered strategies generally become more probable if the opposition does not fulfill its role, if elections lose their character of democratic renewal, and if distrust in the political elite increases. This may happen in both types of democracies. Thus, unveiling scandals and attacking unfair privileges and irregularities constituted a key element of the strategy of the Austrian Liberal Party (FPÖ) after Haider had taken over the party's leadership in 1986. From the start, the FPÖ appealed to the public in terms of its "young dynamism" as opposed to the "inertia of the old parties" (Plasser and Ulram 2000). In a majoritarian democracy similar to Spain, the media also played a crucial role in breaking the "coalitions of silence" at a given moment in time. Pujas and Rhodes (1999) believe that the role of the opposition is increasingly taken over by the press in Spain. Even in Great Britain, the paradigmatic case of a majoritarian democracy, the disinformation practiced by leading politicians and high officials implies that the media increasingly take over the role of the opposition.[8]

While the type of democracy is more pertinent for the strategies of decision makers, *the institutional accessibility of state actors* is more relevant for the strategies of *challengers*. Highly accessible institutional settings invite inside strategies. The reverse, however, does not necessarily apply. A comparative study on the mobilization of new social movements in four Western European countries (Germany, France, the Netherlands, and Switzerland) has shown that poorly accessible institutional settings induce outside collective actors to adopt radical public strategies (Kriesi et al. 1995). But low institutional accessibility does not increase the volume of public strategies. On the contrary, the largest amount of public events was produced in the most accessible settings. This is because public strategies (at least bottom-up ones) depend on political access to achieve

---

[8] Ms. Thatcher for example has never tried to hide her displacement and cover-up strategies: to the great merriment of backbenchers, she used to answer troublesome questions in the parliamentary question hour by citing lists of irrelevant statistics having no relationship with the question (cf. NZZ, International Edition Nr. 14; January 18, 2001; 5: "Kontrollfunktion der britischen Medien").

visibility, resonance, and legitimacy in the public sphere. Challengers, put differently, are more likely to choose public strategies if the institutional accessibility of state actors is high, rather than low. In poorly accessible settings, however, the bottom-up public strategies tend to be more radical.

Note that this typology of the national political context is entirely based on the characteristics of the political system and does not refer at all to the party systems or the media systems in the various countries. As it turns out, the structure of these two systems heavily correlates with the type of democracy: consensus democracies (including Germany and Austria) generally tend to have a strong, independent press and a comparatively strong party system, while majoritarian democracies tend to have a weak press[9] that is less autonomous from the state and weaker party systems,[10] too.

It is likely that in countries in which the parties are no longer able to control their base, public strategies will become increasingly important. Italy presents the paradigmatic case of a collapse of the old party system and the development of new parties from scratch – above all Silvio Berlusconi's Forza Italia, which lacks any established social-structural base. In fact, the strategy of Berlusconi's "media-centered personality party" corresponds rather closely to the proactive version of the strategy of "going public" (Seisselberg 1996). Italy is also the extreme case of a weak press. As is pointed out by Seisselberg (1996, 725), in the 1990s Italy became the television-society par excellence. In Italy, television plays a larger role as a source of information than in other countries and it is also generally accepted as a means of forming political opinion (Gabriel and Brettschneider 1994, 541–3). Ricolfi (1997) adds that more than any other Western nation, Italy has only been linguistically united by television. Finally, television is the only means of communication for a majority of Italians. Italy also illustrates the consequences of a weak press and the concentration of political communication in television. According to

---

[9] Indicators for the strength of the press are the circulation per capita (Lane et al. 1997, 175; Table 8.9) and the share of national publicity expenditures obtained by the press (De Bens and Ostby 1997, 19; Table 2.3). An indicator for the independence of the press can be obtained by the share of the ten largest national newspapers that are rated as "neutral" or "independent" by Banks' *Political Handbook of the World* (Voltmer 2000, 21).

[10] For measuring the strength of party systems we use the share of citizens who still are party members. The newest available data are those presented by Mair and van Biezen (2001, 9). Greece is a partial exception, because it has a strong party system (but no strong media), although it is a majoritarian democracy.

Mancini (2000, 321–2), the experience is a mixed one: political reporting and the traditional political partisanship of the media have not declined, but political sensationalism, and the dramatization and personalization of politics have definitely increased. A neutral distance of journalists to political events is completely lacking. The dramatization of politics by television, which sets the agenda of the press, implies a simplification and exaggeration of political conflict. The effect on the citizens, however, is all but clear: it remains to be seen whether this kind of reporting politicizes the citizens or rather incites them to withdraw from politics altogether.

THE TRANSLATION OF THE PROBLÉMATIQUE INTO A RESEARCH DESIGN

Against the background of the general trend toward an audience democracy, the question of the public sphere's role in the democratic decision-making process is a crucial one in all liberal democracies: Under which conditions and with what kind of success do decision makers, the media, and challengers mobilize public opinion in order to promote their point of view in the political process? And how are the public strategies of the various actors related to the structural contexts of the political systems (including the media system and the party system)? It has been the purpose of this chapter to propose a conceptual framework that may serve as the theoretical starting point for the analysis of questions such as these. This heuristic framework should be translated into a research design that can constitute the basis for an internationally comparative project.

The typology of national context that I have presented in Figure 8.3 suggests that a comparative project should include at least four countries – one representing each of the four ideal combinations of type of democracy and accessibility of state actors (e.g., France, Italy, a Scandinavian country, and Switzerland). Germany, as the typical intermediary case would be an interesting complement. One might also think about extending the study to the new democracies of Central and Eastern Europe. Given that the political process proceeds in issue-specific subdomains, the project design should also carefully select types of issues that allow for a maximum of variation with regard to the choice of public strategies. I would like to suggest that the distinction between issues with an "incremental" and issues with an "eruptive" problem structure may be a particularly promising one in the present context.

Incremental problem structures are predictable, evolve gradually, and are well understood (based on an established policy paradigm); eruptive problem structures are unpredictable, involving "suddenly imposed grievances" and not very well understood (not based on an established policy paradigm). This criterion corresponds to one of the five issue dimensions distinguished by Cobb and Elder (1983, 100).[11] Eruptive issues tend to catch the public eye, which provides a strong incentive for challengers to choose public strategies and forces decision makers to do so, too. In eruptive issue domains, politicians cannot think twice about policy options but have to address public concerns immediately (Livingston 1997). By contrast, for incremental issue domains, it is easier to separate policy making from the public sphere. In such domains, experts and technocrats play an important role. In other words, eruptive issues are prone to symbolic politics (*politique d'opinion*), while incremental issues are prone to problem solving (*politique des problèmes*) (Leca 1996).

In each country and each issue domain, the project would then have to identify and describe the configuration of actors – decision makers, media actors, and challengers – and of their public strategies. I would submit that this task can best be achieved by a two-pronged strategy: a combination of a *political claims' analysis* (Gerhards et al. 1998; Koopmans and Statham 1999, 2000) with a *structural analysis of policy networks* (see Laumann and Pappi 1976; Kriesi 1980; Laumann and Knoke 1987; Kriesi and Jegen 2001). While the claims analysis – a systematic, quantitative contents analysis of the press – allows, above all, reconstructing the events, identifying the actors involved and their mobilizing strategies, as well as determining the relevant public opinion, the interviewing techniques of the policy network analyses serve to identify the coalitional structures and to evaluate the strategies and the influence of the different actors. Finally, the secondary analysis of existing surveys could provide an additional idea of the issue-specific public opinions as measured by the polls.[12]

---

[11] Cobb and Elder call this dimension "categorical precedence" and distinguish between "routine" and "extraordinary" issues. They refer to Lowi (122), who had already maintained in 1964 that this is the most important of all the issue characteristics.

[12] I might add that an internationally comparative research proposal involving nine countries from Western and Central Europe that was based on these general ideas was presented to the fifth framework program of the European Union (EU) in early 2002, but was rejected. The anonymous reviewers thought that the proposal was too expensive and too risky!

REFERENCES

Baumgartner, Frank R., and Bryan D. Jones. 1993. *Agendas and Instability in American Politics.* Chicago: University of Chicago Press.

Beyme, Klaus von. 1994. Die Massenmedien und die politische Agenda des parlamentarischen Systems. In Friedhelm Neidhardt, ed. *Öffentlichkeit, öffentliche Meinung, soziale Bewegungen.* Opladen, Germany: Westdeutscher Verlag, pp. 320–36.

Blumler, Jay G., and Dennis Kavanagh. 1999. The Third Age of Political Communication: Influences and Features. *Political Communication* 16: 209–30.

Burstein, Paul. 1998. *Discrimination, Jobs, and Politics. The Struggle for Equal Employment Opportunity in the United States since the New Deal. With a New Introduction.* Chicago: University of Chicago Press.

Cobb, Roger W., and Charles D. Elder. 1983. *Participation in American Politics. The Dynamics of Agenda-Building.* 2nd ed. Baltimore: The Johns Hopkins University.

Colomer, Josep M. 1996. Introduction. In Joseph M. Colomer, ed. *Political Institutions in Europe.* London: Routledge, pp. 1–17.

Converse, Philip E. 1987. Changing Conceptions of Public Opinion in the Political Process. *Public Opinion Quarterly* 51: 12–24.

Dalton, Russell J., Paul A. Beck, and Robert Huckfeldt. 1998. Partisan Cues and the Media: Information Flows in the 1992 Presidential Election. *American Political Science Review* 92 (1): 111–26.

De Bens, Els, and Helge Ostbye. 1997. The European Newspaper Market. In Denis McQuail and Karen Siune, eds. *Media Policy. Convergence, Concentration and Commerce.* London: Sage, pp. 7–22.

Esser, Frank. 2000. Spin Doctoring. Rüstungsspirale Zwischen Politischer PR und Politischem Journalismus. *Forschungsjournal Neue Soziale Bewegungen* 13 (3): 17–24.

Ferree, Myra Marx, William A. Gamson, Jürgen Gerhards, and Dieter Rucht. 2002. *Shaping Abortion Discourse. Democracy and the Public Sphere in Germany and the United States.* New York: Cambridge University Press.

Fuchs, Dieter. 2000. Typen und Indizes demokratischer Regime. Eine Analyse des Präsidentialismus- und des Veto-Spieler Ansatzes. In Hans-Joachim Lauth, Gert Pickel, and Christian Welzel, eds. *Demokratiemessung. Konzepte und Befunde im internationalen Vergleich.* Opladen, Germany: Westdeutscher Verlag, pp. 27–48.

Gabriel, Oskar, and Frank Brettschneider, eds. 1994. *Die EU-Staaten im Vergleich. Strukturen, Prozesse, Politikinhalte.* Opladen, Germany: Westdeutscher Verlag.

Gais, Thomas L., and Jack L. Walker. 1991. Pathways to Influence in American Politics. In Jack L. Walker, ed. *Mobilizing Interest Groups in America. Patrons, Professions, and Social Movements.* Ann Arbor: The University of Michigan Press, pp. 103–22.

Gamson, William A. 1988. Political Discourse and Collective Action. In Bert Klandermans, Hanspeter Kriesi, and Sidney Tarrow, eds. *From Structure to Action: Comparing Social Movement Research across Cultures.* Greenwich, CT: JAI-Press, pp. 219–44.

Gamson, William A., and André Modigliani. 1989. Media Discourse and Public Opinion on Nuclear Power: A Constructionist Approach. *American Journal of Sociology* 95 (1): 1–37.

Gamson, William A., and David S. Meyer. 1996. Framing Political Opportunity. In Doug McAdam, John D. McCarthy, and Mayer N. Zald, eds. *Comparative Perspectives on*

Social Movements. Political Opportunities, Mobilizing Structures, and Cultural Framings. Cambridge: Cambridge University Press, pp. 275–90.

Gamson, William A., David Croteau, William Hoynes, and Theodore Sasson. 1992. Media Images and the Social Construction of Reality. In Judith Blake and John Hagan, eds. *Annual Review of Sociology* 18. Palo Alto, CA: Annual Reviews Inc., pp. 373–93.

Gerhards, Jürgen, Friedhelm Neidhardt, and Dieter Rucht. 1998. *Zwischen Palaver und Diskurs. Strukturen öffentlicher Meinungsbildung am Beispiel der deutschen Diskussion zur Abtreibung.* Opladen, Germany: Westdeutscher Verlag.

Grande, Edgar. 2000. Charisma und Komplexität: Verhandlungsdemokratie, Mediendemokratie und der Funktionswandel politischer Eliten. *Leviathan* 28 (1): 122–41.

Habermas, Jürgen. 1992. *Theorie kommunikativen Handelns.* Frankfurt, Germany: Suhrkamp.

Hajer, Maarten A. 1995. *The Politics of Environmental Discourse. Ecological Modernization and the Political Process.* Oxford: Clarendon Press.

Hamdan, Fouad. 2000. Aufdecken und Konfrontieren. NGO-Kommunikation am Beispiel Greenpeace. *Forschungsjournal Neue Soziale Bewegungen* 13 (3): 69–74.

Hilgartner, Stephen, and Charles L. Bosk. 1988. The Rise and Fall of Social Problems: A Public Arenas Model. *American Journal of Sociology* 94 (1): 53–78.

Kahn, Kim, and Patrick J. Kenney. 1999. *The Spectacle of U.S. Senate Campaigns.* Princeton: Princeton University Press.

Keck, Margaret E., and Kathryn Sikkink. 1998. Transnational Advocacy Networks in the Movement Society. In David S. Meyer and Sidney Tarrow, eds. *The Social Movement Society. Contentious Politics for a New Century.* Boulder, CO: Rowman and Littlefield, pp. 217–38.

Kernell, Samuel. 1988. *Going Public. New Strategies of Presidential Leadership.* Washington, DC: CQ Press.

Kingdon, John W. 1984. *Agendas, Alternatives, and Public Policies.* Boston: Little Brown.

Kitschelt, Herbert. 1986. Political Opportunity Structures and Political Protest: Anti-Nuclear Movements in Four Democracies. *British Journal of Political Science* 16: 57–85.

———. 2000. Citizens, Politicians, and Party Cartellization: Political Representation and State Failure in Post-Industrial Democracies. *European Journal of Political Research* 37 (2): 149–79.

Klandermans, Bert. 1984. Mobilization and Participation: Social-Psychological Expansions of Resource Mobilization Theory. *American Sociologica Review* 49: 583–600.

Kliment, Tibor. 1998. Durch Dramatisierung zum Protest? Theoretische Grundlegung und empirischer Ertrag des Framing-Konzepts. In Kai-Uwe Hellmann and Ruud Koopmans, eds. *Paradigmen der Bewegungsforschung. Entstehung und Entwicklung von Neuen sozialen Bewegungen und Rechtsextremismus.* Wiesbaden, Germany: Westdeutscher Verlag, pp. 69–89.

Kollman, Ken. 1998. *Outside Lobbying. Public Opinion and Interest Group Strategies.* Princeton: Princeton University Press.

Koopmans, Ruud. 1995. *Democracy from Below. New Social Movements and the Political System in West Germany.* Boulder, CO: Westview Press.

———. 1996. Asyl: Die Karriere eines politischen Konflikts. In Wolfgang van den Daele and Friedhelm Neidhardt, eds. *Kommunikation und Entscheidung, WZB-Jahrbuch.* Berlin: Edition Sigma, pp. 167–92.

Koopmans, Ruud, and Paul Statham. 1999. Political Claims Analysis: Integrating Protest Event and Political Discourse Approaches. *Mobilization* 4 (2): 203–22.

———. 2000. Challenging the Liberal Nation-State? Postnationalism, Multiculturalism, and the Collective Claims-making of Migrants and Ethnic Minorities in Britain and Germany. In Ruud Koopmans and Paul Statham, eds. *Challenging Immigration and Ethnic Relations Politics. Comparative European Perspectives.* Oxford: Oxford University Press, pp. 89–232.

Kriesi, Hanspeter. 1980. *Entscheidungsstrukturen und Entscheidungsprozesse in der Schweizer Politik.* Frankfurt, Germany: Campus.

Kriesi, Hanspeter, and Maya Jegen. 2001. The Swiss Energy Policy Elite. *European Journal of Political Science* 39: 251–87.

Kriesi, Hanspeter, Ruud Koopmans, Jan Willem Duyvendak, and Marco Giugni. 1995. *New Social Movements in Western Europe. A Comparative Analysis.* Minneapolis: University of Minnesota Press.

Lane, Jan-Erik, David McKay, and Kenneth Newton. 1997. *Political Data Handbook. OECD Countries.* 2nd ed. Oxford: Oxford University Press.

Lang, Gladys Engel, and Kurt Lang. 1983. *The Battle for Public Opinion. The President, the Press and the Polls During Watergate.* New York: Columbia University Press.

Laumann, Edward O., and David Knoke. 1987. *The Organizational State. Social Choice in National Policy Domains.* Madison: The University of Wisconsin Press.

Laumann, Edward O., and Franz U. Pappi. 1976. *Networks of Collective Action: A Perspective on Community Influence Systems.* New York: Academic Press.

Leca, Jean. 1996. Ce que l'analyse des politiques publiques pourrait apprendre sur le gouvernement démocratique. *Revue française de science politique* 46 (1): 122–33.

Lijphart, Arend. 1999. *Patterns of Democracy.* New Haven: Yale University Press.

Linsky, Martin. 1986. *Impact. How the Press Affects Federal Policymaking.* New York: W. W. Norton.

Livingston, Steven. 1997. *Clarifying the CNN Effect. An Examination of Media Effects According to Type of Military Intervention.* Research paper R-18 of the Joan Shorenstein Center of Press, Politics, and Public Policy at the John F. Kennedy School of Government, Harvard.

Lowi, Theodore J. 1964. American Business, Public Policy, Case-Studies and Political Theory. *World Politics* 16: 667–715.

Maarek, Philippe J. 1997. New Trends in French Political Communication: The 1995 Presidential Elections. *Media, Culture and Society* 19: 357–68.

Mair, Peter. 1997. *Party System Change. Approaches and Interpretations.* Oxford: Clarendon Press.

Mair, Peter, and Ingrid van Biezen. 2001. Party Membership in Twenty European Democracies, 1980–2000. *Party Politics* 7 (1): 5–21.

Mancini, Paolo. 2000. How to Combine Media Commercialization and Party Affiliation: The Italian Experience. *Political Communication* 17: 319–24.

Manin, Bernard. 1995. *Principes du gouvernement représentatif.* Paris: Flammarion.

McAdam, Doug. 1982. *Political Process and the Development of Black Insurgency, 1930–1970.* Chicago: University of Chicago Press.

McAdam, Doug, John D. McCarthy, and Mayer N. Zald. 1996. *Comparative Perspectives on Social Movements. Political Opportunities, Mobilizing Structures, and Cultural Framings.* Cambridge: Cambridge University Press.

McCarthy, John D., Clark McPhail, and Jackie Smith. 1996. Images of Protest: Dimensions of Selection Bias in Media Coverage of Washington Demonstrations, 1982 and 1991. *American Sociological Review* 61 (3): 478–99.

McCarthy, John D., Jackie Smith, and Mayer N. Zald. 1996. Accessing Public, Media, Electoral, and Governmental Agendas. In Doug McAdam, John D. McCarthy, and Mayer N. Zald, eds. *Comparative Perspectives on Social Movements. Political Opportunities, Mobilizing Structures, and Cultural Framings.* Cambridge: Cambridge University Press, pp. 291–311.

McCombs, Maxwell E. and Donald L. Shaw. 1972. The Agenda-Setting Function of the Mass Media. *Public Opinion Quarterly* 36: 176–87.

Mény, Yves, and Yves Surel. 2000. *Par le peuple, pour le peuple. Le populisme et les démocraties.* Paris: Fayard.

Meyer, David S., and Sidney Tarrow. 1998. A Movement Society: Contentious Politics for a New Century. In David S. Meyer and Sidney Tarrow, eds. *The Social Movement Society. Contentious Politics for a New Century.* Boulder, CO: Rowman and Littlefield, pp. 1–28.

Morris, Dick. 1999. *The New Prince. Machiavelli Updated for the Twenty-first Century.* Los Angeles: Renaissance Books.

Neidhardt, Friedhelm. 1994. Öffentlichkeit, öffentliche Meinung, soziale Bewegungen. In Friedhelm Neidhardt, ed. *Öffentlichkeit, öffentliche Meinung, soziale Bewegungen. Kölner Zeitschrift für Soziologie und Sozialpsychologie Sonderheft* 34. Opladen, Germany: Westdeutscher Verlag, pp. 7–41.

Neidhardt, Friedhelm, Christiane Eilders, and Barbara Pfetsch. 1998. Die Stimme der Medien im politischen Prozess: Themen und Meinungen in Pressekommentaren. *Discussion Paper FS III 98–106.* Berlin: Wissenschaftszentrum Berlin für Sozialforschung.

Neveu, Erik. 1998. Media and Politics in French Political Science. *European Journal of Political Research* 33: 439–58.

Newton, Ken. 2000. Versagt politisches Marketing? In Oskar Niedermayer and Bettina Westle, eds. *Demokratie und Partizipation. Festschrift für Max Kaase.* Opladen, Germany: Westdeutscher Verlag, pp. 177–91.

Page, Benjamin I., Robert Y. Shapiro, and Glenn R. Dempsey. 1987. What Moves Public Opinion? *American Political Science Review* 81 (1): 23–43.

Panebianco, Angelo. 1988. *Political Parties: Organization and Power.* Cambridge: Cambridge University Press.

Pfetsch, Barbara. 1986. Volkszählung '83. Ein Beispiel für die Thematisierung eines politischen Issues in den Massenmedien. In Hans-Dieter Klingemann and Max Kaase, eds. *Wahlen und Politischer Prozess.* Opladen, Germany: Westdeutscher Verlag, pp. 201–31.

———. 1993. Strategien und Gegenstrategien – Politische Kommunikation bei Sachfragen. Eine Fallstudie aus Baden-Württemberg. In Wolfgang Donsbach, ed. *Beziehungsspiele – Medien und Politik in der öffentlichen Diskussion. Fallstudien und Analysen.* Gütersloh, Germany: Bertelsmann Stiftung, pp. 45–110.

———. 1998. Regieren unter den Bedingungen medialer Allgegenwart. In Ulrich Sarcinelli, ed. *Politikvermittlung und Demokratie in der Mediengesellschaft.* Wiesbaden, Germany: Westdeutscher Verlag, pp. 233–52.

Plasser, Fritz, and Peter A. Ulram. 2000. Rechtspopulistische Resonanzen: Die Wählerschaft der FPÖ. In Fritz Plasser, ed. *Das Österreichische Wahlverhalten*. Wien, Austria: Signum-Verlag, pp. 225–41.

Pujas, Véronique, and Martin Rhodes. 1999. Party Finance and Political Scandal in Italy, Spain and France. *West European Politics* 22 (3): 41–63.

Ricolfi, Luca. 1997. Politics and the Mass Media in Italy. *West European Politics* 20 (1): 135–56.

Rochon, Thomas R. 1990. The West European Peace Movement and the Theory of New Social Movements. In Russell J. Dalton and Manfred Kuechler, eds. *Challenging the Political Order*. Cambridge: Polity Press, pp. 105–21.

Sabatier, Paul A. 1993. Advocacy-Koalitionen, Policy-Wandel und Policy-Lernen: Eine Alternative zur Phasenheuristik. In Adrienne Héritier, ed. *Policy-Analyse. Kritik und Neuorientierung*. PVS-Sonderheft 24: 116–48.

————. 1998. The Advocacy Coalition Framework: Revisions and Relevance for Europe. *Journal of European Public Policy* 5 (1): 98–130.

Sarcinelli, Ulrich. 1989. Symbolische Politik und politische Kultur. Das Kommunikationsritual als politische Wirklichkeit. *Politische Vierteljahresschrift* 30 (2): 292–309.

Schmitt-Beck, Rüdiger. 1990. Über die Bedeutung der Massenmedien für soziale Bewegungen. *Kölner Zeitschrift für Soziologie und Sozialpsychologie* 42 (4): 642–62.

Schmitt-Beck, Rüdiger, and Barbara Pfetsch. 1994. Politische Akteure und die Medien der Massenkommunikation. Zur Generierung von Öffentlichkeit in Wahlkämpfen. In Friedhelm Neidhardt, ed. *Öffentlichkeit, Öffentliche Meinung, Soziale Bewegungen. Kölner Zeitschrift für Soziologie und Sozialpsychologie Sonderheft* 34. Opladen, Germany: Westdeutscher Verlag, pp. 106–38.

Schnapp, Kai-Uwe. 2000. Ministerial Bureaucracies as Stand-In Agenda-Setters? A Comparative Description. *Discussion Paper FS III 00–204*. Berlin: Wissenschaftszentrum Berlin für Sozialforschung.

Seisselberg, Jörg. 1996. Conditions of Success and Political Problems of a 'Media-mediated Personality Party.' The Case of Forza Italia. *West European Politics* 19 (4): 715–43.

Snow, David A., and Robert D. Benford. 1988. Ideology, Frame Resonance, and Participant Mobilization. In Bert Klandermans, Hanspeter Kriesi, and Sidney Tarrow, eds. *Structure to Action: Comparing Social Movement Research Across Cultures*. Greenwich, CT: JAI-Press, pp. 97–218.

Snow, David, E. Burke Rochford, Jr., Steven K. Worden, and Robert D. Benford. 1986. Frame Alignment Processes, Micromobilization, and Movement Participation. *American Sociological Review* 51 (4): 464–81.

Stimson, James A., Michael B. MacKuen, and Robert S. Erikson. 1995. Dynamic Representation. *American Political Science Review* 89 (3): 543–65.

Swanson, David L., and Paolo Mancini. 1996. Patterns of Modern Electoral Campaigning and Their Consequences. In David L. Swanson and Paolo Mancini, eds. *Politics, Media, and Modern Democracy. An International Study of Innovations in Electoral Campaigning and Their Consequences*. London: Praeger, pp. 247–76.

Tarrow, Sidney. 1994. *Power in Movement. Social Movements, Collective Action and Politics*. Cambridge: Cambridge University Press.

————. 1998. Social Protest and Policy Reform: May 1968 and the Loi d'Orientation in France. In Marco Giugni, Doug McAdam, and Charles Tilly, eds. *From Contention to Democracy*. Lanham, MD: Rowman and Littlefield, pp. 31–56.

Voltmer, Katrin. 2000. Structures of Diversity of Press and Broadcasting Systems. The Institutional Context of Public Communication in Western Democracies. *Discussion Paper FS III 00-201*. Berlin: Wissenschaftszentrum Berlin für Sozialforschung.

Walgrave, Stefan, and Jan Manssens. 2000. The Making of the White March: The Mass Media as a Mobilizing Alternative to Movement Organizations. *Mobilization* 5 (2): 217–39.

Wolfsfeld, Gadi. 1997. *Media and Political Conflict. News from the Middle East*. Cambridge: Cambridge University Press.

NINE

Political Campaign Communication

Conditional Convergence of Modern Media Elections

Christina Holtz-Bacha

Though not at all a new phenomenon, Americanization as a "useful hypothesis" (Mancini and Swanson 1996, 4) opened the researchers' eyes for common interests and developments in Western democracies and triggered new research efforts. At the same time it became clear that beside some overarching trends, national characteristics of the political structure, including electoral systems and party structure, as well as characteristics of the media system, have an impact on the way electoral campaigns are designed today. Campaign communication proves to be a field that more than any other has stimulated cross-national research and cooperation. The paper's aim is to take stock of this research and discuss the advantages and difficulties of the comparative perspective on this topic. The overview will show that – not least due to the Americanization hypothesis – the majority of the studies took U.S. campaigns as a point of reference while only a few compared campaigns across Europe, for example, thus revealing a need for further research although research efforts have been intensified during recent years.

Until recently the prime interest of electoral research has always been with voter behavior. When Lazarsfeld, Berelson, and Gaudet (1944) published their classical study *The People's Choice*, its subtitle *How the Voter Makes Up His Mind in an Election* already pointed in this direction. At the same time this study, along with its follow-up, *Voting*, by Berelson, Lazarsfeld, and McPhee (1954) laid the basis for the sociological approach in voter research. With the publication of *The American Voter* (1960) by Campbell, Converse, Miller, and Stokes this was supplemented by the sociopsychological approach of the Michigan school. According to the Michigan model or Ann Arbor model as it is alternatively named, party identification plays the central role in voter behavior. Party identification is conceived as being a long-term and comparatively stable attitude. Because sociodemographic variables that are central to the sociological approach, as introduced by Lazarsfeld and his colleagues of the Columbia school, in some way crystalize in party identification, one approach did not replace the other. However, the Michigan model soon dominated research in the United States. It was also one of the early objectives of the Michigan school to test the applicability of the model in other countries (Miller 1994). In Europe, the sociological approach attained at least an equal place beside the Michigan model. It was further supported by the macrosociological perspective of the cleavage model introduced by Lipset and Rokkan (1967). The cleavage theory traces the origins of the West European party structure back to cleavages in the social structure of these countries and at the same time these cleavages are thought to influence voter behavior. Although Anthony Downs had already developed the rational choice model in 1957, this approach has only recently come to compete with the Columbia and the Michigan models. The media, however, are not given a place in any of these models. If at all, only the rational approach conceives the media to be an economical means to provide the information needed to make the electoral choice.

Ever since *The People's Choice* (1944) discussed the mass media as a potential impact factor on voting behavior for the first time, media effects research has been influenced strongly by electoral research. In the interpretation of their findings however, Lazarsfeld, Berelson, and Gaudet regarded the media – at that time only newspapers and radio – as being of minor importance. Therefore the media did not find much attention and were rather neglected in further research. It was only with the presidential election in 1960 when the United States witnessed its first television campaign that research turned to the media again. The fact that the media were attributed the possibility of exerting influence was also due to John F. Kennedy's campaign, which was very much tailored to television, and the legendary television debate between Kennedy and Richard Nixon. As a consequence, communication research focused more and more attention toward the question of the media's influence on the voting decision.

With the growing importance of television during the 1960s the media also became the subject of research in Europe. In 1961, Joseph Trenaman and Denis McQuail published *Television and the Political Image*, which presented the findings of their study about the British parliamentary election in 1959. While television did not have much effect on images, it proved its influential role by improving voters' campaign knowledge. By asking how people used the media during the campaign, the follow-up study on the occasion of the British election in 1964, *Television in Politics*, by Jay Blumler and McQuail (1968) can be regarded as an early example of the uses and gratifications perspective. Some time later Elisabeth Noelle-Neumann published the first articles on her concept of the Spiral of Silence, which propagated the "return to the concept of powerful media" (1973) and also prompted German communication research to turn to elections. The international perspective first arose with the publication of *La télévision fait-elle l'élection?* by Jay Blumler, Roland Cayrol, and Gabriel Thoveron (1978), which studied the role of television for the electorate and the factors influencing the interest in the election by comparing the 1974 electoral campaigns in Belgium, France, and Great Britain.

These studies of the first wave of electoral research in Europe under a communication perspective were primarily interested in how the media affected the electorate. Meanwhile, a new angle emerged in the United States by looking at the way campaigns are conducted and how they are oriented toward the mass media. In a first step, journalists presented descriptions of electoral campaigns. In 1961, the journalist and author Theodore W. White published the first book in what later became a series under the title *The Making of the President* in which he recounted his observations during the 1960 presidential campaign. He used the same format for describing the campaigns of 1968, 1972, and 1976. How campaigns became more and more adapted to the challenge of television became even clearer in *The Selling of the President* (1969) written by journalist Joe McGinnis who had closely followed the 1968 Nixon campaign. In the appendix to the book, McGinnis documented notes by campaign managers on their advertising strategies and thus demonstrated that campaigning has long become a commercial business. Finally, representatives of the newly developing profession appeared in the public themselves. When Joe Napolitan's *The Election Game and How to Win It* was published (1972), this also dealt with the 1968 presidential campaign. It was the first time that a political consultant gave a behind-the-scenes account of the campaign business. Napolitan was also the initiator of the American Association of Political Consultants, which was founded in 1969 and, as a professional association, demonstrated the establishment of a profession that has made politics a business. In 1981, Larry Sabato, at that time a campaign manager, made the profession the subject of his book *The Rise of Political Consultants*.

The growing interest of scientific research in the way electoral campaigns are planned and conducted is a consequence of their professionalization, which is also expressed in the increasing importance of consultants. Professionalization in the sense of shifting the organization of campaigns from the inner circle of the political system to external marketing experts is a consequence of distinctive developments in society that have been termed *modernization*, as well as of changes in the media systems.

Modernization has made campaigning a difficult job. The influence of sociodemographic characteristics or party identification on voting behavior has diminished, leading to much greater uncertainty in predicting the vote. In the United States as well as in European countries voter turnout has fallen – in some cases dramatically. This dealignment process was fostered by a shift in value preferences and even more so by the increase in the general educational level. What had once been an almost automatic decision was replaced by a weighing of alternatives on the part of the voter – not necessarily a deliberate and careful process, but one of taking shortcuts. This is also the starting point for the rational choice approach. However, with the weakening of party ties the chances for gaining voters through the campaign increase. At the same time, with these prospects, the challenge for campaigners has increased as well. In addition to these changes in the electorate, the differentiation of the media systems has further contributed to the necessity of employing sales professionals for electoral campaigns.

All these changes, which have provoked the professionalization of campaigning, could first be observed in the United States. This is also due to the fact that the U.S. political and electoral systems are oriented toward individual candidates and to a media system that has been a commercial one right from its early beginnings. When similar developments became visible in Western Europe and electoral campaigns changed their outlook, these changes were therefore dubbed *Americanization*. It is only at this point that similarities and simultaneously common problems develop and campaign research finally takes on an internationally comparative perspective. A 1987 research overview by Harrop and Miller still concluded: "The study of election campaigns, as opposed to elections, is a major gap" (240).

Thus, international comparisons in this field of research usually do not date back further than ten to fifteen years. The cause for the hesitant emergence of the international perspective may lie in the development of campaigns and campaign research as described here. It is certainly also due to the particular difficulties research in this area has to deal with because of a multitude of context variables that have to be considered. Compared to the impressive number of national campaign studies in some countries, the body of internationally comparative research is still meager.

If research builds on the method of international comparison, which means comparing phenomena in at least two countries, it takes on the systemic perspective: Several of the variables that influence the design of a campaign and therefore have to be taken into account in the study of campaign communication, do not vary within a country, often not even over periods of time, but only between countries. Among these systemic variables are the political system, the electoral system, party structure, regulation of election campaigns, political culture, and the media system (Bowler and Farrell 1992, 7–8; Mancini and Swanson 1996, 17–20).

COMPARATIVE RESEARCH ON CAMPAIGN COMMUNICATION

One of the earliest European studies that compared various countries, was a study initiated by Jay Blumler on the occasion of the first direct election of the European Parliament in 1979. Fifteen researchers from all nine countries that were members of the European Community at that time took the opportunity of a common event for a multimethod study on the role of television during the European election campaign (Blumler 1983a). It included interviews with representatives of the parties and of the broadcasting corporations, content analyses of television campaign reporting, and finally surveys of the electorate. In the interest of an international comparison across countries the national research instruments were kept as identical as possible.

Although high symbolic relevance for the integration process was attributed to the direct election of the European Parliament and even though this was regarded as a further step in the development of European identity, the campaigns in the individual countries proved to be surprisingly different and concentrated more on national than European aspects. It was not so much the common event that determined how campaigns were led. Instead, the new situation was dealt with according to the traditional patterns of existing national campaign models, in particular on the part of the broadcasting stations. These findings thus confirmed the powerful influence of the above-mentioned systemic variables. In addition, the design of the campaign, media reporting, and the reactions of the electorate were influenced by time- and spacebound factors leading Blumler to speak of "spatio-temporal 'noise'" (1983b, 360).

However, besides the national differences and particularities the study revealed some similarities between the nine countries that allow for generalization – at least for West European countries. For one thing, these common features lie in a similar journalistic approach to political events. Regardless of what the media were offered by the political actors, their reporting concentrated more on aspects of the campaign itself than on political issues. They were reluctant to give evaluative comments and preferred conflicts, personalization, and the national side of the campaign. Moreover, the European Election study assessed the victorious advance of television as a campaign channel – in all countries and in almost all sociodemographic groups of the electorate. Finally, cross-national findings supported the passive learning model of mass media effect with television playing a central role.

In his review of the merits of the comparative approach Blumler pointed out that political science could no longer exclude political communication variables: "After all, a network of mobilizing phenomena, linking communicator motivation with message volume, popular interest in and exposure to the campaign and turnout rates, was one of the most cross-nationally consistent patterns in our evidence at both individual-citizen and national-system levels" (1983, 375). Because in the 1979 European Election study, party activities and the climate of opinion in the electorate emerged as influential factors for the way the broadcasting stations dealt with the event, Blumler also made a plea for future research to take into account dynamic variables in addition to structural variables. He thus outlines a theoretical model that is similar to the dynamic-transactional approach that explains the production of media content and its effects on the audience through interactions ("transactions") between communicators (journalists) and their audience on the one hand and between journalists and primary communicators (the political system in this case) on the other (cf. Früh and Schönbach 1982; Schönbach and Früh 1984).

European elections provide a unique chance for internationally comparative research. Nevertheless, after the first direct election of the European Parliament the opportunity has been put to little use and never again on a large scale as in 1979 (cf. however Cayrol 1991; Schulz and Blumler 1994; Scherer 1995). Difficulties seem to outweigh advantages in this case. The advantages lie in the fact that the event takes place simultaneously in all European Union (EU) member states. The campaigns unfold at more or less the same time, thus keeping certain external conditions constant. Because of the fact that national members of the European Parliament are elected and thus the campaign remains a national campaign instead of being transnational, the election allows for comparing how the individual countries deal with the election.

In addition to the usual difficulties of international research cooperations, the event itself posed problems. Findings from research on the European Election can hardly be generalized for all electoral campaigns. The European Election is usually regarded as an election of the "second order," which in turn influences the behavior of all actors. The electorate is barely interested and their knowledge about issues and candidates is very limited. The parties prefer to spend their money on elections where power is at stake and thus conduct the European campaign with less intensity, which is further supported by the fact that their candidates are often unknown to the electorate. The media, respectively, also treat the European Election as a matter of lesser importance. These peculiarities are explained by the mostly symbolic relevance of the European Parliament, which does not elect a government or a prime minister.

Comparative research on European Elections therefore cannot lead to general conclusions about modern campaigns in general. Transnational comparisons, however, can deliver findings about similarities and differences at the macrolevel and about the influence of systemic variables such as, for instance, political culture or the media system, on the political communication processes. At this level, for example, as Jay Blumler points out in his summary of the 1979 European Election study, there was not much support for a discretionary role of the media in the sense of an autonomous function in society. Instead the study proved the dependence of television on the political system.

While European Election studies build on the advantage of the event in common and of governmental systems that are largely similar, difficulties increase in research that tries to compare national elections, particularly when the United States are included. One study that stood up to this challenge was a French-American joint venture published under the title *Mediated Politics in Two Cultures* (Kaid et al. 1991b). This project was conducted in 1988 when presidential elections were held in both countries. The study, however, had to deal with the differences between the electoral systems, the position of the president in France and in the United States, as well as with differences in the regulation of electoral campaigns and in the media systems. In fact, the hypothesis that was put forward in the introduction of the book, generally indicating the Americanization of French election campaigns, has fallen short of a fruitful comparison of the two countries. Instead, the project became an exemplary model of the difficulties that internationally comparative research is facing.

Beyond the differences in important factors that influence political communication processes the project teams from France and the United States had to cope with the different research traditions prevalent in both countries. Disagreements about the theoretical approach, the research questions, and the methods proved to be barriers that could not be overcome in any case. Thus, the project demonstrated that internationally comparative research not only has to deal with a whole network of political and cultural factors that influence the subject but also with difficulties that arise from differences in academic cultures.

Against the backdrop of the experiences from this Franco-American project, David Swanson (1992) discussed strategies of how to manage theoretical diversity in an international research team. As the simplest approach he recommends the avoidance strategy: Problems stemming from theoretical diversity are avoided when researchers in a project share a theoretical approach and therefore have no difficulties in agreeing upon a specific research question and the method for the study. By avoiding theoretical alternatives, this strategy, however, forgoes the potential of cross-national cooperation to bring together diverse theoretical approaches and thus lead to new and fruitful perspectives for research. Nevertheless, because international comparisons have to deal with variance in their subject anyway and, in addition, have to consider a multitude of influential factors, the avoidance strategy is a way to reduce the overall complexity that adds to the difficulties of cross-national research.

A second approach in dealing with theoretical diversity is the pretheoretical strategy that was applied by the 1979 European Election project. Using a pretheoretical strategy means that the international team of researchers agrees upon common research questions and the methods to be employed. Data are collected on this basis, theoretical considerations then come to bear only for analysis and interpretation. Thus, in this case the concept for empirical research is not deduced from theory. Instead the findings are used for theory building. Because it is the general objective of the comparative approach to detect common, transnational phenomena, which can then be used for the development of theoretical concepts, the pretheoretical strategy seems to be particularly suited to international research. This strategy has proved effective, for example, in a study by Rüdiger Schmitt-Beck (2000) on the influence of political communication on electoral behavior in four countries. Esser, Reinemann, and Fan (2000) followed a similar approach in an analysis of the reactions of the British and the German press to spin doctoring during the electoral campaigns in 1997 in Great Britain and in 1998 in Germany.

The third method of dealing with theoretical diversity in international research teams is the metatheoretical approach. According to Swanson (1992), this was the approach of the French-American election project. Due to their divergent theoretical positions the project team could only agree on a vague common objective, which was to study what kind of political reality the campaign constructed for the electorate. A broad research question such as this allows for integration of the interests of "rhetorical and narrative critics, social-scientific media effects researchers, semioticians, linguists, quantitative media content analysts, and others" (Swanson 1992, 23). The original idea, however, to compare specific elements and processes of the campaigns in two countries thus could only be realized to a very limited extent. These problems are mirrored in several chapters of the book that resulted from the project where *individual* authors wrote about aspects of the campaign in *one* country.

These difficulties of international cooperation are avoided by studies that do not aim for direct cooperation. One way of doing this is that researchers from one country conduct a study in several other countries and analyze the results. The comparison in this case is achieved by applying a common design in all countries. This approach has several shortcomings and uncertainties that lie in the applicability of the same instrument, particularly the adequate translation of questionnaires and code books and the comparable application of the instrument in all countries. Foreign researchers therefore have to rely on the cooperation of local colleagues who also help with the interpretation of findings because these require knowledge of the national political culture.

Another possibility is an approach that usually leads to anthologies containing chapters on countries where specific phenomena are described for individual countries. Usually the editors provide the authors of the individual chapters with a more or less detailed structure based on variables whose influence on the matter is assumed or already known. By asking all authors to consider the same variables the editors can hope for comparability across the various chapters on countries and thus go beyond the collection of case studies. The actual comparison is usually done in a summary chapter. Examples in the field of election research are *Electioneering*, edited by Butler and Ranney (1992) and *Electoral Strategies and Political Marketing*, edited by Bowler and Farrell (1992a). Both anthologies offer comparisons of election campaigns in different countries. Another such example is *Politics, Media, and Modern Democracy*, edited by Swanson and Mancini (1996b), which also compares election campaigns across countries but with a particular focus on communication aspects. And finally, *Political Advertising in Western Democracies*, edited by Kaid and Holtz-Bacha (1995) as well as Kaid (1999) – both present findings on the contents and effects of political advertising in various countries. A similar strategy is chosen by authors who collect data from several countries for integration in comparative synopses. Examples here are Smith (1981) who presented an overview of the role of television in electoral campaigns, or Farrell's chapter in *Campaign Strategies and Tactics* (1996), which described the influence of various variables of the political systems and media systems on campaign strategies.

THE AMERICANIZATION THESIS AS A MOTOR FOR COMPARATIVE RESEARCH

It is obvious that the number of international comparisons in the field of election research increased during the 1990s, while at the same time a focus on the organization and design of election campaigns could be noted. The reason why this perspective proved to be particularly fruitful for comparative research at the international level lies in the fact of seemingly similar developments in West European countries that also became visible almost at the same time. This led to the discussion about the Americanization of European election campaigns. The presumption that European campaigns are adapting more and more to the U.S. model implies the call for comparative research but makes the United States the inevitable yardstick. This, for example, becomes obvious in Gurevitch and Blumler's 1990 plea for internationally comparative research: "The practices and ideologies of the American political communications industry are taking hold worldwide. [...] American-style 'video-politics' seems to have emerged as something of a role model for political communicators in other liberal democracies" (311).

In Europe, the term *Americanization* has elicited much critique. Comparisons with the United States must obviously be regarded as problematic because of the obvious differences in the political systems and in the media systems. Nevertheless, the Americanization hypothesis has been used as a starting point for several analyses of modern election campaigns. Similarly, in the introductory chapter of their comparative book on campaigns, the editors Swanson and Mancini argue that Americanization is a useful working hypothesis but stress equally: "We regard the matter as an open question, and offer Americanization not as a conclusion, but as a reference point . . ." (Mancini and Swanson 1996, 4).

Against this background the editors design the analytic frame for comparing campaigns in eleven democracies. This frame takes into consideration the consequences for the political and the media system and their interrelationships that result from the differentiation of society – a process that is also called *modernization*. On the part of the political system these consequences are the deideologization of parties and the rise of "catch-all parties" or "electoral parties" that, in order to maximize votes, remain susceptible to a broad variety of issues. In weakening party structures the career of individual candidates who serve as reference points for specific groups of society and their issues and expectations comes to the forefront. This process of personalization leads to a situation where the person represents the idea. In modern societies, Mancini and Swanson (1996, 11) further argue, the mass media have emerged as autonomous power centers that influence the political process by setting their own issue agenda. In addition, the media, and television in particular, reinforce the personalization process. The commercialization of the broadcasting media that accompanied the market entry of commercial broadcasters has also changed the conditions for the conveyance of politics and forced political actors to adapt to the new situation.

Following these theoretical considerations Mancini and Swanson developed five characteristics of modern campaign communication: personalization of politics; scientificization of politics; detachment of parties from citizens while interpersonal contact is substituted by opinion polls; autonomous structures of communication in which the mass media act independently; and finally, the citizen becomes a spectator following the political spectacle. Context factors, particularly different electoral systems, the structures of party competition, campaign regulation, political culture, as well as the structures of the media systems, constitute differences in electoral campaigns in the various countries.

Comparison of campaigns in North and South America, Western and Eastern Europe, and Israel confirms Swanson and Mancini's (1996a) assumption that there is a common pattern of modern campaigning that can be interpreted as a response to the modernization process. The authors find similarities for the following key features that they interweave in a "modern model of campaigning." A direct cause for campaign innovations is seen in the changing relation between parties and the electorate. This mainly refers to the weakening of party ties: voting is no longer "an expression of solidarity with one's group and its institutions" but rather "an expression of one's opinions" (Swanson and Mancini 1996a, 250). This process goes hand in hand with a detachment of the parties from their ideological basis and their transformation into parties that can accommodate diverse opinions and attitudes that in turn results in a growing interchangeability of these parties.

The necessity for parties to keep the ability to shape public opinion in their own hands as far as possible proved to be another common feature across countries, which can also be regarded as a consequence of the development previously described. Parties thus try to determine themselves the way that politics is presented to the public. The resulting "'marketing' approach to campaigning" (251) is orientated toward the electorate and the media audience and stands for the adaptation of party decisions and activities to the logic of the media and the logic of television in particular. This goes along with "a style of political reporting that prefers personalities to ideas, simplicity to complexity, confrontation to compromise, and heavy emphasis on the 'horse race' in electoral campaigns" (251).

Beyond similar trends that become visible in the various countries und thus confirm the model of a media-centered campaign as developed by Swanson and Mancini, context factors specific to countries affect the design of campaigns and their effects. Political culture is among the most influential factors, used here in a sociological sense comprising the shared values and social practices of a country that shape the expectations vis-à-vis the political system and political behavior. Against this backdrop the editors divide the countries included in their book into three groups. The first group is made up of established democracies with a stable political culture. The second group combines the new or recently restored democracies. Finally, countries with a democratic system but currently or recently undergoing the pressure of destabilizing factors belong to the third group. By adopting this categorization Swanson and Mancini assume that a country's political culture mirrors the historical development as well as the current position of its political institutions and processes (1996a, 260–1). Among the countries of the first group are the United States, Great Britain, Sweden, and Germany. In these countries the modernization process has led to the weakening of traditional structures (religious institutions, trade unions) that formerly influenced voting decisions. Small groups that represent diverse interests have emerged instead. Parties define their programs on the basis of broad and generally accepted values and objectives. The mass media, and television in particular, became established as central agents of political socialization. As a consequence of theses processes, political actors were forced to to take over modern methods of campaigning. A common feature of the three European countries in this group is that the U.S.-style campaigning here is subject to public criticism. In Europe, parties still play a central role in the political process and thus prevent a shift of campaign organization from the parties to external experts, which also explains the comparatively strong commercialization of the campaign in the United States.

Spain, Russia, and Poland belong to the group of newly or recently restored democracies. These countries have adapted to modern campaign techniques with less resistance than the established democracies of the first group. This is explained by the fact that candidates in these countries encounter more difficult political conditions because democratic processes were introduced even before democratic institutions became established. Owing to nationally diverse reasons, the printed press is weak in these countries, which necessarily makes television the central channel of campaigning.

The route to modern campaigning took still another turn in those countries struggling with internal, potentially destabilizing tensions. This group consists of Israel, Italy, Argentina, and Venezuela. In these countries political actors are confronted with – in some cases considerable – loss of trust in the whole electorate or in certain target groups, which leads to specific conditions for campaigning. Where parts of the electorate appear not very susceptible to modern campaigns methods, traditional channels for addressing voters remain relevant (Swanson and Mancini 1996a, 263–5)

CONCLUSION

The way in which modern campaigns are conducted has been widely criticized. In the United States the high costs became the primary subject of discussion, particularly because the candidates have to raise their own funds. Therefore, campaign financing has become a permanent issue. Moreover, low voter turnout, a reason for worries in the United States has raised the question about whether there is a correlation with the way politics is presented during campaigns. In Europe, the Americanization hypothesis, although critically commented upon in the scientific community, stimulated and directly challenged internationally comparative research efforts. Even single-country studies dealing with national campaigns imply the comparative perspective by referring to Americanization and the idea of a U.S.-style model for Europe.

Many similarities can in fact be found across countries. In democratic systems, campaign communication follows similar lines. However, research has given up assigning the character of a model to U.S. campaigns – if there has ever been wholehearted support for the Americanization hypothesis. A plethora of intervening variables, national specifics of the political and the media systems, prevent the adoption of recipes for effective campaigning from one country to another. In the conclusion of their book, Swanson and Mancini therefore speak of an "archetype" of modern campaign practice (1996a, 268): While similarities in social developments lead to similar reactions by political actors and thus lead one to the assumption of convergence, there is still much room for national variance, in particular in comparison with the United States. The findings of Plasser, Scheucher, and Senft (1999) from their survey of European campaign consultants, point in the same direction when they speak of a shopping model as opposed to an adoption model: Campaign organizers in European countries take over from the United States what has proved to be effective there but apply it to national conditions. Campaign consultants maintain a "network of connections" (Swanson and Mancini 1996a, 250) for the exchange of manpower and know-how. Farrell has called this a process of "internationalization of campaign consultancy" (1998), in which American consultants, however, encounter increasing competition from their European colleagues. The assumption that only the United States exports modern campaign techniques is therefore no longer valid.

The hypothesis of Americanization that regards U.S. campaigns as a role model has changed into the modernization hypothesis that regards professionalization as a necessity resulting from the social differentiation and the changes of the media systems (Holtz-Bacha 2000). For international comparisons, modernization – and this is an outcome of the country studies edited by Swanson and Mancini (1996b) – has to be treated as a systemic variable. In addition to other context variables a country's degree of modernization influences the design of campaigns.

Studies that apply a comparative approach across countries have demonstrated which systemic variables are relevant. However, none of these studies has quantified the influence of the system variables. Therefore it is not possible to know which variables are more important and which are less important; how they relate to each other; and if they benefit or hinder the professionalization of campaigns. In this respect, a well-known problem of cross-national studies comes to bear, the fact that they usually work with a small number of cases. Nevertheless, because it is the aim of international comparisons to assess the validity of theoretical assumptions across systems, it is important to exceed the qualitative description of campaign communication and render possible a systematic and quantitative comparison.

Although the Americanization hypothesis proved to be inspiring for comparative election research, it has brought about a focus on the United States for studies by communication researchers that is less visible in election studies stemming from political science (cf. Berg-Schlosser 1998). However, because the United States is often the exception, this questions whether it makes sense to take the United States as the reference system. Finally, comparative campaign research shows a focus on Western industrial democracies although, on the one hand, globalization in politics, economy, and media call for a broader perspective and, on the other, the verification of the supra-national validity of theoretical assumptions makes the inclusion of other political cultures necessary.

REFERENCES

Berelson, Bernard R., Paul F. Lazarsfeld, and William N. McPhee. 1954. *Voting. A Study of Opinion Formation in a Presidential Campaign.* Chicago: The University of Chicago Press.

Blumler, Jay G. 1983a. *Communicating to Voters. Television in the First European Parliamentary Elections.* London: Sage.

––––––. 1983b. Election Communication: A Comparative Perspective. In Jay G. Blumler, ed. *Communicating to Voters. Television in the First European Parliamentary Elections.* London: Sage, pp. 359–78.

Blumler, Jay G., and Denis McQuail. 1968. *Television in Politics. Its Uses and Influence.* London: Faber and Faber.

Blumler, Jay G., Roland Cayrol, and Gabriel Thoveron. 1978. *La Télévision Fait-Elle Election?* Paris: Presses de la Fondation Nationale des Sciences Politiques.

Bowler, Shaun, and David M. Farrell, eds. 1992a. *Electoral Strategies and Political Marketing*. Houndsmills, UK: Macmillan Press.

———. 1992b. Conclusion: The Contemporary Election Campaign. In Shaun Bowler and David M. Farrell, eds. *Electoral Strategies and Political Marketing*. Houndsmills, UK: Macmillan Press, pp. 223–5.

———. 1992c. The Study of Election Campaigning. In Shaun Bowler and David M. Farrell, eds. *Electoral Strategies and Political Marketing*. Houndsmills, UK: Macmillan Press, pp. 1–23.

Butler, David, and Austin Ranney. 1992. *Electioneering. A Comparative Study of Continuity and Change*. Oxford: Clarendon Press.

Campbell, Angus, Philip E. Converse, Warren E. Miller, and Donald E. Stokes. 1960. *The American Voter*. New York: Wiley.

Cayrol, Roland. 1991. European Elections and the Pre-Electoral Period: Media Use and Campaign Evaluations. *European Journal of Political Research* (19): 17–29.

Downs, Anthony. 1957. *An Economic Theory of Democracy*. New York: Harper & Row.

Esser, Frank, Carsten Reinemann, and David Fan. 2000. Spin Doctoring in British and German Election Campaigns. How the Press is Being Confronted with a New Quality of Political PR. *European Journal of Communication* (15): 209–39.

Farrell, David M. 1996. Campaign Strategies and Tactics. In Lawrence LeDuc, Richard G. Niemi, and Pippa Norris, eds. *Comparing Democracies. Elections and Voting in Global Perspective*. Thousand Oaks, CA: Sage, pp. 160–83.

———. 1998. Political Consultancy Overseas: The Internationalization of Campaign Consultancy. *Political Science* (31): 171–6.

Farrell, David M., and Martin Wortmann. 1987. Party Strategies in the Electoral Market: Political Marketing in West Germany, Britain and Ireland. *European Journal of Political Research* (15): 297–318.

Früh, Werner, and Klaus Schönbach. 1982. Der dynamisch-transaktionale Ansatz. Ein neues Paradigma der Medienwirkungen. *Publizistik* (27): 74–88.

Gerstlé, Jacques, Keith R. Sanders, and Lynda Lee Kaid. 1991. Commonalities, Differences, and Lessons Learned from Comparative Communication Research. In Lynda Lee Kaid, Jacques Gerstlé, and Keith R. Sanders, eds. *Mediated Politics in Two Cultures. Presidential Campaigning in the United States and France*. New York: Praeger, pp. 271–82.

Gurevitch, Michael, and Jay G. Blumler. 1990. Comparative Research: The Extending Frontier. In David L. Swanson and Dan Nimmo, eds. *New Directions in Political Communication: A Resource Book*. Newbury Park, CA: Sage, pp. 305–25.

Harrop, Martin, and William L. Miller. 1987. *Elections and Voters. A Comparative Introduction*. New York: New Amsterdam Books.

Holtz-Bacha, Christina. 2000. Wahlkampf in Deutschland. Ein Fall bedingter Amerikanisierung. In Klaus Kamps, ed. *Trans-Atlantik–Trans-Portabel? Die Amerikanisierungsthese in der Politischen Kommunikation*. Opladen, Germany: Westdeutscher Verlag, pp. 43–55.

Holtz-Bacha, Christina, Lynda Lee Kaid, and Anne Johnston. 1994. Political Television Advertising in Western Democracies: A Comparison of Campaign Broadcasts in the U.S., Germany and France. *Political Communication* (11): 67–80.

Kaid, Lynda Lee, ed. 1999. *Television and Politics in Evolving European Democracies*. Commack, NY: Nova.

Kaid, Lynda Lee, and Christina Holtz-Bacha, eds. 1995. *Political Advertising in Western Democracies. Parties and Candidates on Television.* Thousand Oaks, CA: Sage.

Kaid, Lynda Lee, Jacques Gerstlé, and Keith R. Sanders. 1991a. Constructing a Political Communication Project in Two Cultures. In Lynda Lee Kaid, Jacques Gerstlé, and Keith R. Sanders, eds. *Mediated Politics in Two Cultures. Presidential Campaigning in the United States and France.* New York: Praeger, pp. 3–7.

————. 1991b. *Mediated Politics in Two Cultures. Presidential Campaigning in the United States and France.* New York: Praeger.

Lazarsfeld, Paul F., Bernard Berelson, and Hazel Gaudet. 1944. *The People's Choice. How the Voter Makes Up His Mind in a Presidential Election.* New York: Duell, Sloan & Pierce.

Le Duc, Lawrence, Richard G. Niemi, and Pippa Norris, eds. 1996. *Comparing Democracies. Elections and Voting in Global Perspective.* Thousand Oaks, CA: Sage.

Lipset, Seymour M., and Stein Rokkan. 1967. Cleavage Structures, Party Systems, and Voter Alignments. In Seymour M. Lipset and Stein Rokkan, eds. *Party Systems and Voter Alignments: Cross-National Perspectives.* New York: Free Press, pp. 1–64.

Mancini, Paolo, and David L. Swanson. 1996. Politics, Media, and Modern Democracy: Introduction. In David L. Swanson and Paolo Mancini, eds. *Politics, Media and Modern Democracy. An International Study of Innovations in Electoral Campaigning and Their Consequences.* Westport, CT: Praeger, pp. 1–26.

McGinnis, Joe. 1969. *The Selling of the President 1968.* New York: Trident Press.

Miller, Warren E. 1994. An Organizational History of the Intellectual Origins of the American National Election Studies. *European Journal of Political Research* (25): 247–65.

Napolitan, Joseph. 1972. *The Election Game and How to Win It.* Garden City, NY: Doubleday.

Noelle-Neumann, Elisabeth. 1973. Return to the Concept of Powerful Media. *Studies of Broadcasting* (9): 67–112.

Plasser, Fritz, Christian Scheucher, and Christian Senft. 1999. Is There a European Style of Political Marketing? A Survey of Political Managers and Consultants. In Bruce I. Newman, ed. *Handbook of Political Marketing.* Thousand Oaks, CA: Sage, pp. 89–112.

Sabato, Larry. 1981. *The Rise of Political Consultants.* New York: Basic Books.

Scherer, Helmut. 1995. Kommunikationskanäle der Europawahl 1989. Eine International Vergleichende Studie. In Lutz Erbring, ed. *Kommunikationsraum Europa.* Konstanz, Germany: UVK/Ölschläger, pp. 203–21.

Schmitt-Beck, Rüdiger. 2000. *Politische Kommunikation und Wählerverhalten. Ein Internationaler Vergleich.* Wiesbaden, Germany: Westdeutscher Verlag.

Schönbach, Klaus, and Werner Früh. 1984. Der Dynamisch-transaktionale Ansatz II: Konsequenzen. *Rundfunk und Fernsehen* (32): 314–29.

Schulz, Winfried, and Jay G. Blumler. 1994. Die Bedeutung der Kampagnen für das Europaengagement der Bürger. Eine Mehr-Ebenen-Analyse. In Oskar Niedermayer and Hermann Schmitt, eds. *Wahlen und Europäische Einigung.* Opladen, Germany: Westdeutscher Verlag, pp. 199–223.

Smith, Anthony. 1981. Mass Communications. In David Butler, Howard R. Penniman, and Austin Ranney, eds. *Democracy at the Polls. A Comparative Study of Competitive National Elections.* Washington, DC: American Enterprise Institute for Public Policy Research, pp. 173–95.

CHRISTINA HOLTZ-BACHA

Swanson, David L. 1992. Managing Theoretical Diversity in Cross-National Studies of Political Communication. In Jay G. Blumler, Jack M. McLeod, and Karl Erik Rosengren, eds. *Comparatively Speaking: Communication and Culture Across Space and Time.* Newbury Park, CA: Sage, pp. 19–34.

Swanson, David L., and Paolo Mancini. 1996a. Patterns of Modern Electoral Campaigning and their Consequences. In David L. Swanson and Paolo Mancini, eds. *Politics, Media and Modern Democracy. An International Study of Innovations in Electoral Campaigning and Their Consequences.* Westport, CT: Praeger, pp. 247–76.

———. 1996b. *Politics, Media and Modern Democracy. An International Study of Innovations in Electoral Campaigning and Their Consequences.* Westport, CT: Praeger.

Trenaman, Joseph, and Denis McQuail. 1961. *Television and the Political Image.* London: Methuen.

White, Theodore H. 1961. *The Making of the President 1960.* New York: Atheneum.

230

TEN

Political Communication and Electronic Democracy

American Exceptionalism or Global Trend?

Thomas Zittel

The concept of electronic democracy[1] has experienced a remarkable career in the social sciences during the past decade. It is not a new concept, despite the most recent outburst of publications and conferences on the topic. It can be traced back to the early 1970s when normative theorists of democracy perceived new digital media such as telephone and computer networks as tools for democratic reform (cf. Krauch 1972; Etzioni et al. 1975; Becker 1981; Barber 1984). However, it has changed in character since those days. Today, electronic democracy is being used as an empirical-analytical concept that carries the assumption that new digital media in general and computer networks in particular are in the process of changing the nature of political communication and democratic government (Rheingold 1993; Grossman 1995; Browning 1996; Rash 1997).

This so-called cyber-optimism is driven by the far-reaching diffusion of computer networks as a means of communication during the late 1990s. Few people knew about this medium before. It was primarily used by researchers around the globe to communicate and to share their research. This changed significantly during the past decade. The number of those with access to the Internet increased from 26 million in 1996 to 407 million in 2000 worldwide (NUA 2001). Among established democracies significant minorities of one quarter up to one third of the population were online by the end of the year 2000. In the United

[1] This chapter is part of a larger study on democracy in the networked society. I am grateful to the Fritz-Thyssen-Stiftung which supported parts of this research. I am also grateful to many staffers and members of parliament in the Swedish Riksdag, the German Bundestag, and the U.S. House of Representatives who gave large amounts of their time to assist me with my inquiries. I thank Fiona C. Barker who edited this text and the Minda de Gunzburg Center for European Studies at Harvard University that provided a hospitable research environment when I was preparing this paper.

States and Scandinavian countries, the number of those with access to the Internet has already passed the 50 percent threshold (NUA 2001).

The contemporary debate on electronic democracy is also driven by the fact that computer networks have matured in technological terms. They provide new opportunities for networked communication that are now readily available to everyone. Traditional mass media such as radio and television are channel media that enable a limited number of people to broadcast a small amount of information to a homogeneous mass audience in a unidirectional fashion. Contrary to this, the Internet is a network medium that allows for decentralized and interactive mass communication at low cost. It makes no distinction between sender and receiver in technological terms and it increases bandwidth in substantial ways. Every individual who cares to do so is able to broadcast information in various formats such as one-to-many or one-to-few. Every person is also able to enter into conversations with groups of people who may be scattered across the globe (Höflich 1994; Negroponte 1995; Morris and Ogan 1996). Some theorists even argue that the Internet allows for genuine social interaction rather than mere communication. Those students refer to applications such as Multi-User Dungeons (MUDs) that simulate a space independent from the physical world surrounding us (Loader 1997, 2–3; Lyon 1997; Ravetz 1998; Jordan 1999, 20).

The majority of political scientists has been more or less skeptical about these claims and still perceives e-democracy as the domain of techno-maniacs. Some outspoken cyber-skeptics stress that computer networks are being used by political actors in quite traditional ways. On the basis of case studies and impressionistic evidence they conclude that the Internet will reinforce established political structures rather than transforming them (Margolis and Resnick 2000). Hans Kleinsteuber and Martin Hagen added a comparative note to this debate. They perceive electronic democracy to be a secular development that will be restricted to the American political system while leaving many other established democracies untouched (Kleinsteuber 1995; Hagen 1997; Kleinsteuber and Hagen 1998; Hagen 2000).

This paper aims at an empirical test of this latter hypothesis. In its first part we will map the discourse on electronic democracy to delineate a framework for comparative empirical research. This theoretical analysis has to deal with the fact that electronic democracy is a vague and multifaceted concept that does not provide a coherent framework for focused comparative research.

In a second empirical part, we will narrow our focus to the representational dimension of electronic democracy. This theoretical dimension represents one crucial segment of the larger discourse on this concept. We will perform a comparative analysis of the use of personal parliamentary Web sites in order to test for the hypothesis that electronic democracy will be a secular development in American politics. We contrast the U.S. House with the Swedish Riksdag and the German Bundestag to produce general evidence on the similarities and differences between the American and the European context. This analysis goes well beyond the current use of case studies in researching electronic democracy.

In a third part we will discuss the findings of the analysis in order to determine the relationship between computer networks, political context, and political representation. This discussion has to deal with the fact that most theories on electronic democracy stress the macrolevel of political analysis. As a result, they reveal little in the way of details on the politics of electronic democracy. They also suffer from overdetermination and fail to acknowledge the role of social actors as well as the role of third variables they might be exposed to. We believe that much can be gained by an actor-centred approach to electronic democracy. This third part discusses the result of our comparative analysis from this perspective. It aims to utilize this perspective to generate explanations regarding the promises and limitations of computer networks for representative democracy.

WHAT IS ELECTRONIC DEMOCRACY ALL ABOUT?

The evolution of the concept of electronic democracy has done little for its clarification. A short glance at the most recent publications on the topic reveals that electronic democracy is being used as an umbrella concept for all sorts of political uses of the Internet. The term *electronic democracy* is being associated with phenomena such as party Web sites, electronic voting, sending e-mails to political representatives, political discussion fora, and even with administrative services provided over the Internet (see e.g., Browning 1996; Hague and Loader 1999; Kamps 1999).

This usage of the term falls into the trap of conceptual stretching, which produces vague and amorphous analytical categories (Sartori 1970). While comparative research is in need of general categories to travel across the boundaries of single cases, electronic democracy appears to be a category that defines no boundaries at all. As a result, it does not provide a clear and coherent model of the phenomenon at stake and it gives little conceptual guidance to empirical comparative research.[2] For this very reason we have to specify the phenomenon we deal with. The following sketched out model of electronic democracy argues that normative theories of democracy highlight three crucial dimensions of democracy that define coherent models of electronic democracy and that embrace many empirical observations related to this concept at the same time.

Electronic democracy is a segmented concept in the social sciences. During the past decades it has drawn the attention of many different subfields in the discipline, each of which associates different theoretical frameworks and empirical phenomena with the term. Normative theorists of democracy have been among the first to take up new developments in media technology and to consider its relevance for social and political structures. From the perspective of these scholars, new digital media such as telephone or computer networks could serve as tools for more participatory forms of democracy. Figure 10.1 demonstrates that these normative analyses refer to three essential theoretical dimensions of democracy to define the notion of participatory democracy in more specific ways: the jurisdictional dimension, the decisional dimension, and the representational dimension.

The *jurisdictional dimension* is based upon the question of whether decisions should be taken collectively or whether they should be taken by autonomous social actors. It stresses a normative model of social integration that argues that the stability of democracy is dependent upon the existence of social associations and communities performing crucial political functions such as political integration and regulation (Putnam 2000). Theorists of electronic democracy have argued that new digital media possess the capability to strengthen social associations and civic engagement (Etzioni et. al. 1975; Laudon 1977). Some have even argued that the Internet could provide a space for new types of virtual communities (Rheingold 1993). There has been no explicit debate on the constitutional ramifications of virtual communities and shifting jurisdictions in networked societies so far.

---

[2] There are only a few attempts in the literature on electronic democracy to discuss and clarify the concept (Hagen 1997; Bellamy 2000). These considerations have made important contributions to its understanding. However, they aim at real types of electronic democracy that are still closer to the empirical observations than they are to general and coherent models of electronic democracy. From our point of view, ideal models are better suited to guide systematic comparative research.

	Jurisdictional Dimension	Representative Dimension	Decisional Dimension
Constitutional Level	?	Electronic Voting	Electronic Referenda
Institutional Level	Informal and formalized opportunities for horizontal, decentralized, and interactive communication and participation within established political associations using the Internet.	Informal and formalized opportunities for direct, decentralized, and interactive vertical communication and participation between parliaments and citizens using the Internet. Institutionalized opportunities to participate using the Internet in the parliamentary process.	Informal and formalized opportunities to receive information related to e-referenda and to engage in comprehensive horizontal and vertical debates on this information.
Behavioral Level	Individual uses of new opportunities to communicate and to participate within established associations. Individual uses of the Internet to establish new types of organizations.	Individual uses of new opportunities to communicate with representatives and to participate in the parliamentary process.	Individual uses of new opportunities to learn about the issues, to deliberate, and to participate in e-referenda.

Figure 10.1 Electronic Democracy: A Conceptual Map

The *decisional dimension* asks about the mode of decision making. A normative model of direct democracy argues that citizens who are subject to authoritative decision making should be able to have a say in the decisions that affect them. It is therefore critical of schemes of representative democracy because of the dangers of misrepresentation. Theorists of electronic democracy argue that new digital media could foster direct democracy and help to make "[...] public opinion the law of the land [...]" (Becker 1981; Slaton 1992; Budge 1996).

The *representational dimension* focuses on the relationship between political representatives and constituents. It stresses a normative model of representation that sees political representatives as delegates of constituents who are to carry out constituents' policy demands and who are to be held accountable for their policy choices (Miller and Stokes 1963; Pitkin 1967). This perspective is critical of the current representative process, which is perceived as being too removed from ordinary citizens and as granting too much independence to intermediary organizations and political elites. Theorists of electronic democracy have argued that the Internet will help to close the gap between ordinary citizens and representative institutions (Krauch 1972; Dahl 1989; McLean 1989).

These considerations emphasize the fact that electronic democracy is a multidimensional discourse. Each of the dimensions involved represents the basis of a distinct model of electronic democracy. Apart from this, Figure 10.1 stresses that we need to distinguish three different levels of political analysis that apply to each of the dimensions sketched: the constitutional (macro), the institutional (meso), and the behavioral (micro) level. The debate on electronic democracy has not been explicit enough regarding these multiple levels of analysis. At the macrolevel of political analysis some attention has been devoted to the constitutional implications of electronic voting and electronic referenda (Buchstein 2001; Mutter 2002). This research discusses the relationship between constitutional norms such as the authenticity of a vote and the technical and procedural assumptions for electronic democracy, which derive from this legal basis.

Comparativists as well as students of political communication have focused on the institutional level of electronic democracy. This perspective stresses the use of the Internet by political elites to increase opportunities for vertical and horizontal communication and to allow for more political participation. Virtual party conventions, citizen consultations on the Internet, and ways to use the Internet to organize debates prior to direct decision making have been subject to empirical research on electronic democracy at the institutional level (Fishkin 1995, 1998; Coleman 1999; Marschall 2001). Each of these three examples can be related to one of the normative models of electronic democracy sketched previously.

Students of political participation focus on the microlevel of political analysis in their research on electronic democracy. This perspective focuses on individual use of the Internet for the purpose of political communication and political participation.[3] It asks whether the Internet will be able to increase the quantity and quality of political communication and political participation and whether this medium is able to draw into the process groups that have not communicated and participated before (Bimber 1998; Wilhelm 2000; Norris 2001).

These areas of research are integrated by an ethos of cyber-optimism, which assumes that the various scenarios of democratic change will be of significance for the future development of democracy. This ethos has

---

[3] The literature on electronic democracy has been more or less vague about the definition of each of these two concepts and about the problems of making a distinction. We will not elaborate on this problem in the context of this paper. Our conceptual map simply emphasizes that it is important to make a distinction.

three major sources in social science literature, which we will not be able to discuss in great length in the context of this paper. The first source derives from a strand in media studies, which emphasizes the political significance of the media from a historical perspective. According to this point of view, there has been a close relationship between waves of democratization and crucial breakthroughs in media technology such as the invention of the printing press or the introduction of television. This relationship is being perceived as an indicator for the existence of a causal impact of the media on politics (Startt and Sloan 1994). Cyber-optimists stress the scope of technological change along with these historical precedents when they argue that the Internet will be related to a new wave of democratization.

Cyber-optimism secondly touches upon theories of technology, which stress the social significance of technology. Proponents of so-called strong technological determinism argue that social institutions are determined by technological capacities at a given point in time (Street 1992; Sclove 1995). From this perspective, social change can be extrapolated from the emergence of technological innovations (Toffler 1980).

Thirdly, cyber-optimism refers to what can be called the "perfection-ist theory of democracy." This theory emphasizes the ideal of popular sovereignty as the core of democratic government. At the same time, it stresses the fact that large-scale mass democracies raise many obstacles to the implementation of this ideal (Dahl and Tufte 1973). Because of this tension between idea and physical matter, the history of democracy has been perceived as a constant struggle to overcome these obstacles, and new digital media are seen as a structural change that removes obstacles to participatory forms of democracy and that serves as a catalyst of democratic reform.

According to Hans Kleinsteuber and Martin Hagen, these assumptions are far too optimistic regarding the impact of technology in general and of computer networks in particular. These authors argue that technologies as well as the ideals of democracy are cultural artifacts rather than independent and universal forces. On the basis of this assumption they perceive American democracy as the only cultural and institutional environment that is compatible with electronic democracy and that cultivates innovative uses of computer networks (Kleinsteuber 1995; Hagen 1997; Hagen 2000). This secular impact of new digital media on democracy will thus preserve and further foster the distinct character of the American model of democracy rather than trigger a universal transformation of democracy.

This notion of American exceptionalism forms the basis of a long-standing debate in the social sciences. Alexis de Tocqueville sketched in his seminal book on democracy in America, published in 1835 and 1840, the picture of a postfeudal society based upon values such as equality, individualism, anti-etatism, and populism. This type of social structure presented a stark contrast to European feudal systems in the early nineteenth century (Tocqueville 1976). Theorists of American exceptionalism argue that these different historical vantage points patterned the development of democracy over time on both sides of the Atlantic and account for historical continuities and crucial differences across cases (Lipset 1990, 1996). Contemporary students of American politics stress the egalitarian, participatory, and populist character of American democracy compared to its European counterparts (Huntington 1981), and according to Kleinsteuber and Hagen, this is the only environment in which computer networks will be perceived as tools for participatory democracy and will be used in related ways.

The literature on electronic democracy provides little systematic empirical evidence to support this hypothesis. Most available empirical research is based upon atheoretical single case studies, which do not accumulate evidence, and which are thus ill suited to allow for general conclusions. On the theoretical level, this hypothesis suffers from the same weaknesses as its counterparts. It is based upon an overdeterministic theory of politics and political change. It also ignores the fact that political change does after all have to be initiated by autonomous political actors and that explanatory theories of electronic democracy have to focus on the micropolitics of electronic democracy to understand the potential as well as the limits of computer networks.

The following empirical section aims to produce systematic evidence regarding American exceptionalism in the networked society. In order to achieve this goal we will have to narrow our focus. The following analysis stresses the representational dimension of electronic democracy. We perform a comparative analysis of the use of personal Web sites in the German Bundestag, the Swedish Riksdag, and the U.S. House of Representatives. All three countries experienced technological change in telecommunications and have established a critical mass of Internet users. The selection of the cases furthermore allows us to compare the United States with two established European democracies and to learn whether there is a systematic difference between the American and the European case regarding developments in electronic democracy. The empirical indicator selected is well suited to determine whether political representatives are using the Internet to communicate in direct and interactive ways with their constituents, because Web sites are technologically mature and one of the most popular applications on the Internet.

PERSONAL WEB SITES IN THE U.S. HOUSE, THE SWEDISH RIKSDAG, AND THE GERMAN BUNDESTAG: DOES THE INTERNET MATTER TO DEMOCRACY?

The Parliaments of Sweden, Germany, and the United States introduced main parliamentary Web sites in 1995–6.[4] But by April 2000 there were still major differences among these cases regarding the degree to which individual representatives were using the World Wide Web to communicate with constituents in direct ways. This finding is based upon a count of hypertext links that direct users from the main parliamentary Web site to personal Web sites in direct or indirect ways. A personal Web site is defined here as a piece of digitalized information that is published by an individual member of parliament rather than a parliamentary bureaucracy or party, which provides personalized information beyond a uniform handbook format, and which can be retrieved using the World Wide Web.[5] Figure 10.2 demonstrates that these differences are in line with the assumption that electronic democracy would be a secular development in the American political context. While almost all members of the U.S. House of Representatives were using personal Web sites by April 2000, only a minority of members of parliament (MPs) did so in the Riksdag and the Bundestag.

These personal Web sites raise questions regarding their political relevance. After all, they could be nothing other than digital brochures, which have little meaning as a means for direct political communication between members of parliament and their constituents. For the purpose of this analysis, the notion of relevance has been defined by the degree to which personal Web sites utilize the new opportunities for communication provided by the technology. These new opportunities are defined by the interactive capabilities of the Internet, its bandwidth, which allows

---

[4] For the German Bundestag see Fühles-Ubach/Neumann 1998 and Mambrey et al. 1999; for the U.S. Congress see Casey 1996; and Coleman et al. 1999 and Norris 2001, ch. 7, provide an overview on other parliaments.

[5] All three main parliamentary Web sites along with all of the available personal Web sites were downloaded and archived in April 2000 to secure a stable set of data.

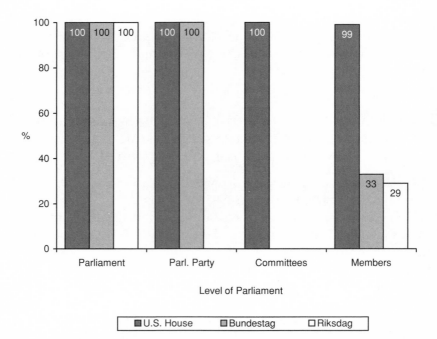

Figure 10.2 The Universe of Parliamentary Web Sites (U.S. House, Bundestag, Riksdag–April 2000)

the broadcasting of massive amounts of information, and its ability to be used as a tool to poll constituents on policy issues in a timely and targeted manner. We performed a content analysis[6] to test the degree to which personal Web sites in the three parliaments under study were taking advantage of these opportunities.

This analysis demonstrates that many MPs were using this new medium in suboptimal ways if we take its technological capabilities as a point of reference. In each of the three cases analyzed, more than 93 percent of personal Web sites provide only the most basic interactive applications such as e-mail or Web mail. These basic interactive applications are hardly any different from traditional means of one-to-one communications such as letters or telephones. They might decrease the cost of communication in marginal ways but they do not take advantage of new opportunities for public interactive communication in various formats such as many-to-many or many-to-few. Discussion fora, for example,

---

[6] The analysis was based upon a scheme that coded the characteristics of personal Web sites in terms of interactivity, the political relevance of information and its use as an instrument to poll citizens.

allow constituents to question political representatives in public and to engage in an interactive and open dialogue. Political representatives rarely use these sophisticated means of interactive communication on the Internet across all cases. In Sweden and Germany around 10 percent and 14 percent of the analyzed Web sites are providing some kind of discussion forum or public guestbook. In the United States, only one single MP (0.3 percent) was providing this kind of interactive feature on his Web site by April 2000.

The Internet also provides opportunities for individual MPs to poll constituents on particular policy issues in a timely and cost-effective manner. Online surveys can be used to inform constituents of pending policy decisions and to learn about their preferences. They can also be used in a proactive, anticipatory way by asking constituents which policies they care most about. This method of using online surveys allows citizens to influence the parliamentary agenda. This type of communication on the Internet could only be found on 6 percent of the personal Web sites in the U.S. House. It was completely absent on the Web sites of Swedish and German MPs.

The political relevance of personal Web sites is also dependent upon their textual content. Digital outlets, which provide comprehensive and accessible policy information, educate citizens on the policy positions, and legislative behavior of their representative and thus increase the accountability of this office holder. In contrast, digital brochures with colorful pictures and some general personal information have little relevance in this respect. The same is true regarding Web sites that are badly structured and do not present crucial information in accessible ways, such as using hypertext links. Figure 10.3 looks at the quantity of textual information on personal Web sites, which could be one empirical indicator for the former type of Web site.

The analysis of the quantity of textual information on personal Web sites again stresses that the Internet is used in suboptimal ways across all cases. Figure 10.3 demonstrates that in each of the three cases only minorities of MPs take advantage of the Internet to publish massive amounts (more than 200 pages) of textual information. Qualitative research reveals that those Web sites with fewer than 100 standard letter-size pages are likely to provide only passing and anecdotal information on the political positions and behavior of MPs.

From a qualitative perspective we furthermore have to ask about the type of information, which is provided on these personal Web sites. Even large amounts of textual information are no guarantee for the existence of

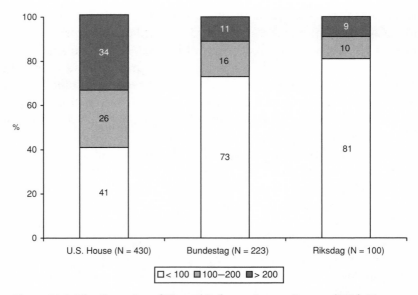

Figure 10.3 The Quantity of Textual Information on Personal Web Sites (U.S. House, Bundestag, Riksdag–April 2000)

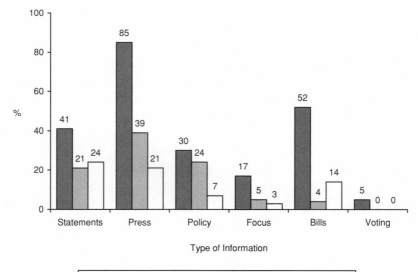

Figure 10.4 Type of Information on Personal Web Sites (U.S. House, Bundestag, Riksdag–April 2000)

politically relevant and accessible information. In Figure 10.4 we report the result of a content analysis, which studied the type of information users were directed to using hypertext links.

Figure 10.4 again demonstrates that MPs use their Web sites in suboptimal ways across all three cases. Most Web sites contain a "welcome page" with a picture of the MP, a postal address for contacting the member, and some basic information such as a biography or his or her committee assignments. Some pages also offer gimmicks such as recipes of the members' favorite dish. Regarding political information, press releases are the most frequent content that can be found on these Web sites almost across all three cases. Other political information that would be of more vital interest for constituents such as the policy positions of a member, his or her public statements, or his or her legislative activities are in spare supply on these Web sites across all three cases. The predominance of press releases indicates that the mass media rather than the ordinary citizen remain the focus for political representatives and that these Web sites are not being used as a direct channel for political communication.

While the previous data report a suboptimal use of the Internet across all three parliaments, they also stress differences between the U.S. House of Representatives on the one hand and the two European national parliaments on the other. Most of these differences are in line with the assumption of models of electronic democracy that pinpoint a secular American development of democracy: While most U.S. Representatives established a presence on the World Wide Web, only one third of their Swedish and German colleagues did so by April 2000. A small minority of U.S. representatives was using online surveys to poll citizens while in neither the Riksdag nor the Bundestag could such applications be found on personal Web sites. A majority of Swedish and German MPs had little textual information on their Web sites compared to a minority in the U.S. House of Representatives. The median is illuminating in this respect. It is 133 for the U.S. House of Representatives, 24 for the German Bundestag, and 1 for the Riksdag.

The American case is also different from its European counterparts regarding the political relevance of the information that is provided on personal Web sites. Figure 10.4 demonstrates that more U.S. representatives publish press releases, public statements, or information about their legislative behavior than their Swedish and German counterparts. The only finding that deviates from this pattern concerns the level of interactivity of personal Web sites. Members of the U.S. House of Representatives are not taking advantage of new forms of public interactivity on the Internet while at least some of their Swedish and German colleagues are experimenting with these opportunities.

ELECTRONIC DEMOCRACY – AN AMERICAN MODEL OF DEMOCRACY WITH RESERVATIONS

The preceding comparative analysis of the use of personal Web sites in the U.S. House of Representatives, the Swedish Riksdag, and the German Bundestag supports the hypothesis that electronic democracy is a secular American phenomenon. However, it also stresses the fact that many Swedish and German MPs do take advantage of the Internet. Some of them even use the Internet in quite far-reaching ways. Our analysis furthermore demonstrates that many U.S. representatives choose to use the Internet in suboptimal ways. This evidence contradicts the notion of any type of deterministic relationship between technology, institutional context, and political change. It stresses the need to study developments in electronic democracy from the perspective of social actors in order to understand the mechanisms that link macrovariables with individual choices and to explain the promises and limits of new opportunity structures in telecommunications.

A set of semistandardized interviews with staffers and MPs in these three parliaments reveals particular institutional features that are perceived as constraining choices regarding the use of computer networks. Many of the Swedish and German MPs we interviewed voiced outright opposition to the idea of using Web sites to enhance their communication with constituents. These members first and foremost emphasize their general role as a representative of their party who has to implement the party platform. A Swedish MP denies outrightly any independent role on his part or the relevance of demands put forward by his constituency:

> I see myself in an organization, I am in a party. And the party made a program [which tells me] what I am supposed to speak [about] and what I am supposed to propose. So, that is my [. . .] guidance to what I have to decide.

As a consequence of this general orientation, other party elites and party officials are perceived as natural points of reference in retrieving information and in discussing policy issues. When asked whom they contact to learn about policy concerns back home in the district, Swedish MPs in particular refer to local party officials and other local organizational elites rather than to constituents in general. Traditional mass media organizations as well as party organizations are being used as the main channels for disseminating information, while direct communication with constituents is considered less relevant and less desirable.

The narratives of those members who express this orientation suggest that the focus on party is a behavioral norm deeply ingrained into the hearts and souls of MPs in European national parliaments. It is hardly raised as an issue or perceived as a particular problem. Some members offer reasons that point to the programmatic closeness among the members of a party that minimizes tensions between the individual and his or her party. A Swedish MP explained when talking about her campaign:

> My personal campaign was all based on speaking for the party. If the people vote for me, they should know that they get a liberal.

This is different in the case of the U.S. House of Representatives. The members of this legislative institution consider themselves primarily as a representative of their district rather than their party. When asked about the goals related to the Web site of his member, a systems administrator explained:

> The goal is always to improve the communication with people in [the district]. It is really great that people in Washington are making use of the site as well but they are really not our interest. We are trying to improve our communication and get information out to our constituents.

The narratives of American respondents reveal that the decision to take advantage of the Internet is based upon strategic considerations as well. In contrast to respondents in Sweden and Germany, they stress electoral incentives as a reason to take advantage of the Internet as a means for communication with constituents. Looking back to the early beginnings of his member's Web site, a systems administrator explained:

> In the beginning we had no real vision. My member represents a very educated district close to Silicon Valley. There was a fear that it might hurt him if he is not proving to be up to date with technological developments.

Many of the respondents also pointed to the legislative structure as a factor that affects their choices. Some of the Swedish and German members we interviewed are quite positive about the use of Web sites to communicate with constituents, but argue that they cannot use Web sites because of a lack of resources. These answers point toward a mechanism that clearly communicates macroinstitutional pressures toward party homogeneity downward to the individual level and thus patterns behavior. Swedish members are in the most desperate situation in this respect. They lack their own budget and rely on allowances provided by their party. Most Swedish members command no more than one third to one quarter of a staffer. They lack the most basic resources to exploit the potential of the Internet to communicate with constituents. A Swedish MP who uses a Web site explains the situation as follows:

> Because I was a computer programmer, I was happy to learn how to design a website. I took a small course from a colleague who is very into it. He taught me how to use FrontPage, which is not very difficult. So, I did it myself. I also update it myself. All the news I put in, I have to do it myself. It takes about one hour every Sunday.

Another Swedish member sets out:

> I read [e-mail] personally and I answer them directly. I have no staff to do this. So, this is more work [. . .]. A website is certainly the thing I'd like to do but what I couldn't do because of restricted resources.

German members are more fortunate with a moderate budget that buys up to three staffers. But even this is no comparison with the situation of U.S. representatives who command a staff of up to eighteen people and a budget of about $500,000 per year. Among this staff there is at least one systems administrator, a press secretary, and several people in charge of constituency communication who come up with ideas on how to apply the Internet for the purpose of constituency relations; who design and update Web sites; and who eventually read, process, and answer incoming e-mail. The lack of staff and money to communicate with constituents on the part of European representatives clearly functions as an incentive to ignore new opportunities for increasing their personal profile and focusing more on geographic constituencies rather than party.

The American political context is not wholeheartedly biased toward electronic democracy. Some interviews suggest that this hesitancy of American representatives in using discussion fora reflects the strong first amendment tradition of the United States. While in Germany and Sweden, the principle of freedom of speech is balanced with the principle of fair speech, in the United States a clear hierarchy of values prevents any kind of censorship, regardless of content. The rulings of the Supreme

Court emphasize this tradition in a very persuasive manner. The risks that come with using public discussion fora can therefore only be controlled in the American case by not using discussion fora at all. Contrary to this, in Sweden and Germany, improper contributions to public discussion fora can be censored on the basis of the principle of fair speech.

The most towering motivation for U.S. representatives to remain on guard regarding electronic democracy was their sense of being after all part of a deliberative institution that has to strike a balance between the representative function and the function of making authoritative decisions. According to some of the MPs under study this requires the ability to bargain, to compromise, and to look into the merits of an issue. The deeply ingrained sense of the need to perform this function appears to be a major roadblock toward a bolder approach toward electronic democracy even in the context of American democracy.

While the institutional context in European democracies is less supportive of electronic democracy it does not completely discourage developments in this direction. Parliaments in modern democracies are based upon the principle of a division of labor. Individual MPs specialize in particular policy fields and function as the spokesperson of their party in their area of expertise. Some of the respondents refer to these professional reasons to explain their interest in computer networks as a medium of communication. A German member who deals with issues of telecommunications policy in his party explains:[7]

> I deal with issues of media technology in the policy areas of education and research. I have the feeling that I have to get first hand experience of everything that is going on in this field.

These latter examples indicate that institutional context can be ambiguous in its impact on choices in networked communication. While some features might encourage developments toward electronic democracy others might work in the opposite way. This observation leads us to conclude that electronic democracy is an American model with reservations. Compared to the European situation, specific features of the American institutional context are more supportive of electronic democracy. But, while American democracy creates some roadblocks to electronic democracy, the European context offers some opportunities too.

[7] The following quote was translated by the author.

REFERENCES

Barber, Benjamin. 1984. *Strong Democracy: Participatory Politics for a New Age.* Berkeley: University of California Press.

Becker, Ted. 1981. Teledemocracy: Bringing Power Back to the People. *The Futurist* 15 (12): 6–9.

Bellamy, Christine. 2000. Modelling Electronic Democracy: Towards Democratic Discourses in the Information Age. In Jens Hoff, Ivan Horrocks, and Pieter Tops, eds. *Democratic Governance and New Technology: Technologically Mediated Innovations in Political Practice in Western Europe.* London: Routledge, pp. 33–53.

Bimber, Bruce. 1998. The Internet and Political Transformation: Populism, Community, and Accelerated Pluralism. *Polity* 31 (1): 133–60.

Browning, Graeme. 1996. *Electronic Democracy: Using the Internet to Influence American Politics.* Wilton: Pemberton Press.

Buchstein, Hubertus. 2001. Modernisierung der Demokratie durch E-Voting. *Leviathan* 29 (2): 147–55.

Budge, Ian. 1996. *The New Challenge of Direct Democracy.* Cambridge: Polity Press.

Coleman, Stephen. 1999. Cutting Out the Middle Man: From Virtual Representation to Direct Deliberation. In Barry N. Hague and Brian D. Loader, eds. *Digital Democracy: Discourse and Decision Making in the Information Age.* London: Routledge, pp. 195–210.

Coleman, Stephen, John Taylor, and Wim van de Donk, eds. 1999. *Parliaments in the Age of the Internet.* Oxford: Oxford University Press in association with The Hansard Society for Parliamentary Government.

Dahl, Robert A. 1989. *Democracy and its Critics.* New Haven: Yale University Press.

Dahl, Robert A., and Edward R. Tufte. 1973. *Size and Democracy.* Stanford: University Press.

Etzioni, Amitai, Kenneth Laudon, and Sara Lipson. 1975. Participatory Technology: The MINERVA Communications Tree. *Journal of Communication* 25.

Fishkin, James F. 1998. Das ganze Land in einem Raum. In Claus Leggewie, and Christa Maar, eds. *Internet & Politik: Von der Zuschauer-zur Beteiligungsdemokratie.* Köln, Germany: Bollmann.

Fishkin, James S. 1995. *The Voice of the People: Public Opinion and Democracy.* New Haven: Yale University Press.

Fühles-Ubach, Simone, and Hans-Peter Neumann. 1998. Zwei Jahre Deutscher Bundestag im Internet: Konzeptionen, Organisation, Erfahrungen, Resonanz und Perspektiven. *Nachrichten für Dokumentation* 4: 205–10.

Grossman, Lawrence K. 1995. *The Electronic Republic: Reshaping Democracy in the Information Age.* New York: Viking.

Hagen, Martin. 1997. *Elektronische Demokratie: Computernetzwerke und Politische Theorie in den USA.* Hamburg, Germany: Lit.

_____. 2000. Digital Democracy and Political Systems. In Kenneth L. Hacker and Jan van Dijk, eds. *Digital Democracy: Issues of Theory and Practice.* London: Sage.

Hague, Barry N, and Brian D. Loader. 1999. Digital Democracy: An Introduction. In Barry N. Hague and Brian D. Loader, eds. *Digital Democracy. Discourse and Decision Making in the Information Age.* London: Routledge.

Höflich, Joachim P. 1994. Der Computer als interaktives Massenmedium. *Publizistik* 39 (4): 389–405.

Huntington, Samuel P. 1981. *American Politics: The Promise of Disharmony*. Cambridge: Belknap Press.

Jordan, Tim. 1999. *Cyberpower: The Culture and Politics of Cyberspace and the Internet*. London: Routledge.

Kamps, Klaus, ed. 1999. *Elektronische Demokratie? Perspektiven Politischer Partizipation*. Opladen, Germany: Westdeutscher Verlag.

Kleinsteuber, Hans. 1995. "Technologies of Freedom": Warum Werden in den USA Medien so Ganz Anders Interpretiert? *Amerikastudien* 40: 183–202.

Kleinsteuber, Hans J, and Martin Hagen. 1998. Was bedeutet "elektronische Demokratie"? Zur Diskussion und Praxis in den USA und Deutschland. *Zeitschrift für Parlamentsfragen* (1): 128–43.

Krauch, Helmut. 1972. *Computer-Demokratie*. Düsseldorf, Germany: VDI-Verlag.

Laudon, Kenneth C. 1977. *Communications Technology and Democratic Participation*. New York: Praeger.

Lipset, Seymour Martin. 1990. *Continental Divide: The Values and Institutions of the United States and Canada*. New York: Routledge.

―――. 1996. *American Exceptionalism: A Double-Edged Sword*. New York: W. W. Norton.

Loader, Brian D. 1997. The Governance of Cyberspace: Politics, Technology and Global Restructuring. In Brian D. Loader, ed. *The Governance of Cyberspace*. New York: Routledge.

Lyon, David. 1997. Cyberspace Sociality: Controversies over Computer Mediated Relationships. In Brian D. Loader, ed. *The Governance of Cyberspace*. New York: Routledge.

Mambrey, Peter, Hans-Peter Neumann, and Kerstin Sieverdingbeck. 1999. Bridging the Gap between Parliament and Citizen – the Internet Services of the German Bundestag. In Stephen Coleman, John Taylor, and Wim van de Donk, eds. *Parliament in the Age of the Internet*. Oxford: Oxford University Press in association with The Hansard Society for Parliamentary Government.

Margolis, Michael, and David Resnick. 2001. *Politics as Usual: The Cyberspace "Revolution."* Thousand Oaks, CA: Sage.

Marschall, Stefan. 2001. Parteien und Internet – Auf dem Weg zu Internet-basierten Mitgliederparteien. *Aus Politik und Zeitgeschichte* (10): 38–46.

McLean, Iain. 1989. *Democracy and New Technology*. Cambridge: Polity Press.

Morris, Merrill, and Christine Ogan. 1996. The Internet as Mass Medium. *Journal of Communication* 46: 39–50.

Miller, Warren E, and Donald E. Stokes. 1963. Constituency Influence in Congress. *American Political Science Review* 57: 45–56.

Mutter, Christa. 2002. Das Rubbelfeld auf dem Stimmzettel. *Die Weltwoche* January 3: 15.

Negroponte, Nicholas. 1995. *Total Digital: Die Welt Zwischen 0 und 1 oder die Zukunft der Kommunikation*. Munich: Bertelsmann.

Norris, Pippa. 2001. *Digital Divide: Civic Engagement, Information Poverty, and the Internet Worldwide*. Cambridge: Cambridge University Press.

NUA. 2001. *How Many Online?* (online) (cited January 2002). Available from World Wide Web: at http://www.nua.ie/surveys/how_many_online/.

Pitkin, Hanna F. 1967. *The Concept of Representation*. Berkeley: University of California Press.

Putnam, Robert D. 2000. *Bowling Alone: The Collapse and Revival of American Community*. New York: Simon & Schuster.

Rash, Wayne Jr. 1997. *Politics on the Nets: Wiring the Political Process*. New York: Freeman.

Ravetz, Joe. 1998. The Internet, Virtual Reality and Real Reality. Brian D. Loader, ed. *Cyberspace Divide: Equality, Agency, and Policy in the Information Society*. London: Routledge.

Rheingold, Howard. 1993. *The Virtual Community: Homesteading on the Electronic Frontier*. Reading, MA: Addison-Wesley.

Sartori, Giovanni. 1970. Concept Misformation in Comparative Politics. *The American Political Science Review* 4: 1033–53.

Sclove, Richard E. 1995. *Democracy and Technology*. New York: Guilford Press.

Slaton, Christa D. 1992. *Televote: Expanding Citizen Participation in the Quantum Age*. New York: Praeger.

Startt, James D, and David Sloan. 1994. The Historical Search for Significance. In James D. Startt and David Sloan, eds. *The Significance of the Media in American History*. Northport, AL: Vision Press.

Street, John. 1992. *Politics and Technology*. London: Macmillan.

Tocqueville, Alexis de. 1976. *Über die Demokratie in Amerika*. Munich: Deutscher Taschenbuchverlag.

Toffler, Alvin. 1980. *The Third Wave*. New York: Morrow.

Wilhelm, Anthony G. 2000. *Democracy in the Digital Age: Challenges to Political Life in Cyberspace*. New York: Routledge.

ELEVEN

Political News Journalists

*Partisanship, Professionalism, and Political Roles
in Five Countries*

Wolfgang Donsbach and Thomas E. Patterson

Most empirical studies of journalists' thinking and decision-making processes have been conducted as case studies of individual countries. They suffer from a considerable shortcoming insofar as they lack a larger context for assessing the validity of their findings. However, the question of how significant these findings are can be answered by use of comparative analyses, which include a range of different countries. The relevance of international comparative studies is demonstrated, for instance, when we examine the influence that journalists' political beliefs exert on their professional actions. To be sure, case studies of a particular national context can provide a basis for describing the beliefs of journalists in the respective country and the impact of these beliefs on the daily work in newsrooms. Yet, such case studies give no clue as to how much their findings have been influenced by characteristics of the respective media and political systems. The national context must therefore be eliminated if we want to get a clear picture of the connection between the political views of journalists and their professional decisions. This can be achieved by conducting a systematic comparison of various countries with differing media systems and political situations. Apart from its cross-national perspective, this approach also provides a formidable basis for categorizing the state of each country on an international scale.

Journalists in Western democratic societies operate under similar legal, political, economic, and cultural conditions. They enjoy formidable legal protections, have considerable access to those in power, and are backed by substantial news organizations. They also share a professional orientation that affects how they see their work. "The height of professional skill," says Denis McQuail, "is the exercise of a practical craft, which delivers the required institutional product, characterized by a high degree of objectivity, key marks of which are obsessive facticity and neutrality of attitude" (1994, 198). Yet, Western journalists operate in societies that are not identical in their press histories and traditions and in their media and political structures. These differences can be expected to produce differences in the way that journalists see and do their jobs.

Generally, studies of journalism fall into two categories both of which have a different objective with regard to the applicability and validity of their findings and theories: In this context, scholars can either study whether descriptions of the field yield universal characteristics of the profession and its members, and whether universally applicable laws determining journalists' professional behavior can be identified by examining explanatory analyses. Or, scholars can try to define the specific factors that shape the journalistic profession and influence professional behavior in different countries, regions, media, and organizations. Indeed, both approaches are sensible and have been amply explored, but studies that claim to belong to the first category produce only results of questionable merit if they have not been replicated in other countries. To claim generalizability for one's own findings is not possible until one has been able to detect the same characteristics and behavioral patterns in different journalistic cultures.

Studies belonging to the second category, in contrast, fail to fully accomplish their own objectives, for example, to trace the characteristics or the "essence" of journalism in a particular country, as long as they exclude the option of international comparison. Or to use a more colloquial expression: in the case of this kind of study, you never know whether the glass is half full or half empty. How relevant is it if a study concludes that in a sample of news journalists x percent agreed with a specific role conception, or that there is a correlation of y between one's own opinion and the news decisions one has made? Basically, the applicability of such findings is limited because, considered in the absolute, the interpretation of a particular frequency or intensity within a statistical complex is almost impossible. This can only be changed by comparing them with the same parameters of similarly structured samples.

Considering this, one is astonished to find that most studies in journalism research manage without comparison or replication. The studies of journalistic roles conducted by Jack McLeod (1964) and his team constitute an exception to this. Originally, the work of these scholars was theoretically grounded in the sociological concept of professionalism. As early as the 1960s, they applied the same survey instrument to journalists in different countries or stimulated follow-up surveys. There are, moreover, studies of editorial control that are also international in scope, albeit considerably smaller in number (cf. e.g., Esser 1998).

Explanatory comparative analyses, however, are virtually nonexistent, even though the field is of high scientific interest, especially where theories of news selection are concerned. How much of the explained variance can be attributed – technically speaking – to general patterns of human behavior and how much to specific circumstances, is an interesting question. We can presume that cognitive patterns of information reception and processing in humans (cognitive dissonance, schemas, etc.) belong to general human features and therefore are probably invariant factors, whereas professional socialization, professional standards, and forms of editorial control belong to specific environmental conditions. This study, for instance, is the first to our knowledge that replicates Kepplinger's (1991, 1992) theory of instrumental actualization in an international context but more comparative research has yet to be carried out.

Our study's aim, now, is to contribute to the "amounts of explained variance" in descriptive and explanatory journalism research. It sought to examine differences and similarities in the way that journalists in Western democracies do their jobs. Funded by a grant from the Markle Foundation, our study included Germany, Great Britain, Italy, Sweden, and the United States as its case studies. They were selected because, as will be seen, they vary in their press traditions and structures. In this chapter, we will describe our methodology; present three examples from our research that illustrate different uses of a comparative survey; and conclude with some observations about comparative research that emerged from our study.

SURVEY DESIGN: CROSS-NATIONAL MEDIA AND DEMOCRACY PROJECT

The five-country project centered on a mail survey of journalists in Germany, Great Britain, Italy, Sweden, and the United States. The questionnaire that the journalists of the different countries received was identical, except in its language (there were English, German, Italian, and Swedish translations) and in its reference to particular organizations, such as a country's political parties and news organizations.

The questionnaire was administered to journalists who were involved in the daily news process and who worked on news of politics, government, and current affairs (including, e.g., coverage of the environment, labor, and business). Journalists who were not involved in the production of daily news were excluded from the survey. For example, journalists who produced television news documentaries or who worked for weekly news magazines were not sampled. Also excluded were daily journalists who concentrated, for example, on sports, travel, fashion, and entertainment.

In terms of the study, a journalist was defined as a person who makes decisions directly affecting news content. The category thus includes both reporters and editors. In some news organizations, other roles, such as that of owner or newsroom manager, were also included in the category. As a consequence, the sole criterion for inclusion in the sample was whether a journalist participated in daily news decisions about politics and public affairs.

Each country's sample was stratified. The stratification occurred on two levels. Medium of communication was one of them. In each country, 50 percent of those sampled were newspaper journalists and 50 percent were broadcast journalists. The broadcast journalists were weighted toward television: in each country, seven of every ten broadcast journalists surveyed worked in television and three of ten worked in radio. The sample was also stratified 50/50 on a national–local basis. Although any such classification is somewhat arbitrary, distinctions can be made. In the United States, for example, CBS News and *The New York Times* are widely regarded as nationally significant news organizations, whereas WIXT (a television station in Syracuse, New York) and the *Sioux Falls Argus-Leader* (a newspaper in South Dakota) are considered locally or regionally important news organizations.

The procedure for random selection varied, depending on the available information. In the case of Italy, the sample was drawn from the membership list of the National Union of Journalists to which all Italian journalists belong. Each of the Italian journalists sampled was contacted directly by mail. Because there is no national roster of journalists in the other four countries, the samples were obtained through random selections made from organizational rosters in some instances and by news editors in others. For example, the British sample included fifteen journalists from the (London) *Daily Telegraph*, a national newspaper, and one journalist from the *Kent Evening Post*, a local paper. To select the fifteen *Daily Telegraph* journalists, we obtained from the *Telegraph* a complete roster of its journalists and randomly selected fifteen individuals from the list who were then contacted directly by mail. In the case of the *Kent Evening Post*, we wrote to the news editor, who was provided instructions on how to randomly select a journalist to whom the questionnaire was to be given. The name and address of the *Post*'s news editor was obtained from *Benn's Media Directory*, a standard reference book on the British media. The selection process in the United States, Sweden, and Germany was the same as that for Great Britain, although the proportion of journalists who were contacted directly and through news editors varied slightly in each case.

The survey included an original mailing and a follow-up. In each country, 600 journalists were contacted. The surveys were done sequentially in the 1991–3 period, beginning with the United States and concluding with Italy. The response rates in the five countries varied from 51 percent (303 replies) for Germany to 36 percent (216 respondents) for Great Britain. The response rates for the United States, Sweden, and Italy respectively were 46 percent (278 respondents), 45 percent (272 respondents), and 49 percent (292 respondents).

The questionnaire was sweeping in its scope. Among the areas it explored were the nature of news organizations; the structures and norms of news processes; journalists' perceptions of public opinion and groups; the factors that play a role in news decisions; journalists' attitudes toward press law and policy; journalists' conceptions of objectivity; journalists' social, economic, and educational backgrounds; how journalists allocate their time and attention across various news tasks; journalists' relationship with political officials; and journalists' partisan and political views.

In the sections that follow, we will discuss some of our findings for the purpose of indicating the power of a comparative design.

CASE 1: JOURNALISTS AS POLITICAL ACTORS

The long-term trend in news organizations has been toward increasing political independence. As McQuail notes, the "party newspaper has lost ground to commercial press forms, both as an idea and as a viable business enterprise" (McQuail 1994, 15). Nevertheless, vestiges of the old-time partisan press remain, particularly in European newspaper systems (Donsbach 1983; Köcher 1986; McQuail 1994, 15). Nor are broadcast organizations completely outside the fray of partisan politics. In Germany, Italy, France, and some other European countries, broadcasting has at times been structured in ways that allow parties or governments to affect news content (McQuail 1994, 172). Finally, allegations of a "hidden" bias among journalists have surfaced in nearly every Western democracy. Journalists have been described as social critics whose personal beliefs, which are more likely to be liberal than conservative, color their reporting (Schulman 1982).

Through our comparative design, we sought to assess the level of partisanship in Western news systems and how it varied across types of news organizations. We used a standard measure – a seven-point Left-Right scale – to assess journalists' political leanings. We found, as Schulman (1982) suggested, that journalists identify more with the Left than with the Right, although not to the same extent in all countries. Italian journalists with a mean score of 3.01 were the most liberal group. British and Swedish journalists with average scores of 3.46 and 3.45 respectively were the least liberal.

One way that journalists could promote their partisan values is to seek a position with a news organization that subscribes to the same values. However, the opportunities for such employment vary substantially (Patterson and Donsbach 1993; Curtice 1997; Donsbach 1999a). The United States provides few opportunities in any area. The British national newspaper system provides numerous opportunities for right-of-center journalists but relatively few for those on the Left. *The Guardian* and the *Mirror* are among the few national newspapers on the political left, while the *Daily Telegraph, The Times, Daily Mail, Sun, Express,* or *Star* are among the many on the Right. (After our study was completed, some of these papers changed their editorial stance and supported Tony Blair's New Labour Party in the 1997 and 2001 British general elections.) In contrast to Great Britain, *Il Giornale* is one of the few right-of-center national papers in Italy; most of the other national dailies have a liberal bias. Germany and Sweden are more evenly balanced in the Left-Right distribution of their national newspapers; in both countries, there are several major news organizations on each side of the political spectrum. In general, broadcast organizations and local newspapers provide less opportunity for partisan journalism, although some opportunity does exist.

These differences in partisan opportunities were associated with journalists' organizational affiliations. As Table 11.1 indicates, there was virtually no correlation between U.S. journalists' political beliefs and their perception (measured on seven-point Left-Right scales) of the editorial position of the news organization for which they worked. In the European news systems, there was a closer connection between journalists' partisanship and that of their own news organization. The correlation (Pearson's *r*) was particularly strong among Italian (.47) and

Table 11.1 The Correlation (Pearson's *r*) Between Journalists' Partisan Beliefs and Their Perception of the Partisan Editorial Position of the News Organization in Which They Work

	United States	United Kingdom	Germany	Italy	Sweden
All Respondents	.03	.03	.13*	.20**	.10
National Newspaper Journalists	.03	.24*	.54**	.47**	.23*
National Broadcast Journalists	.03	−.31*	−.03	.23*	−.15
Local Newspaper Journalists	.09	.03	.16	.11	−.01
Local Broadcast Journalists	−.11	−.28*	−.03	−.17	.03

*p < .05; **<.001

German (.54) journalists who worked for the leading national papers but was also relatively high among their British (.24) and Swedish (.23) counterparts. When local newspapers in Europe were considered, the correlations were positive in direction (except for Sweden) but much weaker than at the national level. In the case of European broadcasting, on the other hand, there was a significant positive correlation only among Italian national broadcasters. It would appear that, unless journalists work in an arena where news organizations are overtly partisan, their partisanship is a small factor in determining the job they hold.

Partisanship in the media, however, is not merely a question of the news organizations within which journalists work. In the final analysis, the issue of journalists' partisanship is a question of whether it affects their news decisions. If, as news professionals, they make their choices almost entirely in the context of prescribed journalistic norms and practices, their partisan beliefs are largely immaterial. Content analysis has been the primary method for examining this issue. This method, however, is limited in its ability to isolate and identify bias. It is exceedingly difficult to determine, for example, whether negative or positive coverage of a politician or issue is a result of partisan bias, the nature of events, or other factors. The problem of inference is magnified when country-to-country differences are at issue because the watchdog role is emphasized more heavily in some news systems than it is in others.

Accordingly, we developed a quasi-experimental survey method for measuring bias that exploits the fact that journalists are accustomed to making news decisions on the basis of event descriptions. Respondents were presented textual descriptions of four situations and asked to make six news decisions (a headline decision, a newsworthiness decision, and four visual-item decisions) about each of them (thus making a total of twenty-four decisions). The situations were developed from actual news stories and were identical in each of the five questionnaires except for references to country-specific institutions. The following example (British version) involving the issue of industrial pollution is one of the four situations contained in the survey (the other three situations dealt with taxes, prisons, and Third World debt obligations):

Situation: Broad government regulations aimed at eliminating thousands of tons of air pollutants at chemical plants each year were put into effect today. The regulations, developed under authority of environmental protection laws, were put into effect despite company arguments that the cost of plant modifications to meet the new standards could cripple the industry.

A chemical industry spokesperson contended that the rules could cost more than £50 million over the next decade, although environmental officials have estimated the cost to be much lower. The chemical industry has also asserted that the new rules would have little effect because companies are already removing more than 90 percent of the pollutants at issue.

Newsworthiness: How would you rate this situation in terms of its newsworthiness?

LOW   HIGH
1   2   3   4   5   6   7

Heading: How would you rate the following as a possible heading for a news story based on the situation?

"Chemical Industry Predicts High Cost and Little Effect from New Regulations"

UNACCEPTABLE   ACCEPTABLE
  1   2   3   4   5   6   7

Visual: Suppose an editor asked you to select a visual to accompany a story based on the situation. If the following visuals were available to you, what would be your preference among them? Please rank them from 1 (first preference) to 4 (last preference).

Rank:

_____ a photo showing dark smoke emerging from a plant's smoke stacks

_____ a photo of the chemical industry spokesperson at the press conference called to protest the new regulations

_____ a graph that shows the decline in air pollution over the last ten years

_____ a graph showing the projected improvement in air quality as a result of the new regulations

As in this case, each situation dealt with an issue that is a source of partisan conflict. In addition, seventeen of the twenty-four news decisions were purposely framed in a way that favored a partisan view (the other seven were purposely neutral in tone). For example, the proposed headline in the pollution situation ("Chemical Industry Predicts High Cost and Little Effect from New Regulations") was presumed to have a right-of-center bias because it conveyed the chemical industry's view of the situation rather than the regulatory agency's perspective. On the other hand, the last of the visual options ("a graph showing the projected improvement in air quality as a result of the new regulations") highlighted the expected benefits of the new regulations and hence was assumed to reflect a left-of-center and proenvironmental protection bias.

In developing the survey's four news situations, we aimed to construct decision options where the partisan bias was subtle. We sought to create plausible options that the respondents might actually face in the newsroom rather than blatantly partisan options that a professional journalist would reject out of hand. In this way, if the respondents expressed a preference for options that were slanted toward their point of view, we could reasonably infer that partisanship had influenced the decision.

We correlated journalists' decisions with their partisanship as measured by our Left-Right scale (see previous). Because of the small size of the samples (the average n is about 250 respondents), we examined the significance of the aggregate distribution of decisions. Each of the seventeen news decisions can be compared to the toss of the coin. If the relationship between partisanship and news decisions is random, a single test is as likely to yield a negative correlation as a positive one. On the other hand, if partisanship affects news decisions, a single test is more likely to yield a positive correlation and most of the seventeen decisions will be positive in direction. The probability of a particular outcome (Prob) where the assumed likelihood of a positive or negative correlation is equal can be determined by the binomial probability formula (Weinberg and Goldberg 1990, 187):

$$\text{Prob} = (^{n!}/_{(k!)(n-k)!})p^k q^{n-k}$$

where: p = probability of positive correlation = 1/2
q = probability of negative correlation = 1/2
n = number of tests = 17
k = number of successes (positive correlations)
n−k = number of failures (negative correlations)

When the probabilities for all possible outcomes (zero positive correlations through seventeen positive correlations) are determined, a binomial probability distribution for seventeen tests can be constructed. Statistically, if twelve or more of the seventeen tests are positive, the chance probability of the outcome is about .05. If fourteen or more are positive, the chance probability is about .01. And if fifteen or more are positive, the chance probability is about .001.

In all five countries, journalists' partisanship was significantly related (p < .01) to their news decisions. The individual correlations (Pearson's r) were not particularly large, however. The average positive correlation using the Left-Right scales was highest for Germany (.16) and nearly as high for Italy (.13) and Britain (.12); it was lowest for the United States (.09) and Sweden (.05). The correlations suggest that the hues of journalists' partisanship tend to shade the news rather than coloring it deeply and that the degree of shading is affected by the news culture in the respective country. Herbert Gans's conclusion (1979) that most journalists hold "progressive" but "safe" views is a reasonably precise summary of the findings of the five-country survey.

CASE 2: JOURNALISTS AS NEWS PROFESSIONALS

As in the previous example, comparative research is usually intended to explore similarities and differences between each case in the study. But it can also be used to illuminate a particular case. Through comparisons with the other cases, the exceptionalism of a particular case can be confirmed or disconfirmed. We sought to do this in the case of U.S. journalists.

Unlike European democracies, which developed in the nineteenth and twentieth centuries, American democracy dates back to the eighteenth century when liberty rather than equality was the dominant ideal. As a result of this historical background, U.S. journalists are thought to have a heightened sense of their rights. The American press also changed more quickly and completely from a partisan orientation to a commercial one (Schudson 1978). The news became a full-blown business with profits outweighing politics in the minds of most publishers (Schiller 1981). This development culminated in the development of a distinctive objective style of reporting that centered on "facts" and was "balanced" in the sense that it fairly presented both sides of partisan debate (Peterson 1956). As a consequence, new professional roles were created: the reporter who is sent out to get the news, and the editor who is responsible for the quality of what is finally printed. And "quality" meant not only factual accuracy but also balance and fairness to those who were covered in the news. The journalist became mainly a broker of relevant information.

These tendencies were not uniquely American, but they may run more deeply among U.S. journalists. Consider briefly the contrasting history of German journalism. From its beginning the German press was dominated by a strong belief in the superiority of opinion over news. Influential journalists, such as Joseph Goerres of *Der Rheinische Merkur*, promoted press freedom on the idea that journalists collectively would reflect public sentiment (Baumert 1928). The opinionated editor and commentator became the epitome of the journalistic profession (Engelsing 1966). German journalism was influenced by the continental ideology that objective or even neutral accounts of reality are not possible (Janowitz 1975). Unlike the liberal consensus in America, European philosophy claimed that an individual's *Weltanschauung* would always determine his or her interpretation of reality, which hindered the emergence of the type of objectivity that typified American journalism (Rothman 1979). Studies indicate that German journalists see themselves chiefly as social analysts and critics who seek to present a well-reasoned interpretation of political reality (Köcher 1986; Donsbach 1999b). To the German journalist, objectivity is seen less as an issue of impartiality than as a question of getting to the "hard facts" underlying partisan debate. Although American journalists would describe this type of reporting as "subjective," German journalists would defend it as more "realistic" and in this sense more "objective" than the American style.

Journalists in the British, Swedish, and Italian news systems employ interpretive styles that rest between the American and German styles. The Swedish style, for example, combines the interpretive qualities of the German model with the less partisan tone of the American model.

The surveys indicate that American journalists are, indeed, a relatively distinctive group. They are the most aggressive fighters for a free press. We collapsed our respondents' opinions on six different issues concerning freedom of the press into a single index. The six questions concerned free access to any government documents; disagreement with legal consequences in cases where a journalist breaks confidentiality promised to a news source; the right to protect sources in the courtroom; difficulty for libel suits by public officials; disagreement with a private citizen's right to reply when he or she has been falsely criticized; and disagreement with the government's right to stop publications in cases of national security. United States respondents supported these rights to a much greater extent than their colleagues in the other countries, particularly in Italy.

However, a stereotype that seems weak in the light of the empirical data is the notion that U.S. journalists are usually attuned to commercial considerations. We compiled four different questions on this issue into a single index: the importance of leading competitors as guidance for news decisions; the frequency with which news the respondent has prepared is changed to increase audience interest; limitation of his or her work by the necessity for capturing the audience's attention; and whether it is typical of the respondent's work to seek audience attention rather than to inform the audience. United States journalists were in the middle range of this index of "competition and commercialization."

But U.S. journalists were the most distinctive in the material they used for their news stories. The survey included a question that asked respondents to think about the most recent news story on which they had worked and to indicate the sources that were used, such as eyewitness observation, person-in-the-street interviews, wire service material, archives, and so on. This question was not intended to measure individual-level behavior; we made no assumption that a journalist's most recent story was typical of his or her work. The question was designed instead to uncover patterns that typify news systems. Are journalists in one system more likely than those in another to rely, say, on person-in-the-street interviews or wire service copy? The U.S. journalists relied far more heavily on personal initiative (e.g., obtaining interviews with newsmakers and people in the street) in covering stories than did their international colleagues, who relied more heavily on other-initiated material (e.g., wire service copy).

United States journalists are also rather distinctive in their sharp separation of the work of the reporter, the editor, and the editorial

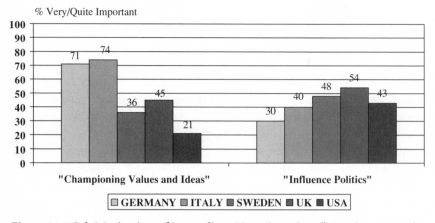

% Very/Quite Important

Figure 11.1 Job Motivation of Journalists. *Note:* Question: "How important is each of the following aspects for your work as a journalist?" (very, quite, slightly, not at all)

commentator. We asked our respondents how much time they spend with several professional activities, some of which described the roles of the reporter ("preparing reports based on personal observation and investigation"), the editor ("making content decisions about news other journalists produce"), and the commentator ("writing editorial commentary"). For reasons of cross-national comparison we avoided the labeling of these roles with terms that might have a different meaning in the five countries. A simple cross tabulation of the three roles showed to what extent in each of the countries the same person exercises different professional roles. United States journalists showed the highest degree of role segregation. Only one in four indicated exerting at the same time reporter and editor functions, only one in ten indicated combining reporter and editor roles, and almost nobody combines editing *and* commentary. In all of these cases the German journalists scored highest. Three in four indicate that they spend a lot of time on covering events and at least some time on writing commentaries, often on the very same event.

In all countries journalists were motivated primarily by the task of gathering and disseminating information about current public developments. But they differed in the degree to which they claimed an interest in influencing politics. United States journalists ranked near the top on this indicator, which contradicted what we had otherwise found. However, another survey item puts the finding into perspective (see Figure 11.1).

United States journalists ranked the lowest (21 percent) in terms of the importance to them of "champion[ing] particular values and ideas." Their German (71 percent) and Italian (74 percent) colleagues ranked the highest. It was the means of influence that separated the Americans from the Europeans. Simplifying our data one might say that U.S. journalists primarily want to affect politics and the public through information (almost 100 percent say that it is very or quite important for them to impart information to others) and *not* through advocating their subjective ideas, values, and beliefs in news writing.

To sum up, our look at U.S. journalists from a cross-national perspective shows them as a relatively peculiar breed within the profession. They are aggressive defenders of press freedom, sometimes at the expense of the rights of those covered in the news. They have by far the highest degree of division of labor between different journalistic tasks, and they face the strongest editorial control for the sake of factual accuracy and balance. Although they like political influence, they do not pursue this goal by championing their subjective values and beliefs – as do their German and Italian colleagues – but by digging out relevant information through their own research.

CASE 3: POLITICAL ROLES AND NEWS SYSTEMS

Although our study focused on journalists, we were also interested in identifying differences in news systems. The news organizations and professionals within a country can be said to constitute a news system (Seymour-Ure 1974). Such systems could be expected to vary in important ways.

We sought, for example, to distinguish news systems by the emphasis placed on certain functions, such as the oversight of public officials. Bernard Cohen (1963) was one of the first scholars to devise a typology of journalists' roles; he separated the "neutral" role from the "participant" role. Johnstone et al. (1976) applied this typology in one of the first surveys ever of American journalists. A decade later, based on their survey of U.S. journalists, Weaver and Wilhoit (1986) proposed a three-role typology: the "interpreter," "disseminator," and "adversary" roles. In a Swedish study, Fjaestad and Holmlov (1977) identified the "watchdog" and "educator" roles as the dominant orientations of Sweden's journalists. In a comparative study, Köcher (1986) described British journalists as "bloodhounds" and used the term "missionaries" to identify German journalists. Other analysts have proposed other roles, including that of "gatekeeper" and "advocate" (Janowitz 1975).

Although these typologies are suggestive, they are not overly helpful in a comparative context. All roles found in one Western system are found in varying degrees in all other Western systems. Typologies based on fixed descriptive categories, such as Weaver and Wilhoit's, cannot describe these variations. Those typologies that are based on a continuum (e.g., Cohen's neutral-participant dimension) could be employed, but each is based on a single dimension only. Our five-country survey suggests that two dimensions must be used to adequately describe the cross-national variation in journalists' roles.

One of these dimensions is a passive-active dimension and the other is a neutral-advocate dimension. The first is based on the journalist's *autonomy* as a political actor. The passive journalist is one who acts as the instrument of actors outside the news system, such as government officials, party leaders, interest group advocates, or others. The key point is that the journalist takes his or her cues from these actors, rather than operating independently. In contrast, the active journalist is one who is more fully a participant in his or her own right, actively shaping, interpreting, or investigating political subjects.

The second dimension is based on the journalist's *positioning* as a political actor. The neutral journalist is one who does not take sides in political debate, except for a preference for good (clean, honest) government as opposed to bad (corrupt, incompetent) government. The key point about the neutral journalist is that he or she does not routinely and consistently take sides in partisan or policy disputes. In contrast, the advocate journalist takes sides and does so in a consistent, substantial, and aggressive way. These sides do not have to be those of the opposing political parties. The journalist could act, for example, as an advocate of a particular ideology or group.

The two dimensions are largely independent. There was virtually no correlation ($r = .01$) between our passive-active and neutral-advocate indices (each was created from four separate survey questions). Although it might be assumed that an advocate role conception would be associated with an active role conception, the absence of a relationship is, by itself, a justification for the use of a two-dimensional rather than one-dimensional framework.

Each of the dimensions is, in practice, a continuum, but it is instructive to temporarily regard each dimension as having two discrete categories – passive or active, neutral or advocate. When viewed this way, there are

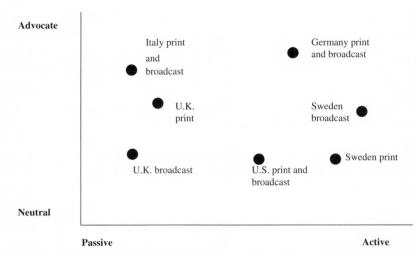

Figure 11.2 Role Positions of Journalists in Five Countries. *Note:* The active-passive scale is based on five survey items indicating to what degree the journalists hold a critical, adversarial position or a supportive, mediating position toward political leaders. The advocate-neutral scale consists of five items indicating to what degree the journalists prefer an advocacy or a detached type of reporting. Positions are based on deviances for each country's journalists from the grand mean for all five countries.

four combinations, and they encompass nearly all of the role conceptions and metaphors found commonly in the scholarly and popular literature on the news media:

Passive-Neutral: neutral reporter, mirror, common carrier, disseminator, broker, messenger
Passive-Advocate: hack reporter, partisan press
Active-Neutral: critic, adversary, watchdog, Fourth Estate, progressive reporter
Active-Advocate: ideologue, missionary, interpreter

Although this typing capacity is another indicator of the utility of our two-dimensional framework, a more critical test is whether it has the capacity to describe a variety of news systems. Figure 11.2 shows where the journalists from the five countries are positioned in the two-dimensional space. They are positioned by their mean scores on the passive-active and neutral-advocate indices. It will be noted that British print and broadcast journalists are located at different points, an indication that their journalistic cultures differ substantially. And in fact, the partisan-tinged world of British newspapers is different from the air of neutrality that pervades British broadcasting. Sweden is another country where the news cultures of print and broadcast journalists are measurably different.

In the three other countries – the United States, Germany, and Italy – the differences in the mean scores of the print and broadcast journalists are so small as to be insignificant. Journalists in these countries work through different mediums, but they have a shared conception of news. In other words, they have a common journalistic culture.

It is important to keep in mind, of course, that these cross-national differences describe news systems that also have much in common, including their primary task: the gathering and dissemination of the latest information about current events. It is probably fair to say that Western news systems are more alike than different, although their differences are important and consequential.

LESSONS LEARNED

The power inherent in a comparative design is evident in these examples. The chronic problem of a single-country study is that of a weak context in which to assess the results. They are much richer in a comparative study because it provides bases for comparison and thus for judging the significance of a particular tendency or relationship. For example, when partisanship in the news is examined simultaneously through the lens of five countries, additional leverage is gained beyond even what five separate studies could provide. We understand the impact of partisanship more fully by being able to examine it across news systems that differ in their media and political structures. We also understand each separate case better because of the ability to see it through precisely the same lens as the other cases. For example, as Case 2 illustrated, we have a much clearer picture of the professional culture of U.S. journalism through comparison with those of four other countries.

A comparative survey, however, places unusual demands on the researcher. Not only must the survey instrument be a precise one – which is always the case – but it must also be exact in terms of its applicability to each case. Anyone undertaking such a survey should not underestimate the time and effort required to ensure that questions asked of journalists in separate countries are identical in their meaning. If this goal is not accomplished, the researcher is at the mercy of measurement error. Are observed differences real ones or are they methodological artifacts? The survey researcher gets some protection from the fact that, when numerous questions are asked, a faulty question will stand out because the responses it yielded are markedly inconsistent with other distributions. Nonetheless, the burden on survey research is greater in a comparative study than in a single-country study.

For this reason, a comparative survey requires a substantial initial investment of time. It took us roughly a year to develop our questionnaire. As a first step, the two authors conducted in-depth interviews with a dozen U.S. and foreign correspondents in Washington, DC to explore the various theoretical dimensions of the study. Original drafts of the questionnaire were then prepared by the principal authors and were reviewed by scholars in the countries where the survey would be conducted. English-language versions of the country-specific questionnaires were then pilot tested. The U.S. version was tested on American journalists while the other versions were tested on foreign correspondents working in the United States. Final versions of the questionnaires were then developed and translated. A double system of translation was employed. After the questionnaire was translated into another language, it was reverse translated to determine its fidelity to the original. Altogether, the survey progressed through nearly two-dozen drafts before the final version was settled upon. Anything less than this type of effort would have subjected our study to substantial errors of inference. There is no doubt we made some errors of this type anyway. But they did not occur because of hasty execution of the survey.

Although we were careful, we were not tentative. We took advantage of the fact that journalists are an elite population and could handle a complex survey, which enabled us to treat it as a flexible instrument. It would have been enormously expensive for us to conduct a content analysis of news outputs in five countries of local and national broadcast and newspaper outlets. Our quasi-experimental news decision questions allowed us through survey research to address issues that normally would have required a content analysis component.

The study also indicates that a survey of this type can be a means of obtaining system-level measurements. For some of our questions, we used our survey respondents as "expert judges." Although this chapter does not provide an example, we had our respondents assess, for example, the Left-Right positioning of major news organizations within each country.

Finally, our study indicates that comparative surveys of journalists do not require large foundation grants. Although we had some financial support, the fact that we were able to employ a mail survey kept the costs to a modest level. Journalists are accustomed to working with pen and paper and thus suitable subjects for a mail survey.

Throughout the study, we benefited from the built-in stimulation that comparative research provides. When cross-national variation is found, the analyst's curiosity is immediately triggered. Why the differences? Many of the questions in our survey provoked from us this type of response. The pattern we found was either different from what we had expected or the variation was substantially greater or less than we had expected. In every case, the finding launched us on a search for explanation, which, after all, is what inspires all of us in the research community to do what we do.

REFERENCES

Baumert, Dieter Paul. 1928. *Die Entstehung des Deutschen Journalismus.* Munich: Verlag von Duncker.

Curtice, John. 1997. Is the Sun Still Shining on Tony Blair? The Electoral Influence of British Newspapers. *Press/Politics* 2 (2): 9–26.

Cohen, Bernard. 1963. *The Press and Foreign Policy.* Princeton: Princeton University Press.

Donsbach, Wolfgang. 1983. Journalists' Conception of Their Roles. *Gazette* 32: 19–36.

Donsbach, Wolfgang. 1999a. Sieg der Illusion. Wirtschaft und Arbeitsmarkt in der Wirklichkeit und in den Medien. In Elisabeth Noelle-Neuman, Hans Mathias Kepplinger, and Wolfgang Donsbach, eds. *Kampa.* Freiburg, Germany: Alber, pp. 40–77.

Donsbach, Wolfgang. 1999b. Journalism Research. In Hans-Bernd Brosius, and Christina Holtz-Bacha eds. *German Communication Yearbook.* Cresskill, NJ: Hamilton Press, 159–80.

Engelsing, Rolf. 1966. *Massenpublikum und Journalistentum im 19. Jahrhundert in Nordwestdeutschland.* Berlin: Duncker u. Humblot.

Esser, Frank. 1998. Editorial Structures and Work Principles in British and German Newsrooms. *European Journal of Communication* 13: 375–405.

Fjaestad, Bjorn, and P. G. Holmlov. 1977. *Dagspressen och Samhallet.* Stockholm: PAN/Norstedt.

Gans, Herbert. 1979. *Deciding What's News.* New York: Vintage.

Janowitz, Morris. 1975. Professional Models in Journalism. The Gatekeeper and the Advocate. *Journalism Quarterly* 52: 618–26, 662.

Johnstone, John W. C., Edward J. Slawski, and William W. Bowman. 1976. *The News People: A Sociological Portrait of American Journalists and Their Work.* Urbana: University of Illinois Press.

Kepplinger, Hans Mathias, with Hans-Bernd Brosius, and Joachim Friedrich Staab. 1991. Instrumental Actualization: A Theory of Mediated Conflicts. *European Journal of Communication* 6: 263–90.

Kepplinger, Hans Mathias. 1992. Put In The Public Spotlight – Instrumental Actualization of Actors, Events and Aspects in the Coverage on Nicaragua. In Stanley Rothman, ed. *The Mass Media in Liberal Democratic Societies.* New York: Paragon House, pp. 201–19.

Köcher, Renate. 1986. Bloodhounds or Missionaries: Role Definitions of German and British Journalists. *European Journal of Communication* 1: 43–64.

McQuail, Denis. 1994. *Mass Communication Theory.* London: Sage.

Patterson, Thomas, and Wolfgang Donsbach. 1993. *Press-Party Parallelism. A Cross-National Comparison.* Paper presented at the International Communication Association meeting, Washington, DC.

Peterson, Theodore. 1956. The Social Responsibility Theory of the Press. In Fred Siebert, Theodore Peterson, and Wilbur Schramm, eds. *Four Theories of the Press.* Urbana: University of Illinois Press.

Rothman, Stanley. 1979. The Mass Media in Post-Industrial Society. In Seymour Lipset, ed. *The Third Century America as a Post-Industrial Society.* Stanford, CA: Stanford University Press, pp. 346–499.

Schiller, Dan. 1981. *Objectivity and the News: The Public and the Rise of Commercial Journalism.* Philadelphia: University of Pennsylvania Press.

Schudson, Michael. 1978. *Discovering the News: A Social History of American Newspapers.* New York: Basic Books.

Schulman, Bob. 1982. The Liberal Tilt of Our Newsrooms. *Bulletin of the American Society of Newspaper Editors* 654: 3–7.

Seymore-Ure, Colin. 1974. *The Political Impact of Mass Media.* Beverly Hills, CA: Sage Publications.

Weaver, David, and G. Cleveland Wilhoit. 1986. *The American Journalist.* Bloomington: University of Indiana Press.

Weinberg, Sharon, and Kenneth Goldberg. 1990. *Statistics for the Behavioral Sciences.* New York: Cambridge University Press.

TWELVE

Political Communication Messages

Pictures of Our World on Television News

Patrick Rössler

Television news is an excellent means of comparing political communication across countries. News programs are part of almost every television system in the world. They are usually broadcast at prime time and audiences consistently rate them as the most important of all available information programs (Straubhaar et al. 1992; Hajok and Schorb 1998). Television news provides "survival-relevant information about novel events" (Newhagen and Levy 1998, 10). It also influences political orientation, informs opinion building, and serves as a control mechanism of state power. In the pluralist societies of the western world, television news exerts a strong influence on the very nature of political communication (Kamps 1999, 141).

According to Schaap et al. (1998) the research literature on television news can be organized according to the fields of mass communication, with a focus on *journalist working routines* (Esser 1998), *audience reception* and the *effects of television news at the individual level* (Jensen 1998; Zillmann et al. 1998), and *public opinion formation* at the societal level. Thus, Iyengar and Kinder note for the United States: "television news obviously possesses the potential to shape American public opinion profoundly" (Iyengar and Kinder 1987, 1). This chapter will elaborate on a fourth approach to examining television news: the *content and structure of television* news (Bonfadelli 2000, 33–6). In a comparative empirical study, we have analyzed news programs from different countries according to three main categories of content and structure: news geography, issue/actor representation, and topical integration.

TELEVISION NEWS CONTENT AND STRUCTURES:
EMPIRICAL EVIDENCE FROM SELECTED STUDIES

Comparing media content in different languages is a demanding task that raises fundamental methodological questions. This is particularly the case when languages other than English (as a *lingua franca*) or the researcher's own are involved. Distributing fieldwork to in-country teams may reduce difficulties concerning the collection of raw material and coder training, but it causes huge problems with coding reliability (Lauf and Peter 2001). This may be the reason why international comparisons of news coverage are rare, and why those that do exist tend to focus on print news material, such as newspapers and magazines, rather than on broadcast news (Stevenson 1985). Comparative research on television news across countries and cultures is currently limited to a handful of empirical studies.

The Foreign Images Project is a landmark study in the field that was conducted by a group of researchers organized by the International Association for Media and Communication Research (Sreberny-Mohammadi et al. 1985) and supported by the United Nations Educational, Scientific, and Cultural Organization (UNESCO). This study explored the extent to which different regions and continents appeared within the foreign news reporting of countries (see the News Geography section). Using both qualitative and quantitative methods, it assessed news in print and audiovisual media from twenty-nine countries for a fictitious and an actual week in 1979. National teams of coders in thirteen countries shared a coding manual; native speakers living in the United States completed the coding for sixteen further countries (Sreberny-Mohammadi et al. 1985, 14–15).

Unlike the Foreign Images Project, the studies by Cohen et al. (1990), Straubhaar et al. (1992), and Cooper Chen (1989) included all coverage and not just foreign news in their samples. Cohen, Adoni, and Bantz (1990) were interested in the amount of conflict represented in the news in five industrialized nations. Their analysis of news programs in 1980 and 1984 revealed that there was more conflict in British and Israeli television news than in German, South African, and U.S. news. Their study also showed that foreign news was generally more conflict oriented than domestic news (Cohen et al. 1990, 156). Straubhaar et al. (1992) used translated transcripts to compare the structure of news in China, Germany, India, Italy, Japan, Colombia, the Soviet Union, and the United

States. Contrary to their expectations, there was a strong correspondence of the conceptualization, format, and issues in television news in all countries, whether emanating from industrialized, socialist, or developing societies. These results are supported by Cooper Chen (1989), who studied the main news programs in the United States, Japan, Sri Lanka, Jamaica, and Colombia but used a rather limited sample of twenty-three news shows for analysis.

A study by Heinderyckx (1993) of television news from seventeen programs in eight West European countries analyzed four weeks of coverage in the winter of 1991. He found that news in all countries exhibited great conformity (Heinderyckx 1993, 448), due to its common emphasis on political issues and the relative balance between national and international coverage. He attributed differences in coverage to a German or Roman news culture, which he based on both formal criteria (program duration, item number, and length and presentation) and content criteria (issue selection and personalization).

A study by Meckel (1996) comparing news formats of national (German ARD, BBC, French TF2) and international (Arte, CNN, Euronews, ITN) broadcasts, encompassing formal, topical, and geographic aspects of coverage, found that news programs in all countries are structured similarly and make use of a limited set of visual features (Meckel 1996, 198–9).

The Foreign News Study was conducted by some of the scholars involved in the initial UNESCO project (Stevenson, 2003). In response to the renewed discussion of international news flows, the group used a modified code scheme for the analysis of two newspapers and the main television news program in each of the thirty-eight participating countries. However, as with the original study, this project only considered international coverage, leaving out the domestic news. The analysis revealed the profile of news values guiding the selection of foreign news in the countries under study (Hagen et al. 1998; Wu 2000; Stevenson, 2003).

The brief overview of comparative research into television news allows us to identify three crucial fields of interest in the study of information coverage:

News geography: evidence of how, where, and how intensively topics concerning a certain country are covered
Country-specific representation of *issues* and *actors*
Issue diversity or *issue convergence* in and across different countries

NEWS GEOGRAPHY

The UNESCO study was the first to introduce into the debate about a "new world information order" the way in which countries are portrayed in the foreign news of other countries (Sreberny-Mohammadi 1991). A basic and unsurprising characteristic of almost all television news is its orientation toward the territory (city, region, or country) where it is distributed. Information offered by the media concentrates on developments in the broadcaster's local (home) region, thereby fulfilling one of media's basic informational functions (see Stevenson and Cole 1984, 37). This orientation of media as overwhelmingly "local" corresponds with observations made within international audience research, in which television viewers unanimously emphasized the difference between *here* and *there* as an important dimension of television news (Jensen 1998, 165). Schulz (1983, 283) found a pattern that he called "universal regionalism": No matter where a program was distributed, the home (local) region always played the most important role in news coverage. This result has regularly been confirmed by studies in single countries (for an overview see Kamps 1999, 278).

In a study done in Germany, purely domestic news amounted to about 50 percent of coverage for the ARD, ZDF, and RTL in the mid-1990s (Kamps 1999, 284). Similar results were reported by Heinderyckx (1993, 431, 440) for different European news programs, with Italian RAI 1 coming out on top, broadcasting 69 percent domestic news. Compared internationally, the share of domestic news varies markedly, from Belarus (38 percent) and Mexico (45 percent) to more Western-oriented countries with more than two thirds of coverage (United States: 72 percent; Israel: 73 percent; Italy: 79 percent; see Jensen 1998, 201). Even for explicitly internationally oriented channels such as CNN or ITN, a high portion of coverage deals with the locality, although the percentages do not reach the level of domestic channels (Meckel 1996, 202–3).

Of course, national news programs also include coverage of foreign and international events. Such coverage varies insofar as it focuses on different countries. The term *communication magnetism* reflects the extent to which events in one country are reported on by another country. "Some nations cover each other, regularly reporting on the events in the other country; these nations attract each other in their coverage, while other nations are ignored" (Kamps 1999, 111 [translated by the author]). In German and Anglo-American news programs, France, Great Britain, and the remaining G7-countries play the most important role (apart from Germany and the United States), while other European Union (EU) countries or even nations with the same language (Austria and Switzerland, in the case of Germany) seldom appear.

As a result, four different types of countries were identified (Kamps 1999, 241–2):

(1) *News Centers*: countries that are consistently presented in coverage (usually the United States and the broadcasting country itself)
(2) *News Neighbours*: countries that are frequently included in coverage (e.g., the G7 countries or political organizations)
(3) *Topical News Neighbors*: countries that are covered mainly because they are central to ongoing political issues and themes (e.g., Bosnia, China, or Iraq)
(4) *News Periphery*: countries that make news only arbitrarily or very occasionally (in the case of natural disasters or accidents)

This typology reflects a consistent pattern of news construction, in which pure geographical proximity is not the dominant factor per se in news selection. Centrality is a relational factor: Apart from the United States as an international news center, the respective broadcasting country is a second center that is connected to a distinct set of news neighbors. Topical news neighbors and the news periphery do not vary greatly between broadcasters located in the same region, because coverage of these groups is mostly event driven.

It is a tradition in the television news business that most coverage is related to the country of broadcast, even if the developments reported on occur in other countries. Gans (1979, 38) described this phenomenon in the American media as the *domestication* of international news: "As in most other countries, American foreign news is ultimately only a variation on domestic themes." Events that take place in a faraway nation are "made" part of the domestic issue agenda by pointing out similarities with events at home, by focusing on nationals affected, or by emphasizing the relevance of the event for domestic affairs. In the United States, for instance, it is largely such "domesticated" events that make up the international agenda for the American public (Wanta and Hu 1993).

In German television news, Schulz (1983) showed that no more than 58 percent of international reports actually dealt with foreign affairs; the remainder of international coverage was related to Germany or even qualified as domestic news, with some implications for other countries. This phenomenon, called the *Aberdeen Effect*[1] was also prevalent in a study by Kamps (1999, 284–5), where almost a quarter of international news items made explicit reference to Germany. These findings, however, do not indicate how legitimate it was for broadcasts to relate international news to domestic issues. In other words, it is not clear whether the domestication was an inherent part of the event, emphasized, or merely constructed by the media themselves.

ISSUES AND ACTORS

Television news research usually compares the amount of coverage a program dedicates to different issues. Not surprisingly, Meckel (1996, 194–5) found that political and economic issues are the dominant themes in television news programs all over the world accounting for roughly two thirds of coverage. In contrast, about one out of ten reports dealt with natural disasters or catastrophes.

When considering the portrayal of countries (news geography), imbalances emerge if nations from the news periphery predominate in coverage of disasters, catastrophes, or other negative events, such as violence, war, or conflict. Western media in particular have been accused of covering developing countries negatively because of the economically dominant position of industrialized countries in the news market (Nordenstreng and Kleinwächter 1989). However, the evidence is thus far inconclusive: The UNESCO study showed that negativism was a general characteristic of news coverage, but was more pronounced in coverage of Third World countries. Meanwhile, positive news was often limited to coverage of industrialized countries (Sreberny-Mohammadi et al. 1985). Another interpretation of the same data is provided by Schulz (1983, 289; translated by the author), who argues that "news media selection focuses on current conflicts and crisis, but there is no obvious bias in coverage of third world countries." Similar results were reported by Stevenson and Cole (1984), Stevenson and Gaddy (1984), and Straubhaar et al. (1992).

Nevertheless, the Politics in TV News Study found that reports on countries in the news periphery reflect a limited set of topics, such as conflicts and crisis, natural disasters, or sporting events. For a considerable number of countries, no coverage of political affairs was found at all

---

[1] A Scottish newspaper reported on the Titanic catastrophy in 1912 with the headline "Aberdeen Man Lost at Sea."

(Kamps 1999, 289–90). Within Europe, this same result emerged when small and less important EU nations were reported on infrequently, and then only outside a political framework (Meckel 1996, 205).

The predictability of events provides another criterion for the differentiation of issues across broadcasters. *Predictability* refers to the ability to characterize events as genuine, taking place without media coverage (e.g., disasters); or as mediated, staged with an aim to create news media resonance (e.g., press conferences). Across channels and different countries there is a rather high percentage of coverage of predictable events, which are planned and announced in advance. However, because it was not always possible to classify events as predictable, a large part of coverage remained ambiguous or unidentified (Kamps 1999, 294).

Meckel (1996, 200) showed that the position of selected news events varied on the agenda of different countries. This does not mean, however, that different criteria for selection were applied. Instead, the same events were rated differently because of regional proximity or other interests such as the target group of the broadcast. Although the first items on news programs consistently deal with international issues, they preferably stem from the news centers and news neighbours (Kamps 1999, 313).

In terms of the actors represented in television news, politicians and government officials contribute to the coverage more often due to their elite status in political and public life. In fact, news programs usually focus either on political and societal elites, prominent sports athletes, or on criminals and individuals accused of crime. Furthermore, the concentration in news programs on news centers is also relevant to the portrayal of actors, as events in other countries are covered more frequently, if fellow nationals from the home country are involved (Kamps 1999, 155, 254–5). A European case study supports these results: stations largely reported on the Maastricht EU summit by interviewing political actors from their own country (Heinderyckx 1993, 445), which also refers to the domestication effect previously mentioned.

Eventually, news coverage relies on *symbolic visuals* for topics that do not lend themselves easily to visual material. "Political action then manifests itself in ritualised media routines: approaching limousines, hand shaking, ceremonies, debates, speeches and the welcome gestures of laughing politicians" (Kamps 1999, 81; translated by the author). Such visuals account for an increasing part of political coverage, as political events are portrayed using a set of standardized motifs. Again, a discrepancy can be observed when pictures from nations in the news periphery contain more arrival and departure scenes (e.g., visits of statesmen and other important politicians) than those from news centers and news neighbors, where press conferences dominate (Kamps 1999, 334).

Pulling the results of his various studies together, Kamps (1999, 348) concludes that news centers are most frequently and consistently covered; feature earlier-in-the-news line up and are part of the longest stories; and appear in conjunction with a large variety of topics and visuals.

DEGREE OF ISSUE DIVERSITY AND INTEGRATION

One basic function of mass media in society refers to agenda setting, which is to provide a set of issues for public debate. Thus, news media fosters a mutual understanding of which political and social problems are the most necessary to solve (Rössler 1999). The analysis of media coverage reveals the tension between issue diversity and issue convergence; the former leads to negative (plurality/fragmentation) and the latter to positive (integration/monopolisation) societal consequences (McQuail 2000, 72). News is information critical for the public life of the nation (Newhagen and Levy 1998, 10), and issue diversity and convergence is most often relevant to issues at the national level. For instance, if there is a discussion going on in the United States about a tax reform, issue integration and/or diversity must be determined primarily for the U.S.-American audience and related to the media coverage in the United States. A similar logic can be applied for different levels of analysis: On the local level, relevant issues should be communicated to a local audience by local media; and consequently, on the transnational level, issues such as the War Against Terrorism should be communicated by media in different countries to an international audience. Assuming greater social-spatial integration (Jarren 2000) in a globalized world, a basic set of issues that are relevant for more than one country could be communicated to generate international public awareness in them (Shaw 1997).

Most empirical studies of this aspect of international coverage – the representation of issues in different national media – only compare the structure of coverage. To describe the diversity or convergence of issues, a different approach is required, one that takes as its basis each report and determines its representation in the broadcasts of different countries (for a detailed description of the procedure, see Rössler 2000, 2001). At country level, there are few systematic studies of news content.[2]

---

[2] For an overview of German research, see Rössler (2002).

From a transnational point of view, only Cooper Chen (1989, 7) has produced some results: During one week of coverage, no more than four common events were covered in three out of five countries, and the issues in the news of the five countries varied heavily. Coverage converged most strongly in the case of an air crash in California and a hijacking event in Pakistan, but no single political issue was covered in all countries. Looking at the formal criteria of television coverage, Heinderyckx (1993, 443–7) analyzed news on the EU summit in Maastricht and found differences among countries in the length and choice of topics. The author concluded that, from a formal news structure point of view, European audiences did not receive a homogenous picture of the event.

RESEARCH QUESTIONS AND METHODOLOGY

The following comparison of television news in nine European countries and the United States is based on a quantitative content analysis. It assesses news geography, the representation of issues and actors, and the degree of issue convergence and divergence, providing some initial answers to the following four research questions:

- Were the four dimensions of news geography still valid at the end of the 1990s, and do they hold true for countries other than the United States and Germany?
- To what degree and for which types of issues can we observe a domestication of issues?
- How does news geography relate to issues and actors in media coverage?
- Do common news topics in different countries exist that may indicate a topical integration across different nations?

The present study extends the Politics in TV News Study to a wider array of countries (as the Foreign News Study did), but is not limited to the analysis of foreign news.[3] Furthermore, by including countries other than the United States and Germany, the study allows for a perspective beyond that of television news broadcast from news centers. The study analyzes the complete coverage of main news shows on eighteen

---

[3] The study avoids coding in different countries, because lack of cross-national reliability tests makes it difficult to conclude whether national differences in results are due to factual differences in coverage or are artifacts of differences in coding.

television channels in eight European countries and the United States[4] that were broadcasted in one week in December 1998. The content analysis was based on a detailed, multilevel coding scheme. For the program, formal characteristics were recorded. Then, the content of the coverage was coded for length, representation of issues and persons, partisanship of politicians, and additional characteristics, such as the depiction of violence, the differences between pictures and text, the degree of scandal, the inclusion of prototypical exemplars, and the way the audience was addressed. According to Lauf and Peter (2001, 200–1), there are different approaches to coding and reliability testing in cross-national studies. In the present case, we chose a *project language* approach, where the coding manual, coder training, and all coding are done in the native language of all the researchers.[5] Reliability testing is then conducted in the project language.[6]

Overall, the study reviewed forty-five hours of television news from 124 different news shows.[7] In these shows, we identified 1,727 reports,

[4] For the week between December 14 and December 20, 1998 the following news programs were collected: *Germany:* Tagesschau (ARD, 8 p.m.), heute (ZDF, 7 p.m.), RTL aktuell (RTL, 6:45 p.m.), 18:30 Nachrichten (SAT.1, 6:30 p.m.), PRO 7 Nachrichten (PRO 7, 7:30 p.m.), Kabel 1 Nachrichten (Kabel 1, 8 p.m.), and RTL 2 News (RTL 2, 8 p.m.). *Switzerland:* Tagesschau (SF DRS, 8 p.m.). *Austria:* ZiB (ORF 1-2, 8 p.m.). *France:* Journal (France 2, 8 p.m.). *Spain:* Telediario 1 (TVE 1, 3 p.m.). *Italy:* Telegiornale (RAI 1, 8 p.m.). *Norway:* Dagsrevyen (NRK, 7 p.m.) and Nyhetene (TV2, 9 p.m.). *Denmark:* TV-Avisen (DR 1, 9 p.m.). *United States:* World News Tonight (ABC, 6:30 p.m.), NBC Nightly News (NBC, 6:30 p.m.), and CBS Evening News (CBS, 6:30 p.m.). Due to technical problems we were not able to include two programs from Great Britain into the sample as it was originally planned. The most important events during these days were the attack of American forces against Iraq and the possible impeachment of the American president Bill Clinton.

[5] This method requires some compromises in field organization – for example, the media outlets of different languages cannot be distributed randomly to the coders. It also limits the reliability of data, which cannot be controlled within countries. Nevertheless, this was the most effective and valid approach for researchers who are all native speakers of the same language.

[6] Intercoder reliability was tested using a German program (PRO 7 news, December 14). We chose a day prior to the Iraq crisis to ensure greater variety in news reporting, which requires more coder decisions. We calculated the equivalence in the work of all coders (Merten 1995, p. 304, type 2), which is a stronger criterion than the mutual agreement of two coders. Our test was performed for all ten teams of coders and on all three levels of analysis. Our overall intercoder reliability of 0.88 across all categories indicates a satisfying quality of coding, if we take into account the complexity and variety of dimensions to be coded. Selected single coefficients were as follows: identification of reports 0.98; identification of report element 0.91; issue coding 0.88; location of events 0.76; valence of coverage 0.87; and relevant persons 0.75.

[7] Two shows could not be included in the sample: one from RAI1, due to recording problems, and one from NBC, due to a change in programming caused by breaking

consisting of 3,397 content elements. We found that formal features of the news displayed the expected differences in the duration of programs, ranging from 11.7 minutes on average for a program on RTL2 to 39.8 minutes on average for a program on France 2. We also found that the number and length of reports varies heavily among news programs. To produce results comparable across channels, we weighted all reports by their length in seconds; for cross-national comparisons, we aggregated data for channels and countries. To examine news diversity, we rearranged the data set, resulting in 914 single events representing the number of cases for analysis (Rössler 2001, 147).

FINDINGS ON NEWS GEOGRAPHY, ISSUES, AND PERSONALIZATION

Our data corroborate the findings of previous studies of television news: *Universal regionalism* is a central characteristic of news coverage. Weighted by the length of a report, more than half of the time available in a news show is filled with domestic events related to the broadcasting country (see Figure 12.1). This tendency is less obvious in the German-speaking countries (particularly in Austria, with just 36 percent domestic coverage), but was predominant in the United States and even stronger in Italy and France. In the latter countries, two-thirds or more of the news time is devoted to domestic information. However, these results depend on the news context: events with an international impact (e.g., the Clinton impeachment) are coded as domestic in one country (the United States) but international in all others.

To further illustrate the influence of breaking news on news geography, we divided our sample in two parts, one before and one following the Iraq crisis. Comparing both parts, there is a dramatic shift: Although speculation about a forthcoming attack was discussed early in the week, there was still a strong concentration on domestic events in Spain, Italy, Norway, and Denmark. In the second half of the week, domestic coverage in the latter two Scandinavian countries was reduced to half. A similar shift is observed in the Austrian news.

Figure 12.1 shows the location of events and the countries they refer to in detail. The Iraq crisis was the most important issue during the week sampled, which is why we displayed its share of coverage separately in

news. We took this into account by performing weighting procedures where applicable in our analysis.

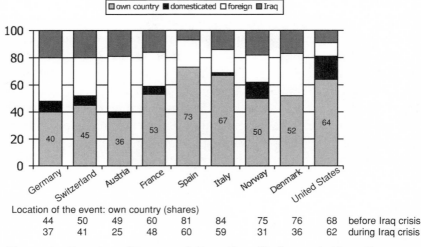

Figure 12.1 Location of Events and Countries of Reference in News Coverage (percentages; n = 1,727 reports, weighted by their length in seconds)

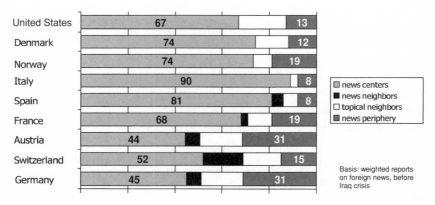

Figure 12.2 News Geography in Foreign News by Countries (percentages)

each column. Except for the United States, the Iraq crisis amounts to about 20 percent of coverage in each country. As the United States was directly involved in military operations in Iraq, a larger part of the Iraq coverage had to be coded as "referring to the broadcasting country." But apart from the United States, the "domestication" of foreign events was rather low, except in the German and Norwegian news.

To look at the news geography, all foreign news items were coded according to a country-specific definition of news centers, news neighbors, topical news neighbors, or news periphery (Kamps 1999, 241–2).

Table 12.1 News Geography – Topical Background and Issue
Categories (Percentages)

	Topical Background		Issue Categories			
	Before Iraq Crisis	During Iraq Crisis	Politics	War	Other Issues	Sports
News Centers	69	56	62	1	29	8
News Neighbors	4	1	53	0	36	11
Topical News Neighbors	11	28	63	37	1	1
News Periphery	16	15	62	9	21	8

Figure 12.2 illustrates the distribution for each country in the time period preceding the attack on Iraq; per definition, Iraq had to be coded
as a "topical news neighbor" as it had become part of the coverage due
to a single, but very important, event.

Our results indicate the predominance of news centers, which account
for more than two thirds of coverage in all but the German-speaking
countries. News centers attain an even higher share of coverage in Italian
and Spanish news programs, where the focus on the home country correlates with an emphasis on news centers in the remaining foreign coverage. In Germany, Austria, and Switzerland foreign news is less focused
on news centers. Instead, the news periphery plays an important role,
comprising up to a third of coverage. In all countries, news neighbors
and topical news neighbors are not important for the period before the
Iraq crisis.

We also sought to explain how an extraordinary event (such as the
Iraq crisis) would influence news geography. Based on Figure 12.2, we
calculated mean values for all countries and compared these shares with
the results for the period during the Iraq crisis (see Table 12.1). As expected, the asymmetry in foreign news coverage is somewhat reduced:
Only 56 percent of the coverage focuses on news centers during the crisis itself (as compared to 69 percent before the attack on Iraq), while
the share of topical news neighbors (meaning Iraq) rises from 11 to
28 percent in the second half of the week. However, this increase is not
part of a trade-off with the news periphery, whose coverage remains almost constant (16 percent). The change in communication magnetism
caused by events in Iraq shifts emphasis only from the news centers to
the topical news neighbors.

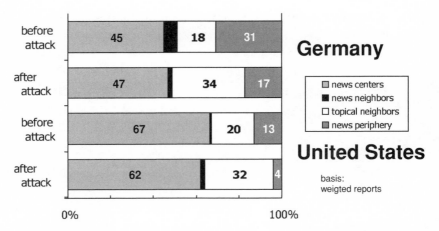

Figure 12.3 Influence of the Iraq Crisis on News Geography in Foreign News Coverage (Germany and the United States, percentages)

If we take a closer look at the results for news programs in Germany and the United States, the results found at the aggregate level for all countries need modification (Figure 12.3). In contrast to the general trend, coverage of news centers in Germany is not reduced but remains at about the same level in both parts of the week (45 versus 47 percent). Here, the dramatic increase in coverage of topical news neighbors (again, Iraq) coincides with a loss in influence of the news periphery (from 31 to 17 percent). The same holds true for American news programs, where the move toward topical news neighbors reduces the share of the news periphery to a mere 4 percent. After the attack on Iraq, U.S. news contained almost no coverage of countries in the news periphery.

In terms of the issues covered in the news, our study confirmed that political events dominate the content of news programs. Comparing across countries, coverage in the United States, Germany, and Norway focused to a higher degree on the Iraq issue. In the United States, this was combined with a second focus on domestic policy (the Lewinsky scandal). In Italy, television news showed more accidents and crime; in Spain, more sports. But evaluating issues in the context of news geography (see Table 12.1) does not support the argument that countries from the news periphery only become part of coverage due to negative events, such as disasters or crime. This type of news (other issues) focused less on countries from the news periphery (21 percent) than on news centers (29 percent). Attention to direct news neighbors is based on higher shares of sports and other news issues, while the strong emphasis on the "war" category in the case of topical neighbors can almost completely be explained by the Iraq crisis. Hence, there is no evidence that coverage of the news periphery was limited to events with little political relevance.

Obviously, the important role of political issues in television news coverage has an influence on the type of persons represented in news reports (Table 12.2): Politicians were the main actors in all countries under study. In the United States, Bill Clinton was included in about every third report, as he was involved in the Iraq crisis as well as in the Lewinsky scandal. Except for Saddam Hussein, politicians from other countries appear only occasionally in the American news. News items in European countries are more likely to include other nation's politicians (among them Bill Clinton) in their coverage, particularly in Denmark. News reports in Austria and Italy portray their own political leaders most frequently. A considerable share of coverage in Germany and Norway is devoted to nonpolitical actors such as sports athletes or "people on the street" involved in events.

For our analysis of issue diversity, we used all 914 single events that were reported at least once in any country during our one-week sample period.[8] The distribution of frequencies shows that nine out of ten events make the news in only one country (Figure 12.4). In other words, national coverage focuses on events that are rarely mentioned in another country. In our sample week, less than 100 events were prevalent in the news of at least two countries, and only five issues were able to attract the attention of newsmakers in seven or more countries. However, the attack on Iraq was covered in all nine countries (comprising 3,829 seconds of coverage); seven countries also covered reactions to the attack (3,449 seconds) and a summary of the air raid against Iraq (1,327 seconds.). Significant attention was also given to the possible impeachment of Bill Clinton (6,749 seconds) and the collapse of a house in Rome that killed twenty-seven people (1,612 seconds).

The level of issue convergence seems rather small at a first glance, but the results need to be reinterpreted in the context of the amount of coverage. We weighted each issue according to the length of reports, measured in seconds. Then almost 20 percent of the coverage refers to issues that were represented in six or more countries. To put it differently: if we consider all news broadcast in our sample, nearly one fifth deals with issues

---

[8] In the following, only cross-national results are reported. The country-specific analysis for Germany is published in Rössler (2002).

Table 12.2 Actors Appearing in News Coverage, Divided by Countries (Percentages, Based on Weighted Reports; Coding of a Maximum of Four Persons Per Report; Excluding Spanish Programs)

Persons	Country							
	Germany	Switzerland	Austria	France	Italy	Norway	Denmark	United States
Head of Government	23	10	26	15	23	12	11	13
Clinton	13	10	11	11	15	9	13	50
Hussein	3	6	6	4	11	6	1	13
Other Politician	25	38	36	48	43	34	55	50
Foreign Politician	22	36	26	24	16	9	77	7
Institutions	28	40	20	47	45	55	39	27
Sportsmen	40	34	7	9	22	27	1	2
Criminals	10	9	4	5	6	6	7	3
Citizens Involved	8	13	10	26	19	39	17	3

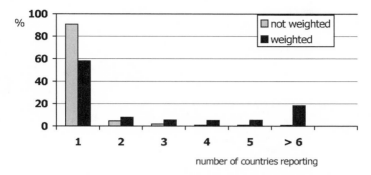

Figure 12.4 Issue Diversity in News Shows of Different Countries (percentages; unweighted events = number of countries only; weighted events = including story length)

presented to television news viewers in more than six European countries. This result may seem improbable, but it holds true for other media as well (Rössler 2002). It can best be explained by two coinciding factors. First, reports that were calculated only singly when counting events become more influential with the weighting procedure, as their multiple representation is also considered. Second, according to the research on news values, coverage of important events is longer by nature.

How can we describe those issues that were the focus of coverage in several countries? Additional analysis reveals that those issues that were a part of coverage in more than four countries mostly dealt with political issues (80 percent) or war and conflict (12 percent). Apart from these, only accidents and disasters are covered in multiple countries' coverage. In contrast, events that appear only in one country are mostly economic issues or topics related to domestic policy (22 and 14 percent respectively). Furthermore, cultural events, human-interest stories, crime, and sports are also largely country specific.

Issue convergence varies both among countries but also among channels within one country, depending on whether we compare the unweighted story count or those weighted by story length (Figure 12.5). If we look at the overlap in story selection among ABC, CBS, and NBC in the United States, the result is low – 3.5 percent of events in the news of all three – and seems hard to believe. But these few events were absolutely dominant, and accounted for 34.7 percent of the news coverage in these programs. In other words, more than one third of the main American broadcast news at that time was devoted to the same events. The same tendency was found in the four main German news

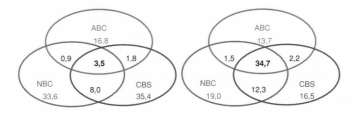

Issue diversity: channels in the United States (113 single events, unweighted versus weighted values)

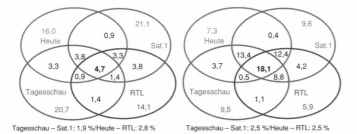

Tagesschau – Sat.1: 1,9 %/Heute – RTL: 2,8 %   Tagesschau – Sat.1: 2,5 %/Heute – RTL: 2,5 %

Issue diversity: channels in Germany (213 single events, unweighted versus weighted values)

Figure 12.5 National Issue Convergence in the United States and Germany (unweighted and weighted percentages, relations between areas not proportional)

shows: the number of common events was rather low, but their portion of the overall coverage was substantial. More than half of the news time included issues presented by at least three of the four German programs.

LESSONS LEARNED: ONE WORLD – DIFFERENT PICTURES?

Our comparison of main news programs from several European countries and the United States proved that, beyond rather similar visual formats, significant differences exist with regard to the issues and actors represented in news coverage. In this study, the fourfold model of news geography is neither valid in all nations, nor at all times. The data supported the fact that news centers play a dominant role in coverage. The Iraq crisis illustrates how the borderline between general and topical news neighbors can become blurred under certain political circumstances. News programs in all countries favor domestic events, but foreign news coverage consistently portrays countries from the news periphery. Indeed, the news selection process in newsrooms around the world is likely driven by an internalized schema that guarantees a certain quota of coverage of news from the periphery. This coverage does not only include catastrophes and disasters, as suggested by earlier research, but also contains "serious" political events. Furthermore the "domestication" of events is commonplace, but events are not always linked to the broadcasting country in our sample. In terms of actors, the emphasis in all countries is on coverage of politicians, with domestic politicians appearing most often on the screen. A main exception is globally important actors such as Bill Clinton or Saddam Hussein. Almost no events were covered by broadcasters in all nations, but selected events did obtain a substantial portion of overall coverage, due to their length. Nevertheless, we conclude that television news does not substantially contribute to the emergence of an integrated "transnational public."

Despite these conclusions about the nature of international news, additional research is needed.[9] Thus far, research on news factors, as one of the mid-range approaches in media effects theory, already includes aspects of news geography and actor representation. We may want to ask whether similarities and differences in the coverage in different countries is caused by the application of a common set of news factors (with varying results in selection), or if the set of news factors differs among nations and their news cultures.

Communication research thus far does not offer a sufficient theoretical framework to integrate the impact of differential coverage across countries into a general model. To create such a framework, we could imagine extending of the cultivation hypothesis: The description of news coverage in different countries can be perceived as a type of "message system analysis" (Shanahan and Morgan 1999). The variation in the selection of issues and actors represented in each country's coverage may lead to distinct perceptions of (political) reality in the respective country. For nonfictional news content, which aims at the construction of valid pictures of reality, the hypothesis of a mid-term and long-term cultivation of regional or topical stereotypes (independent from a certain news

---

[9] The limitations of our pilot study include (1) the short time period analyzed, making single events overly influential on the results; (2) the limited number of channels: not all channels in all countries could be considered; (3) the absence of other information programs and other media, which undoubtedly exert a strong influence on public opinion formation; and (4) the lack of data on the selection mechanisms in the newsrooms of our media outlets.

background) may form the basis for further comparative research on international television news.

REFERENCES

Bonfadelli, Heinz. 2000. *Medienwirkungsforschung II. Anwendungen in Politik, Wirtschaft und Kultur.* Konstanz, Germany: UVK Medien.

Cohen, Akiba A., Hanna Adoni, and Charles R. Bantz. 1990. *Social Conflict and Television News.* Newbury Park, CA: Sage.

Cooper Chen, Anne. 1989. Televised International News in Five Countries: Thoroughness, Insularity and Agenda Capacity. *International Communication Bulletin* 24 (1–2): 4–8.

Esser, Frank. 1998. Editorial Structures and Work Principles in British and German Newsrooms. *European Journal of Communication* 13 (3): 375–405.

Gans, Herbert J. 1979. *Deciding What's News. A Study of CBS Evening News, NBC Nightly News, Newsweek and Time.* New York: Pantheon.

Hagen, Lutz, Harald Berens, Reimar Zeh, and Daniela Leidner. 1998. Ländermerkmale als Nachrichtenfaktoren. Der Nachrichtenwert von Ländern und seine Determinanten in den Auslandsnachrichten von Zeitungen und Fernsehen aus 28 Ländern. In Christina Holtz-Bacha, Helmut Scherer, and Norbert Waldmann, eds. *Wie die Medien die Welt erschaffen und wie die Menschen darin leben.* Opladen, Germany: Westdeutscher Verlag, pp. 59–82.

Hajok, Daniel, and Bernd Schorb. 1998. Informationssendungen europäischer Fernsehanbieter in der Prime Time. *Media Perspektiven* 7: 331–6.

Heinderyckx, Francois. 1993. Television News Programmes in Western Europe: A Comparative Study. *European Journal of Communication* 8 (4): 425–50.

Iyengar, Shanto, and Donald Kinder. 1987. *News that Matters. Television and American Opinion.* Chicago: The University of Chicago Press.

Jarren, Otfried. 2000. Gesellschaftliche Integration durch Medien? Zur Begründung normativer Anforderungen an Medien. *Medien & Kommunikationswissenschaft* 48 (1): 22–41.

Jensen, Klaus Bruhn. 1998. *News of the World. World Cultures Look at Television News.* London: Routledge.

Kamps, Klaus. 1999. *Politik in Fernsehnachrichten. Struktur und Präsentation internationaler Ereignisse – ein Vergleich.* Baden-Baden: Nomos.

Lauf, Edmund, and Jochen Peter. 2001. Die Codierung verschiedensprachiger Inhalte. Erhebungskonzepte und Gütemasse. In Werner Wirth and Edmund Lauf, eds. *Inhaltsanalyse. Perspektiven, Probleme, Potentiale.* Köln, Germany: von Halem, pp. 199–217.

McQuail, Denis. 2000. *McQuails Mass Communication Theory.* 4th ed. London: Sage.

Meckel, Miriam. 1996. Informationsleistungen nationaler und internationaler Nachrichtensendungen: Anspruch und Wirklichkeit. In Peter Ludes, ed. *Informationskontexte für Massenmedien.* Opladen, Germany: Westdeutscher Verlag, pp. 187–211.

Merten, Klaus. 1995. *Inhaltsanalyse. Einführung in Theorie, Methode und Praxis.* 2nd ed. Opladen, Germany: Westdeutscher Verlag.

Newhagen, John, and Mark Levy. 1998. The Future of Journalism in a Distributed Communication Architecture. In Diane Borde and Kerric Harvey, eds. *The Electronic*

Grapevine: Rumor, Reputation and Reporting in the New On-Line Environment. Mahwah, NJ: Lawrence Erlbaum, pp. 9–21.

Nordenstreng, Karle, and Wolfgang Kleinwächter. 1989. The New International Information and Communications Order. In Molefi Kete Asante and William B. Gudykunst, eds. *Handbook of International and Intercultural Communication*. Newbury Park, CA: Sage, pp. 87–113.

Rössler, Patrick. 1999. The Individual Agenda-Designing Process. How Interpersonal Communication, Egocentric Networks and Mass Media Shape the Perception of Political Issues by Individuals. *Communication Research* 26 (6): 666–700.

————. 2000. Vielzahl = Vielfalt = Fragmentierung? Empirische Anhaltspunkte zur Differenzierung von Medienangeboten auf der Mikroebene. In Otfried Jarren, Kurt Imhof, and Roger Blum, eds. *Zerfall der Öffentlichkeit?* Opladen, Germany: Westdeutscher Verlag, pp. 168–86.

————. 2001. Visuelle Codierung und Vielfalts-Analysen auf Mikroebene. Kategorisierungs- und Auswertungsstrategien für die ikonographische Untersuchung journalistischer Berichterstattung. In Werner Wirth and Edmund Lauf, eds. *Inhaltsanalyse. Perspektiven, Probleme, Potentiale*. Köln, Germany: von Halem, pp. 140–56.

————. 2002. Viele Programme, dieselben Themen? Vielfalt und Fragmentierung, Teil 2: Konvergenz und Divergenz in der aktuellen Berichterstattung – eine Inhaltsanalyse internationaler TV-Nachrichten auf der Mikroebene. In Kurt Imhof, Otfried Jarren, and Roger Blum, eds. *Integration und Medien*. Opladen, Germany: Westdeutscher Verlag, pp. 148–67.

Schaap, Gabi, Karsten Renckstorf, and Fred Wester. 1998. Three Decades of Television News Research: An Actional Theoretical Inventory of Issues and Problems. *Communications* 23 (3): 351–82.

Schulz, Winfried. 1983. Nachrichtengeographie. Untersuchungen über die Struktur der internationalen Berichterstattung. In Manfred Rühl and Heinz-Werner Stuiber, eds. *Kommunikationspolitik in Forschung und Anwendung. Festschrift für Franz Ronneberger*. Düsseldorf, Germany: Droste, pp. 281–91.

Shanahan, James, and Michael Morgan. 1999. *Television and its Viewers. Cultivation Theory and Research*. Cambridge: Cambridge University Press.

Shaw, Martin. 1997. The Theoretical Challenge of Global Society. In Annabelle Sreberny-Mohammadi, Dwayne Winseck, Jim McKenna, and Oliver Boyd-Barrett, eds. *Media in Global Context. A Reader*. London: Arnold, pp. 27–36.

Sreberny-Mohammadi, Annabelle. 1991. The Global and the Local in International Communications. In James Curran and Michael Gurevitch, eds. *Mass Media and Society*. London: Arnold, pp. 118–38.

Sreberny-Mohammadi, Annabelle, Karle Nordenstreng, Robert Stevenson, and Frank Ugboajah. 1985. *Foreign News in the Media: International Reporting in 29 Countries*. Paris: UNESCO.

Stevenson, Robert. 1985. Other Research and the World of the News. In Annabelle Sreberny-Mohammadi et al., eds. *Foreign News in the Media: International Reporting in 29 Countries*. Paris: UNESCO, pp. 71–80 (Appendix 5).

————. 2003. Mapping the News of the World. In Brenda Dervin and Steven H. Chaffee, eds. *Communication, a Different Kind of Horse Race: Essays Honoring Richard F. Carter*. Cresskill, NJ: Hampton Press, pp. 149–65.

Stevenson, Robert, and Richard R. Cole. 1984. Patterns of Foreign News. In Robert Stevenson and Donald Shaw, eds. *Foreign News and the New World Information Order.* Ames: The Iowa State University Press, pp. 37–62.

Stevenson, Robert, and Gary D. Gaddy. 1984. "Bad News" and the Third World. In Robert Stevenson and Donald Shaw, eds. *Foreign News and the New World Information Order.* Ames: The Iowa State University Press, pp. 88–97.

Straubhaar, Joseph, Carrie Heeter, Bradley Greenberg, Leonardo Ferreira, Robert Wicks, and Tuen-Yu Lau. 1992. What Makes News. Western, Socialist, and Third-World Television Newscasts Compared in Eight Countries. In Felipe Korzenny and Stella Ting-Toomey, eds. *Mass Media Effects Across Cultures.* Newbury Park, CA: Sage, pp. 89–109.

Wanta, Wayne, and Yu-Wei Hu. 1993. The Agenda-Setting Effects of International News Coverage: An Examination of Different News Frames. *International Journal of Public Opinion Research* 5 (3): 250–64.

Wu, Denis. 2000. Systemic Determinants of International News Coverage: A Comparison of 38 Countries. *Journal of Communication* 50 (2): 110–30.

Zillman, Dolf, K. Taylor, and K. Lewis. 1998. News as Nonfiction Theater: How Dispositions Toward the Public Cast of Characters Affect Reactions. *Journal of Broadcasting & Electronic Media* 42 (2): 153–69.

THIRTEEN

Political Communication Effects

The Impact of Mass Media and Personal Conversations on Voting

Rüdiger Schmitt-Beck

In recent years there has been a revived interest in the question of whether the media can not only inform, but also persuade their audiences. Opinions, attitudes, and even behavior are no longer believed to be totally immune from media influences (Page et al. 1987; Ansolabehere et al. 1993; Bartels 1993; Kepplinger et al. 1994; Joslyn and Ceccoli 1996; Zaller 1996; Dalton et al. 1998; Kinder 1998; Schmitt-Beck 2000; Denemark 2002; Farrell and Schmitt-Beck 2002). This chapter will discuss this theme in comparative perspective, with a particular focus on voting decisions.[1] Two different angles of comparison will be applied. One concerns differences and similarities between various countries and societies. As Blumler and Gurevitch note, inspecting political communication in more than one systemic context can serve as an "essential antidote" against ethnocentrism and premature generalizations (Gurevitch and Blumler 1990, 308–9). The empirical basis for analytical statements is extended, and above all it becomes clear to what extent observed relationships are tied to specific settings and contexts (Dogan and Pelassy 1984, 5–19; Kohn 1989, 21–2).

Another dimension of comparison concerns different modes of political communication. Voters not only participate in processes of mass communication, thus opening up avenues for media influence; to varying degrees, they also talk to other people and discuss political matters. The messages they receive during such conversations may also influence their attitudes and behavioral intentions (Huckfeldt and Sprague 1995). As a consequence, it may be asked which form of political communication – mass communication or interpersonal communication – is more important with regard to the formation and change of political orientations.

[1] The chapter profited much from helpful comments by David Farrell.

Logically such a comparison between different modes of communication is equivalent to a comparison of the role of the same type of communication across countries or societies (van Deth 1995). By comparing the influences of mass communication and interpersonal communication the study reconsiders a theme that was already discussed in the classic studies of the Columbia school of social research (Lazarsfeld et al. 1944; Katz and Lazarsfeld 1955), but rarely subjected to stringent empirical scrutiny, least of all comparative scrutiny.

The next section will discuss these two types of comparison in more detail. Taking into account the problems of conceptualization and measurement raised by the two comparative research problems dealt with in this chapter, the subsequent section will outline a strategy of analysis. The final section presents the findings of empirical analyses. Using cross-nationally comparable surveys of voters the study investigates how individual voting decisions are influenced by the voters' exposure both to the mass media's political reporting and to political conversations in their everyday lives, and how these patterns vary in five societies: Britain, East Germany, West Germany, Spain, and the United States.

TWO COMPARATIVE RESEARCH QUESTIONS

COMPARING SOCIETIES

Societies differ in many respects. One of these is the degree of change in electoral behavior, which is manifest in smaller or larger shifts in the parties' or candidates' vote shares at elections. Table 13.1 provides an example. Based on the well-known Pedersen Index of electoral volatility (Pedersen 1990), the table displays the average aggregate vote shifts for all elections since 1960 in Britain, East Germany, West Germany, Spain, and the United States,[2] revealing huge differences across these five cases. The index values are on the relatively low side in West Germany and Britain over the past four decades (ranging from 6 to 7 percent), whereas they are much higher – in fact nearly twice as high – in the other three cases.

How can these differences be explained? Following a simple model proposed by Converse election results can be decomposed into two components (Converse 1966; Zaller 1992). The first is a baseline determined by the distribution of core political predispositions within a given society.

---

[2] In Spain and East Germany only democratic elections, that is, since 1977 in Spain, since 1990 in East Germany.

Table 13.1 Electoral Volatility in Five Societies (1960–2001)

Britain	West Germany	East Germany	Spain	United States
6.8	6.2	13.4	13.0	12.0

Basic predispositions, such as partisanship, ideology, and social group identifications, are ingrained in citizens' minds by processes of early socialization. These define a basic distribution of electoral preferences that is highly stable, with any change tending to occur only in the course of generational succession. The second component of the model consists of short-term oscillations around this baseline. These fluctuations are the consequence of responses by voters to political information that reaches them through processes of political communication. The information component in political decision making is the necessary precondition for any short-term or medium-term change of political preferences within societies. Hence, in this model political predispositions represent a static component of inertia and continuity, while political information, conveyed through political communication, and received and processed by voters, is the source of electoral dynamics. Were voters never reached and influenced by new information, election results would invariably mirror the baseline distribution of traditional political loyalties.

According to this view, the information conveyed through processes of political communication is crucial for any electoral change. If this assumption about the relationship between the intensity and nature of societal flows of political information and electoral volatility is correct, the differences displayed in Table 13.1 should correspond to similar differences with regard to the importance of political communications for electoral behavior in these societies.

In this chapter this proposition is explored by means of comparative analyses. To develop a research strategy for testing this proposition empirically, a theory of political influence is needed, where "influence" means that in response to information a person acts differently than he or she would have were they not exposed to this information (Dahl 1957, 202–4; Chaffee and Mutz 1988, 30). Such theoretical guidance can be derived from the Receive-Accept-Sample (RAS) model of political influence (Zaller 1992, 1996). According to this model, political decisions come about as the result of a succession of distinct steps. The first step is the reception of some information by an individual, where it is crucial that this information bears some evaluative content – favorable or unfavorable – about the political object, say, a political party or candidate, to which the decision refers. Some, but not all recipients of such persuasive messages will accept them as valid statements about this attitude object. The recipients' political predispositions filter the received information and induce some selectivity in the acceptance process. Once accepted, the persuasive messages are stored in recipients' long-term memories. In subsequent decision situations regarding the attitude object, such as an election, individuals will sample some of these considerations from their memories, and use them as reasons for deciding one way or the other. The outcome of the decision depends on the specific mix of retrieved considerations with regard to their evaluative content. The latter is subject to the composition of all considerations that are stored, and in principle available, for such retrieval within one's memory, as well as on cues emerging from the specific circumstances of the situation.

According to this model, political information may be influential, and thus relevant for the outcome of decisions, if it carries evaluative content. Both the amount and the directional composition of the evaluative information to which an individual is exposed are crucial for the extent and direction of its influence. Following the RAS model, persuasion by political communication cannot be expected to come about in reaction to one or even a few particularly effective messages. Editorial endorsements are not likely to be very effective in this regard, and neither is an occasional chat about a party or a candidate. Only by means of the cumulative effect of a larger number of evaluative messages, disseminated, received, and accepted over a protracted period of time, can media reporting and political conversations gain a potential to influence voting decisions. Similarly, under this perspective media or discussant influence on voting behavior takes the form not of a punctuated conversion, but of a gradual shifting of the probability of a particular choice at an election, caused by the continuous reception of a steady stream of persuasive messages that on the whole are rather favorable to a particular alternative.

COMPARING MODES OF POLITICAL COMMUNICATION

There is no denying that for citizens the mass media are an important source of political information. But they are not their only source. Political messages also reach voters during the conversations in which most people engage more or less regularly with members of their primary environments. Spouses, relatives, friends, co-workers, neighbors, and other persons with whom they interact in everyday life are all potential sources of politically influential information. However, it is not clear which of the two sources of information – mass communication or interpersonal communication – is more important with regard to political persuasion. Beginning with Lazarsfeld's Erie County and Decatur studies, many authors have maintained that political discussion is the stronger – or even the only relevant – force in the process of political influence (Lazarsfeld et al. 1944; Katz and Lazarsfeld 1955; Chaffee 1972, 1986; Chaffee and Mutz 1988).

Summarizing their findings, Katz and Lazarsfeld noted that "the effect of the mass media was small as compared to the role of personal influences" (Katz and Lazarsfeld 1955, 3). However, only indirect evidence and inductive reasoning could be referred to in support of this claim. In addition, this proposition dates from pretelevision times. Media systems and media usage have undergone striking transformations since then. The assumption that political conversations are more influential than watching the news or reading a newspaper lacks sufficient empirical support and cannot be taken as a proven fact. In fact, surprising as this may appear, there are few studies that have attempted to analyze both mass communication and interpersonal communication simultaneously (cf., e.g., Robinson 1976; Lenart 1994). One of the main reasons for this unsatisfactory state of affairs is the theoretical fragmentation of political communication research. "Communication theory lacks integration. Today there is one set of theories for interpersonal communication, and a different set of theories for mass media communication" (Reardon and Rogers 1988, 295).

Without a model that is similarly applicable to both types of political communication, no theoretical guidance is available for a systematic comparison of mass communication and interpersonal communication. Fortunately, the RAS model is general enough to allow for the necessary theoretical integration. As a general theory of political influence, it allows for the development of a research strategy to study simultaneously the influence of both modes of political communication on voters' political decisions.

In the remainder of this chapter, I will concentrate on two research questions:

(1) Is the importance of political communication for voting behavior higher in societies that are characterized by higher levels of electoral volatility, and lower in societies characterized by lower levels of electoral volatility?

RÜDIGER SCHMITT-BECK

(2) Does mass communication have an impact on electoral behavior, and/or does interpersonal communication have an impact on electoral behavior? If so, which of the two types of political communication is more influential?

These questions involve different forms of comparison. Question 1 requires a comparison *between societies* with regard to the relevance of political communication in general for electoral behavior. Question 2 aims at a comparison *between two forms of political communication* with regard to their importance in influencing electors' choices. In addition, both questions need to be combined, because it is of interest whether the relationship between mass communication and interpersonal communication is the same or differs across the various societies.

CONCEPTUAL CONSIDERATIONS AND THE LOGIC OF COMPARISON

The starting point in this chapter was the highly abstract notion of societal information flows through processes of political communication. One step down the "ladder of abstraction" (Sartori 1970) and thus somewhat less general is the distinction between political information flows that originate from the mass media or from individuals (Figure 13.1; cf. Schmitt-Beck 1998). Mass communication involves information that is produced by media organizations and disseminated by means of technical carriers to audiences that are potentially unlimited, heterogeneous, and anonymous to the producers of the messages. It is predominantly unidirectional, because the audience has only limited possibilities to respond to the media's messages. In contrast, interpersonal communication is typically not public but private, and it involves only a small number of participants, often not more than two. It is unmediated and bidirectional, and it usually takes the form of personal conversations (Rogers 1973).

For the purpose of comparing mass communication and interpersonal communication with regard to their influence on voting, this level of abstraction may still be too general. As Zukin notes, "all media are not created equal" (1977, 245). The general concept of mass media is a "catch-all term" (Semetko 1996, 255), and may mask differences between various media that are of key importance for their persuasive potential. They should, therefore, be taken into account when trying to analyze the media's political influences. Similarly, Knoke maintains that the general

298

POLITICAL COMMUNICATION IN GENERAL

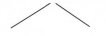

FIRST STEP OF SPECIFICATION
BY TYPE OF POLITICAL COMMUNICATION

Mass communication:

- Number of habitually used media
- Frequency of usage of each of these media

Interpersonal communication:

- Number of political discussants
- Frequency of political conversations with each of these discussants

SECOND STEP OF SPECIFICATION
BY QUALITATIVE ATTRIBUTES OF COMMUNICATION CHANNELS
AND SOURCES

Media formats:

- Type of medium (print vs. television)
- Factual reporting (daily newspapers, television news) vs. opinionated presentation of politics (magazines, talk shows)
- For factual reporting: information quality (quality press vs. 'middle market press' vs. tabloids; news of public broadcasters vs. news of private broadcasters)

Role relationships:

- Primary relationships vs. secondary relationships
- For primary relationships: spouses vs. relatives vs. friends
- For secondary relationships: co-workers vs. neighbors vs. acquaintances from clubs and churches vs. other relationships

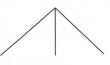

THIRD STEP OF SPECIFICATION
BY POLITICAL DIRECTIONS OF MESSAGES

Political directions of media (content analyses and audience perceptions):
Pro vs. contra party or candidate 1,
Pro vs. contra party or candidate 2, etc.

Political preferences of discussants (perceptions of respondents):
Pro vs. contra party or candidate 1,
Pro vs. contra party or candidate 2, etc.

Figure 13.1 Reception of Political Information: Dimensions of Operationalization

notion of interpersonal communication may be too unspecific to allow for meaningful analyses of phenomena of persuasion through political discussion (Knoke 1990, 33–4). Apparently, the concepts of mass communication and interpersonal communication are still too general. More specification is needed, and it can be attained by moving further down the ladder of abstraction.

However, this descent should stop short of the level of "proper names" (Przeworski and Teune 1970). For obvious reasons this must in any case apply to studies of interpersonal communication: Social scientists are not interested in particular individuals. When it comes to analyses of media effects, this is even more complex. Under certain conditions studies of the relationship between particular newspapers or television programs and their audience's political behavior may make sense, for instance if we are interested in explaining the outcomes of specific elections. A notable example is Curtice's (1997) study of the influence of the British tabloid *Sun* on its readers' party preferences in the 1990s. However, such case studies lack generalizability and have no clear implications for research interested in the general mechanisms and regularities of media influence on political behavior. Comparative studies in particular must take note of the fact that – with the exception of transnational media such as the *International Herald Tribune* or CNN – the media are national institutions. Hence, in order to become cross-nationally comparable, their "proper names" must be substituted by variables, that is, dimensions with a well-defined range of attributes (Przeworski and Teune 1970).

Cross-national studies of media influence are by definition multilevel analyses, because they are inquiries into the relationships between individuals and specific aspects of their social contexts, namely the institutions of mass communication (van Deth 1995). To allow for meaningful cross-national statements about their importance for political behavior, they must be carefully conceptualized in theoretical terms. The concepts used must be abstract enough to "travel" between various national contexts, that is, they must be so general as to allow for the classification of media from diverse contexts into a common conceptual framework. Otherwise they would not be comparable, and there would be no basis for genuine comparative analysis.

To determine the appropriate level of abstraction for our comparative study of persuasive communication two dimensions must be taken into account for both mass communication and interpersonal communication. Choosing a more general level of analysis would entail the risk that communication influences would become empirically blurred and remain undetected, even if genuine.

One dimension concerns *qualitative attributes* of communication channels beyond the general distinction between communication originating from mass media and communication originating from other people. Perhaps some channels with particular attributes are more influential than others. If so, chances to observe effects are enhanced by distinguishing analytically between these attributes.

In the case of the mass media we may think of various "media formats" (Altheide and Snow 1988). Often it is assumed that because of its vividness television has a higher capacity to influence its audience than the "dry" press (Noelle-Neumann 1979). In addition to the rather general differentiation between audiovisual and print media it is possible to draw some further distinctions. One concerns the difference between media whose political reporting is rather factual and those whose presentation of politics is more opinionated. While daily newspapers and television news are of the more factual type, magazines typically offer more space for opinions. Perhaps media outlets with a special emphasis on opinion are more persuasive than news seeking to concentrate on the "plain facts."

In addition, news media can be further distinguished by their information quality, that is, the amount and complexity of the information they convey (Kleinnijenhuis 1991). With regard to the press there is the common threefold distinction between the quality press on the one hand, tabloids on the other, and the "middle-market" press in between. In the case of television, the news programs of public broadcasters can be contrasted to those of private stations. While the former tend to present politics in a more serious fashion, the latter are characterized by a stronger emphasis on "infotainment" (Pfetsch 1996). Previous research has shown that with regard to knowledge gain, these differences are crucial. People tend to learn more about politics from media of higher information quality (Schmitt-Beck 1998). Perhaps these different styles of presenting the political world are also important moderators of persuasive media effects.

A qualitative distinction that may be relevant with regard to the impact of political conversations concerns the roles within which people interact with each other. In particular it has been assumed that the distinction between "strong" primary relationships and "weak" secondary relationships mediates the effects of interpersonal exchange (Schenk 1989). The early studies of personal influence focused on primary groups and tended to ignore secondary relationships altogether (Katz and Lazarsfeld 1955; McClosky and Dahlgren 1959). In recent years, authors such as Huckfeldt and Sprague emphasized that secondary relationships may also be important sources of political influence (1995).

Further differences within these two more general categories may also be relevant. Relationships between spouses, relatives, and friends are all of a more or less intimate kind, but nonetheless they may not all be similarly influential when it comes to the effects of political discussion on political behavior. Similarly, with regard to secondary relationships, the distinction between, for instance, neighbors and co-workers may also be relevant (Simon 1976).

Communication effects can be hard to detect if such mediating attributes of the channels or sources of communications are overlooked and not specified with sufficient precision. A further dimension of differentiation concerns the *political direction* of the communicated messages. According to the RAS model, political persuasion is a consequence of the reception of messages that carry evaluative content. Only one-sided information can be expected to lead to persuasion. Thus, what is crucial about the messages a person receives is the degree to which they favor one party or candidate over the others. In trying to identify communication influences this gives rise to the methodological problem of mutual cancellation. The mass media may differ considerably with regard to the political tone of their reporting. Media audiences are therefore usually exposed to information flows consisting of many competing voices. The same applies for people discussing political matters with associates of different sympathies and positions on parties, candidates, or issues.

Failing to take this into account may produce misleading findings because, due to mutual neutralization, influences in opposing directions remain invisible. In order to solve this problem it is necessary to identify "influence gaps whereby individuals receive and accept messages from one campaign but not from the other" (Zaller 1996, 42). Political information flows must be decomposed according to their political direction. With regard to mass media this can be accomplished by distinguishing media of different political tendencies. Similarly, concerning political conversations, discussants need to be distinguished according to the different parties or candidates they support. All of these dimensions need to be taken into account when developing a strategy for operationalizing the key independent variables for the analysis of communication effects.

DATA AND VARIABLES

This study is based on a unique collection of cross-nationally comparable surveys of voters, conducted during the early 1990s in four Western democracies, on the occasion of national elections: Britain (1992 parliamentary election); Germany, with independent samples of East and West Germans (1990 parliamentary election); Spain (1993 parliamentary election); and the United States (1992 presidential election).[3] Representative random samples of the voting-age population were probed for their political communication habits and electoral preferences.

The dependent variables of the analyses reported in this section are voting decisions. Both multinomial and binary logistic regression analysis are used to estimate the effects of political communication on these decisions. Multinomial models are applied to get an impression of the overall importance of blocks of variables for voting decisions in general within each of the five societies. Binary analyses are used to model voting decisions for or against particular parties or candidates. For each party in the European cases a dichotomous variable was constructed, indicating whether a respondent chose this party or any of the competing parties. The same procedure was applied with regard to candidate choices in the United States. Nonvoters were excluded.

Strictly speaking, the approach of this study is static. Given the interest in the importance of political information for electoral volatility, a dynamic perspective focusing on changes in political preferences between two elections would be clearly more appropriate. Panel data linking two consecutive elections would be ideal for such an approach. Unfortunately, only cross-sectional data are available for the present analysis.[4] Thus, the story told by the analyses in this chapter is whether long-term exposure to political communication may be consequential for political behavior, allowing also for the possibility that this behavior may be

---

[3] Data were collected by national project teams cooperating in the Comparative National Elections Project (CNEP). The British CNEP survey was conducted as a postelection survey in the context of the British Election Study 1992 (ESRC archive no. 2981; N = 2,855, weighted to correct for oversampling in Scotland); principal researchers were John Curtice, Anthony Heath, and Roger Jowell. Principal researchers of the German project were Max Kaase, Hans-Dieter Klingemann, Manfred Kuechler, and Franz Urban Pappi; the project was directed by Rüdiger Schmitt-Beck. The survey (ZA archive no. 2517) was realized by means of personal face-to-face preelection interviews (N = 1,340). The analyses for Spain are mostly based on data collected in the second wave of a two-wave panel survey (face-to-face; N = 1,448 and N = 1,374, for the first [preelection] and second [postelection] waves respectively). The Spanish project was directed by Richard Gunther, Franceso Llera, José Ramón Montero, and Francesc Pallarès. In the United States the CNEP survey (ICPSR archive no. 6541) was conducted as a postelection survey (CATI; N = 1,318). Principal researchers were Paul Allen Beck, Russell J. Dalton, and Robert Huckfeldt. The author wishes to thank these colleagues for allowing him to use their data for the analyses presented in this paper.

[4] Given the cross-sectional design of the surveys, a dynamic analysis could be applied only by relying on a comparison of present preferences with vote recall. However, recall data are typically biased toward the present preference to a degree that such an approach would by necessity produce results of very dubious validity (cf. Weir 1975).

stable and not changing over time. In other words, the analysis indicates if, and to what extent, electoral choices at a given point in time can be attributed to political communication, and whether there are variations across countries and between modes of communication.

The regression models include three blocks of independent variables. Both to take care of the partial dependence of the political coloring of voters' personal environments on their political predispositions (Rogers and Bhowmik 1970), and to control for the possibility that voters let themselves be guided by these predispositions when deciding which mass media to use (Klapper 1960), a broad array of political predispositions is taken into account. These include partisanship, cultural predispositions (ideological identifications, value orientations), and social-structural predispositions (class, affiliation to trade unions, religious denomination, affiliation to churches; for U.S. voters also region and race [cf., e.g., Lipset and Rokkan 1967; Conover 1984; Erikson et al. 1989; Inglehart 1990; Richardson 1991; Listhaug et al. 1994; Miller and Shanks 1996; Levine et al. 1997]).

The second and third blocks of independent variables consist of detailed measures of respondents' exposure to mass communication and to interpersonal communication. As discussed previously, the RAS model requires measures that register the habitual reception of political information (Zaller 1992). Because information reception cannot be measured directly with survey data, exposure to information through mass communication and interpersonal communication is used instead. The exposure measures serve as proxies for the number of – potentially influential – persuasive messages received by the voters. The more frequently voters expose themselves to political communications, the more messages they are likely to receive. To operationalize respondents' exposure to mass communication and interpersonal communication, measures need not be identical. In fact, it is hard to see how they can be identical, given the differences between these two forms of communication. However, measures need to be equivalent in registering the typical aspects of each form of communication in a valid way (Chaffee and Mutz 1988).

In the surveys used, media exposure was registered in an unusually fine-grained fashion, by means of open-ended questions for up to two newspapers read, and by means of closed, though highly specific, questions for the main television news programs watched. Exposure to magazines was measured by somewhat simpler instruments. On the whole, the surveys delivered very detailed data on respondents' usage of a broad array of mass media: daily newspapers, weekly newsmagazines, television news programs, television magazines, and – only in the United States – television talk shows. Characteristic features of respondents' participation in processes of interpersonal communication were explored by means of detailed questions on their ego-centered networks (Burt 1984), including up to five *alteri* in Germany and the United States, and up to three in the other countries.

The frequency of media exposure was measured in days per week for daily newspapers and television news programs, with the exception of Britain where a less fine-grained scale was used (ranging from 0 to 4). For magazine formats both in print and on television, a scale ranging from 0 = "no exposure" to 3 = "regular exposure" was used. The same scale was used to register the intensity of political discussion between respondents and each of their network associates. In addition, the network questions also probed the role relationships between the respondents and each of their *alteri*, as well as their perceptions of the *alteri's* voting intentions.

The amount of potentially influential information obtained by a voter through mass communication is a function of both the *number of media* used, and the *frequency* with which each of them is used. Hence, the more media one attends to, and the higher the frequency of the usage of each, the stronger their influence on a recipients' voting decision can be expected to be (see Figure 13.1). Analogous to this, the number of persuasive messages received through interpersonal communication is determined by the *number of other persons* with whom one discusses politics, and the *frequency* of such conversations with each discussant. The more associates one talks to and the more often this occurs, the more information is obtained, and accordingly the greater the expected influence on voting decisions.

However, as discussed in the previous section, such pure exposure measures cannot be expected to deliver an unveiled view on communication effects. They can only serve as a starting point. In addition to the mere extent of exposure to mass communication and interpersonal communication, we must also take into account qualitative attributes of the various sources and channels of information, as well as the direction of the political messages they convey. To classify the mass media by formats, descriptive studies of national media systems prove helpful (e.g., Østergaard 1997; Gunther and Mughan 2000; for details cf. Schmitt-Beck 2000, 182–95). The role relationships between respondents and their discussants were registered directly in the surveys.

Apart from these qualitative attributes of sources and channels, the political direction of the conveyed messages is also crucial. Indications of the media's political leaning can be obtained from content analyses and from the perceptions of these media's audiences. Of course, as party media are no longer important in most Western democracies, and most media subscribe to the principle of objective reporting, clear-cut partisanship is likely to be an exception rather than the norm. Still, if significant segments of the audience of a newspaper or a television channel believe that this medium favored a particular party or candidate in its reporting, one may conclude that some degree of political one-sidedness is present. Correspondingly, content analyses confirm that not all parties or candidates are portrayed similarly in all media (cf. Schmitt-Beck 2000, 236–55; 2003). At closer inspection, an important difference between European and American media becomes obvious. European newspapers and to some degree also television stations are characterized by clear alignments along the left-right axis of party-political conflict. In contrast, as Page et al. observed, American media "are very much of a piece. They all tend to report the same kinds of messages. [. . .] [T]he contents of one medium is a good indicator of the content of many media" (Page et al. 1987, 39). During the 1992 campaign in most media the Democratic candidate Bill Clinton was portrayed more positively than his competitors. On the whole, the pattern of reporting of American media is indicative of a clear "structural bias," while European media appear more characterized by varying "political biases" (Hofstetter 1976).

What follows from these findings is that European and American media should be treated differently when constructing the exposure measures for the regression analyses. In the European countries the danger of mutual cancellation of opposing influences can be avoided only by distinguishing as far as possible between specific newspapers and single broadcasters when measuring respondents' media exposure. Only in some cases, where methodological reasons left no alternative, are media classified into summary categories.[5] These summary categories are then constructed according to the qualitative dimensions (media formats) previously discussed. In contrast, the American media can be generally combined into broader categories, distinguishing media only by formats. As a rule, if respondents used several media of the same format,

---

[5] The reasons for subsuming media to summary categories were high correlations of exposure measures for various news magazines (West Germany); no distinction between specific news magazines, television magazines, and talk shows in survey questions (Spain, United States); and too small numbers of cases for readers of specific newspapers (regional press in general, West German quality press and tabloids). Newspapers were combined with others if they were read by less than twenty respondents.

the respective frequencies of exposure are combined into an additive index. For instance, if an American respondent habitually read two quality papers, say the *Washington Post* on a daily basis and the *New York Times* on Sundays, he or she is assigned a value of 8 (7 + 1) on the index of exposure to the quality press.

Effects of media exposure on voting are expected to be in line with the political leanings of the various media, but perhaps moderated by the format properties of these media. Television may be expected to exert stronger influences than the press. Media with an emphasis on opinion should be more influential than media with a more factual style of presenting politics. And media of higher information quality should be more influential than media of lower information quality. If measures of media exposure, controlling for political predispositions (and exposure to interpersonal communication), reveal statistically significant effects on voting decisions, indicating that the likelihood of preferring a particular party or candidate varied with the amount of information respondents received from particular media, it can be concluded that these media exerted a positive or negative influence on the vote.

Because the content of political conversations is impossible to measure directly in survey-based studies, respondents' perceptions of their discussants' party-political leaning are used as a surrogate indicator. Respondents infer their discussants' political leaning usually from the content of their statements during political conversations, so this proxy measure for unobservable actual communication content should be sufficiently valid. For each of the various parties or candidates, binary regression models and for all types of role relationships, specific indices of exposure to interpersonal communication are constructed that are based on the same dichotomization of discussants' partisanship as the dependent variable. This means that for each model discussants who were supporters of the respective parties or candidates (pro) were distinguished from supporters of any of the other parties or candidates (contra). The multinomial models contain all provariables, but no contravariables.

The final indices of exposure to interpersonal communication that are entered in the regression analyses are constructed by summarizing the frequency of political discussions across all *alteri* of the same role relationship and the same party or candidate preference. Take the example of the models estimating communication effects on the vote for or against Bill Clinton in 1992: If a respondent named one relative with whom he talked from time to time, but not regularly, about politics and whom he perceived to be a supporter of Bill Clinton, an index value of 2 is assigned for exposure to political conversations with relatives supporting Clinton (pro). If the same respondent named two other relatives who were sympathizers of either George Bush or Ross Perot, and with each of whom he discussed political matters regularly, the corresponding index of exposure to interpersonal communication with relatives supporting candidates other than Clinton (contra) is assigned a value of 6. Similar indices are constructed for spouses, friends, and other types of relationships.

Effects of exposure to political discussions on voting are expected that are in line with the perceived political preferences of the discussants, but perhaps not similarly strong for all kinds of role relationships between respondents and discussants. Within primary relationships political discussions may be particularly influential. And perhaps there are also differences between various kinds of relationships. For instance, because of the particularly intimate character of their relationship, spouses may be expected to be particularly influential. If indices of exposure to interpersonal communication, again controlling for political predispositions (and exposure to mass communication), reveal statistically significant effects on voting decisions, indicating that the likelihood of preferring a particular party or candidate varied with the amount of information respondents received during political conversations with other people, it can be concluded that these communications exerted a positive or negative influence on the vote.

FINDINGS

Despite the high specifity of the communication variables in the models the main focus of my analyses is on fairly global comparisons. Nonetheless, it is essential to work with such fine-grained measures of communication exposure, since, as discussed previously, otherwise it would be unlikely for patterns of influence on voting decisions to become manifest. Accordingly, in the following I will restrict myself mostly to inspections of goodness-of-fit measures that capture the global importance of whole sets of variables. The indicator used for that purpose is a modified version of McFadden's Pseudo-R^2 that adjusts for the variable number of parameters in the equations and thus allows for more precise comparisons (cf. Andress et al. 1997).

I start my analysis with a global view of the importance of political communication for voting behavior in each of the five societies. The

Table 13.2 Global Explanatory Power of Mass Communication and Interpersonal Communication for Voting Decisions (Adjusted Pseudo-R^2 from multinomial logistic regression analyses)

	(M+D)|P	M|(P+D)	D|(P+M)
Britain (N_{min}=1,803)	.030**	.007**	.019**
West Germany (N_{min}=781)	.079**	.044**	.034**
East Germany (N_{min}=424)	.141**	.023**	.128**
Spain (N_{min}=928)	.119**	.029**	.082**
United States (N_{min}=929)	.191**	.005*	.182**

**$P < .01$, *$P < .05$

Note: (M+D)|P   Interpersonal communication and mass communication, controlling for political predispositions. M|(P+D) Mass communication, controlling for political predispositions and interpersonal communication. D|(P+M) Interpersonal communication, controlling for political predispositions and mass communication.

left column of Table 13.2 is based on multinomial regression models and displays the combined explanatory power of all communication variables on voting behavior in each of the five societies.[6] The displayed values are increments, indicating the difference in explanatory power between restricted reference models including only political predispositions, and full models including also the entire range of communication variables. The significance of these incremental differences is evaluated by means of likelihood ratio tests. In all five societies, knowledge of voters' exposure to political communications increases significantly one's ability to predict their voting decision, over and beyond the explanatory contribution of a broad range of political predispositions, including structural, cultural, and party-political identifications. With an incremental Pseudo-R^2 of almost .20, the largest contribution of communication variables is to be found in the United States. In East Germany and Spain, the importance of political communication for electoral behavior is also remarkably high, well over .10. In contrast, the contribution of communication variables to predicting voting decisions is far lower in the remaining two societies, Britain and West Germany. On the whole, across all five societies, the pattern pertaining to the explanatory power of societal information flows

---

[6] Categories of the dependent variables–Britain: Conservatives, Labour Party, Liberal Democrats, other parties; West and East Germany: CDU[/CSU], SPD, FDP, Greens; Spain: PSOE, PP, IU, other parties; United States: Clinton, Bush, Perot.

for electoral behavior nicely matches the pattern for electoral volatility displayed in Table 13.1.

Next, I am interested in the independent contributions of mass communication and interpersonal communication to predicting voting decisions. Because both modes of political communication may be correlated, a stringent comparison requires that the contribution of each type is estimated while controlling for the other mode. The findings of these analyses are displayed in the remaining columns of Table 13.2. The second column shows the incremental goodness-of-fit values for mass communication, over and above the combined impact of political predispositions and interpersonal communication. Column three contains the corresponding values for interpersonal communication. They are, again, based on multinomial logistic regression models.

In four of the five societies, voters' engagement in political discussions had more sizable consequences for their voting decisions than their exposure to mass media. In the United States the impact gap between mass communication and interpersonal communication appears especially large, but in Spain and East Germany it is also substantial. In Britain, both forms of political communication do not seem to have been very relevant for electoral behavior. However, in direct comparison, political conversations again appear more consequential. These findings support the common assumption, initially formulated by Lazarsfeld and his colleagues, that the informal political exchange between voters in their everyday life world has a higher capacity to influence their votes than the mass media. Yet, this rule does not seem to be universal: West German voting behavior was influenced more by the mass media than by political discussions. On the whole, however, the analysis suggests that in comparison to mass communication, interpersonal communication is indeed the stronger force when it comes to influencing decisions at national elections.

A closer look at the decisions for or against particular parties or candidates by means of binary regression analyses reveals the same basic pattern, but with interesting details. Table 13.3 is constructed analogous to Table 13.2. These findings suggest that within societies the importance of political communications in general, and of mass communication and interpersonal communication in particular, is not necessarily the same for all parties or candidates. Particularly striking is that in West Germany media exposure is clearly more important than political conversations only with regard to voting for one of the two small parties: the liberal FDP and the Greens. However, on the whole – including the

Table 13.3 Explanatory Power of Mass Communication and Interpersonal Communication for Specific Voting Decisions (adjusted Pseudo-R^2 from binary logistic regression analyses)

	(M+D)|P	M|(P+D)	D|(P+M)
Britain (N_{min}=1,938)			
Conservatives	.027**	.013**	.011**
Labour	.027**	.005*	.018**
Liberal Democrats	.035**	.005+	.030**
West Germany (N_{min}=814)			
CDU/CSU	.089**	.042**	.043**
SPD	.075**	.016**	.054**
FDP	.148**	.101**	.042**
Greens	.095**	.065**	.029**
East Germany (N_{min}=424)			
CDU	.130**	.023**	.113**
SPD	.151**	.009	.144**
FDP	.164**	.030+	.153**
Greens	.088**	.006	.090**
Spain (N_{min}=928)			
PSOE	.128**	.023**	.124**
PP	.109**	.004	.099**
IU	.098**	−.005	.107**
United States (N_{min}=929)			
Clinton	.137**	.009*	.125**
Bush	.185**	.006*	.177**
Perot	.192**	.006+	.176**

** $P < .01$, * $P < .05$, + $P < .10$

Note: (M+D)|P   Interpersonal communication and mass communication, controlling for political predispositions. M|(P+D)   Mass communication, controlling for political predispositions and interpersonal communication. D|(P+M)   Interpersonal communication, controlling for political predispositions and mass communication.

two large parties in West Germany – we again find consistent evidence for the superior capacity of interpersonal communication to influence votes.

These analyses have taken a general perspective, inspecting only the total net impact of mass communication and interpersonal communication. A closer look at the detailed findings of these analyses is necessary to see if the assumptions about qualitative differences between the various sources and channels of communication that guided the construction of our measures are justified with respect to media effects. The patterns of relationships between these communication activities and voting can be inspected, and we can explore whether these patterns are the same in all societies, or whether there are important differences. Table 13.4 displays the parameter estimates corresponding to the goodness-of-fit values shown in Table 13.3. For the sake of simplicity, only the statistically significant coefficients are displayed in the table. Insignificant coefficients as well as coefficients for political predispositions and constants are not shown. In terms of the RAS model the size of the effects indicates the extent to which received persuasive messages were accepted by their recipients and referred to as reasons for voting one way or the other. The models include a number of interaction terms between communication exposure and partisanship as the strongest political predisposition. To represent – again in terms of the RAS model – selectivity in the acceptance of persuasive messages within the regression equations, such interaction terms were constructed for all forms of political communication that prove influential, but only retained in the models if they attained sufficient levels of statistical significance.

First of all it should be noted that the overwhelming majority of the media effects we see in Table 13.4 has the right sign, given the political leaning of the respective media (cf. Schmitt-Beck 2000, 236–55; 2003). But the patterns of media effects are complex, and to some degree at odds with our assumptions about the influence of mass media on voting. For instance, they suggest that the press is no less important than television, at least in Europe. In Britain, Germany, and Spain newspapers seem to be no less influential on electors' decisions than television (perhaps they are even more so) – arguably a consequence of the (moderate) partisanship of the European press. In contrast, apart from a positive effect of exposure to news magazines on voting for Bill Clinton, American voting behavior appears responsive only to television. Thus, the general distinction between audiovisual media and print press does seem to be of some importance, although with important variations by country that most likely mirror crucial differences between media systems. However, there are no systematic indications that differences in the media's information quality, or in the degree to which they openly express opinions are of relevance for the persuasive effects of mass communication. All kinds of media seem to bear a potential for influencing voting decisions, whether these be daily newspapers, news magazines, television news programs, television magazines and even talk shows, and outlets of high

Table 13.4 Effects of Exposure to Mass Media and Political Conversations on Specific Voting Decisions (exp(B))

Britain ($N_{min}=1{,}938$)	Conservatives	Labour	Liberal Democrats
Independent (QP)	1.28^{+}		
Daily Express (MP)	1.26^{*}	1.22^{-1+}	
Daily Mail (MP)	1.48^{**}	1.27^{-1*}	1.25^{-1*}
Today (MP)	1.44^{-1*}		1.26^{+}
Sun (TP)	1.27^{**}	1.13^{-1+}	
Daily Mirror (TP)		1.11^{+}	
ITN news (PubTV)		1.14^{*}	
Spouse pro	1.59^{**}	1.59^{*}	2.14^{**}
Spouse contra	1.61^{-1**}	1.72^{-1**}	1.20^{-1+}
Relatives pro			1.57^{**}
Relatives contra		1.42^{-1**}	
Friends pro | PId contra		1.53^{*}	
Neighbors pro	2.00^{-1+}		
Neighbors contra	2.45^{-1+}		
Same clubs pro			1.67^{*}

West Germany ($N_{min}=814$)	CDU/CSU	SPD	FDP	Greens
Leftist quality press (QP)		1.17^{+}	1.36^{-1*}	
Regional press (MP)			1.26^{-1**}	
Regional press (MP) | PId pro	1.25^{*}			
Bild (TP)		1.13^{+}	1.32^{-1*}	
Spiegel and *Zeit* (MagP)			1.56^{**}	1.81^{**}
Spiegel and *Zeit* (MagP) | PId pro	1.86^{-1**}	1.64^{-1**}		
ARD news (PubTV)	1.13^{**}			1.20^{-1**}
SAT1 news (PrivTV)				1.51^{**}
Spouse pro	1.38^{+}	1.97^{**}	3.26^{*}	4.22^{**}
Spouse pro | PId contra	2.69^{**}			
Spouse contra	2.20^{-1**}	1.39^{-1+}	1.73^{-1*}	
Relatives pro	1.54^{**}	3.77^{**}		
Relatives pro | PId contra		3.51^{-1+}		
Relatives contra				1.57^{-1*}
Relatives contra | PId contra			2.37^{-1*}	
Friends pro		1.52^{**}		1.43^{+}
Friends contra	1.21^{-1+}	1.30^{-1*}		
Co-workers pro	1.62^{*}			
Neighbors/same club/other relationships pro	—	—	5.21^{+}	

(continued)

Table 13.4 (continued)

East Germany ($N_{min}=424$)	CDU	SPD	FDP	Greens
Regional press (MP)	1.08^{-1}+		1.18*	
DFF news (PubTV)	1.14^{-1}**			
ARD and ZDF magazines (MagTV)		1.06+		
DFF magazines (MagTV)	1.12*			1.23*
Spouse pro	1.31*	2.36**	2.80**	2.20**
Spouse contra	1.89^{-1}**			
Relatives pro	1.23*		2.44*	2.56**
Relatives contra		1.29^{-1}*		
Friends contra		1.29^{-1}*		
Co-workers pro	1.29**	1.23+		
Co-workers contra		1.32^{-1}**		
Neighbors/same club/other relationships pro	1.25+		3.83**	
Neighbors/same club/other relationships contra	1.49^{-1}*	1.57^{-1}**		

Spain ($N_{min}=928$)	PSOE	PP	IU
El País (QP)	1.18^{-1}+		
ABC (QP)		2.07*	
El Mundo (QP)	1.66^{-1}**		1.32+
Vanguardia (QP)	1.40^{-1}*		
Regional press (MP)	1.14^{-1}*		
News magazines (MagP)	5.19*		
TVE news (PubTV)	1.07**		
Canal+ news (PrivTV)	1.67**		
Spouse pro	2.71**	3.02**	2.59**
Spouse pro | PId contra	7.44**		
Spouse contra	2.14^{-1}**	3.42^{-1}**	2.06^{-1}**
Relatives pro		3.26**	2.62*
Relatives pro | PId contra		5.35^{-1}**	
Relatives contra	2.96^{-1}**		
Friends pro	2.29*	2.36**	2.10**
Friends contra	1.46^{-1}*	2.86^{-1}**	
Co-workers pro		8.23**	

(*continued*)

Table 13.4 (continued)

United States (N_{min}=929)	Clinton	Bush	Perot
News magazines (MagTV)	1.20*		
National TV news (PrivTV)	1.09[+]		1.14^{-1}*
TV magazines (MagTV)	1.31*	1.31^{-1+}	
Talk shows (MagTV)	1.27^{-1}*		
Spouse pro	1.77**	2.23**	2.27**
Spouse contra	1.88^{-1}**	2.10^{-1}**	
Relatives pro	1.31**	1.48**	1.56**
Relatives contra	1.33^{-1}**		1.21^{-1}**
Friends pro	1.25*		1.87**
Friends contra	1.25^{-1}*		1.30^{-1}**
Co-workers pro	1.19[+]		1.31[+]
Co-workers contra			1.18^{-1+}
Neighbors pro	1.25[+]	1.33*	1.55*
Neighbors contra		1.76^{-1}**	
Same church pro			2.05**

** $P < .01$, * $P < .05$, [+] $P < .10$

Notes: Constants and effects of political predispositions as well as insignificant effects of political communications not shown (for an overview of all independent variables and their effects cf. Schmitt-Beck 2000, 272–4, 338–9). Media formats: Quality press (QP), Middle market press (MP), Tabloid press (TP), News magazines (MagP), News programs of public broadcasters (PubTV), News programs of private broadcasters (PrivTV), TV magazine formats (MagTV).

information quality (quality press, public television) just as well as media of low information quality (tabloids, private television).

In sum, none of the hypotheses guiding my classification of media appears to be fully supported by these findings. The general ideal that the difference between print and television matters, is justified to some degree. However, only in the United States do we find a pattern that is consistent with the hypothesis that television is the stronger force, whereas the European results suggest that on the other side of the Atlantic print media bear the greater potential for political influence. The more specific considerations about the role of media formats for media effects are not supported by the findings displayed in Table 13.4.

In contrast to the somewhat ambiguous media effects, the patterns of results concerning interpersonal communication are very clear. In all five societies, the potential of discussants to influence votes runs consistently in the right direction, but depends crucially on the nature of their relationship to the respondents. Political conversations held within primary relationships were far more influential than discussions that took place in the context of secondary relationships, like those between co-workers and neighbors. To be sure, even that kind of exchange, taking place not between intimate associates but between more distant acquaintances, is by no means irrelevant. However, it manifests itself primarily in those societies where the total impact of interpersonal communication is high, and much less so in the other societies. Yet, on the whole there is no denying that the personal exchange taking place on an everyday basis between spouses, relatives, and (close) friends is a major factor of influence on decisions taken by voters on election day. In addition, the data suggest that even among these more intimate relationships, spousal relationships stand out as particularly conducive to interpersonal influence.

DISCUSSION

This chapter started with the observation that the extent of electoral volatility differs between electorates. From election to election, in some societies there is considerable movement between parties, while others remain fairly stable, and the outcomes of the contests fluctuate only by a narrow margin. Comparing five societies in four countries, it became obvious that two of them – Britain and West Germany – are characterized by only a limited degree of aggregate electoral change, while in the remaining three – East Germany, Spain, and the United States – the extent of mobility between parties or candidates is quite substantial. The patterns of differences with regard to the importance of habitual political communication for voting behavior support the assumption that societal information flows are the source of electoral change.

Remarkably, a complementary pattern can be detected with regard to the relevance of political predispositions for electoral behavior (Table 13.5). In those cases where we observed high degrees of electoral volatility, the incremental impact of political communication, over and above the impact of political predispositions, is high. However, as Table 13.5 reveals, these same societies are also characterized by a rather limited importance of political predispositions for citizens' electoral behavior. The combined effect on the vote of identifications with social groups, ideological identifications, value orientations, and partisanship is quite low, and in the case of East Germany extremely low. The small

Table 13.5 Global Explanatory Power of Political
Predispositions for Voting Decisions (adjusted Pseudo-R^2
from multinomial logistic regression analyses)

Britain	West Germany	East Germany	Spain	United States
.544**	.491**	.070**	.443**	.288**
(2,196)	(840)	(474)	(999)	(969)

** $P < .01$ (N in parentheses)

role of political predispositions for explaining voting behavior can be
put down to several factors. Electoral procedures are one of them. At
Presidential elections American voters choose persons, not parties, and
that makes for a much more limited effect of political predispositions on
voting than in established European democracies, where parties are at
the core of the electoral process. In addition, the United States has gone
through a period of delignment, and the proportion of voters with firm
loyalties to a political party has decreased substantially. In contrast, the
postauthoritarian societies of East Germany and Spain are characterized
by a state of "prealignment." With democratization having taken place
only in the recent past, parties in these countries did not have sufficient
time to take root in society – arguably something that in some of the new
democracies actually may never happen, as they "leapfrogged" (Pasquino
2001) from their authoritarian past directly into the age of "postmod-
ern" politics, bypassing the stage of mass politics with its strong mutual
linkages between party organizations and social groups (Norris 2000).

As it seems the importance of political communication for electoral
behavior increases as the grip of political predispositions on electoral
behavior gets weaker, leading to more electoral mobility. If current di-
agnoses are correct that we are witnessing a general trend toward a
more "individualized" electoral behavior, that is decoupled from its
social-structural foundations and cultural underpinnings (Dalton and
Wattenberg 2000), then we can expect to see further increases in the
importance of political communication for the outcomes of elections,
more mobile electorates, and, ultimately, less predictable election results
(Schmitt-Beck and Farrell 2002).

Political information can reach its recipients through various channels. Mass media and personal conversations with other people are
among the most important of these. This blends into a general renaissance of the idea that mass media can affect their audiences' orientations

not only by means of complex cognitive processes, such as priming or framing (Ansolabehere et al. 1993), but also in a more directly persuasive way. The analysis presented in this chapter suggests that the reception of persuasive messages, carrying evaluative content, from the mass media can indeed be consequential for individual electoral behavior. Depending on which media they use, citizens differ systematically with regard to the likelihood of voting for or against particular parties or candidates at national elections. This was shown for different countries. However, the importance of the media for electoral behavior turns out not to be the same in each society. Arguably, conditions for the influence of the mass media are particularly favorable in media systems that are characterized by a significant, though moderate "press-party parallelism" (Seymour-Ure 1974), where reporting by a particular media organization tends to advantage specific parties, but not in such a blatant way that it becomes strikingly obvious for each and every recipient. Thus, the hurdle of selective exposure may be overcome. Media market structures may also play a role. Media influences are more likely when there is a shortage of genuine alternatives, because readers' inclinations toward selective exposure are preempted by a lack of choices. Processes of press concentration in press landscapes that are mostly regional and not national, ultimately limiting readers' choices to one or two outlets, or government interference in the operation of public broadcasters are examples of developments that may lead to such constellations. These features are typical of the media systems of West Germany and Spain (Gunther and Mughan 2000) – the two countries where according to this analysis the media's impact on electoral behavior is strongest.

If such a constellation coincides with a rather limited importance of political discussions for electoral behavior, one may well find that mass communication is the stronger source of political influence. This peculiar pattern is characteristic of the small parties in West Germany. Apart from this, however, electoral decision making depends more on who voters discuss politics with, rather than on which media they use. In each of the three societies that is characterized by weak political predispositions the sizable impact of political communication is to a large extent due to the strong effects of interpersonal communication, especially between intimates such as spouses, relatives, or friends, but to a lesser degree also between co-workers, neighbors, and other more distant acquaintances. As Lazarsfeld and his colleagues maintained half a century ago, on the whole we may conclude that interpersonal communication is more important than mass communication when it comes to influences on "the people's choice" (Lazarsfeld et al. 1944).

REFERENCES

Altheide, David L., and Robert P. Snow. 1988. Toward a Theory of Mediation. In James E. Anderson, ed. *Communication Yearbook* 11. Newbury Park, CA: Sage, pp. 194–223.

Andreß, Hans-Jürgen, Jacques A. Hagenaars, and Steffen Kühnel. 1997. *Analyse von Tabellen und kategorialen Daten. Log-lineare Modelle, latente Klassenanalyse, logistische Regression und GSK-Ansatz.* Berlin: Springer.

Ansolabehere, Stephen, Roy Behr, and Shanto Iyengar. 1993. *The Media Game. American Politics in the Television Age.* New York: Macmillan.

Bartels, Larry M. 1993. Messages Received: The Political Impact of Media Exposure. *American Political Science Review* 87: 267–85.

Burt, Ronald S. 1984. Network Items and the General Social Survey. *Social Networks* 6: 293–339.

Chaffee, Steven H. 1972. The Interpersonal Context of Mass Communication. In Gerald F. Kline and Phillip J. Tichenor, eds. *Current Perspectives in Mass Communication Research.* Beverly Hills, CA: Sage, pp. 95–120.

Chaffee, Steven H., and Diana C. Mutz. 1988. Comparing Mediated and Interpersonal Communication Data. In Robert P. Hawkins, John M. Wiemann, and Suzanne Pingree, eds. *Advancing Communication Science: Merging Mass and Interpersonal Processes.* Newbury Park, CA: Sage, pp. 19–43.

Conover, Pamela Johnston. 1984. The Influence of Group Identifications on Political Perceptions and Evaluation. *Journal of Politics* 46: 760–85.

Converse, Philip E. 1966. Information Flow and the Stability of Partisan Attitudes. In Angus Campbell, Philip E. Converse, Warren E. Miller, and Donald E. Stokes, eds. *Elections and the Political Order.* New York: Wiley, pp. 136–57.

Curtice, John. 1997. Is the *Sun* Shining on Tony Blair? The Electoral Influence of British Newspapers. *Press/Politics* 2: 9–26.

Dahl, Robert A. 1957. The Concept of Power. *Behavioral Science* 2: 201–15.

Dalton, Russell J., Paul Allen Beck, and Robert Huckfeldt. 1998. Partisan Cues and the Media: Information Flows in the 1992 Presidential Election. *American Political Science Review* 92: 111–26.

Dalton, Russell J., and Martin P. Wattenberg, eds. 2000. *Parties Without Partisans: Political Change in Advanced Industrial Democracies.* Oxford: Oxford University Press.

Denemark, David. 2002. Television Effects and Voter Decision Making in Australia: A Re-Examination of the Converse Model. *British Journal of Political Science* 32: 663–90.

Dogan, Mattei, and Dominique Pelassy. 1984. *How to Compare Nations. Strategies in Comparative Politics.* Chatham, UK: Chatham House.

Erikson, Robert S., Thomas D. Lancaster, and David W. Romero. 1989. Group Components of the Presidential Vote, 1952–1984. *Journal of Politics* 51: 337–46.

Farrell, David M., and Rüdiger Schmitt-Beck, eds. 2002. *Do Political Campaigns Matter? Campaign Effects in Elections and Referendums.* London: Routledge.

Gunther, Richard, and Anthony Mughan, eds. 2000. *Democracy and the Media: A Comparative Perspective.* New York: Cambridge University Press.

Gurevitch, Michael, and Jay G. Blumler. 1990. Comparative Research: The Extending Frontier. In David L. Swanson and Dan Nimmo, eds. *New Directions in Political Communication. A Resource Book.* Newbury Park, CA: Sage, pp. 305–25.

Hofstetter, C. Richard. 1976. *Bias in the News. Network Television Coverage of the 1972 Election Campaign.* Columbus: Ohio State University Press.

Huckfeldt, Robert, and John Sprague. 1995. *Citizens, Politics, and Social Communication. Information and Influence in an Election Campaign.* Cambridge: Cambridge University Press.

Inglehart, Ronald. 1990. *Culture Shift in Advanced Industrial Society.* Princeton: Princeton University Press.

Joslyn, Mark R., and Steve Ceccoli. 1996. Attentiveness to Television News and Opinion Change in the Fall 1992 Presidential Campaign. *Political Behavior* 18: 141–70.

Katz, Elihu, and Paul F. Lazarsfeld. 1955. *Personal Influence. The Part Played by People in the Flow of Mass Communication.* Glencoe, IL: Free Press.

Kepplinger, Hans M., Hans B. Brosius, and Stefan Dahlem. 1994. *Wie das Fernsehen Wahlen beeinflußt. Theoretische Modelle und empirische Analysen.* Munich: R. Fischer.

Kinder, Donald R. 1998. Communication and Opinion. *Annual Review of Political Science* 1: 167–97.

Klapper, Joseph T. 1960. *The Effects of Mass Communication.* Glencoe, IL: The Free Press.

Kleinnijenhuis, Jan. 1991. Newspaper Complexity and the Knowledge Gap. *European Journal of Communication* 6: 499–522.

Knoke, David. 1990. *Political Networks. The Structural Perspective.* Cambridge: Cambridge University Press.

Kohn, Melvin L. 1989. Introduction. In Melvin L. Kohn, ed. *Cross-National Research in Sociology.* Newbury Park, CA: Sage, pp. 17–31.

Lazarsfeld, Paul F., Bernard Berelson, and Hazel Gaudet. 1944. *The People's Choice. How the Voter Makes Up his Mind in a Presidential Campaign.* 3rd ed. New York: Columbia University Press.

Lenart, Silvo. 1994. *Shaping Political Attitudes. The Impact of Interpersonal Communication and Mass Media.* Thousand Oaks, CA: Sage.

Levine, Jeffrey, Edward G. Carmines, and Robert Huckfeldt. 1997. The Rise of Ideology in the Post-New Deal Party System, 1972–1992. *American Politics Quarterly* 25: 19–34.

Lipset, Seymour Martin, and Stein Rokkan. 1967. Cleavage Structures, Party Systems, and Voter Alignments: An Introduction. In Seymour Martin Lipset and Stein Rokkan, eds. *Party Systems and Voters Alignments: Cross-National Perspectives.* New York: Free Press, pp. 1–64.

Listhaug, Ola, MacDonald, Stuart Elaine, and George Rabinowitz. 1994. Ideology and Party Support in Comparative Perspective. *European Journal of Political Research* 25: 111–49.

McClosky, Herbert, and Harold E. Dahlgren. 1959. Primary Group Influence on Party Loyalty. *American Political Science Review* 53: 757–76.

Miller, Warren E., and J. Merrill Shanks. 1996. *The New American Voter.* Cambridge, MA: Harvard University Press.

Noelle-Neumann, Elisabeth. 1979. *Öffentlichkeit als Bedrohung. Beiträge zur empirischen Kommunikationsforschung.* 2nd ed. Munich: Alber.

Norris, Pippa. 2000. *A Virtuous Circle: Political Communications in Post-Industrial Democracies.* Cambridge: Cambridge University Press.

Østergaard, Bernt Stubbe, ed. 1997. *The Media in Western Europe: The Euromedia Handbook.* London: Sage.

Page, Benjamin I., Robert Y. Shapiro, and Glenn R. Dempsey. 1987. What Moves Public Opinion? *American Political Science Review* 81: 23–43.

Pasquino, Gianfranco. 2001. The New Campaign Politics in Southern Europe. In Nikiforos Diamandouros and Richard Gunther, eds. *Parties, Politics, and Democracy in the New Southern Europe.* Baltimore: Johns Hopkins University Press, pp. 183–223.

Pedersen, Mogens N. 1990. Electoral Volatility in Western Europe, 1948–1977. In Peter Mair, ed. *The West European Party System.* Oxford: Oxford University Press, pp. 195–207.

Pfetsch, Barbara. 1996. Convergence Through Privatization? Changing Media Environments and Televised Politics in Germany. *European Journal of Communication* 11: 427–51.

Przeworski, Adam, and Henry Teune. 1970. *The Logic of Comparative Social Inquiry.* New York: Wiley.

Reardon, Kathleen K., and Everett M. Rogers. 1988. Interpersonal Versus Mass Media Communication. A False Dichotomy. *Human Communication Research* 15: 284–303.

Richardson, Bradley M. 1991. European Party Loyalties Revisited. *American Political Science Review* 85: 751–75.

Robinson, John P. 1976. Interpersonal Influence in Election Campaigns: Two-Step-Flow Hypotheses. *Public Opinion Quarterly* 40: 304–19.

Rogers, Everett M. 1973. Mass Media and Interpersonal Communication. In Ithiel de Sola Pool, Frederick W. Frey, Wilbur Schramm, Nathan Maccoby, and Edwin P. Parker, eds. *Handbook of Communication.* Chicago: Rand McNally, pp. 290–310.

Rogers, Everett M., and Dilip K. Bhowmik. 1970. Homophily-Heterophily: Relational Concepts for Communiation Research. *Public Opinion Quarterly* 34: 523–38.

Sartori, Giovanni. 1970. Concept Misformation in Comparative Politics. *American Political Science Review* 64: 1033–53.

Schenk, Michael. 1989. Massenkommunikation und Interpersonale Kommunikation. In Max Kaase and Winfried Schulz, eds. *Massenkommunikation. Theorien, Methoden, Befunde.* Opladen, Germany: Westdeutscher Verlag, pp. 406–17.

Schmitt-Beck, Rüdiger. 1998. Of Readers, Viewers, and Cat-Dogs. In Jan W. van Deth, ed. *Comparative Politics: The Problem of Equivalence.* London: Routledge, pp. 222–46.

―――. 2000. *Politische Kommunikation und Wählerverhalten. Ein internationaler Vergleich.* Wiesbaden, Germany: Westdeutscher Verlag.

―――. 2003. Mass Communication, Personal Communication and Vote Choice: The Filter Hypothesis of Media Influence in Comparative Perspective. *British Journal of Political Science* 33: 233–59.

Schmitt-Beck, Rüdiger and David M. Farrell. 2002. Do Political Campaigns Matter? Yes, But It Depends. In David M. Farrell and Rüdiger Schmitt-Beck, eds. *Do Political Campaigns Matter? Campaign Effects in Elections and Referendums.* London: Routledge, pp. 183–93.

Semetko, Holli A. 1996. The Media. In Lawrence LeDuc, Richard G. Niemi, and Pippa Norris. eds. *Comparing Democracies. Elections and Voting in Global Perspective*. Thousand Oaks, CA: Sage, pp. 254–79.

Seymour-Ure, Colin. 1974. *The Political Impact of Mass Media*. London: Constable.

Simon, Klaus. 1976. Einfluß von Gruppenzugehörigkeiten auf politisches Verhalten. In Paul Kevenhörster and Horst Kanitz, eds. *Kommunales Wahlverhalten*. Bonn: Eichholz, pp. 59–113.

Van Deth, Jan W. 1995. Comparative Politics and the Decline of the Nation-State in Western Europe. *European Journal of Political Research* 27: 443–62.

Weir, Blair T. 1975. The Distortion of Voter Recall. *American Journal of Political Science* 19: 53–62.

Zaller, John R. 1992. *The Nature and Origins of Mass Opinion*. Cambridge: Cambridge University Press.

———. 1996. The Myth of Massive Media Impact Revived: New Support for a Discredited Idea. In Diana C. Mutz, Paul M. Sniderman, Richard A. Brody, eds. *Political Persuasion and Attitude Change*. Ann Arbor: University of Michigan Press, pp. 17–78.

Zukin, Cliff. 1977. A Reconsideration of the Effects of Information on Partisan Stability. *Public Opinion Quarterly* 41: 244–54.

PART III

Perspectives and Challenges

FOURTEEN

State of the Art of Comparative Political Communication Research

Poised for Maturity?

Michael Gurevitch and Jay G. Blumler

This chapter attempts an assessment of the current status of comparative political communication research. Its core concept is *maturity*. Comparative approaches to political communications, albeit promising and sometimes impressive, can seem ragged when compared, say, with the solidity of their application in other social sciences (e.g., sociology and political science). Our central point is that the quality of comparative research can vary not only in scientific rigor but also, and perhaps more importantly, in its ability to reveal fundamental and broadly influential features of the structures and cultures of the societies being examined. Our concern throughout this chapter therefore is that of how to recognize and to achieve such maturity in the subfield of comparative political communication scholarship.

In fact, this is our third attempt to take stock of the "state of the art" of comparative political communication research. In the first such effort, more than a quarter century ago (Blumler and Gurevitch 1975) we depicted comparative political communication research as a "field in its infancy." The dominant tone was one of uncertainty, illustrated by the opening paragraph of the essay:

> Writing in 1975, nobody could claim to be able to paint an assured portrait of the field of investigation to be described in this essay. It is not merely that few political communication studies have been mounted with a comparative focus. More to the point, there is neither a settled view of what such studies should be concerned with, nor even a firmly crystallized set of alternative options for research between which scholars of diverse philosophic persuasions could choose.

Reviewing the field again fifteen years later (Gurevitch and Blumler 1990), we were more positively struck by its growth and emergent identity. But some qualifications remained. As we summed up:

> The results of a number of scientifically motivated comparative research efforts have by now seen the light of published day. Although, taken as a whole, their fruits may still appear patchy, quite a few have demonstrated the theoretical fertility and empirical utility of macrocomparative approaches to political communication analysis. It is as if comparative research has progressed from infancy to, if not yet full adulthood, at least late adolescence.

What follows then, carrying the biological metaphor forward, focuses on the issue of *maturation*. Can encouraging signs of such maturation be discerned in approaches to comparative political communication enquiry published after 1990? If so, how might these be built on and strengthened? By what criteria may such maturity be identified?

WHY "POISED"?

A fundamental change has taken place in attitudes to comparative research from the earlier periods of our writing. There is no longer that need to urge others to "go comparative," to proselytize for more involvement in comparative political communication research, which animated us in both 1975 and 1990. There is now a widespread appreciation of its potential. Mentions of its value and calls for its further adoption abound. Bennett and Entman (2001), for example, call for "comparative dialogue about the impact of market forces on media systems, the blurring of traditional boundaries between entertainment and news, and the political uses of new communication technologies" as well as for study of "the comparative qualities of, and the deliberative outlets for, citizen information both within and between societies." Reese (2001) considers that, "The many opportunities available for cross-national research have the potential for providing important new insights into global journalism, particularly as US and British media sociology is compared and tested against experience and evidence from other systems." Corner (2001) recommends creation of a "stronger European and then international network for media research" to exploit "those comparative opportunities which do so much to illuminate both what is specific to certain situations and what is more general and requires, perhaps, broader terms of explanation." And Schudson (2001) declares that, "whatever phenomenon I look at I try to see located in space (how does it compare with the same or similar things in other countries or other locations?) and located in time (how does it compare with the same or similar things in earlier or later historical periods?). Far from being neglected, comparative political research has almost become fashionable!

Many factors are probably responsible for this increased interest. One is awareness of globalization as a process driven by communications technology, raising the prospect of an increasing homogenization of political communication across previously more diverse societies, polities, and cultures (as in Mancini 2000). The increased conglomerization of media organizations and their assembly into an ever smaller number of corporate behemoths has also triggered concerns over a threatened homogenization of the voices and interests given space to express themselves and to be heard in the globally disseminated media.

Other incentives to engage in comparative work may also be mentioned. In a world shrunk by easier travel and by instant electronic communication, researchers from different points on the globe are now able to meet more frequently, to converse almost as if face to face, to exchange ideas, and sometimes to mull over new projects of a collaborative nature. International conferences and workshops proliferate. Visiting lectureships in other countries have become more common. Research proposals wing their way electronically from one country to another. Awareness of the similarities and differences between cultures and social and political systems becomes more widespread. The growth and increasing use of the Internet has also played a part, facilitating easier access to information and databases on political communication arrangements in different societies. Data that were once difficult to come by have now become accessible through the application of computer-based search engines. But here pitfalls begin to emerge. The easier availability of data is not always unalloyed gold. Sifting out what is comparatively most significant can be difficult. The task of standardizing such data to allow truly comparative analysis is also daunting.

And *more* comparative work doesn't necessarily equate with *better*. The easier it becomes to undertake cross-societal research, the easier it is to neglect or fail to exploit its distinctively *comparative* potential. This may encourage what may be termed a *comparativism of convenience*, which uses other countries merely as places to situate the same investigation that one would have conducted at home, instead of designing research that aims to find out how key characteristics of diverse political-media systems differently shape political communication processes within them.

We need therefore to distinguish between more conventional cross-country investigations and more ambitious comparative research. Unfortunately, the two are often conflated and the boundaries between them have become blurred. Observance of this distinction and greater commitment to demanding comparative conceptualizations and design could further the maturation of the field.

Nevertheless, several fine specimens of political communication research in this more ambitious sense have appeared in the literature since we last reviewed the field. What can we learn from them about the criteria of mature comparative scholarship? After briefly summarizing the approaches of eight such pieces of work in the following text, we generalize about the elements that make them exemplary.[1]

Some Recent Studies

An outstanding effort was Swanson and Mancini's (1996) analysis of the innovations in election campaigning techniques adopted in recent years by political parties and leaders in eleven different societies. The locales ranged across long-established democracies, new or recently restored ones, and ones that have latterly experienced destabilizing pressures. The participating scholars, who were invited to write national case studies, received in advance a remarkably elaborated theoretical essay (Mancini and Swanson 1996), which included hypotheses about the underlying generators of change in campaign communication tactics (the increased "modernization" and complexity of social organization allied to processes of "Americanization"); a specification of the kinds of changes most likely to happen have emerged; and a discussion of systemic factors by which the processes of change might have been mediated or modified in different democracies (such as the countries' election systems, media systems, structures of party competition, and political cultures). Provision of this brief ensured that the national case studies could be composed along comparable lines and that their authors could comment on the applicability of the framework to their national situations.

---

[1] These should not be regarded as our top eight list of best comparative analyses of political communication conducted in the 1990s. They reflect what impressed us as illustrative of good comparative practice only among the readings we happen to have consulted – which we do not claim to have been comprehensive. We realize that other equally valuable studies could have been included.

It enabled Swanson and Mancini (1996) to revisit that framework in light of the completed case studies, stating how far its expectations had been confirmed, and along what lines it required amendment. Some of the changes were not minor, including, for example, significant reservations about the concept of Americanization.

A number of national case studies shaped by a comparative purpose also appear in Gunther and Mughan (2000). This team operated on a broader and more overtly normative canvass than Swanson and Mancini, aiming to explore the relationship of political communication to the health of democracy generally in light of the increasingly vocal criticism in recent times of media roles in politics. Although the approach was less theoretical than that followed by Swanson and Mancini, the national contributors (coming, respectively, from established democracies and transitional ones that had emerged from formerly totalitarian or author-itarian regimes) were armed in advance with several lines of guidance: to relate their analyses to specified criteria of democratic media perfor-mance (mainly impartiality plus provision of a volume and substance of political coverage sufficient to inform citizens' voting choices); to be sensitive to the reciprocal interactions of communication and political influences; and to identify those macrolevel factors that appeared most conducive to a well-functioning democracy. Three broad conclusions emerged from this project. First, media roles in politics differed greatly in the two kinds of democracies chosen for analysis – mixed at best in the established ones but often positively supporting adoption of demo-cratic norms in transitional ones. Second, there was clear cross-national evidence of a reduction and dilution of information dissemination by the media in the established democracies. And third, the most impor-tant macrolevel factors resistant to such deterioration appeared to be the presence and civic mission of strong public service broadcasting orga-nizations and firm regulation of the broadcasting media. Also evident from the comparisons were the distinctiveness of the U.S. case (hosting the most commercial and adversarial and least regulated journalism in the democratic world) and uneven tendencies for other democracies to approach, without yet fully adopting, the American model.

In Pfetsch (2001), a pivotal but empirically rarely explored area is opened to a detailed and revealing comparative U.S.-German analysis: the culture that governs interactions over media publicity between politi-cians and journalists. Based on interviews with both groups of commu-nicators, the area for investigation was theoretically predefined in terms of a "political communication system as jointly fashioned by political and media roles, both transcending their purely sectional interests" (drawing here on Blumler and Gurevitch 1981). The cultural codes of such systems, it was further postulated, could be more politically or more media-driven (adapting Mazzoleni's distinction between political and media "logics," Mazzoleni 1987). Also postulated were potentially relevant structural differences between the United States and Germany, such as the former's weaker party system, the tendency for its presidential political system to favor communication strategies of "going public" (in Kernell's sense, Kernell 1986) and a stronger public element in the German broadcasting system. All this served to generate prior expectations about likely cross-national similarities and differences in the interviewees' role orientations; to focus the questions put to those interviewees; and to guide the analysis of the resulting data. The findings revealed more differences than similarities in the culturally governed interactions between politicians and journalists in the two societies; confirmed the validity of the distinction between more politically and more media-driven sources of such influence; and countered "popular ideas about Americanization trends in German political communication" – at least in the mid-1990s when the research was conducted.

A predefined conceptual framework of a different kind organized the Semetko et al. (1991) examination of political and media influences upon the formation of campaign agendas in television and press coverage of U.S. and British elections in the 1980s. This was based on five systemic factors or dimensions, which the researchers considered likely to favor or inhibit journalistic intervention into the agenda-setting process – namely, the degree of esteem for politics and politicians in the culture; newspersons' more "pragmatic" or "sacerdotal" attitudes to politics and politicians; the degree of professionalization of electioneering by parties and candidates; a public service versus commercial organization of the broadcast media; and strength of media competition for audiences and revenue. This framework led the team to expect more journalistic influence on coverage in the United States than in the United Kingdom. It suggested ways in which such influence could be operationalized in content analysis. And it anchored the concluding interpretation of the empirical findings, which broadly confirmed the impact of the posited dimensions.

But the authors also cautioned that the systemic dimensions of the framework might themselves be "undergoing gradual change," which could lessen differences in the campaign roles of the media in the two societies in the future. Following this up, Blumler and Gurevitch (2001) revisited that 1980s portrait of two quite contrasted political communication systems to see how far it still prevailed or had been blurred, when account was taken of what was known about media performance during the U.S. presidential and U.K. general elections of 1996 and 1997, respectively. They thus aimed to combine a temporal with their spatial comparison of election communication in the two societies. Two main conclusions emerged from their analysis. First, the abiding utility of the five originally specified dimensions of system difference was confirmed – in the sense that they had helped to make sense of the later comparisons of Anglo-American data. Second, complex light was shed on the Americanization hypothesis: whereas the evidence suggested that by the 1990s the British political communication system had moved closer to the American model along three of the dimensions, the American system appeared to have moved *away* from the British pattern along two of them. It was not that the U.S. system was fixed while others evolved toward it; it too was caught up in dynamic processes of change.

A more specific, recently emergent, and highly significant political communication phenomenon was the focus of Esser, Reinemann, and Fan (2001): coverage in the United States, the United Kingdom, and German newspapers of "spin doctoring" and the related news management practices of politicians. Like the other examples of comparative research reviewed previously, the empirical work of these authors was preceded by extensive prior conceptualization. This centred on (a) the idea that the press is increasingly becoming a collective political institution in its own right (as defined by Cook 1998); (b) the notion of "metacoverage" as a new stage of political journalism in which reporters comment on their own roles in political communication (citing Johnson et al. 1996); (c) its division into "self-referential" and "process" news (where stories of spin doctoring belong); and (d) the assumption that many political journalists are disposed to resist news management by aggressively exposing it (as Blumler 1997 had suggested). After presenting the results of their comparative content analysis, the authors specified three macrolevel influences that seemed responsible for differences in the amounts and framing styles of stories about spin doctoring in the three countries' press systems: the extent of national politicians' commitment to strategic public relations and campaign news management, resulting in more extensive and pejorative coverage; the longevity of national politicians' involvement in such practices, defusing pejorative coverage as journalists became accustomed to and made their peace with spin doctoring over the longer term; and linkages between national political and media systems, with closer ties tending to reduce the amount and aggressiveness of the coverage.

Wilke and Reinemann (2001) is interesting for showing how even a single-country study can make a significant contribution to comparative knowledge, if deliberately designed to do so. Their point of departure was suggestions in the literature that certain trends, especially characteristic of U.S. campaign coverage, were recasting political journalism in many other democracies – notably reduced attention to politics, increased personalization, increased negativity, and increasingly interpretative reporting (entailing less scope for politicians to be heard due to the "shrinking sound bite"). After analyzing the content of German newspaper coverage of election campaigns from 1949 to 1998, the authors found an overall trend in line with only one of the hypothesized developments – toward more interpretative coverage, including a marked reduction in the latter part of the period in the length of politicians' statements quoted. They ascribed the failure to confirm the other expected trends to a number of mutually reinforcing macrolevel differences between the United States and Germany, such as their election systems, strength of party systems, structures of political competition, media systems, lines of access of politicians to the media, politicians' and journalists' communication cultures (as in Pfetsch 2001), and peculiarities in the criteria by which German political journalists select campaign news (drawing here on the research of Schönbach and Semetko 2000).

Awareness of a normatively defined problem was the point of departure of Schönbach et al.'s (1999) comparison of trends over time in newspaper reading in the United States and Germany. "Newspapers," they said, "were an endangered species," a cause for concern because, among other things, the press tends to be a more substantial and effective conveyor of civic information than television. But the decline has been less precipitate in Germany than in the United States, and the scholars postulated three possible macrolevel differences that could have been responsible for this: differences in competition for audiences from other media; differences in the attempts of newspapers to make themselves stylistically and linguistically attractive to readers; and differences in the impact on readership habits of sociodemographic trends. Although the results (combining content analyses with readership surveys) gave somewhat more weight to the first two explanations, a closer look at some of the sociodemographic evidence proved more interesting. Newspapers in the United States were increasingly serving as what the authors termed "an instrument of social distinction" (whereby readers separated themselves from the lower-strata groups in which newspapers circulated less extensively). Not only was this process less advanced in Germany; other social relationships were more important there, such as being married, and having deeper roots and more ties in the local community.

CRITERIA OF MATURITY: INDIVIDUAL PROJECTS

Six criteria of maturity in the design, conduct, and analysis of comparative political communication research appear common to these cases. We state them as prescriptions in the following text.

First, the purpose of going comparative should be explicated. Why have the scholars involved in the research chosen to do so? What particular benefits do they hope to gain by situating their studies in more than one society or more than one time frame? All this should be articulated, not taken for granted.

Second, the research should be situated in a theoretical or conceptual perspective, which will not only determine the phenomena to be investigated but will also shape their comparative treatment. Often that perspective will draw from theoretical ideas that were initially proposed by scholars for application to their own national conditions. The transnationalization of such ideas through comparative research enlarges and enriches our field by exposing them to, and refining them in, more diverse testing grounds. Involvement in prior theorizing has another advantage. It ensures what may be termed the *comparative sufficiency* of the research – that it focuses not on "any old bits and pieces" that happen to be open to comparison but on those features and trends of political communication, which matter because of their organizing power and influence or their normative implications.

Third, comparative research should be designed to realize "double value." That is, it should aim to shed light not only on the particular phenomena being studied but also on the different systems in which they are being examined. In other words, more mature comparative research will be "system sensitive." This can be achieved by trying to specify in advance certain macrolevel dimensions along which the political communication systems concerned may vary in their impact on the empirical phenomena. This may be accompanied by a rationale for basing the research in the selected places or time periods. And as the findings of such system-sensitive research cumulate, our understanding of what matters most in the organization of political communication systems and the influences that play on them should increase.

Fourth, initial conceptualizations should include a prior statement of expectations (or hypotheses if appropriate) about what might emerge from the empirical comparisons. This will usefully guide both the research design and analysis of the findings.

Fifth, more mature work will revisit some of the preconceived ideas and expectations about comparative similarities and differences in light of the results of the empirical research. This will identify what has been confirmed, what has not (with suggested explanations where possible), and what unanticipated additions to comparative knowledge or the framework of comparative analysis seem to have emerged.

Sixth, although it is natural to think of comparative research as a predominantly spatial (i.e., cross-national) exercise, its temporal component should always be borne in mind. After all, almost everything to do with political communication is in flux these days: social formations and lifestyles; strategies of persuasion; politician-journalist relations; and media technology, organization, and finance (Blumler 1999). Such changes, or trends allegedly resulting from them, provided a context for most of the examples of comparative research reviewed previously. The preoccupations of several of the authors with the validity or otherwise of the concept of Americanization illustrate this. And a master theme of political communication research for some time to come is likely to be how far posited processes of change are taking place universally and how far they are being blocked or modified by enduring structural differences in present-day political communication systems.

COLLECTIVE CRITERIA OF MATURITY

Maturity is manifested, however, not only in how individual scholars or teams conceive and pursue the comparative task. For the political communication subfield collectively, two other criteria apply.

One is the criterion of "comparative scope." How broadly have comparative designs been applied across the political communication terrain as a whole? The short answer to this question at present is "not very!"

Much recent comparative work (as the examples reviewed in the preceding text tend to show) has focused on the conduct of election campaigns. An overarching theme has been the notion of Americanization, an offshoot of the debate on the globalization of politics and the media. Arguments have been put both in support of this notion (with campaign practices in many countries said to be approximating the U.S. model) and against it (stressing the persistence of cultural differences and resistant or mediating structural factors). Heavily examined in this work both nationally and cross-nationally have been processes of political marketing (e.g., Newman 1999) and party publicity professionalization (e.g., in Plasser's surveys of the deployment, roles, and status of political consultants, Plasser 2001).

In itself, this is neither surprising nor unwelcome. The question is whether this focus has been at the expense of other significant issues and trends to which comparative effort could and should also be devoted.

POLITICAL CULTURE: A FRAMEWORK FOR FUTURE RESEARCH

But how might the objects of comparative investigation be most effectively expanded? What intellectual strategy might broaden our comparative lines of attack? Rather than produce a shopping list of discrete features of political communication, for comparativists to address (which could be endless), we prefer to concentrate instead on the relationship of political culture to political communication as an organizing framework for future attention. Political culture may be defined for the sake of this discussion as "the values, norms, beliefs, sentiments and understandings of how power and authority operate within a particular political system. Generally, political culture sets informal and unwritten ground rules as to how the political process is to be performed" (Amin 2002) – and, we would add, how relationships between key actors within them should be conducted and managed.

We regard the notion of political culture as particularly useful for our purpose because of its all-encompassing character. It constitutes a framework within which all political communication takes place. It is certainly multifunctional, for it can be regarded as facilitating and legitimizing existing forms of political communication; implying standards by which existing arrangements may be criticized and pressured to change; and constraining proposed changes within limits of acceptability (including ruling out some as beyond the pale). Its essential usefulness for comparative research is that it allows and enables consideration of the differences between political communication arrangements in different societies and hence it is a unifying conceptual framework for such work.

Just as comparative communication research can be regarded as a subset of the comparative study of culture, comparative political communication research should be seen as the examination of political cultures and their impact on political communication in different societies. The main concern here would be to generate a broad conceptual approach, designed to identify key dimensions along which political cultures may differ, resulting in different forms of political communication in turn. Yet the role of political culture in political communication has been little explored to date and rarely been subjected to comparative investigation.

To demonstrate the wide-ranging impact of political culture, we mention here some facets of political communication that are influenced by it and that could provide fertile areas for comparative research. These are merely illustrative and not an exhaustive or definitive list.

The encoding of political messages. Culture is the context, the framework within which all forms of communication, be they interpersonal or mass, takes place. Political culture is thus key to understanding the construction and encoding of political messages. It shapes political rhetoric; the symbols commonly invoked; appeals for support; claims to rights and needs; and ways of framing political issues and controversies in the news.

Political culture and the vocabulary of politics. Closely related to the encoding of political messages is "the semiotic turn," which has led media scholars to pay increasing attention to the meaning systems that undergird the flow of mediated messages. The manner in which political cultures impinge on the uses of language and the diversity of possible meanings embedded in media messages is of major significance for the comparative analysis of political communication. Clearly, the language of politics varies from one society to another, not only in terms of sheer vocabulary but also in terms of the meanings it carries. The vocabulary of democratic politics is obviously different from that deployed in nondemocratic regimes. But even among different democratic societies political vocabularies vary, rooted as they are in different political cultures, historical legacies, and traditions.

Constraints on the decoding of political messages. The counterpart of the encoding of political messages would be comparative study of the processes of decoding. Just as political cultures define and shape encoding, so they impinge on the meaning systems that message receivers deploy to interpret those messages. The role of audience members in decoding media messages is the core issue of reception analysis, as it has evolved over the past two decades. Much of this work, however, has focused on single-country audiences. Applying that approach to comparative studies of audiences across diverse societies would be beneficial in identifying the similarities and differences between the processes of decoding prevalent among audiences in different countries and different cultural settings.

Political culture and the culture of journalism. An intriguing area for comparative work concerns the culture of journalism in different societies. The issue here is how the culture of journalism is articulated to the political culture of different societies. Because political cultures may vary, do they also generate variations in the culture of journalism – or is the latter relatively immune to such influences? How do the principles of different political cultures relate to the character and degree of professionalization of media practitioners in diverse political systems? An often-presumed attribute of professionalism is its universality, that is, that the profession's values and basic principles are shared by its practitioners everywhere. Yet the connection of media systems to political cultures implies a cultural specificity that precludes the profession's universality. Comparative research could help to sort this out.

Interrelationships of media institutions and political institutions. More comparative research has probably been devoted to this area than to any of the others listed here but little attention has been paid to the cultural influences that play on and possibly variegate these relationships in different societies. In question here are the values and norms that prescribe and guide these relationships and the rules and practices derived from them to specify the normative guidelines and the boundaries of the permissible in the reciprocal interaction between both sides. Pfetsch (2001) has made an excellent start in empirically discovering and comparing the role and systemic origins of such cultural influences in the United States and Germany. This is enormously promising and should be built on in other societal contexts.

Reciprocal relations of citizens and elites. Citizenship is above all a culturally impregnated idea. It is also essentially relational, prescribing how the members of a society should regard and participate in their political institutions. It is a rich notion as well, incorporating, among others, attitudes to political authority (e.g., deferential or skeptical); entitlements to participate, be heard, have one's claims satisfied; all degrees of partisanship or its opposite; sentiments of duty and efficacy; even attitudes toward the rightful place of reason and emotion in politics. Yet this cornucopia has almost entirely escaped comparative scrutiny – other than through a cross-national charting of citizens' increasing disengagement in recent years from mainstream politics in many advanced democracies.

Of course much conceptual work will be required to develop the idea of *political culture* into a strong comparative tool. This is not the place to embark on such a project, but we close this part of our discussion by mentioning a particular need that arises from what we have emphasized so far.

Dimensions of Political Culture

The notion of political culture is at this point quite broad and open to different interpretations. To advance comparative research, its dimensions need to be specified and defined more clearly. In earlier work we have suggested certain dimensions along which political cultures may vary. These include "the valuation of politics as such" (Blumler and Gurevitch 1975), that is, the extent to which politics is valued highly rather than denigrated; the degree to which different political cultures embrace or resist populism (Blumler and Gurevitch 2001); and degrees of cultural support for international or nationalist/ethnocentric goals (Blumler 1983).

While these dimensions may well be useful in specific studies, they are evidently ad hoc. Political culture must be structured before it can be broken down into a set of field-spanning dimensions. The structure of a political communication system offers one basis for such a framework. This points to three areas of potentially fruitful dimensionalization. The first concerns the prescriptions of different political cultures about the relationship between their media and political systems. The second consists of the norms that define the roles and functions of the media for society. And the third concerns the relationship between citizens and their political system.

For example, a key dimension of the relationship between the media and the political system is the continuum of autonomy versus subordination (which, however, may subsume a host of subsidiary dimensions). Probably all societies can be placed at different points on this continuum, according to the degree to which their political cultures accord the media a relatively high measure of autonomy from the political system or conversely subordinate the media to that system. Democratic societies will thus be placed closer to the autonomy pole of the continuum while authoritarian societies will be located nearer the subordination pole – but there will be considerable variation within both camps as well.

Political cultures also prescribe norms concerning the functions of the media in society. Defining and sorting these could be a worthwhile endeavor. For example, certain cultures may expect the media to perform an essentially critical/watchdog function, exposing abuses of power by all social institutions; while others might support a nation-building role for the media, as if maintaining or guiding society toward an idealized state and thus collaborating with the political leadership, or elements within it, who view themselves as the vanguard in pursuit of the appropriate goals.

Finally, a cluster of dimensions could apply to varying orientations in the political culture toward the relations of citizens to government. We have already noted the many-faceted richness of the concept of citizenship. Again, some of these facets might be dimensionalized as continua with positive and negative poles at opposite ends. The former would encourage high levels of political engagement among citizens, while the latter would entail alienation or apathy. However, many distinctions would have to be kept in mind when entering this area. There are different sorts of positive and negative sentiments (e.g., disengagement does not necessarily equate with indifference). There are different parts of the political system to which they might be applied. And different population groups might be under the influence of different cultural orientations.

Thus, the areas recommended for dimensionalizing cover the three key elements of a political communication system – political system, media system, and citizenry.

THE NEED FOR THEORETICAL EXCHANGE

The extent and vigor of theoretical debate that permeates a field is a second criterion of its collective maturity. On this count, comparative political communication analysis still falls lamentably short. Subfields of political science and sociology are far more advanced in this respect. The literature on political parties, for example, is rich with frameworks for analyzing them cross-nationally, connected and advanced by a vein of cumulative debate about their respective merits and demerits. There is no such tradition in comparative political communications.

It is not that conceptual frameworks are absent from its literature but that they are almost never critically discussed after their publication. In fact, a near abundance of conceptual frameworks have been proposed to guide the comparative investigation of diverse facets of political communication – for example:

- On the media's subordination to or autonomy from political power – as in Alexander's (1981) differentiation theory and in Blumler and Gurevitch's (1975) specification of four dimensions of subordination-autonomy, including hypotheses about their implications for political content in the media and its effects on audience members.

339

- On the media's subordination to or autonomy from economic power – including the often used distinction between public-service and commercial broadcast media; hypotheses about the effects on political communications of increased competition between news media; and John McManus' (1995) "market model of news communication."
- On journalists' roles in political communication – including not only the long-standing adversarial-exchange dichotomy but also Patterson's (1998) two-dimensional typology, combining "passive-active" with "neutral-advocate" distinctions and hypothesizing consequences for media content and audience reception there from.
- On politicians' efforts to secure positive coverage in election news – including such distinctions as professional versus amateur; capital-intensive versus labor-intensive; proactive versus reactive, and so forth.
- On influences upon the access of sources to political news – as in Schlesinger's (1990) model of competition for such access (taking account of the distribution of symbolic and material resources plus opportunities for strategic action) and Blumler and Gurevitch's (2000) discussion of the impact of media abundance on the terms of such competition.
- *On sources of change in the overall organization and workings of political communication systems* – such as change in communication technologies; changes in the structure and culture of surrounding social and political systems; the dynamics of politician-journalist relations; and changes in the values, lifestyles, civic concerns, and attitudes to authority of audience members.

It is not the discreteness of these frameworks and their lack of integration into a more comprehensive comparative theory that most concerns us. The preceding listed examples may be regarded as specimens of what Merton once termed *middle range theories*, and, given both the multi-level complexity of political communication and its linkages to many other institutional domains, it is probably no bad thing that scholars have tailored frameworks to suit particular areas of the field. But left uncriticized, there is no spur to conceptual improvement or indeed to broader integrative theorizing.

In the future the situation we have described may become less lamentable. As more scholars break out of their national shells, pursue their interests collaboratively with colleagues from other societies, seek systemic explanations of discovered similarities and differences, and compare their findings and conclusions with those of other researchers, theoretical exchange may become more natural, common, and productive. Productive opportunities for such discussion should arise when Dan Hallin and Paolo Mancini publish a path-breaking attempt they are making to generate a framework of three distinct *media system models*, each with interrelated characteristics, which have not co-occurred accidentally but have arisen from different sociopolitical and cultural patterns of historical development. A taster of what may eventually emerge from their project can be consulted in Hallin and Papathanassopoulos (2002).

CONCLUDING NOTE

The inadequacy of research that stops short at fielding identical or similar instruments in several societies and reporting the results was an opening theme of this essay. In a sense, our argument now comes full circle. If conceptual analysis, and critical discussion thereof, were to become higher priorities and were more prominent in the literature, more scholars might be encouraged to engage in genuinely comparative rather than merely cross-national political communications research.

REFERENCES

Alexander, Jeffrey C. 1981. The Mass News Media in Systemic, Historical, and Comparative Perspective. In Elihu Katz and Tamás Szecskö, eds. *Mass Media and Social Change*. London: Sage, pp. 17–51.

Amin, Hussein. 2002. Freedom as a Value in Arab Media. Perceptions and Attitudes Among Journalists. *Political Communication* 19 (2): 125–36.

Bennett, W. Lance, and Robert M. Entman. 2001. Mediated Politics. An Introduction. In W. Lance Bennett and Robert M. Entman, eds. *Mediated Politics. Communication in the Future of Democracy*. Cambridge: Cambridge University Press, pp. 1–29.

Blumler, Jay G. 1997. Origins of the Crisis of Communication for Citizenship. *Political Communication* 14 (4): 394–404.

———. 1999. Political Communication Systems All Change. A Response to Kees Brants. *European Journal of Communication* 14 (2): 241–9.

Blumler, Jay G., ed. 1983. *Communicating to Voters. Television in the First European Parliamentary Elections*. London: Sage.

Blumler, Jay G., and Michael Gurevitch. 1975. Towards a Comparative Framework for Political Communication Research. In Steven H. Chaffee, ed. *Political Communication. Issues and Strategies for Research*. Beverly Hills, CA: Sage, pp. 165–93.

———. 1981. Politicians and the Press. An Essay on Role Relationships. In Dan D. Nimmo and Keith R. Sanders, eds. *Handbook of Political Communication*. Beverly Hills, CA: Sage, pp. 467–93.

_____. 2000. Rethinking the Study of Political Communication. In James Curran, and Michael Gurevitch, eds. *Mass Media and Society*. 3rd ed. London: Edward Arnold, pp. 155–72.

_____. 2001. "Americanization" Reconsidered: U.K.-U.S. Campaign Communication Comparisons across Time. In W. Lance Bennett and Robert M. Entman, eds. *Mediated Politics. Communication in the Future of Democracy*. Cambridge: Cambridge University Press, pp. 380–403.

Cook, Thomas. 1998. *Governing with the News. The News Media as a Political Institution*. Chicago: Chicago University Press.

Corner, John. 2001. Towards the Really Useful Media Researcher? *Nordicom Review* 22 (1): 3–10.

Esser, Frank, Carsten Reinemann, and David Fan. 2001. Spin Doctors in the United States, Great Britain and Germany. Metacommunication about Media Manipulation. *The Harvard International Journal of Press/Politics* 6 (1): 16–45.

Gunther, Richard, and Anthony Mughan. 2000. *Democracy and the Media. A Comparative Perspective*. Cambridge: Cambridge University Press.

Gurevitch, Michael, and Jay G. Blumler. 1990. Comparative Research. The Extending Frontier. In David L. Swanson and Dan Nimmo, eds. *New Directions in Political Communication. A Resource Book*. Newbury Park, CA: Sage, pp. 305–25.

Hallin, Daniel C., and Stylianos Papathanassopoulos. 2002. Political Clientilism and the Media. Southern Europe and Latin America in Comparative Perspective. *Media, Culture & Society* 24 (2): 175–96.

Johnson, Thomas J., Timothy Boudreau, and Chris Glowski. 1996. Turning the Spotlight Inward. How Five Leading News Organisations Covered the Media in the 1992 Presidential Election. *Journalism & Mass Communication Quarterly* 73 (3): 657–71.

Kernell, Samuel. 1986. *Going Public. New Strategies of Presidential Leadership*. Washington, DC: Congressional Quarterly Press.

Mancini, Paolo. 2000. Political Complexity and Alternative Models of Journalism: The Italian Case. In James Curran and Myung-Jin Park, eds. *De-Westernizing Media Studies*. London: Routledge, pp. 265–78.

Mancini, Paolo, and Daniel L. Swanson. 1996. Politics, Media and Modern Democracy. Introduction. In Daniel L. Swanson and Paolo Mancini, eds. *Politics, Media and Modern Democracy. An International Study of Innovations In Electoral Campaigning and Their Consequences*. Westport, CT: Praeger, pp. 1–28.

Mazzoleni, Gianpietro. 1987. Media Logic and Party Logic in Campaign Coverage. The Italian General Election 1983. *European Journal of Communication* 2 (1): 81–103.

McManus, John M. 1995. A Market-Based Model of News Production. *Communication Theory* 5 (4): 301–38.

Newman, Bruce, ed. 1999. *Handbook of Political Marketing*. London: Sage.

Patterson, Thomas E. 1998. Political Roles of the Journalist. In Doris Graber, Denis McQuail, and Pippa Norris, eds. *The Politics of News, the News of Politics*. Washington, DC: Congressional Quarterly Press, pp. 17–32.

Pfetsch, Barbara. 2001. Political Communication Culture in the United States and Germany. *The Harvard International Journal of Press/Politics* 6 (1): 46–67.

Plasser, Fritz. 2001. Parties' Diminishing Relevance for Campaign Professionals. *The Harvard International Journal of Press/Politics* 6 (4): 44–59.

Reese, Steve D. 2001. Understanding the Global Journalist. A Hierarchy of Influences Approach. *Journalism Studies* 2 (2): 173–87.

Schlesinger, Philip. 1990. Rethinking the Sociology of Journalism. Source Strategies and the Limits of Media-Centrism. In Majorie Ferguson, ed. *Public Communication. The New Imperatives.* London: Sage, pp. 61–83.

Schönbach, Klaus, Edmund Lauf, Jack M. McLeod, and Dietram A. Scheufele. 1999. Sociodemographic Determinants of Newspaper Reading in the USA and Germany, 1974–1996. *European Journal of Communication* 14 (2): 225–40.

Schönbach, Klaus, and Holli A. Semetko. 2000. Gnadenlos Professionell. Journalisten und die aktuelle Medienberichterstartung in Bundestagswahlkämpfen 1976–1998. In Hans Bohrmann, Otfried Jarren, Gabriele Melischek, and Josef Seethaler, eds. *Wahlen und Politikvermittlung durch Massenmedien.* Wiesbaden, Germany: Westdeutscher Verlag, pp. 69–78.

Schudson, Michael. 2001. Politics as Cultural Practice. *Political Communication* 18 (4): 421–31.

Semetko, Holli A., Jay G. Blumler, Michael Gurevitch, and David H. Weaver. 1991. *The Formation of Campaign Agendas. A Comparative Analysis of Party and Media Roles in Recent American and British Elections.* Hillsdale, NJ: Erlbaum Associates.

Swanson David L., and Paolo Mancini. 1996. Patterns of Modern Election Campaigning and Their Consequences. In David L. Swanson and Paolo Mancini, eds. *Politics, Media and Modern Democracy. An International Study of Innovations in Electoral Campaigning and Their Consequences.* Westport, CT: Praeger, pp. 247–76.

Wilke, Jürgen, and Carsten Reinemann. 2001. Do the Candidates Matter? Long-Term Trends of Campaign Coverage – A Study of the German Press since 1949. *European Journal of Communication* 16 (3): 291–314.

FIFTEEN

From Political Culture to Political Communication Culture

A Theoretical Approach to Comparative Analysis

Barbara Pfetsch

The scholarly debate on the development of political communication in modern democracies makes reference to concepts of Americanization, modernization, and globalization (Chapter 2, in this volume). The framing of political communication in connection with macropolitical economic and societal processes of change raises the question of the convergence of political communication processes, which elicits ambivalent answers depending on the level of analysis, the point in time, the country, and the cultural context. While one can best speak of convergence in electoral campaign communication, the issue of parallel development tendencies in other areas of political communication still largely remains to be investigated. This is because, firstly, we have neither convincing theoretical concepts nor a comprehensive body of empirical studies on the processes of everyday political communication between elections, communication between government and citizens, or interaction between political actors and the media (Chapter 14, in this volume). Secondly, political communication in national arenas is often considered a constant factor in the policy process and scarcely conceded to have an independent explanatory contribution to make to political analysis.

The most routinized communication relationships between political actors and journalists are nevertheless a critical factor in the democratic process in all Western countries. Democratic systems of government depend on political action and political decisions being publicly communicated and legitimated. The structures and rules of political communication are therefore an important variable in understanding the public representation of political objects. The analysis of interaction between politics and the media is not least of all a challenge for international comparative research. Why is political public relations successful in one country and not in another? Why is the same political problem an issue for the media in one country but not in another? Why do news broadcasts tend to give politics a populist format in one country while in another they tend to bespeak the state?

The demand for international comparative research in political communication has far-reaching consequences, for it requires implicit premises and national particularities to be left aside in both politics and media communication in the search for generalizable patterns in communicating political content and, above all, in the consequences thereof. Thus, in speaking about the modernization of political communication (Swanson and Mancini 1996) or the global convergence of political communication systems, or even seeking to demonstrate them empirically, it is not sufficient to describe only isolated phenomena in the outward manifestations of electoral campaigns, television appearances by politicians, or the practices of political public relations. In order to explain similarities and differences in political communication in different countries, it is necessary to understand the processes of political communication and the public forms it assumes in the context of both actors *and* structures. That is to say, political communication in Western democracies is to be understood firstly as a process of interaction between political actors and media actors. Secondly, these processes take place in different structural contexts of the political system (e.g., the mechanisms of the electoral system or the constellation of the party system) and of the media system (e.g., in media markets with a strongly differing degree of commercialization).

One upshot of these considerations is that political communication is to be regarded in comparative approaches as a system that has a structural and a cultural dimension. The structure of political communication involves the institutional conditions of the political system and the media system at the macrolevel and the mesolevel. The cultural dimension involves describing actors and the subjective action orientations, attitudes, and norms of actors in professional political communication roles. If political communication processes are seen as interplay between the actors' behavior and structural conditions, the comparative approach offers considerable potential for analyzing these processes. Comparison makes it possible to vary structural and contextual conditions and to ask what constellations of actor orientations correspond.

Nevertheless, comparative research designs mark not only a strategy of empirical inquiry. They also require the issues and theoretical concept of the subject under study to be sufficiently specified. This is the motivation for the present chapter. The aim is to develop a conceptual perspective for the comparative study of interaction between political actors and media actors in modern democracies. The focus is on actors in political communication, who supply political information in exchange for media publicity, and whose orientations form a political communication culture. It is assumed that the interaction space at the interface between politics and the media in which political communication actors move is crucial in understanding the representation of political objects in national public arenas. This milieu is characterized by the orientations of journalists and political spokespersons, which, following Blumer and Gurevitch (1995, 19), can be termed the *political communication culture* of a country. The political communication culture plays a central role in how politics is thematized, and this has implications for the democratic process. In Dahl's democracy theory terms (1989, 111), the quality of political communication can be measured by whether it contributes to an "enlightened understanding" among citizens. What is meant is the possibility and capacity of the individual to judge the performance and decisions of political decision makers in order to participate on the basis of this knowledge. It is therefore a democracy-theoretical test of every political communication culture whether it permits or generates discourses that allow a rational understanding of political processes on the part of the public. Vice versa, a political communication culture is dysfunctional for the democratic process if it impairs the rationality of the political discourse.

This chapter addresses the thesis that the political communication culture is an essential component of the political culture of a country. The relationship between politics and the media is thus a central factor for the legitimacy and stability of the democratic process and for the style and quality of the political discourse. Given these premises, the concept of political communication culture is to be presented and discussed as a possible approach for the comparative analysis of political communication. The approach focuses on the role-specific conditions for the action and attitude patterns of political communication actors that shape the profile of different types of political communication depending on the actor constellation and structural conditions in the given country. It is also assumed that the public representation of politics varies with the structure and culture of political communication.

A first step toward underpinning this thesis is to deal in greater detail with the conceptualities and the notion of political communication culture and its substantive dimensions. The second step is to present a heuristic concept for the typification of political communication cultures useful for international analysis. This is followed by a consideration of what types of political communication culture are conceivable under what structural conditions in different national arenas, and what profiles of political discourse are to be expected in each case. The goal is to make a contribution toward the theoretical conceptualization of political communication that can serve as a basis and point of departure for the international comparative empirical study of political communication systems.

POLITICAL CULTURE AND POLITICAL COMMUNICATION CULTURE: SPECIFICATION AND DIMENSIONS OF THE CONCEPTS

CLARIFICATION OF THE ORIGINAL CONCEPT OF ALMOND AND VERBA

The concept of political communication culture was introduced in communication research by Blumler and Gurevitch (1977, quoted as Blumler and Gurevitch 1995) in the 1970s. The issue and point in time were no accident, for the authors were in the direct tradition of political culture research, which had begun in the 1960s with the study "Civic Culture" by Almond and Verba (Almond and Verba 1963; Almond 1980). Political culture research is interested in the interplay between subjective orientations of citizens, that is, the ideas and value codes that regulate political action (Verba 1965), and the structural conditions of democratic systems. "When we speak of the political culture of a society, we refer to the political system as internalized in the cognitions, feelings, and evaluations of its population.... The political culture of a nation is the particular distribution of patterns of orientation toward political objects among the members of the nation" (Almond and Verba 1963, 13). On the assumption that a political system can be stable only if the fundamental values and orientations of the members of society are compatible with the sociopolitical and institutional structure, political culture research seeks to describe the attitudes and norms of the citizens who act *within* the framework of political institutions (Verba 1965, 514).

If the concern of political culture research is transferred to the subarea of political communication, the political communication system is to be explained not only through indicators of the institutional structure of the political and the media systems. It is rather the subjective orientations of actors in politics and the media that lend meaning to this system. What is decisive in this view of political communication is that exchanges between political actors and journalists are regulated by a set of orientations and norms within the media and political context, in other words, by the political communication culture[1] (Blumler and Gurevitch 1995, 19). One can go so far as to say that the attitudes of the actors are a decisive criterion for the quality and stability or change in the political communication of a country.

If one basically accepts the idea of a political communication culture, certain questions arise on the status and content of the concept, which have to be put not least of all because political culture research has had a critical reception history (cf. Almond 1980; Kaase 1983; Pappi 1986). However, the criticism directed at political culture research does not lend itself to question that political communication culture can be understood as a component of general political culture of a country, and that by comparing political communication cultures across countries the fabrics of political communication systems can be analyzed in a systematic way.

In the debate on political culture it has been questioned whether the national-state level is a meaningful unit of reference for analysis, because the aggregation from individual orientations up to the level of the nation state is quite a large step (Pappi 1986). Thus, Verba (1980, 406) suggests that the units of analysis be kept smaller. Instead of large, national aggregates, it would be useful to examine specific subcultures and their value structures. Kaase (1983, 161–3) and Pappi (1986, 281) stress that one could just as well choose smaller political units or social systems, for example, a regional, cultural, or structural subsystem for the fruitful analysis of political culture. Studies of specific subcultures have the advantage over total analyses of being closer to social reality.

Against this background, it seems obvious and plausible to choose the political communication system as a relevant subsystem of political culture and as a unit for analysis. The focus then is on the orientations of actors in political communication, that is, political spokespersons and journalists. In analogy to political culture, political communication culture can be defined as *the empirically observable orientations of actors in the system of production of political messages toward specific objects of political communication, which determine the manner in which political actors and media actors communicate in relation to their common political public.*

[1] This culture concept has little to do with the usual semantics of "Kultur" as the totality of intellectual and artistic forms of expression in general German usage. It refers rather to the observable norms and rules that regulate interactions between mutually dependent actors in a given relationship.

Dimensions	Objects of Orientation
System in General	Political communication system as interpenetration system of media and politics
Input	Public opinion
Output	Political public relations, news management, strategic communication
Self-Image	Communication roles, interaction norms

Figure 15.1 The Dimensions of Political Communication Culture

THE OBJECTS OF POLITICAL COMMUNICATION CULTURE

As for the concept of political culture, the dimensions of the political communication culture and its empirical desiderata need to be clarified. By analogy with political culture research on this point, the dimensions[2] proposed by Almond and Verba (1963) can also be useful for the Political Communication system (Figure 15.1). The following objects can be identified: the system of producing, processing, and communicating political messages; the input side of this system; the output side of the system; and the role allocations and norms that ensure the maintenance of political communication.

THE POLITICAL COMMUNICATION SYSTEM. In contrast to other societal subsystems such as politics, law, or the economy, which can largely be distinguished from one another by their functions and codes, the political communication system is a construct composed of elements from two other social systems, politics, and the public sphere in its mass-media format. If this is the case, German proponents of systems theory, in particular, will ask what mechanisms integrate the two subsystems to form the political communication system. Münch offers a solution to the problem of integrating functionally differentiated subsystems (1997, 89). He argues that the integration of two social systems occurs to the extent in which the subsystem-specific media of communication (e.g., power in the political system or attention in the public) transport the input and the output of the subsystems across their borders. The idea is that the generation of power in the political system depends explicitly on the import of resources from other social systems, for example, attention, value commitments, and material resources. Similarly, the production of attention in the media depends on resources from other systems, such as political autonomy, freedom of speech, information, certainty of the

---

[2] Almond and Verba (1963, 16) propose an analytical schema based on Parsons that identifies four objects of the political system as attitude dimensions: the political system in general, input structures, output structures, and the self-image of the individuals acting in the system.

law, money, and so forth. According to Münch, integration then means institutionalizing the exchange process between the subsystems.

The political communication system can be regarded as such an institutionalization in the sense of the integration of two functionally differentiated subsystems. In other words, the political communication system regulates cross-border communication between politics and the media, and develops a "common language of communication that is assigned to no subsystem," and the more contacts are maintained, the more a "sense of belonging together over and beyond systems and group borders" develops (Münch 1997, 90). From this point of view the political communication system is an "empirical system" (Münch 1997, 93). The concept of empirical system is concerned with both the institutionalization of exchange relations and with the actors. Renate Mayntz (1988) argues that one can speak of a differentiated subsystem if the functions ascribed to it are to be found in the subjective orientations of the actors operating both within the system itself and in the environment of the system.

THE OUTPUT SIDE OF THE POLITICAL COMMUNICATION SYSTEM. The output side of the political communication system is concerned with the production, processing, and communication of political messages. The functional area of cross-border communication in the political system is political public relations. At the level of concrete organization, the job of political public relations workers is to generate issues, to frame and evaluate issues, and to time when they are to be made public (Baerns 1985). The issue-generation function of political public relations is fraught with consequences, for the choice of issues has an impact on the image of the actors involved. This means that political public relations not only offers issues but, using these issues, can influence the generation of public opinion about organizations and actors, and does so with persuasive intent, that is, with the aim of generating consent (Gerhards 1994, 97–100).

THE INPUT SIDE OF THE POLITICAL COMMUNICATION SYSTEM. The common unit of reference for actors of the political communication system is the public. The preferences and demands of the media audience with certain information needs and the preferences and demands of the electorate with specific political demands converge in the construct of public opinion. From a democracy theory point of view, public opinion is a central normative factor in public choice in democratic systems, which provokes and sustains communication about politics. In this sense the social construction of public opinion on the part of political communication actors can be understood as the input side of the political communication system and as a central dimension of the political communication culture.

THE SELF-IMAGE OF ACTORS IN THE POLITICAL COMMUNICATION SYSTEM.
The orientations of system members toward their roles as actors in political communication, which are endowed with specific competencies, can be described as the fourth dimension of the political communication system. Members' own roles are concerned with the understanding spokespersons and journalists have of themselves and the expectations they have of their interlocutors in the process of producing political messages. As far as journalism is concerned, communicator studies suggest that the orientation of journalists toward their professional role depends strongly on the professional environment and functional context (Scholl and Weischenberg 1998, 221). Nevertheless, national media cultures can be described in terms of the specific orientation patterns of journalists (Chapter 11, this volume).

It is difficult, however, to assess the role understanding of political spokespersons uniformly, just as it is difficult to delimit the area of activity and socialization background of these actors. With regard to the development of spokesperson roles in political communication, two types can initially be distinguished: Politicians who act as "communication managers for their own cause" (Bentele 1998, 136) and the "special category of experts" (Neidhardt 1994, 15), who operate in professional communication positions that have emerged through the differentiation of political communication. Tenscher (2003) describes the latter as "political communication experts," that is, people who work in or for a political institution or actor without himself or herself holding political office. Their job is the public presentation of politicians and their messages in a manner adapted to the media logic.

The areas of action for actors in political communication, both in journalism and in political public relations, are underprofessionalized, because socialization in both areas takes the form of "learning on the job." It is important to note in the present context that the self-image of political spokespersons and journalists, that is, their norms and values, are characterized by tensions resulting from their situation as cross-border "commuters" of their organization of origin.

TYPES OF POLITICAL COMMUNICATION CULTURE

The political communication system develops firstly through an intendedly lasting exchange relationship between political spokespersons and journalists and, secondly, through tensions between these groups. The constellation and type of tension can be taken as a theoretical criterion

for categorizing political communication culture. The opposing orientations of political spokespersons and journalists can theoretically relate
to all the dimensions of political communication culture. Realistically,
however, the relationship of tension between the two sides is manifested
primarily on two levels, firstly the self-image level, that is, the norms of
one's own professional action, and secondly the level of action orientations in relation to the output of interaction, that is, specifically the
gearing of political public relations to the production and framing of
political messages. In these aspects of the political communication culture, the differing interests and profiles of the systems and organizations
of origin collide most violently.

SELF-IMAGE AND ROLE: PROXIMITY VS. DISTANCE

The fact that the images – of themselves and of others – held by political
spokespersons and journalists differ is typical of every political communication culture. Sarcinelli (1998, 255) accordingly calls for empirical
studies of interaction relations between political and media actors "that
permit statements about the institutionally and normatively appropriate
and inappropriate proximity or distance between politics and journalism." It is nevertheless difficult to find a yardstick for "appropriate"
proximity or distance between political spokespersons and journalists.
Realistic analyses of communication relations can therefore seek only
to ascertain greater or lesser proximity, greater or lesser freedom for a
given side. Communication cultures can therefore be distinguished only
by the extent of the differences or distance between the normative orientations of the two groups. The two extreme positions recorded in the
literature on the relationship between journalists and politicians or their
spokespersons are occupied by the United States with comparatively
strong tensions and Japan with markedly close, symbiotic relations.

OUTPUT: MEDIA LOGIC VS. PARTY-POLITICAL LOGIC

At the output level of the political communication culture, orientations toward the goals of action in political public relations are the
relevant factor likely to influence the nature of a political communication culture. Mazzoleni (1987, 85) has developed a dichotomy for
electoral campaign communication that proposes two basic directions
in the production of political messages. *Media logic* is concerned with
the values and formats of the media through which events and issues are
addressed, treated, and interpreted. The media-oriented variant of political public relations aims directly and exclusively to attain positive media

		Self-Image (communication roles and norms)	
		Great distance between political spokespersons and journalists	Small distance between political spokespersons and journalists
Communication Output (orientation toward political public relations)	Dominance of media logic (media attention as primary goal)	Media-oriented political communication culture	Public relations-oriented political communication culture
	Dominance of political logic (political rule as primary goal)	Strategic political communication culture	(Party) political communication culture

Figure 15.2 Types of Political Communication Culture

presentation and the broadest possible attention. This orientation can be more or less equated with political marketing, in which communication forms have been fixed beforehand and substantive messages formulated only subsequently. The political content or substance of the message is secondary. In *party logic*, the normative and power political aspects and calculations of political actors and parties are the focus in the production of political messages. In this variant of political public relations, the media are a means to an end. Communication therefore aims to position political actors favorably and to their strategic advantage in the political competition between parties and vis-à-vis the public, and to put through political programs.

In classifying political communication culture on the two dimensions of self-image and political communication output, the combination of the two levels and their attributes produces a four-field schema offering a heuristic procedure for classifying political communication cultures. The combination of differences in the self-image of political communication actors (distance versus proximity) and the orientation of political public relations (media logic versus political logic) produces four possible types of political communication culture (Figure 15.2).

(1) *Media-Oriented Political Communication Culture*: Characteristic of a *media-oriented political communication culture* is that political spokespersons have to accept the maxims of media production as their own rules if they are to be in any position at all to

communicate their messages. In view of the distance between the two groups, acceptance of the rules of the media game is prerequisite for all communication, because no other social mechanisms – such as personal trust or esteem – are available to overcome the clash of interests.

(2) *Public Relations–Oriented Political Communication Culture*: In a *public relations–oriented political communication culture*, mutual agreement develops between actors that political messages are to be generated by the rules of mass-media attention generation. This agreement is backed by social proximity and personal consensus. This variant of political communication culture, which lives primarily from the close relationship between journalism and public relations, corresponds to what Bentele (1998) calls "intereffication."

(3) *(Party) Political Communication Culture*: In a *(party) political communication culture*, political logic, especially the power-political calculations of political parties or governments, determines communication relationships, as expressed in the determination hypothesis (Baerns 1985). When social or political relations between political spokespersons and journalists are close, political public relations can succeed comparatively easily in determining both issues and timing and, ideally, also opinions in media reporting. Communication proceeds in accordance with the rules of the political actors, even though this means a loss of autonomy for the media.

(4) *Strategic Political Communication Culture*: The dominance of political logic with simultaneously greater role distance produces a communication culture in which political spokespersons have to deploy strategic measures to communicate their messages. They do so by taking political public relations as a strategic political resource and use their technical knowledge about the production and impact of political messages purposively for the specific and short-term objectives of political elites (Manheim 1997). Characteristic of a *strategic political communication culture* is that political spokespersons seek to instrumentalize the media with the aid of their own rules of the game in the pursuit of their power-political goals.

One of the problems of heuristic proceedings is that demarcation is difficult and cannot be powerful on all dimensions. It is therefore realistic to assume that there are intermediate areas between the types of communication culture presented here. But it can be expected that exploring the orientations of actors in political communication will provide at least some indication of whether one is dealing with a more media-oriented, (party) political, public relations–oriented, or strategic political communication culture. This involves two considerations.

- First, every actually observable political communication culture is an expression of specific structural constellations of conditions in the political system and in the media system. The question is therefore what structural conditions of political communication and what types of political communication culture correspond.
- From a democracy theoretical point of view and with regard to the general problem of political communication in Western democracies, it must secondly be asked how different types relate to the democratic process. In other words, which communication cultures tend to be functional from the democracy theory perspective and which tend to be dysfunctional for the representation of issues or for political discourses?

INTERNATIONAL COMPARISON OF POLITICAL COMMUNICATION CULTURES

The special charm of the concept of political communication culture is that it provides a heuristic basis for the international comparison of political communication processes. Only comparative analyses can help answer the question as to whether the types of political communication culture presented here are empirically acceptable and generalizable. International comparative political communication research will have taken a major step forward if it can be shown that certain structural contexts of political communication in the political system and the media system can be related to the development of certain types of political communication culture. One of the few works that deal with the structural conditions of the mass media and the public sphere as explanatory factors for processes of political communication is by Dan Hallin and Paolo Mancini (1984, quoted from Hallin 1994, 125). "Political structure thus comes to be embodied in certain ways of speaking about politics, conventions of communication that in their turn profoundly affect the possibilities for political discourse in the society." The link between the structural conditions of political communication and the given dominant constellations of actor attitudes is an empirical issue and would therefore have to be the subject of a large-scale comparative research program. Nonetheless, such research requires a notion about the relevant dimensions and criteria of the structural contexts that could influence the political communication culture of a country. This is to be outlined as a basis for well-directed hypothesis formation in future research.

Structural Conditions in the Media System and the Political System

It is in the nature of the political communication culture that the key structural framework conditions for interaction between political spokespersons and journalists are located in both the media and the political system. The structural conditions of the media system are associated with specific expectations vis-à-vis media organizations on the part of politics and with political mechanisms and opportunities for exerting influence on the media. On the other hand, the structural conditions of the media system influence how media organizations position themselves in a national media system and in the public sphere. This is relevant for political communication because it is associated with a specific commitment to the public and the intention or obligation to service certain segments of the public. Finally, the structural conditions of the media influence the norms of professional orientations and modes of behavior, the way political spokespersons and journalists deal with one another, and the content of media reporting on politics.

Hallin and Mancini (quoted from Hallin 1994) introduce commercialization as the decisive and obvious criterion in the domain of the media system. Media organizations in highly commercialized media systems obey profit-oriented imperatives of maximum audience reach and thus higher advertising revenues. Although commercial systems are also subject to certain regulative mechanisms, the market-economy logic is at the same time associated with a high degree of media freedom and autonomy from government and political institutions. This is in contrast to media systems that are either dominated by the party press or characterized by structures of press-party parallelism (Seymour-Ure 1974). Media organizations in such systems obey political-ideological imperatives that are imposed by media owners who are themselves political actors or openly commit themselves to a given political line. The opposition between party press and commercial press is not realistic insofar as, in almost all Western media systems, the party press no longer plays any role. The media systems in the vast majority of modern countries follow some form of dual model.

Basically, however, the difference in the structure of media systems lies in the distinction between commercial and political logics. In the organizational forms of the electronic media, the dichotomy – commercial versus public – is associated with the assumption that commercial systems may operate largely without obligation toward the public interest. For public systems, in contrast, such an obligation is politically charged because political elites legitimate their communication and publicity demands with the argument that publicly subsidized media organizations are committed to the public interest and to offering a comprehensive information service. For the processes of political communication it can thus be said that profit-oriented structures are associated with political autonomy and strong orientation toward the audience, and public system structures with politicization and relevance for elites, producing (according to the hypothesis) specific variants of political communication relationships and actor attitudes.

There is a functionally equivalent distinction in the field of the press, which in Western countries is traditionally in private hands. Crucial for political communication in the press is whether pluralism is constituted by a multiplicity of politically independent print media or by a spectrum of newspapers and magazines committed to a particular politics or to specific parties and that reflects the party system (Voltmer 2000). The commercialization/politicization dichotomy can also apply for national systems of print media. Politicization in the sense of elite orientation appears to be particularly marked in print media systems with a range of newspapers and magazines that show a party-political profile. By contrast, in media systems with a large number of politically uncommitted, internally autonomous newspapers and magazines, the profit motive is much more important.

Establishing the structural context conditions on the side of the political system is difficult insofar as the constitutional arrangements of modern Western democracies offer many different government and party systems that shape the political process and political communication in combination with cultural and historical traditions. According to Hallin and Mancini (quoted from Hallin 1994), the decisive substantive dimension in classifying political structural conditions in relation to communication processes is how major political agenda-building institutions structure the political public sphere. This may sound abstract, but what is meant is whether the political public sphere is interpenetrated by strong political organizations and interest groups who claim the power to define issue agendas and political decisions, and which actively perform this role. The contrasting notion is that political organizations and interest groups are so weak and fragmented that the definition of political issues and decisions and their public interpretation is left to the media. To this extent, every system of government can be examined to see if institutional design and constitutional arrangements produce a politicized or mediatized public sphere.

As far as the structural parameters of political systems are concerned, constitutional arrangements have a decisive influence on other institutional factors of the political process. They include the characteristic profiles of government practice in a parliamentary system of government as opposed to a presidential system, which have to do with the control mechanisms of parliament, the functions and strength of political parties, and the structure of interest representation. Ideally one can cite a presidential system of government with an elaborate system of control mechanisms operating between government and parliament (checks and balances), a weak role for political parties, and a highly fragmented system of highly specialized interest and lobby groups. In contrast to this system are representative systems of government with a government carried by parliament, where political parties play a strong role, and where interest groups are less strong and corporatistically interdependent. These constitutional differences are generally named when distinguishing between European party democracies and the American presidential system. In European party systems the processes of political agenda building and the interpretation of political issues are driven by parties and interest groups along ideological cleavages and decided in the parliamentary negotiating arenas. In the American model, by contrast, the organization of parties as electoral campaign machines for gaining political office according to Schumpeter and Down's competitive democracy model and the specialization and fragmentation of interest groups mean that the interpretation of politics depends on two institutions: the president and the media (Hallin 1994). Because the president is strongly controlled by Congress and has no right to initiate legislation, he has to embrace a strategy of "going public" (Kernell 1986) to ensure the support of the media, which assume the real role of interpreting politics in the public sphere.

Structural Conditions, Political Communication Cultures, and Public Discourses

Combining the proposed dimensions and distinctions between structural conditions in the political system and those in the media system produces four constellations of political communication context, which can be confronted with the outlined types of political communication culture. The first constellation is a commercialized broadcasting system and a pluralistic, internally autonomous press with a high degree of political autonomy combined with a political public structure where political agenda building and the interpretation of politics is in the hands of the media owing to the weak role of political parties and the fragmentation of societal (interest) groups. Under these conditions, it seems plausible that political communication is largely dominated by the media and that a media-oriented political communication culture consequently develops.

The consequences of a media-oriented political communication culture for the public discourse on politics are contradictory. At any rate, it can be assumed that what the media report in the way of messages emanating from the political system predominantly uses media formats that promise high audience reach. Such high public attention is in keeping with the economic requirements of the media, especially television. The literature discusses tendencies in media reporting such as the personalization of politics, a preference for political human-touch aspects, and a predilection for visual and (television) dramaturgical infotainment formats. In the long term, this way of representing political issues could lead to situations in which material politics no longer plays a role in the public discourse, although, from a superficial point of view, it has occasioned the message. Thematization in a media-oriented political communication culture tends to develop a dynamic of its own, which, in extreme cases, builds up to such an extent that the political content is no longer perceptible. In a worst-case scenario, this would depoliticize the public discourse on politics. A situation would arise in which the public can no longer recognize the connection between issues and political performance and decision making.

It is no wonder that the media-oriented political communication culture described here corresponds closely to what is to be observed of political communication and the public sphere in the United States. Many different studies on processes of political communication (Bennett 1988; Entman 1989) and electoral campaign communication; analyses of communication relations between the American government and the media (Pfetsch 2003); and studies on the representation of politics on television show that a media-oriented political communication culture can be a plausible explanatory pattern for the way in which communication about politics takes place in the United States.

The second variant of communication context produced by combining structural characteristics is the constellation of a dual broadcasting system with radio and television stations committed to the public interest and thus politically robust in combination with a press more or less reflecting the structure of the party system, in other words, the media system is comparatively strongly politicized. If this constellation is combined with a structure of the political public sphere in which the political agenda and the interpretation of issues is determined by ideologically oriented parties and interest groups and structurally safeguarded by the parliamentary system of government, there is a good chance that interaction between the media and politics will be accompanied by a (party) political communication culture.

As far as the consequences of a (party) political communication culture for the political discourse are concerned, the political instrumentalization of journalism is to be feared. Political actors must ideally be suspected of seeking to enhance their image in public primarily through their ideologically charged positions on certain substantive programs or decisions. From this point of view, this constellation of political communication culture would be more likely to lead to the thematization of different policy options by competing actors. From a democracy theory perspective, one could thus expect this type of political communication culture to contribute to citizens being able to comprehend alternative policy options and the process of their generation. However, this idealized view of a possible outcome of the (party) political communication culture presupposes that the actors participating in political competition do indeed offer alternative policy options. Realistically, divergence in material policy tends to be small, and the symbolic dramatization of political differences (Schmidt 1996) is now to the fore.

The Federal Republic of Germany might offer an example for a (party) political communication culture in a national context. In any case, studies on communication in internal party decision-making processes (Jarren et al. 1993); analyses of the milieus in which government and journalists act (Pfetsch 2003); and studies on electoral campaign communication (Sarcinelli and Schatz 2002) show that the functional logic of party democracy has a still stronger influence on the style and substance of political communication. Nevertheless, changes in the media environment, notably growing commercialization and competition between media, exert strong pressure to adapt the external public presentation of political actors and issues. This may blur political-ideological differences

Types of Political Communication Culture (PCC)	Structural Conditions	Possible Consequences for the Public Discourse on Politics
Media-oriented	Commercial, autonomous media/weak parties	Depoliticization
Public relations-oriented	Dual, political media/ weak parties	Dominance of symbolic politics and surrogate politics
(Party) political	Dual, political media/ strong parties	Dominance of party (political) surrogate politics and policy options
Strategic	Commercial media/ strong parties	Dominance of issue of populist power preservation

Figure 15.3 Types of Political Communication Culture and Possible Consequences for the Public Discourse on Politics

between parties in public (media) presentation in favor of meaningless surrogate politics (Sarcinelli 2001, 138) (Figure 15.3).

The third, a broadcasting system at least partly committed to the public interest together with a politically committed press may produce a constellation in which the media are highly responsive to the communication interests of the political elites, and the political public sphere and political agenda building are structured by weak parties and low-profile (interest) groups. This situation suggests that political communication processes are driven notably by the professionalization and strategies of political public relations. In this case, interaction between political spokespersons and journalists is strongly influenced by a public relations–oriented political communication culture.

Discourses dominated by symbolic politics and media-friendly surrogate politics are to be expected from a public relations–oriented political communication culture. It, too, can contribute little to public transparency in material politics. Nevertheless, the total depoliticization of public thematization is unlikely because journalists, too, when they consider it opportune, become involved with political spokespersons and their interests. A changeable and hybrid discourse on politics is thus to be expected, in which political performance and decision making are symbolically overdramatized and taken out of context. From this perspective, the hope that authors such as Bentele (1998, 142–3) and Ronneberger and Rühl (1992) entertain with regard to the consequences of the political public relations culture, namely that the performance of political public relations generates public trust and societal understanding seem unrealistic.

On the basis of the given structural conditions, one could expect a political public relations culture to have developed in a country such as

Switzerland, where, owing to weak parties and strong consensus democracy elements in the political process accompanied by media responsiveness toward elites, styles of a status-quo-oriented public statement politics develop. At any rate, a study by Saxer (1992, 73) shows that the political communication culture in Switzerland is driven by the "emotional integration" of political actors and journalists, whose relationship is fostered by social proximity. This not only inhibits the journalistic inclination to criticize dignitaries harshly (Saxer 1992, 59), but also means that the presentation of politics has hardly any ideological profile, the focus shifting to symbolic consensus.

The fourth constellation of structural conditions unites a strongly or predominantly commercial broadcasting system with a pluralistic press not oriented on party-political elites in a media system whose public and profit orientation is accompanied by a high degree of political autonomy. It is joined by a political system with strong, ideologically entrenched political parties and (interest) groups. They control political agenda building and the interpretation of politics, and safeguard these processes institutionally. In this situation strong political actors with their communication interests confront strong media with their public orientation. The processes of political communication are thus characterized by strong competition for attention, in which interaction between political spokespersons and journalists are mostly determined by a *strategic* political communication culture.

In a strategic political communication culture, spokespersons instrumentalize the organizational goals and control of media enterprises for their purposes (Manheim 1998, 100–1). The objective of this form of communication is to gain political competitive advantages by thematizing intraparty and interparty altercations; personnel and coalition debates; and the tactical ploys of government politics. From a substantive point of view, the dramatization of these aspects of the political process appear to be best suited to satisfy the attention criteria of the media, even when the distance between political actors and journalists is great. In essence, however, it is the utilitarian goals of political actors that are in play (Manheim 1991, 8–9). According to Manheim (1997, 64–5), "the irony" of this form of communication is that it "is absolutely democratic, because the management of communication is based fundamentally on the observation of the values and needs of target groups, and messages are designed for the optimum satisfaction of established interests" (Manheim 1997, 64–5). Nonetheless, dysfunctional effects arise in relation to what citizens perceive publicly as politics. Because the public depends on the information provided by the mass media and these media are susceptible to "manipulation by the elite of strategic communicators" (Manheim 1991, 10), the rational political discourse is undermined, because the difference between material and publicly dramatized politics can no longer be recognized.

A political communication culture corresponding to this model could be suspected in Italy, where the fact that the head of government is the biggest media owner increases the chances of the media being strategically instrumentalized for political purposes. This is all the more likely now that personnel changes have brought the public television system into line with the government. The public representation of politics is thus prestructured from a political-ideological point of view. At the same time, the media dramatization and styles of political thematization are designed to bring competitive advantages for the government vis-à-vis the public.

CONCLUDING REMARKS

On the basis of the reflections on and discussion of political culture, this chapter argues that the concept of political communication culture as a component in the overall political culture of a country can make an important explanatory contribution to analyzing interaction between politics and the media in modern democracies. As a basis for typifying communication relationships between journalists and political actors against the background of the structural conditions prevailing in politics and the media, the concept can provide a heuristic foundation that may give impetus to the comparative analysis of political communication. In this sense, this chapter is to be understood as a first step and encouragement for the further conceptual development of research, which will require greater substantive and methodological elaboration.

However, the basic idea is established: under differing structural conditions in the political system and the media, specific milieus of interaction between political actors and journalists develop that can be described in terms of empirically observable role constellations and norms. Depending on the given constellation, a political communication culture develops that can be dominant for a spatially and culturally definable system. The relevant consequences of different political communication cultures for democracy theory are particularly how the media represent political or pseudopolitical discourses and how they present politics in the public sphere. It is assumed that ascertaining an empirically observable, dominant political communication culture in a country can help explain the mode and quality of the public discourse on politics, and, not least of all, influence the quality of the democratic political process. This chapter offers an outline and illustrative treatment of this idea by localizing the various types of political communication culture in different countries. To underpin the analytical value of the concept and test its empirical utility requires further comparative studies.

REFERENCES

Almond, Gabriel A. 1980. The Intellectual History of the Civic Culture Concept. In Almond A. Gabriel and Sidney Verba, eds. *The Civic Culture Revisited*. Boston: Little, Brown and Company, pp. 1–36.

Almond, Gabriel A., and Sidney Verba. 1963. *The Civic Culture. Political Attitudes and Democracy in Five Nations*. Princeton: Princeton University Press (reprint 1989. Newbury Park, CA: Sage).

Baerns, Barbara. 1985. *Öffentlichkeitsarbeit oder Journalismus? Zum Einfluss im Mediensystem*. Köln, Germany: Verlag Wissenschaft und Politik.

Bennett, Lance W. 1988. *News: The Politics of Illusion*. 2nd ed. New York: Longman.

Bentele, Günter. 1998. Politische Öffentlichkeitsarbeit. In Ulrich Sarcinelli, ed. *Politikvermittlung und Demokratie in der Mediengesellschaft*. Opladen, Germany: Westdeutscher Verlag, pp. 124–45.

Blumler, Jay G., and Michael Gurevitch. 1995. *The Crisis of Public Communication*. London: Routledge (original edition: Blumler, Jay G., and Michael Gurevitch. 1977. Linkages Between the Mass Media and Politics. In James Curran, ed. *Mass Communication and Society*. London: Edward Arnold, pp. 270–90).

Dahl, Robert A. 1989. *Democracy and Its Critics*. New Haven: Yale University Press.

Entman, Robert. 1989. *Democracy without Citizens. Media and the Decay of American Politics*. Oxford: Oxford University Press.

Gerhards, Jürgen. 1994. Politische Öffentlichkeit. Ein system- und akteurstheoretischer Bestimmungsversuch. In Friedhelm Neidhardt, ed. *Öffentlichkeit, öffentliche Meinung, soziale Bewegungen. Kölner Zeitschrift für Soziologie und Sozialpsychologie Sonderheft* 34. Opladen, Germany: Westdeutscher Verlag, pp. 77–105.

Hallin, Daniel C. 1994. *We Keep America on Top of the World. Television Journalism and the Public Sphere*. London: Routledge, pp. 113–132 (original edition: Hallin, Daniel C., and Paolo Mancini. 1984. Speaking of the President: Political Structure and Representational Form in US and Italian Television News. *Theory and Society* 13: 829–50).

Jarren, Otfried, Klaus-Dieter Altmeppen, and Wolfgang Schulz. 1993. Parteiintern – Medien und innerparteiliche Entscheidungsprozesse. Die Nachfolge Genschers und die Kür Engholms zum SPD-Kanzlerkandidaten. In Wolfgang Donsbach, Otfried Jarren, Hans Mathias Kepplinger, and Barbara Pfetsch, eds. *Beziehungsspiele – Medien und Politik in der öffentlichen Diskussion. Fallstudien und Analysen*. Gütersloh, Germany: Verlag Bertelsmann Stiftung, pp. 111–57.

Kaase, Max. 1983. Sinn oder Unsinn des Konzeptes "Politische Kultur" für die vergleichende Politikforschung, oder auch: Der Versuch, einen Pudding an die Wand zu nageln. In Max Kaase and Hans Dieter Klingemann, eds. *Wahlen und politisches System. Analysen aus Anlass der Bundestagswahl 1980.* Opladen, Germany: Westdeutscher Verlag, pp. 144–71.

Kernell, Samuel. 1986. *Going Public. New Strategies of Presidential Leadership.* Washington, DC: Congressional Quarterly.

Manheim, Jarol B. 1991. *Image Making as an Instrument of Power: The Representation of Foreign Interests in the United States.* Paper presented to the 41st Annual Conference of the ICA, Chicago, May 23–7, 1991.

————. 1997. Strategische Kommunikation und eine Strategie für die Kommunikationsforschung. *Publizistik* 42 (1): 62–72.

————. 1998. The News Shapers: Strategic Communication as a Third Force in News Making. In Doris Graber, Denis McQuail, and Pippa Norris, eds. *The Politics of News. The News of Politics.* Washington, DC: Congressional Quarterly Press, pp. 94–109.

Mayntz, Renate. 1988. Funktionelle Teilsysteme in der Theorie sozialer Differenzierung. In Renate Mayntz, Bernd Rosewitz, Uwe Schimank, and Rudolf Stichweh, eds. *Differenzierung und Verselbständigung. Zur Entwicklung gesellschaftlicher Teilsysteme.* Frankfurt, Germany: Campus, pp. 11–44.

Mazzoleni, Gianpietro. 1987. Media Logic and Party Logic in Campaign Coverage: The Italian General Election 1983. *European Journal of Communication* 2: 81–103.

Münch, Richard. 1997. Elemente einer Theorie der Integration moderner Gesellschaften. Eine Bestandsaufnahme. In Wilhelm Heitmeyer, ed. *Was hält die Gesellschaft zusammen? Bundesrepublik Deutschland: Auf dem Weg von der Konsens – zur Konfliktgesellschaft.* Frankfurt, Germany: Suhrkamp, pp. 66–109.

Neidhardt, Friedhelm. 1994. Öffentlichkeit, öffentliche Meinung, soziale Bewegungen. In Friedhelm Neidhardt, ed. *Öffentlichkeit und soziale Bewegungen. Kölner Zeitschrift für Soziologie und Sozialpsychologie Sonderheft* 34. Opladen, Germany: Westdeutscher Verlag, pp. 7–41.

Pappi, Franz Urban. 1986. Politische Kultur. Forschungsparadigma, Fragestellungen, Untersuchungsmöglichkeiten. In Max Kaase, ed. *Politische Wissenschaft und politische Ordnung. Analysen zu Theorie und Empirie demokratischer Regierungsweise.* Opladen, Germany: Westdeutscher Verlag, pp. 279–91.

Pfetsch, Barbara. 2003. *Politische Kommunikationskultur. Eine vergleichende Untersuchung von politischen Sprechern und Journalisten in der Bundesrepublik und den USA.* Opladen, Germany: Westdeutscher Verlag.

Ronneberger, Franz, and Manfred Rühl. 1992. *Theorie der Public Relations. Ein Entwurf.* Opladen, Germany: Westdeutscher Verlag.

Sarcinelli, Ulrich. 1998. Legitimität. In Otfried Jarren, Ulrich Sarcinelli, and Ulrich Saxer, eds. *Politische Kommunikation in der demokratischen Gesellschaft. Ein Handbuch.* Opladen, Germany: Westdeutscher Verlag, pp. 253–68.

————. 2001. Politische Klasse und Öffentlichkeit. In Hans Herbert Arnim, ed. *Politische Klasse und Verfassung.* Berlin: Duncker und Humblot, pp. 123–44.

Sarcinelli, Ulrich, and Heribert Schatz. 2002. *Mediendemokratie im Medienland? Inszenierungen und Themensetzungsstrategien im Spannungsfeld von Medien und Parteieliten am Beispiel der nordrhein-westfälischen Landtagswahl im Jahr 2000.* Opladen, Germany: Leske + Budrich.

Saxer, Ulrich. 1992. Bericht aus dem Bundeshaus. Eine Befragung von Bundeshausjour-nalisten und Parlamentariern in der Schweiz. *Diskussionspunkt* 24. Zürich: Seminar Publizistik der Universität Zürich.

Schmidt, Manfred G. 1996. Germany. The Grand Coalition State. In Josep M. Colomer, ed. *Political Institutions in Europe.* London: Routledge, pp. 62–98.

Scholl, Armin, and Siegfried Weischenberg. 1998. *Journalismus in der Gesellschaft. Theorie, Methodologie und Empirie.* Opladen, Germany: Westdeutscher Verlag.

Seymour-Ure, Colin. 1974. *The Political Impact of Mass Media.* London: Constable and Sage.

Swanson, David L., and Paolo Mancini, eds. 1996. *Politics, Media, and Modern Democracy. An International Study of Innovations in Electoral Campaigning and Their Consequences.* Westport, CT: Praeger.

Tenscher, Jens. 2003. *Professionalisierung der Politikvermittlung?* Wiesbaden, Germany: Westdeutscher Verlag.

Verba, Sidney. 1965. Conclusion: Comparative Political Culture. In Lucian W. Pye and Sidney Verba, eds. *Political Culture and Political Development.* Princeton: Princeton University Press, pp. 512–61.

———. 1980. On Revisiting the Civic Culture: A Personal Postscript. In Gabriel A. Almond and Sidney Verba, eds. *The Civic Culture Revisited.* Boston: Little, Brown and Company, pp. 394–410.

Voltmer, Karin. 2000. Structures of Diversity in Press and Broadcasting. The Institutional Context of Public Communication in Western Democracies. *WZB Discussion Paper FS III* 00–201. Berlin: Wissenschaftszentrum Berlin.

SIXTEEN

Problems of Comparative Political Communication Research

Culture as a Key Variable

Robert L. Stevenson

Wilbur Schramm, one of the true founding fathers of communication science in the United States, once described the field as "an academic crossroad where many have passed but few have tarried." Later Berger and Chaffee (1987, 15) noted that the crossroad had developed into a large urban center, complete with academic departments, research traditions, and journals. By those criteria, they decided that communications qualified as an academic discipline. An updated metaphor for the beginning of the new century might be a busy international airport, with the mixture of cultures and languages, shopping malls, and frenzied activity that one finds in almost every international airport in the world.

If anything, the field is more successful than ever. In the United States, there are departments of communication, schools of communication, and even colleges of communication with specialized communications departments within them. Total enrollment in journalism and mass communication programs alone – by no means the entire field – is more than 100,000. In most other countries, communication has also established a beachhead in traditional universities. In some – Germany and Britain come to mind – there is almost the same confusion of organization and definition even as universities create their own versions of suburban shopping centers. International conferences bring together specialists in animal behavior, hearing problems, cognitive science, journalism, cultural studies, new technologies, public policy, artificial intelligence, and post-Marxist ideology. By any reasonable criteria, communication is riding the crest of an expansive wave in almost all parts of the world. Yet one cannot survey the field – or spend much time in it – without a sense that success in creating a global academic enterprise is not matched by success in creating useful new theories, accumulating persuasive empirical support for existing theories, or even taking advantage of opportunities offered by a global discipline. In this chapter, we will consider the state of political communication research as a global academic enterprise and point out how future research might benefit from an international perspective.

LOCATING COMMUNICATION RESEARCH

In 1984, Paisley provided a useful matrix for locating communication within the academic structure. He points out a group of disciplines, mostly traditional sciences, that are defined by the unit of analysis they focus on. They are all-inclusive in the sense that they are interested in all aspects of the behavior of the systems at that level. At the highest level are the social sciences – anthropology, sociology, and psychology; followed by the biological sciences – physiology and biology; and the physical sciences – chemistry and physics. At the highest level of all – which he doesn't consider – is the global system as a single unit. It assumes that political and economic elements of the planet operate as a single system similar to the environment. In the era of globalization, economics, politics, and environment get the lion's share of attention, but some studies of global news and entertainment adopt this approach. It is central to the dependency theories that were in vogue during debates about cultural imperialism and a new world information and communication order.

Studies based on a global systems approach are never very satisfying because we cannot get outside the system to see if other worlds operate differently. We cannot disprove any argument about the global system because there is only one, and any investigation is inevitably a case study of one. Arguments about the global system tend to become polemics – starting with a conclusion and amassing evidence that supports it – or at a minimum, tautologies that make their arguments with definitions.

Paisley argues that the goal of these traditional sciences is reduction: to explain the behavior of one in terms of its component elements. Thus, we try to explain the behavior of a – or the – global system on the basis of its components, typically nations or cultures. A focus on cultures as complex units or systems defines the traditional field of anthropology. A nation or culture is composed of groups, the traditional focus of sociology. Groups are composed of individuals. Explaining the behavior of individuals is the focus of psychology, the lowest level of the social sciences. Below the social sciences are the biological sciences, then the natural sciences, and, finally, classical physics, which reduces the natural world to a handful of mathematical formulas. In theory, one could begin with the primal mathematical laws of physics and from them, reconstruct chemistry; from principles of chemistry, reconstruct physiology and biology, then rebuild self-aware human beings and social structures.

Paisley contrasts the traditional sciences with a newer set of disciplines that are defined by a specific behavior or set of behaviors that can be studied at almost any level. The goal of these disciplines is generalization, to define each behavior as part of a broader or more complex behavior. One can study communication as a part of education (learning), economics (wealth), or political science (power); communication also includes cybernetics and systems theory as subsets. Feedback and system maintenance are part of communication, which itself is larger and more inclusive. When the two sets are crossed, a typology emerges that allows us to locate most communication studies and to see possibilities that are usually ignored.

We can define communication as a behavior that is part of learning, governance, and wealth creation and comprises elements such as information exchange, feedback, and adaptation. It can be studied at any level, from a single global system to single cells or atoms. Some cells at the outer edges of the typology are appropriately blank, of course. An examination of representative communication research journals or conference programs would demonstrate that most communication research in virtually all countries where it is carried out falls into a narrow group of cells from Paisley's model: Most studies look at communication exclusively from the perspective of individuals or small groups. In Europe, the traditional perspective is broader, as befits the birthplace of the discipline of political economy and methodology of critical research. In the United States, the focus is more on individuals and small groups, perhaps a reflection of American communication's academic roots in psychology and sociology.[1] A few studies – the number is probably increasing – expand in one direction to see communication as part of an economic or political structure. A few others train a microscopic lens on communication within physiological systems, perhaps focusing

---

[1] American scholarship is more at ease in professional schools than in some other countries where journalism is not recognized as a skill to be learned in a university. The tradition of public service – working to improve media along with teaching practical skills – is also rooted in American pragmatism. Scholars can argue whether the distinction between "administrative" and "critical" research – no longer very large or strong – reflects the difference between a European collectivist identity and American individualism or the accident of historical development and differences in academic structure on the two sides of the Atlantic.

on a component of communication, such as how organs in the body use feedback to maintain functional equilibrium.[2]

At the upper end of possible combinations of behavior and unit, not much is new. Marxism in some form survives in most universities, although Habermas's undefined public sphere probably has replaced Marx's socialist utopia as the favored ideal against which to measure the sins and failures of the Western world. The main claims of Western hegemony are recycled from theories of imperialism to globalization with little modification. The disappearance of virtually all experiments in communism eliminates the occasional useful if unpopular case study that failed to demonstrate any difference – certainly any improvement – between the dominant West and societies that had resisted capitalism. Developing countries that opted for socialism or some form of traditional nationalism failed more often than those that embraced Western politics and economics. But most of the clash of ideologies is now history.

At the lower end of the disciplinary matrix, the situation is different. Efforts to understand the human mind as a physiological system, research to probe the mysteries of animal behavior, projects in artificial intelligence and "thinking" computers have produced explosions of knowledge and insights into how the human being functions as a complex biological organ. If we ever make the leap to understanding how we function as thinking, self-aware organisms that create social and economic systems, it probably will come from the bottom up, not from grand social theories that have survived for more than a century despite a lack of academic development and a long record of failure in practice.

THE FAILURE OF CULTURAL STUDIES

A major problem of political communication as a subfield of communication occupying a cell of Paisley's matrix is that so much of it derives from cultural studies and is more polemic than scholarship. Polemic

---

[2] If one keeps up with the literature – increasingly difficult as the number of organizations, journals, and conferences expands almost exponentially – one is struck by how little new information is presented. A lot of current research is replication of well-established findings or a fleeting description that becomes obsolete as quickly as yesterday's headlines. There must be some useful limit to the number of studies demonstrating a correlation between perceptions of the climate of opinion and willingness to speak out or the correlation between knowledge of public affairs and attention to the news. The flood of studies following every war documenting governments' efforts to influence public opinion reinforces the suspicion that the phenomenon under scrutiny is more a constant than a variable and, therefore, of limited intellectual interest.

is argument rather than investigation; it is an effort to support a pre-determined conclusion rather than an effort to pursue a question or hypothesis with a conclusion left open to evidence or lack of it. Some of the most clever ideas have failed to establish themselves because of a lack of evidence to support them, but others persist despite the lack of evidence.

Part of the problem can be attributed to the tradition of critical research, which started with ideological assumptions about advanced capitalism and never tested the key assumption, which was that Western civilization was the problem. Media systems are assumed to be part of the Western-dominated global system. Criticism tends to be predictable and rarely original. Evidence, when it is offered, is selective and incomplete.

One way of describing the problem of critical research is that it uses an incomplete formulation of its core assumption. It can be put this way: If (A leads to B because of C), then D. In this formulation, A and B represent elements of the media or political system and some effect of them. The C is capitalism or Western society, and the simplest and most important D is that without C, A will not lead to B. Useful studies of non-Western societies are typically written as descriptive case studies but rarely framed as data appropriate for tests of global theories. As the number and variety of case studies increase, they can be arrayed into a simple meta-analysis of the underlying assumption of critical analysis, but this is rarely done, in part, because the wonderful diversity of political, cultural, and media systems fails to fit the critical research model.

And communication? There are exceptions to the excessively commercial media in the United States, but alternatives are European public broadcast systems and old-fashioned socially responsible newspapers not focused exclusively on the bottom line – perhaps even vigorously partisan newspapers that collectively create a marketplace of ideas or its modern equivalent of a public sphere. "Development news," which was touted in earlier decades as an alternative to Western news-as-exception, foundered as thoroughly as Lenin's use of news as an instrument of propaganda and control.

You can array lots of evidence that Country X is poor because of Western meddling, but the general statement that global wealth/poverty, strength/weakness, success/failure is a product of capitalism requires more than a single case study. Think of a simple 2 × 2 table. One dimension represents a nation's experience with capitalism and the West: colonizer/colony, capitalist/socialist, or independent/controlled media system. The other dimension represents some measure of development: high/low gross domestic product (GDP), democratic/totalitarian system. A more complex model is certainly required, but the core of the issue can be reduced to this simple relationship.

One problem, as will be noted later, is a lack of covariance. A recurring problem in communication research is our inability to demonstrate that differences in individuals, in media systems, or even in nations really are correlated with factors that ought to be a product of those differences. A more pressing problem for studies that use a collective entity such as a nation or an external factor such as Western imperialism as the explanatory factor is that they represent at most a single data point. Without at least two data points in opposing diagonal cells, there is no covariance, no correlation, no possibility of demonstrating that C is, in fact, why A leads to B.

Comparative studies do provide additional data points, but we do not see them very often. They are expensive and complicated, but without them, a large part of the body of comparative communication research continues to rely on traditional polemic, citing other polemics instead of evidence that challenges the conventional wisdom of critical research or even addresses the core questions.

REASSERTING CULTURE'S IMPORTANCE

There is, however, an exception to the generalization that higher-order theories have failed to produce useful insights into human behavior. It is resurgence in interest in the importance of culture in human affairs, which to a large degree is a product of the end of the cold war. And good timing. Fukuyama (1992) added the phrase "the end of history" to the vocabulary of political debate with an essay that anticipated the collapse of communism in Europe. The phrase, of course, came from Hegel's assertion that "history" would end when the world agreed on a single form of social organization. Fukuyama's interpretation was that the cold war was a battle between the last two ideologies of communism and multiparty democracy within a market system and that the West won. His short-lived optimism was replaced by another culture-centric global overview, Huntington's (1996) equally famous "clash of civilizations," in which he argued that future conflict would take place along the fault lines of nine distinct civilizations, most defined by religion.

The headline interest in culture/civilization came at times when old clichés of the cold war failed, and Fukuyama and Huntington, in turn, provided a compelling explanation of the new, unfamiliar world. Others had covered the same material, but with less public response. In a series of books, Sowell (1983; 1994; 1996; 1998) explored why some cultures prospered, even in the Diaspora. Diamond (1999) explored the influence of guns, germs, and steel on the fate of human societies, and Landes (1998) asked why some nations are rich and others poor (answer: aspects of culture). After considering how culture values shape economic and political success, Harrison (1992) joined Huntington (2000) in an edited volume that brought together many of the controversial thinkers in the collective effort to articulate the influence of culture. The book's title summarizes the conclusions: *Culture Matters; How Values Shape Human Progress.*

Culture also entered the debate over the clash between Islam and the West and the old issue of the development gap between the West and the rest of the world. Lewis (2002) asked what went wrong with the once-influential Muslim world (answer: lack of freedom). The United Nations Development Program (UNDP) (2002a), after tiptoeing around questions of culture for many years, produced a remarkable report on the sad state of the Arab world – the poorest and least-developed region of the world – and highlighted key "deficits" in freedom, women's empowerment, and knowledge. In its annual global report, the UNDP (2002b) also for the first time highlighted "Western" qualities of good governance. Nobel-Prize winner Sen (1999) also emphasized political freedom as the core of economic development. Peruvian economist De Soto (2000) also asked why capitalism triumphs in the West and fails everywhere else (answer: ownership of property transforms wealth into capital) and argued that every nation had the resources to become rich. A very different view of the world than the old warhorses of imperialism and racism.

Culture as a unit of analysis has not received much attention in communication research, despite the popularity of *intercultural communication* and *cross-cultural communication* as academic buzzwords. Three reasons can be offered as explanation. One is the difficulty of defining the boundaries of a culture. It is usually not quite the same as a nation. Even in relatively homogenous nations, there are cultural hierarchies and overlapping cultures. Cultures can be defined by language, religion, or tribe, even a vague sense of who belongs and who is an outsider. We all belong to several cultures, and sorting out all of the connections is often difficult. Using culture as the basis of explanation of human behavior can be impossible.

It can certainly lead to political trouble, which is the second reason why researchers have avoided culture. Explanation – always a key element in any theoretical research – inevitably leads to comparison: Why is one culture stronger/weaker, more successful/less successful than another? Or it leads to cultural relativism. Huntington was criticized for pointing out that a lot of contemporary conflict occurs at the boundaries of civilizations, the highest level of cultures, and that modern Islam in particular has bloody borders. Only a few writers, including notably Friedman (2002) of the *New York Times*, have pointed out that much of the Islamic hostility toward the West reflects the frustration resulting from the failure of Islamic civilization. Modern Islamic nations are, without exception, undemocratic and corrupt and, except for the handful that are located on oil reserves, poor. It takes courage of the kind rarely seen in academic conferences to point out that the problem of the clash between Islamic and Western civilizations might be in Islam, not in the failure of the West to understand Islam. Or that the failure of other cultures and nations to achieve the level of economic development and political stability that are the basis of modern Western dominance results from a failure of Western cultural values to take root in other parts of the world. Or that free media in the Western model are, whatever their excesses and failures, infinitely better than just about any alternative.

The third reason for the lack of comparative studies is the expense and difficulty of collecting appropriate data. This problem is moving quickly toward at least a partial solution with projects such as the International Social Survey Program (www.issp.org), now with thirty-eight members; the Eurobarometer surveys, which have expanded from the European Union (EU) nations to candidate nations; and a increasing number of multinational commercial surveys (e.g., www.gallup-international.com). Individual researchers who operate on a near-global scale include Inglehart (1990) and the multiwave World Values Survey now operating in more than sixty-five countries (http://wvs.isr.umich.edu). With easy access to data from these sources, there is little excuse not to test the influence of culture.

Communication as a force for social and economic change is another old idea that persists without persuasive evidence. Even dictatorships, which try to enforce a monopoly of information, are rarely successful for long. A new interest in the potential of communication to support national development accompanied the collapse of communism but without noticeable evidence of success. The "emerging democracies" or "transitional nations" of Central and Eastern Europe replaced the "developing" countries of the Third World as the focus of development aid and academic research. Arguments in favor of "authentic non-Western" models and exhibition of a handful of unproven success stories – mostly China, Cuba, and Tanzania – as evidence of "alternative" development largely disappeared amid a global consensus about what it means to be a developed nation. Schramm's (1964) litany of the benefits of Western-style development – health, food, education, and self-government over disease, hunger, ignorance, and dictatorship – were even incorporated into a universal Human Development Index (HDI) adopted by the UNDP. The HDI did not include democracy because the creators of the index could not agree on its measurement and hesitated to emphasize its "Western" components. That changed in the 2002 report, which included for the first time Freedom House ratings of civil and political liberties; measures of government effectiveness; and various indices of gender equity, civil society, and transparency. This was another example of the end of history as well as a new opportunity for cross-cultural research.

The HDI documented what any casual traveler notices on arrival at the international airport: some countries – especially in Asia – have closed the development gap rapidly and dramatically. A few others – notably in the Middle East – have used oil money to create the shell of development. Too many others – particularly in Africa and parts of Asia – have used vast oil revenues merely to reinforce corrupt and brutal regimes. Some countries – Israel, Singapore, and Taiwan come immediately to mind – created "modern" societies without the benefit of oil reserves. While in others – Nigeria and Mexico are good examples – huge oil revenues disappeared without noticeable improvement in the lives of most people. The core question of development remained: If wealth does not influence national growth toward Western modernity, what does? The partial answer may be culture.

Cultural difference is, of course, the basis for this volume, but it also represents a potentially important trend in communication research in general. It is probably not a true paradigm shift that Kuhn described, but it may indicate that we have been looking in the wrong place to understand differences in people and social systems. If so, we need to shift from a telescope to a microscope, or possibly the other way around.

ROBERT L. STEVENSON

FINDING THE SOURCE OF CHANGE

One of the frustrations of studying communication is the apparent lack of variance. Without variance, we cannot establish covariance. And without covariance, we cannot explain differences among people, among cultures, or within a single global system. But maybe we're looking in the wrong place. Consider the typical study of media influence. We survey a population and measure some aspects of media exposure and some things we think are likely to be influenced by media exposure: opinions, knowledge, willingness to express an opinion in public, preference for political candidates, or brands of soap. Correlations between the two sets of variables are usually close to zero, barely above randomness, trivial at most. Gerbner would argue from his mainstreaming perspective the lack of variance is meaningless: we are all so overwhelmed by media that their influence can be accepted as a given (Signorelli and Morgan 1996). Trying to differentiate that influence is like asking a fish to describe living in water. It has no basis for comparison, any more than we can escape the media world enough to assess its influence.

The problem with this approach is that there is variance but no co-variance. Some people surround themselves with information, while others manage to avoid media completely. For some, 100-plus television channels aren't enough while others – not many, but the number is increasing – live their lives without exposure to television and news-papers. Most of us, of course, are spread out along the continuum of exposure and along a similar continuum of opinions, knowledge, and other probable effects of media exposure. The problem is that the two don't co-vary much, hence, the near lack of correlation between media variables and effect variables. We seem to be sentenced to a world of minimum effects, a world where the core of the field is at best peripheral to the experience of human behavior.

The situation is similar in studies that focus on a bigger picture. The literature is full of comparative studies of coverage of Issue-X or Country-Y or Group-Z, but almost all of them find little variance. Foreign coverage in the *New York Times* is pretty much like foreign coverage in *Pravda*, and news values in the *Guardian* are about the same as those in the *Daily Telegraph*. Such findings are contrary to common sense and even a casual perusal of the media in most countries. An argument can be made that most U.S. media are homogeneous; it doesn't make much difference if you watch NBC or ABC, or read the *Los Angeles Times* or *New York Times*. But other countries still have ideologically grounded media that are different. The *Frankfurter Allgemeine Zeitung* is different from the *Süddeutsche Zeitung; le Monde* is not at all like *le Figaro*. Why, then, can't we demonstrate differences and show that these differences explain differences in what people know and think?

Variance does exist in the media content and in people, even if we can rarely find it and even more rarely link the two. A conceptually modest but clever study in 1996 (Bennett et al.) demonstrated by lack of findings that the real source of differences may be, not in individuals or media, but in cultures – individuals' values and behavior aggregated to large groups that share some sense of identification. In this case, cultures were coterminus with nations, but other studies have recognized that the two are not always the same and have separated them. In surveys of a dozen countries, respondents were given a simple test of world affairs. In an analysis of part of the results, Bennett and his colleagues looked at the usual demographic and media-use variables as predictors of knowledge of the world outside of the respondent's own country.

Results followed the pattern of other similar studies: media use explained almost no variance, even though the media systems varied considerably; demographics were minimally correlated with world affairs knowledge in predictable ways. Men were more knowledgeable than women, better educated more than less educated, and age had little influence. The real difference, however, was among cultures. To be German – and to a lesser degree, British and French – was to be aware of the world; to be from the New World, strongly in Mexico, less so in the United States, and much less so in Canada, was to be oblivious to international affairs. While the complete data set was not available for secondary analysis and the multiple regression strategy did not directly assess the overall influence of national differences, it is clear that the single largest predictor was national identity of the respondent. When differences in individuals and differences in their use of news media were factored out of the equation, differences among the countries – cultures – remained. And they accounted for most of the variance in the level of knowledge of world affairs in countries that varied considerably in economic and political development and structure.

It is easy and possibly useful to speculate on the findings. In Europe, geography and history make people more attentive to their neighbors and the rest of the world; the media are less constrained by economic interests and, therefore, give more coverage to international affairs; and the educational system is more oriented toward traditional disciplines that emphasize world affairs. In the three North American countries in the study, despite economic and political differences, there is some commonality of life in a relatively isolated part of the world. The precise cultural reasons are still to be found.

In another simple analysis of the results of a very large content analysis of foreign news in thirty-seven countries, we used the percentage of stories that were either reported by women or featured women as the focus of the news (Campbell and Stevenson 2001). The unit of analysis was the medium – television or newspapers – nested within each country with the level of freedom as a covariate.

In both analyses, the results were not startling but intriguing, nevertheless. Women appeared as newsmakers more frequently in open societies than in those classified by Freedom House as "partly free" or "not free." The United Nations HDI did not influence the frequency of appearance of women in the news. Women reported the news more on television than in print media, regardless of political control of the media and level of development. The results, though modest, do tell us something about how women fit into the news around the world and do point to areas where cultures and media systems do matter and where there is relatively little variance.

Looking at culture as a source of variance is getting easier but is still difficult. In most cases, it requires individual-level measurements in multiple cultures so that individual-level differences can be nested within cultural differences and the two levels assessed simultaneously. Communication variables can be both individual – media use – and cultural – characteristics of national media. Other cultural-related variables can be included as well. They can be individual attributes, which when aggregated do represent cultural differences that matter. Americans, on the whole, are different from Europeans on some key variables; Germans are different from French and British; and so on. Within nations, there are also cultural differences: European-Americans are different from African-Americans and Asian-Americans and probably from the fast-growing subcultures of Hispanic-Americans and Arab-Americans. Scots are probably different from English and Welsh; Germans from the old communist East are different from Westerners; and Bavarians are still probably different from Saxons and Prussians. These differences have implications for levels of national, cultural, or subcultural development. Europeans, Chinese, and some other Asians do well wherever they find themselves in the world diaspora, while Africans and Muslims do not. Hindu Indians are generally prosperous and successful in Britain while Muslin Pakistanis and Bangladeshis are not, even though all of them encounter similar obstacles to assimilation and advancement.

The influence of differences in media systems has not been examined extensively or systematically, but the possibilities are intriguing. Old-fashioned controlled systems or those mobilized in the name of national development cannot claim any success in promoting development, of course, but the nature and direction of the links between communication and social and economic change are still in dispute. To the disappointment of Western development advocates, press freedom seems to be more a product of economic growth than a spur to it. But what about public broadcasting and vigorously partisan newspapers compared to the excessively commercial, entertainment-oriented broadcast channels and bland, neutral newspapers in the United States? Here is a rich area for investigation that has been largely ignored. And data, while still a problem, are better and more easily available.

LIVING AT THE MARGIN

We tend to think that communication research is at the center of academic studies and that our field has something to say to the disciplines surrounding communication in Paisley's matrix. After all, communication can be studied at all levels of organization and is a component of the newer fields that our research touches. A word of caution is in order, however, from personal experience.

The subfield of communication and development (or communication and social change) is reasonably well recognized. Every year, several dozen papers are produced, along with more than a few journal articles and books. There are a handful of university centers devoted to the topic and at least one or two journals. Almost enough, according to Berger and Chaffee, to qualify as an academic discipline in itself. But if you check the really vast literature of development produced by economists, political scientists, anthropologists, and the policy makers responsible for dispensing the several billion dollars allocated annually for development, there is almost no mention of communication. About ten years ago, I looked at the projects of the UNDP in its "communications and transportation" sector. The sector represented a small segment of the full UNDP budget, and most of the projects were related to transportation, not communication. Airports, not broadcast centers; roads, not telephones. What appears to be the critical center of a vital field from our perspective is barely on the radarscope from other perspectives.

Another example is communication and international relations. We all read the claims about "media diplomacy," and "TV wars," and "new-age propaganda." But take a look at the current literature of international relations. Read the memoirs of recent world leaders. Review studies of recent international crises. Communication is rarely mentioned at all, almost never as a critical element in diplomacy. After considering the impact of communication technologies over history, Neuman (1996) concluded that technical innovation speeded up the process of global diplomacy but didn't change the options available to government and was not a decisive factor in the decision to go to war and rarely an important factor in the conduct of war. The memoirs of global leaders rarely even mention modern communication, let alone admit that their actions were influenced by it or that it was an important tool in the conduct of diplomacy.

Another exercise in humility is to examine standard introductory text-books in fields that are closely linked to communication. In most cases, the broad undergraduate surveys of books in sociology, psychology, and political science mention communication peripherally, often with a reference to studies or concepts we would consider outdated or marginal to the field. In our neighbor disciplines in the social and policy sciences, the perspective of communication is certainly different, probably more realistic. Until we can demonstrate persuasively that communication does play a meaningful role in our societies and in others – until we can do a better job establishing evidence of communication effects – we will probably continue to be at the edge of the academic and political worlds, not at the center where we would like to be.

DIRECTIONS FOR RESEARCH

When we got involved in one of the first major comparative studies of foreign news twenty years ago (Stevenson and Shaw 1984), one of the participants found himself in a civil war and asked us to analyze his data. The deck of then-standard eighty-column punch cards hand to be hand-carried by several couriers until they finally reached Chapel Hill several months later; queries back and forth took a week or two by air mail in each direction. Even exchanging data sets with the United States or across the Atlantic often required weeks or months of work to get a computer system to read an imported tape. For the most part, analysis of the kind suggested above was impossible because comparative studies were rare and comparative analysis was subverted by an inability to get the right data in the right form in a spot where it could be analyzed to sort out the relative influence of factors at different levels of explanation.

The situation has changed dramatically (Stevenson, 2003). The number and variety of multinational studies have increased. The venerable General Social Survey (GSS) in the United States is part of an international research enterprise that collects comparable data in a number of countries around the world. The Eurobarometer series interviews across EU countries on a wide variety of communication-relevant topics. Even individually designed projects and commercial research surveys typically are multinational in scope. The World Bank's database of national indicators gets larger, more reliable, and more accessible each year. Better data combined with computer programs open possibilities for exploration that could only be imagined a few years ago.

Many of these data sets are archived in accessible libraries, and an increasing number – though far from all – can be accessed and downloaded using the Internet (Chapter 6, this volume). No more shipping of decks of computer cards from country to country; no more frustrations trying to get one computer system to read a tape produced by another. Well, a lot fewer frustrations, and a lot more opportunities to explore data, increased possibilities of addressing a wider range of questions and hypotheses, better chances to discover new patterns that might not be apparent in single-country studies.

Over the years, a number of medium-range theories have appeared, usually flourished for a while, then receded. Many are reproduced in different countries – usually without reference to any cultural factors – then fade into a general metaphor of media influence. Just about anything becomes agenda setting, the spiral of silence, or framing. You can find similar evidence in just about every country where systematic research is carried out. Even within the relatively small field of international communication, the opportunity to introduce culture as an explanatory is ignored and often deliberately avoided.

Culture as a key variable in political communication is not the magic bullet that the first generation of communication researchers looked for and may in the end be as unproductive as most of the concepts that have appeared fleetingly in the field. But now that we have the data and the analytical tools to examine its influence, we ought to try it. Globalization is a popular buzzword, but it does apply to the twenty-first century unlike any other time in history. It applies to education as well as to culture, politics, and economics, and it ought to apply to political communication as well.

REFERENCES

Bennett, Stephen E. et al. 1996. Citizens' Knowledge of Foreign Affairs. *Harvard International Journal of Press/Politics* 1 (2): 10–29.

Berger, Charles R., and Steven H. Chaffee. 1987. The Study of Communication as a Science. In Charles R. Berger and Steven H. Chaffee, eds. *Handbook of Communication Science.* Beverly Hills, CA: Sage Publications, pp. 15–19.

Campbell, W. Joseph, and Robert L. Stevenson. 2001. Women as Global Newsmakers and Correspondents: Where Press Freedom Matters. In Karen Ross, Deniz Derman, and Nevena Dakovic, eds. *Mediated Identities.* Istanbul: Istanbul Vilgi University Press, pp. 303–12.

De Soto, Hernando. 2000. *The Mystery of Capital. Why Capitalism Triumphs in the West and Fails Everywhere Else.* New York: Basic Books.

Diamond, Jared. 1999. *Guns, Germs, and Steel. The Fate of Human Societies.* New York: Norton.

Friedman, Thomas L. 2002. *Attitudes and Longitudes. Exploring the World After September 11.* New York: Farrar, Straus & Giroux.

Fukuyama, Francis. 1992. *The End of History and the Last Man.* New York: Free Press.

Harrison, Lawrence E. 1992. *Who Prospers? How Cultural Values Shape Economic and Political Success.* New York: Basic Books.

Harrison, Lawrence E., and Samuel P. Huntington, eds. 2000. *Culture Matters. How Values Shape Human Progress.* New York: Basic Books.

Huntington, Samuel P. 1996. *The Clash of Civilizations and the Remaking of World Order.* New York: Simon & Schuster.

Inglehart, Ronald. 1990. *Culture Shift in Advanced Industrial Society.* Princeton: Princeton University Press.

Landes, David S. 1998. *The Wealth and Poverty of Nations. Why Some Are So Rich and Some So Poor.* New York: Norton.

Lewis, Bernard. 2002. *What Went Wrong? Western Impact and Middle Eastern Response.* Oxford: Oxford University Press.

Neuman, Johanna. 1996. *Lights, Camera, War: Is Media Technology Driving International Politics?* New York: St. Martin's Press.

Paisley, William J. 1984. Communication in the Communication Sciences. In Brenda Dervin and Melvin J. Voigt, eds. *Progress in Communication Science* V. Norwood, NJ: Ablex, pp. 1–44.

Schramm, Wilbur. 1964. *Mass Media and National Development: The Role of Information in the Developing Countries.* Stanford: Stanford University Press.

Sen, Amartya Kumar. 1999. *Development as Freedom.* New York: Knopf.

Signorelli, N., and M. Morgan. 1996. Cultivation Analysis: Research and Practice. In Michael B. Salwen and Don W. Stacks, eds. *An Integrated Approach to Communication Theory and Research.* Mahwah, NJ: Lawrence Erlbaum, pp. 111–26.

Sowell, Thomas. 1983. *The Economics and Politics of Race. An International Perspective.* New York: Morrow.

———. 1994. *Race and Culture. A World View.* New York: Basic Books.

———. 1996. *Migrations and Cultures. A World View.* New York: Basic Books.

———. 1998. *Conquests and Cultures. An International History.* New York: Basic Books.

Stevenson, Robert L. 2003. Mapping the News of the World. In Brenda Dervin and Steven H. Chaffee, eds. *Communication, A Different Kind of Horse Race: Essays Honoring Richard F. Carter.* Cresskill, NJ: Hampton Press, pp. 149–65.

Stevenson, Robert L., and Donald L. Shaw, eds. 1984. *Foreign News and the New World Information Order.* Ames: Iowa State Press.

United Nations Development Program. 2002a. *Arab Human Development Report.* New York: United Nations Development Program.

―――. 2002b. *Deepening Democracy in a Fragmented World.* New York: United Nations Development Program.

SEVENTEEN

Meeting the Challenges of Global Communication and Political Integration

The Significance of Comparative Research in a Changing World

Frank Esser and Barbara Pfetsch

This volume argues in favor of increasing consideration of international comparison in political communication research. From our point of view, the potential of comparative research to contribute to knowledge is promising in many respects (Blumler and Gurevitch 1995a):

- Comparative analysis expands the existing database, and by doing so, simplifies generalization and refines theories of political communication research.
- Comparative analysis provides an antidote to naïve universalism, countering the tendency to presume that political communication findings from one's own country also apply to other countries. It thereby helps to prevent parochialism and ethnocentrism.
- Comparative analysis is a way of enhancing the understanding of one's own society by placing its familiar structures and routines against those of other systems. Comparison makes us aware of other systems, cultures, and patterns of thinking and acting – casting a fresh light on our own political communication arrangements and enabling us to contrast them critically with those prevalent in other countries.
- Comparative analysis can be used as a key to discern general findings from culture-specific ones by rendering visible the specific identity of political communication arrangements within a given system. Only a cross-national perspective can draw our attention to the macrosocietal structures and imperatives that are taken for granted within our own system, and can thus only be detected from an outside perspective, that is, by comparing.
- Another advantage of comparative analysis lies in the wealth of practical knowledge and experience it offers. As we gain access to a

wide range of alternative options, problem solutions, and reforms, comparative research can show us a way out of similar dilemmas or predicaments – as long as these solutions can be adapted to our own national context.

- Researchers can benefit from comparative research by using it as an instrument for analyzing processes of transnational diffusion and integration of politics, communications, economics, and technologies in a globalized world where approaches confined to isolated regions are increasingly deemed parochial.

In regard to these advantages, we call for a reorientation of political communication research toward greater consideration of comparative approaches. As stated in the introductory chapter, comparative political communication research can be defined as comparisons between a minimum of two political systems or cultures (or their subelements) with respect to at least one object of investigation relevant to communication research. In doing so, correlations with explanatory variables are considered on the microanalytical actors' level; the mesoanalytical organizational and institutional level; and on the macroanalytical systemic or cultural level. Comparative political communication research differs from noncomparative political communication research in three points. It involves a particular strategy to gain insight, which is essentially of an international nature; attempts to reach conclusions, the scope of which cover more than one system and more than one culture; and explain differences and similarities between objects of analysis with the contextual conditions of the surrounding systems or cultures. Comparative research contributes to theory building in two important ways. First, it helps us to assess the general validity and geographic range of a theory (or hypothesis) by testing it in different social-cultural and systemic settings. Second, it helps us to contextualize middle-range theories by discerning those system factors in the presence of which a theory is mainly valid.

The topics and objects of comparative political communication research are as diverse as those of the field of comparative politics because it is becoming increasingly impossible to separate the "production" of politics (or policy making) from its "depiction" (or political communication). As Pfetsch notes (Chapter 15, this volume), democratic regimes must communicate their political actions and decisions to the public in order to obtain legitimization for them. The times when questions concerning the public presentation of politics could be neglected are long gone. Today, attendance to communication through the media forms an integral part of the political process. Although much decision making still takes place behind closed doors, far from the media spotlights, Jarren and Donges (2002) argue in favor of viewing politics as a process that is inseparably interwoven with political communication. They define political communication as the central mechanism in the articulation, aggregation, production, and implementation of collectively binding policies. To them, political communication is not only an instrument of politics; it is politics (see also Mazzoleni and Schulz 1999, p. 250).

THE SYSTEM OF POLITICAL COMMUNICATION

A theoretical framework that is capable of integrating the various approaches discussed in this volume is the input/output model developed by Almond and Powell (1966; see also Almond et al., 2003). It offers to political science and communication science a common stock of basic concepts that can be applied to different political systems and helps bridge the gap between the two disciplines. Within this model, politics and the media can be seen as two autonomous, distinctive systems with different rationales and objectives: politics primarily aims at generating universally binding decisions, whereas the media aim at generating publicity for political actors and issues. Almond and Powell's input/output model can play an important role in the comparative analysis of the relationship between politics and media communication because it offers four essential advantages:

- It offers a general cross-national terminology that enables us to become independent of country-specific terms and institutions and reach a higher level of abstraction. We can search for structures and functions that are universally valid, and that we can compare in general.
- The model connects system-orientated theoretical analysis with variable-oriented empirical research. The input/output model provides a framework that researchers can use to systematize the findings of empirical research, and to integrate these into theoretical concepts. On the basis of this model, researchers can also infer hypotheses that are to be tested in subsequent studies.
- It belongs to the small group of models in political science that address the relationship between politics and communication, and take their respective influences and reciprocal effects into account.

- It connects the structural and the cultural component of politics and political communication. By including the "psychological" dimension of culture, the model gives us the opportunity of integrating the individual opinions, attitudes, knowledge, and actions of actors on a microlevel into the macrocontext of a political communication system.

When Almond and Powell developed their model for cross-country comparisons, they presumed that the functions of political communication were not performed by the same institutions everywhere. Consequently, the task of comparative communication research was to identify the political and media institutions that emerged in different systems to perform those functions. As political institutions (such as interest groups, political parties, legislatures, executives, bureaucracies, or courts) are organized in dramatically different ways in different countries, Almond and Powell rather look at universal functions and processes (such as interest articulation, interest aggregation, policy making, or policy implementation). The same is true for media institutions. The central political function of media communications lies in the "mediatization" of politics (Mazzoleni and Schulz 1999). The media have become the predominant player in informing the public about political processes. They are increasingly indispensable to the communication of social organizations. At the same time, political actors must adapt to the requirements of an environment shaped by the media. Hallin and Mancini (Chapter 2, this volume), characterize "mediatization of politics" as an element of modernization. Although most authors of this book used it as a basis for their argumentation, we still lack precise information as to its varying intensity and consequences in different political systems. Mediatization is caused by processes rooted in the media system (Figure 17.1). It can be traced back to the media's primary function: the creation of publicity by selecting, processing, and conveying information according to media-specific criteria, formats, and presentational styles. The authors of this volume discuss many aspects of the news media's primary function.

According to the input/output model, the "generation of publicity" serves as a means to "articulate" and "aggregate" interests, issues, and problems (see Figure 17.1). Access to the media (and thereby to the general public), however, is highly restricted. Media attention is often granted to those who have high social status or political power (e.g., celebrities and politicians), who have public relations professionals at their disposal (e.g., interest groups and multinational corporations), or

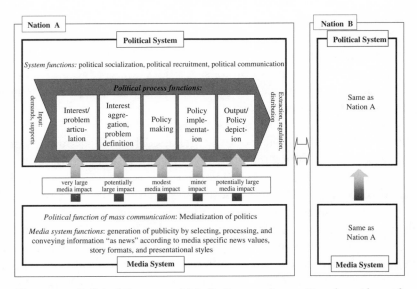

Figure 17.1 Political System and Media System. *Source:* Based on Almond et al. (2003); Jarren and Donges (2002); Mazzoleni and Schulz (1999)

who resort to "alternative" public relations tactics such as spectacular protests or violent pseudoevents (e.g., opposition groups not represented in Parliament). Kriesi offers in this volume a comparative analysis of the different strategies geared at generating media attention and winning public support in different national contexts. The specific ways in which the media "select, process and convey information" refers to their news value criteria, editorial routines, and the format in which the news is presented. News decisions can be explained by intrinsic professional norms and extrinsic personal attitudes. The first category mainly comprises of the criteria of newsworthiness (e.g., negativity, status, proximity) identified by news value theory. These criteria affect the selection of news and thereby impose a systematic bias upon the media reality of politics. As a result, international television news displays a uniform orientation toward disasters, elite actors, or regional events, as Rössler observes in this volume. The second category contains extrinsic effects – such as personal views or political preferences of individual journalists – on news selection. As Donsbach and Patterson note in this volume, news workers' political orientations have a detectable, albeit weak, influence on their news decisions in many Western countries.

By looking at the mediatization of politics from a comparative perspective, four processes have attracted particular attention by the contributors to this volume:

- The process of political socialization, which plays a key role in the maintenance and change of political systems.
- The perception of political processes and the impact of election campaigning on the formation of public opinion – both are key processes in the transformation of input into output.
- Political public relations and its effects on the depiction of system output in the media and the public.
- The reciprocal interactions between political communication structures and political communication culture.

POLITICAL SOCIALIZATION

Political socialization is a precondition for maintaining, altering, and adapting a system to a changing national and international environment (see Figure 17.1). Political socialization entails the adoption of central elements of a given political culture, political knowledge, attitudes, and models of political actions by citizens from an early age on. From the perspective of comparative political communication, it is interesting to explore the respective roles of the mass media as an institution of political socialization in different systems. In a comparison of Europe and North America, Norris (2000) examined the relationship between media usage and political knowledge, opinions, and attitudes. By contrasting media content analyses and public opinion surveys on an international level, she could demonstrate to which degree the mass media in the United States and the European Union (EU) member states promote citizens' willingness and competence to participate in the political process. Moreover, she addressed the question of whether the media contribute to public cynicism and political distrust to the same degree everywhere (cf. Norris 2000).

This question is extremely relevant to comparative political communication research: Similar to Hallin and Mancini, Swanson reports in this volume that "many believe news about politicians has become more negative in its tone [and] more skeptical of leaders' motives." According to Swanson, "such journalism has been cited as a cause of growing public cynicism and mistrust of political actors and institutions. High levels of cynicism about politics have been noted in all the Western democracies." However, the empirical analyses presented by Norris (2000) do not support the existence of an unambiguous relationship between media coverage and political cynicism – at least for Western Europe. Of course, empirical research is still in its infancy here. Yet, it is evident that only a systematic comparison of two or more countries can produce findings that are both reliable and precise.

THE PERCEPTION OF POLITICAL PROCESSES

A further aspect of the impact of media communication on the political process is the interaction of "input/demands," "interest or problem articulation" and "interest aggregation or problem definition." In order to be suitable for policy making, the performance expectations of society, that is, the electorate or the media audience, must be transformed into "issues" and "problems" (see Figure 17.1). This transformation of expectations or demands is not organized like clockwork. It is the result of a socially constructed process aiming at defining these issues and problems. Given this background, comparative political communication research inquires how and why similar topics are covered in vastly divergent ways by different (political and media) systems. The variable considered to be most appropriate to explain differences in coverage is political culture, that is, social and cultural values (cf. Semetko and Mandelli 1997; Lee, Chan, Pan, and So 2000). However, international agenda-setting research started identifying the conditions responsible for shaping culture-bound media agendas only recently (Wanta et al. 1995; Weaver et al. 1998). As shown by Rössler in his analysis of international television news, it is indeed very rare for the media of different countries to cover the same topics – with the exception of international crises, wars, and disasters.

THE MEDIA AND ELECTION CAMPAIGNING

Voting is the most direct form of political participation and can be interpreted as an expression of support for a given system. Studies in this area target the relationship between "input/support," "interest or problem articulation," and "interest aggregation or problem definition." Comparative research into mass media elections now has three models at its disposal that put the relevant variables into a complex framework and at the same time are sensitive to national context factors: the Modern Model of Campaigning by Swanson and Mancini (1996), the model of the Discretionary Power of the Media as summarized by Blumler and Gurevitch (1995b, 2001), and the Model of Campaign Communication by Norris (2002). From a comparative perspective, processes of transformation in campaign management and campaign coverage – usually referred to as Americanization, modernization, and globalization – are especially interesting. In a prototypical study, Plasser (2002) discussed these processes thoroughly. On the basis of an international survey of campaign managers, he concluded that although knowledge and personnel are exchanged on a global scale and although most campaign managers orient themselves toward American models, a global standardization of campaign practices does not occur. Instead, national and culture-specific campaign traditions are supplemented with selected components of a universal media-centered and marketing-oriented campaign style (see also Norris 2002). Today, we are familiar with the culture-specific factors affecting this process of transnational adaptation (Plasser 2002, 79):

- The electoral system (e.g., majority vote versus proportional representation; candidate versus party elections);
- The system of party competition (e.g., number of party activists, ability to mobilize party followers, member versus voter parties);
- The legal regulations of election campaigns (e.g., private versus public campaign financing, limits on expenditures, access to television advertising, procedures for candidate nomination, and time limits for official campaigns);
- The degree of professionalization of election campaigning (professional sophistication at campaign management, use of political consultants);
- The media system (e.g., public versus dual versus private media systems, differentiation of the media system, professional roles of journalists, autonomy of the mass media, degree of media competition);
- The national political culture (e.g., homogeneous versus fragmented cultures, hierarchical versus competitive political cultures, degree of trust in the political process, high versus low turnout cultures); and
- The degree of modernization in society (e.g., degree of societal differentiation, industrialized versus information society).

POLITICAL PUBLIC RELATIONS AND ITS IMPACT ON PUBLIC OPINION

As the pressures to gear the "output" of the political system toward the media grow, the "depiction of politics" according to news-value criteria becomes increasingly important (see Figure 17.1). This process of "self-mediatization of politics" is driven by two motives (Meyer 2002). First, political elites have an inescapable need for legitimacy that feeds a permanent urge to justify themselves and their actions publicly. Secondly, they are motivated to seek an edge over their rivals in the court of public opinion by cultivating a positive image and using the media to win public approval and gain political power. Political public relations, political advertising, marketing, and campaign management move to the focus of attention. Pfetsch (1998) compared the styles and strategies of government public relations in Germany, Great Britain, and the United States. She explained the different approaches by pointing to the role of central actors within the system of government (head of state, government spokesperson, press offices, etc.), the different organizational settings and characteristics of the media system (including the degree of commercialization and competition), and the media culture (which is shaped by the professional roles of journalists and their attitudes toward the political system). Pfetsch (2001) then examined the effects of these structural differences on communication culture, distinguishing between a media-oriented (American) style of interaction between political spokespeople and journalists and a politically motivated (German) interaction style. She found that the norms, objectives, and roles of political public relations reflect the differences between the styles of interaction.

POLITICAL (COMMUNICATION) STRUCTURES AND POLITICAL (COMMUNICATION) CULTURE

Pfetsch's work (Chapter 15) emphasizes the close ties between the structural and the cultural component of political communication – a connection already featured in Almond and Powell's model. *Structure* here refers to the institutional characteristics of the political and media systems on a macrolevel and mesolevel. In contrast, the culture of political communication is defined as the interactions between politicians and journalists on the actor level. Gurevitch and Blumler (Chapter 14, this volume) propose a conceptual framework that combines both dimensions. This framework, "within which all political communication takes place," classifies nations according to their communication structure. Furthermore, Gurevitch and Blumler recommend comparative research in five areas that they regard as fertile for a better understanding of the relationship between political (communication) structures and political (communication) culture. The authors approach these areas in different ways:

- Three authors deal with the construction, communication, and encoding of political messages: Zittel (Chapter 10, this volume) probes into the conditions shaping the national context for the construction and communication of web-based messages by political actors. Kriesi studies the strategies of communication and mobilization that established and alternative political actors employ to attain their goals. Rössler analyzes the country-specific presentation of political issues and actors on television news, comparing different political communication systems.

- Schmitt-Beck (Chapter 13, this volume) examines the reception and effects of political messages by media audiences and their dependence on national context variables.
- Hallin and Mancini as well as Donsbach and Patterson address the relationship between political culture and the culture of journalism: According to Hallin and Mancini, the critical attitude prevalent in the cultures of journalism in Western democracies is linked with the secularization of political culture. Donsbach and Patterson relate differences between Anglo-American and continental European journalists to different professional cultures that are a product of press history and present media structures.
- Zittel and Lang analyze in their respective chapters the reciprocal relations between citizens and political elites from the angle of comparative participation research.
- Pfetsch integrates the interrelationships of media institutions and political institutions into a model for comparing the interactions between political actors and media actors in modern democracies. By connecting this model with her concept of political communication culture, her chapter (Chapter 15, this volume) closely follows the recommendations of Blumler and Gurevitch.

According to Pfetsch, political communication culture can be defined as the empirical reconstruction of actors' attitudes vis-à-vis specific objects of political communication. These attitudes, in turn, determine the way in which political actors and media actors communicate in regards of their common political audience. Pfetsch's work constitutes the most concrete and most consistent adaptation of Almond and Powell's original model. Moreover, it is also consistent with the direction suggested by Gurevitch and Blumler for the further development of comparative political communication research.

THE ROLE OF NATIONAL CONTEXT AND THEORY
IN COMPARATIVE RESEARCH

The model of political (communication) systems developed by Almond et al. (2003) and the model of political communication culture developed by Gurevitch and Blumler and Pfetsch (Chapters 14 and 15, this volume), which is based on Almond's model, seem to fill a conceptual gap in comparative research. Because of their universal applicability and neutrality, they can also serve as tertium comparationes, that is, independent yardsticks enabling us to compare one country with another – even though the role of political communication can differ substantially depending on the object of study, whether it is an established democracy or an instable democracy in the process of transformation (cf. Gunther and Mughan 2000). The models prove to be particularly resourceful where the integration of structure and culture is concerned. They can also serve as frameworks within which we can discuss and categorize concrete middle-range theories.[1] In comparative research, one of the primary objectives consists in generalizing, contextualizing, and building middle-range theories of communication. The nation[2] – or systemic-cultural context with which theories are connected – plays a pivotal role in achieving this. Regarding the role of the nation, Kohn (1989) distinguishes four types of cross-national comparative research:

- "Nation as context": In such research, nations are treated as different contexts in which the phenomenon studied is exposed to various stimuli. One is interested, for example, in testing the generality of findings about how media systems operate or whether the impact of political television advertising changes in the settings observed. If replications in different countries show the same stable effect, the mechanism and its underlying theory can be gradually generalized. Reversed, such an approach can use national context as an explanation for different levels of the dependent variable. In this volume, Schmitt-Beck and Pfetsch (Chapters 13 and 15) both use nations as context.

---

[1] Examples of such middle-range theories include Gatekeeping and News Value Theories, Agenda Setting and Agenda Building, Priming and Framing, Knowledge Gap and Diffusion Theory, Spiral of Silence, Cultivation Theory, News Learning and Reception Theories, or Theories of Media Politics.

[2] The term *nation* refers to an ethnic group with a homogeneous identity. Almond et al. (2003, 19) define *nation* as follows: "When we speak of a 'nation,' we thus refer to the self-identification of a people. That common identity may be built upon a common language, history, race, or culture, or simply upon the fact that this group has occupied the same theory." History has shown that a nation can be divided (e.g., the Federal Republic of Germany and the German Democratic Republic); that several nations can be part of one state (until this state disintegrates, as was the case with the USSR, Yugoslavia, and Czechoslovakia); or a nation can remain without a state of its own (e.g., Kurds, Palestinians, and Basques). As a rule, nation and state are mostly identical (e.g., France, Japan, and Sweden).

- "Nation as unit of analysis": In the second type of comparative research, the investigator's concern is to understand variations in national characteristics. One no longer speaks of countries by name, "but instead classifies countries along one or more dimensions" (Kohn 1989, 22). Typologies resulting from this type of study distinguish between various aspects, for example, information-rich versus information-poor countries, newspaper-centric versus television-centric communication systems, or libertarian-unrestricted versus authoritarian-restricted media systems. Moreover, Kohn's second type of cross-national research translates Przeworski and Teune's (1970, 26–30) idea "to convert country names into variables" into practice. In this volume, both Norris and Kriesi (Chapters 6 and 8) chose this approach in their studies.
- "Nation as object": Such research deals with nations as homogeneous, independent objects of study. It focuses on the national identity of nations and institutions. The purpose of this comparison is to gather information about nations by analyzing the whole context, and to enhance understanding thereof. The quantity of countries studied is usually low and the explanation involved is extensive. An example of this type of research would be investigating which factors make up the identities of different national journalism cultures. Here, particular elements are interpreted as an expression of the culture or the system itself. Kleinsteuber reports in his chapter (Chapter 4) on several such examples.
- "Transnational research": In Kohn's fourth type of research, the investigator regards nations as elements of a larger international system. It focuses on the influence of specific transnational and supranational treaties, organizations, and regimes (e.g., international agreements such as the International Telecommunications Union [ITU], General Agreement on Trade and Services [GATS], and the EU directive "TV Without Frontiers"). Furthermore, the investigator's interest is on the impact of the cross-national flow of information and international elites (e.g., the exchange of campaign consultants or methods and strategies of media-oriented campaign practices) on processes, actors, and structures of political communication in different countries. These aspects of modernization and globalization are examined by various contributors, for example, Hallin and Mancini, Swanson, and Holtz-Bacha (Chapters 2, 3, and 9, this volume).

Table 17.1 Role of National Context and Theory in Comparative Designs

		Orientation Toward	
		Hypothesis-Testing (theory driven)	Exploration (fact driven)
Consideration of Contextual Factors	High (systemic multilevel approach)	Contextualization Studies	Validation Studies
		Always Possible: Theory Building	
	Low (focused-variable approach)	Generalization Studies	Differences Studies

Source: Adapted from van de Vijver and Leung (1997, 2000).

The degree to which comparative studies can contribute to theory building varies depending on what function the nation performs within a study's design. This question addresses the two central dimensions characterizing comparative studies:

- The degree of contextualization (i.e., studies are divided into groups that consider national context variables either to a high, systemic or a low, selective extent), and
- Their orientation toward hypothesis testing or exploration (i.e., studies either choose a strongly theory-driven approach or a less theoretical, more fact-finding approach).

For the sake of simplicity, the two dimensions are dichotomized. Crossing them will then reveal four types of study (Table 17.1). The resulting typology is based on the conceptions of van de Vijver and Leung (1997, 2000) and Wirth and Kolb (Chapter 5, this volume), and stresses the tremendous potential of comparative research: Depending on the four possible approaches shown in Table 17.1, cross-national studies either focus on contextualizing theories, generalizing theories, verifying the validity of concepts, or merely on identifying similarities and differences. To a larger or lesser extent, all four approaches can contribute to the formulation of new theories.

We speak of highly contextualized comparative studies, when the analysis of different systems, cultures, and nations systematically considers contextual factors and builds on an analytical framework divided into microlevel, mesolevel, and macrolevel. A well-founded explanation of the similarities and differences observed can then point to the context variables that have been systematically gathered. Obviously, this type of study corresponds to Kohn's "nation as context" approach. This demands substantial knowledge prior to the study. Also, this method routinely requires collaboration with experts in the respective countries. A specific difficulty of this approach lies in the safeguarding of functional equivalence of all the factors considered (for a discussion of this problem see Chapter 5, this volume).

However, such an extensive systemic approach is not always necessary. In many cases, a more focused approach that considers only few contextual factors may be sufficient. Here, the investigator concentrates exclusively on the variables necessary for the testing of a specific theory or hypothesis. Frequently, one intends to find out how nations react in respect to differences in relevant variables. This approach treats a nation as Kohn's "unit of analysis," yet it also enables us to study the specific impact of "transnational effects." In terms of research resources it is also more economical, but its lack of context variables constitutes a major weakness: the potential for interpreting unexpected phenomena and drawing universal conclusions is small.

Regarding the second dimension of Table 17.1, a study may be theory driven and more orientated toward hypothesis testing. Ideally, a study begins with a theory, or at least a well-based research question. The function of this theory, then, is the selection of variables to be considered. On the one hand, comparative research is founded on theory; on the other hand, it is a means to further the development of existing theories. For this purpose, investigators frequently take middle-range theories developed in a particular national context and test their validity in a cross-national comparison. An instructive example of a theory-driven study can be found in the work of Stevenson (1998) who examined Noelle-Neumann's Spiral of Silence Theory in different national settings (see also Csikszentmihalyi 1991). In order to investigate the transnational applicability of middle-range theories, one must treat "nation as context."

When researchers enter a new field of study and are interested in a specific object about which there are no (known) theories, they usually employ an approach that is not theory based but characterized by an original curiosity for systemic differences. This strategy, which is orientated more toward exploration, is widely used in pilot studies and aims primarily at organizing and classifying data. At best, this results in important groundwork, at worst, it shows the investigator's carelessness in regards to theory. Indeed, Gurevitch and Blumler complain (Chapter 14, this volume) that, in terms of "extent and vigor of theoretical debate [. . .] comparative political communication analysis still falls lamentably short."

CONTEXTUALIZATION STUDIES

As shown in Table 17.1, one may expect a study to belong to one of the four types of comparative research. A "contextualization of existing theories" is possible in a theory-driven study considering contextual factors. Countries are consciously selected according to their theory-validating value and according to either the *most similar systems design* or the *most different systems design* (cf. Chapter 5, this volume). By systematically considering context variables, one can discern those system factors in the presence of which a theory is mainly valid. Aside from refining existing theories, it is also possible to expand a theory's potential for contributing to knowledge: Ideally, culture-specific influences can be completely removed and the theory can be administered globally. A good example for this is modernization, as demonstrated by the edited volume of David Swanson and Paolo Mancini (1996): At first, the two editors drafted an elaborate theoretical framework on modernized elections campaigns that collaborators then used as a base for standardized case studies in many different countries. After the national election studies had shown much more complex and differentiated findings then originally thought, Swanson and Mancini transformed their framework into a comprehensive and contextualized Model of Modern Campaigning. The consideration of national characteristics (contextual factors) induced Swanson and Mancini (1996) to assess the applicability of their model according to whether they observed established democracies, new democracies, or instable democracies (for details see the respective chapters of Holtz-Bacha [Chapter 9, this volume] and Gurevitch and Blumler [Chapter 14, this volume]). Further examples of "contextualizing existing theories" in international comparative communication research include News Value Theory and Agenda Setting Theory.[3] In both cases, system-specific macrovariables for specifying these theories were found.

---

[3] As to News Value Theory, Semetko (1996) concludes that German television journalists strictly stick to conventional news values even in times of election campaigns whereas their British and American colleagues ignore customary news value during campaigns. In Germany, campaign events rank lower on the news agenda because they have to compete with other important domestic or foreign news events. This situation, however, favors the incumbents' visibility on television (as found in German election news) because news factors such as power or elite status also apply to them. British and American journalists, in contrast, emphasized campaign events (by playing up their

GENERALIZABILITY STUDIES

Another type of comparative studies attempts to establish the internationalization or "generalizability of existing theories" (see Table 17.1). Generalizability studies assess the general validity and geographic range of a theory (or hypothesis) by testing it in different social-cultural and systemic settings. As a rule, such tests refer only to the relevant target variables. Therefore, the outcome is mostly either "theory confirmed" or "theory not confirmed." Alternative interpretations are often neglected because respective context variables have not been collected. However, the appeal of this procedure consists in its increasing abstraction and well-founded generalization of useful theories. In this respect, Donsbach and Patterson offer (Chapter 11, this volume) a cross-cultural confirmation of Kepplinger's Theory of Instrumental Actualization. By adopting Kepplinger's (1991) survey instrument, the authors can demonstrate that political journalists in many Western countries seem to have an inclination to select and publish in particular those news items that are close to their own political ideas. In a similar fashion, Norris confirms (Chapter 6, this volume) that the core claims of classic liberal theories of democracy (i.e., that free access to the media and an independent press are closely interconnected with indicators for good governance and human development) are universally applicable. Zittel (Chapter 10, this volume), tested the generalizability of the concept of Electronic Democracy developed in the United States to European countries and found little evidence for its applicability.

VALIDATION AND DIFFERENCES STUDIES

In the form of exploratory pilot studies, validation and differences studies are quite common, yet theory is scarce in these two types of comparative designs (see Table 17.1). At best, investigators using them can gain unusual insights that can then be systematically authenticated in

news value) to a disproportionately high degree in order to inform even disinterested voters about party platforms and candidates. They aimed at balancing the news about all candidates quantitatively, which prevents a visibility advantage of the incumbent but qualifies News Value Theory. As to Agenda Setting Theory, Semetko et al. (1991) prove in their comparison of British news coverage in the 1983 election campaign with American coverage in the 1984 election campaign that agenda setting cannot be understood as a uniform homogeneous process. The struggle between political and media actors for control of the agenda takes place on a continuum from active "agenda setting" to passive "agenda reflecting." The authors describe the reluctant and reactive role of British journalists as "agenda amplifying" and the role of their more proactive, powerful American colleagues as "agenda shaping" (cf. Blumler and Gurevitch 1995b; Gurevitch and Blumler [Chapter 14, this volume]).

larger, theory-driven studies (cf. van de Vijver and Leung 1997, 2000). It is important to acknowledge, though, that all four types of studies fulfill specific and legitimate purposes. Similar to the other types, this type of study is of particular use in comparative research. At an initial stage, when the causes of and information about cross-national similarities and differences with regard to a phenomenon are largely unknown, exploratory validation and differences studies are preponderant. A good example for this is the work of Sabine Lang (Chapter 7, this volume). She stresses that "the scope of existing research is limited [and] results from this inquiry are at best preliminary." Her argument, she states, "is based on a comparative reading of a small number of existing case studies, thus leaving some issues underrepresented and others unaddressed." The new findings gathered in this way must later be linked to established theories in systematic follow-up studies – evidently, these are necessary steps in the development of every science. Lang's work offers a foundation for this because she points out the universal factors determining the "structural transformation of local media publics" and defines perspectives for further comparative research into local public spheres. Pfetsch, by contrast, is a step ahead of her: Chapter 15 proposes a comprehensive, theory-driven framework for comparing the interactions of political and media actors in different types of modern democracies.

THE CONSTRUCTION OF NEW THEORIES

As we consider these issues, we understand that, in principle, building theories by comparing is always possible and not subject to choosing an approach based on theory (with the objective to contextualize or generalize existing theories) or exploration (which classifies findings first, in order to lay a basis for subsequent hypotheses, models, or theories). Theories, on the one hand, provide essential orientation. On the other hand, innovative comparatists may also perceive them sometimes as an obstacle because they leave no room for new discoveries and creative methods. The same is true for established methods and research strategies. But in the present period of turbulent social, political, and media change, comparative research should strive for innovative approaches (Landman 2003). As a matter of fact, in the face of the new challenges posed by globalization, comparative political communication requires new theories and methods. As there is no such thing as an ideal theory or method in comparative research, new challenges demand extended designs.

THE NEW CHALLENGES TO COMPARATIVE POLITICAL COMMUNICATION RESEARCH: GLOBAL COMMUNICATION, POLITICAL INTEGRATION, AND WORLD SYSTEM TENDENCIES

Political systems or cultures are the central units of analysis (or "cases") in comparative political communication research. In times of growing globalization and supranational integration, however, it is becoming increasingly difficult to treat societies and cultures as isolated units (Shaw 1997). Traditionally, international comparison defines a "case" as a bound unit of dependent and independent variables – an example of this would be placing one political system with its characteristic political culture against another system and culture. In each case, investigators assume that the factors leading to variations of the phenomenon observed (e.g., the question of why personalized campaign practices and campaign coverage play a more significant role in the United States than in Europe) can be found among the features determining the concrete political and media environments (e.g., weak parties, majority vote, and commercialized broadcasting media in the United States versus powerful parties, proportional representation, and public service broadcasters in many European countries). However, the notion of countries as bound entities no longer seems to be substantiated by reality. European parties tap U.S. campaign expertise and hire U.S. campaign managers in order to plan successful campaigns; similarly, European newspaper publishers and broadcasting companies consult with American media experts in order to profit from their know-how as to designing successful news casts and entertainment shows. These exogenous impulses may lead to a significant increase in candidate-focused campaign practices and personalized campaign coverage in Europe. If we generalize this example, we encounter serious methodological questions for comparative research. Indeed, the more intensive and institutionalized such cross-border exchange processes become, the more likely a single communicative world system will emerge, where boundaries no longer exist and global mass communication becomes the defining feature. This option appears in the literature under different metaphors including McLuhan's "global village" (1962) and Luhmann's "world society" (1997). As Rosengren, McLeod, and Blumler (1992, 285–6) point out, comparative studies depend on the comparison of independent systems. If, however, communication systems merge with each other and cease to be autonomous, they can no longer serve as objects of comparative analysis. In this case, we would, in fact, observe nothing but the flow of communication and the processes of diffusion occurring within an all-encompassing global system. This poses a challenging question: *Could this already be the end of comparative political communication research?*

Indeed, theoreticians of globalization criticize that sociological research has relied far too long on the "artificial" concept of the territorial nation-state as unit of analysis (Beck 2000; Crofts Wiley 2004). According to them, comparative studies in particular have an inclination to focus excessively on the state and to presume it to be the political heart that integrates society and, by doing so, safeguards collective identity, social cohesion, and cultural homogeneity. In contrast to this, the critics suggest that in a world shaped by massive diffusion, interdependence, and performance on both the level of the global economy (with multinational companies and products, integrated financial markets, and world trade agreements) and global politics (with military alliances, supranational organizations, and membership in international organizations and conventions) the sovereignty of national governments has been reduced so much that one could speak of the denationalization of politics. This criticism must be taken seriously, because similar processes of diffusion, dependence, and performance can also be observed in mass communication (Chapter 4, this volume) where they seem to render the nation-state or national context superfluous, too. In the field of communication, such processes are often discussed under the labels *Americanization, cultural imperialism,* or *globalization.* As Hallin and Mancini explain (Chapter 2, this volume), they are connected to the underlying fear that a "trend towards homogenization" of the media systems could "weaken national characteristics" and "undermine" traditional relationships. From their point of view, the central question is whether changes in political communication arrangements are a consequence of exogenous processes such as diffusion or endogenous processes such as functional differentiation of all modern societies. By posing this question, Hallin and Mancini address a fundamental challenge to comparative analysis, which in the literature is known as "Galton's problem." Can we explain similar phenomena occurring in different societies as a functional differentiation caused by domestic factors or as the imitation of foreign models caused by foreign factors? In the first case, a phenomenon is interpreted according to modernization theory: The phenomenon exists because it performs indispensable functions for its social-political environment; similar environmental conditions require similar solutions and produce similar structures without foreign intervention. In the latter case, a phenomenon is explained by diffusion theory: it exists because national elites decided to adopt a foreign model. This decision is based on the conviction that the foreign model is worth imitating and that it can be modified to fit into traditional national regulatory and institutional structures; comparable phenomena can thus emerge within different contexts.

The question of whether a phenomenon can be attributed to internal or external causes is a dilemma that today, more than ever, is of topical interest. Comparative political communication research must react to these new challenges by updating its theoretical and methodological concepts. First, theories of international communication must be integrated; secondly, exogenous variables must be collected in addition to the endogenous variables of national context. Both conclusions need further explanation.

CONSIDERING THEORIES OF INTERNATIONAL COMMUNICATION

Various theories – ranging from transformation, (cultural) imperialism, modernization, dependency, and diffusion – appear to be helpful in bridging the gap between the concepts of international communication and comparative communication research. To this end, several authors in this volume lay the necessary foundation.

Hallin and Mancini, Swanson, and Gurevitch and Blumler argue in favor of focusing on transformation research: They criticize that comparative research puts too much emphasis on comparing the status quo, and that, by doing so, it neglects the rapid changes in the conditions determining political communication that demand dynamic explanations and designs. According to these authors, comparative research needs to clarify the role of the media (which cause and reflect this change) in the process of transformation. Linking these concepts with theories predominant in transformation research, then, entails more longitudinal section designs.

Modernization, dependency, and (cultural) imperialism are theories that in the course of history have come into and gone out of fashion, and as Stevenson notes (Chapter 16, this volume), carry different meanings in different fields. Today, (cultural) imperialism is associated – in the context of political communication – with the thesis of the Americanization of electoral campaigns, journalism, and entertainment. In comparative communication research, Americanization means a directional, one-way convergence process between the political communication practices of the United States and a second country (see Chapters 1, 2, and 3). Hallin and Mancini (Chapter 2, this volume), try to overcome such sweeping assumptions and refer us to the globalization concept developed by Thompson and Tomlinson, who concentrate on, what they call, "complex connectivity." Complex connectivity results from the all-encompassing communication linkages between localities. These locations are altered by such linkages, but do not disappear. In a globalized world, distances between cultures do not necessarily shrink, yet, the ways in which these cultures communicate with each other multiply. As a consequence, the globalization of media communication does neither create cultural homogeneity nor the cultural proximity of a neighborhood evoked by McLuhan's metaphor of the "global village," nor does it abolish differences. Instead, the globalization of the media produces an ocean of translocal, mediatized cultures where nations are reduced to mere islands whose coastlines become increasingly blurred due to a multitude of new influences (cf. Tomlinson 1999). This differentiated understanding of globalization has also contributed to a better understanding of modernization that today directs us toward intranational processes affecting society, politics, and the media (see Chapter 2 and 3, this volume). As noted by Holtz-Bacha (Chapter 9, this volume), modernization must be factored in as an additional national context variable in international comparative studies.

Another topical theory in the field of international communication is dependency – a theory that today also has a different meaning than it did in the 1960s and 1970s. In today's understanding, dependencies result less from colonial relationships but more often from international treaties (e.g., GATS or ITU), or from membership in supranational intergovernmental institutions (e.g., the EU) or international organizations (e.g., the United Nations). Legislative acts of the EU, for instance, account for approximately 60 percent of the legislation passed in Germany. This quiet Europeanization of national institutions renders comparisons between EU-member states and nonmember states increasingly difficult: If we compared, for instance, the German and the Canadian media system, we would have to consider not only the German media policies as an important variable, but also the telecommunication policies of the EU. This example illustrates our problem quite well: To what extent are these cases still comparable, if different levels of comparison and influence are relevant for them? The same applies to comparisons between EU member states. National context no longer suffices to explain common phenomena. We must include the EU level, too. This dilemma is explicitly addressed in Chapters 2 and 4 (this volume). It requires the conventional principles of comparative research

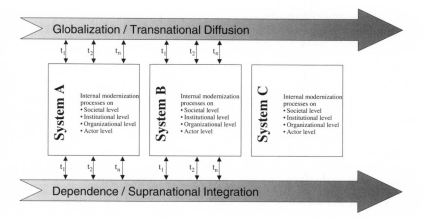

Figure 17.2 Distinguishing External Influences (Globalization, Integration) and Internal Influences (Modernization) in Comparative Research

to be reexamined. This becomes even more urgent when we keep in mind that the tendency toward integration and internationalization of media policies, media regulation, and media economy has relativized the importance of the nation-state and denationalized international communication.

Considering Additional External Variables

From a methodical point of view, comparative political research needs to react to the problems described previously by considering additional sources of data. Figure 17.2 is an illustration of how this might be realized. Comparative studies in political communication can no longer concentrate on comparing systems A, B, and C alone, but must observe a variety of external variables, too. Analysis includes examining, first, internal variables of the respective national context (A, B, C); second, external factors stemming from transnational diffusion and globalization processes; third, external factors from supranational integration processes; and fourth, measuring over time in order to identify the degree to which the mentioned processes affect the respective systems at several points in time (t_1, t_2, t_n). It is prudent to heed Blumler and Gurevitch (2001, 381), who warn that "in the present period of turbulent social, political, and media change, the validity of one-time cross-national analyses cannot be accepted unless they are regularly updated." As a rule, these influential processes of globalization and dependency are transactional or reciprocal. In order to measure their impact, we must first look at the question of whether all systems studied are exposed to the same external processes (such as A and B in Figure 17.2), or whether this is not the case for one of the systems under observation (C). It is extremely important to distinguish accurately effects motivated by diffusion and globalization or dependency and integration on the one hand and from internal effects motivated by modernization on the other hand. During analysis, we have to take the zero-impact hypothesis into account, according to which these external process factors do not influence the object of our study in the systems we compare. As to alternative hypotheses, we can make different assumptions about the impact of external factors. Following Kleinsteuber (Chapter 4, this volume), we can, for instance, distinguish between voluntary and coercive adoption of a model ("dependency," "performance") or between immediate imitation and delayed learning effects ("temporality"). If applied to comparative political communication research, such effects would have to be operationalized and isolated from internal factors.

Only such extended designs will provide reliable evidence for what many authors in this volume assume to be the case, that is, that the adoption of American models is opposed by "persistent cultural differences and resisting or mediating factors" (Gurevitch and Blumler), and that European countries have "often modified [US models] significantly" (Hallin and Mancini), and "adapted them to the national context" (Holtz-Bacha). None of the authors in this volume, however, advocates the idea that Americanization is a form of cultural imperialism. Indeed, recent comparative studies substantiate the view that national context is still a considerable influence. The decisive concept is "hybridization" (cf. Norris 2000; Blumler and Gurevitch 2001; Chan 2001; Plasser 2002).

The hybridization model proposed by modernization theory has been especially successful in gaining acceptance in the international comparison of electoral campaign communication (cf. Plasser 2002, 348–51). It means the implementation of selected components of a cross-national and cross-cultural style of campaigning in order to supplement country-specific and culture-specific traditional styles of campaigning and campaign coverage. Hybrid styles constitute a combination of modern techniques – influenced by the American standard model – with country-specific traditions of one's own political and media culture. The results of recent comparative studies do not support the notion of a directional Americanization or global standardization. Instead, autonomous adaptation processes take place. These processes are the elements of a structural change of the political and media systems. In many mass democracies, this change occurs in the form of an internally motivated process that gradually modifies traditional styles, practices, and routines, and that varies in different countries depending on their system-specific and culture-specific arrangements.

The empirical findings concerning hybridization are excellently compatible with the concept of globalization based on complex connectivity and the concept of modernization based on endogenous changes. Furthermore, hybridization underscores that it is too early to speculate about the irrelevance of the nation-state and national culture. An insight from the field of comparative politics applies here, too: "It seems that national actors are still key institutions that translate international trends into national policies and these policies do vary among nations" (Jahn 2002, 8; see also Morris and Waisbord 2001). Globalization does not simply do away with traditional institutions in politics and the media. Consequently, we can conclude that with regard to the basic principle of comparing separate cases there is no reason to dismiss proven strategies of comparative studies as long as these strategies are completed with the modifications suggested herein. Yet, even those colleagues who advocate the existence of a uniform world system, a world society, or a world public cannot presume that this is the end of comparative studies as they have to consider a new method in comparative research: "incorporated comparison." In contrast to classical international comparison, this method does not view cases as independent units, but as relational parts of a singular arrangement. [4]

CONCLUSION

In this chapter, we have attempted to describe the state of the art of comparative political communication studies. We used the articles contained in this volume as a basis to develop an umbrella concept that shall contribute to the establishment of comparative research as a discipline of communication studies in its own right. To this end, we have tried, above all, to convey the complexity and the fascination emanating from comparative studies. Just how much comparative studies and

---

[4] This arrangement can be a sequence of historical and cumulative developments or a current common experience or influence. Cases are no longer selected according to external criteria – such as in the quasi-experimental design described previously – but according to the relations they establish with each other and their relation to the overall arrangement that they form. Incorporated comparison has been designed for analyzing globalization and can also be applied to analyzing the world system (cf. McMichael 2000). Its proximity to Kohn's (1989) study type of "transnational research" is obvious.

communication studies are interconnected is stressed by the problems that globalization pose: The shrinking importance of national boundaries will lead to a merger of comparative studies with theories of international communication, which, in turn, will necessitate a modification of customary comparative designs. In doing so, intranational and extranational effects and variables must be considered. If this is accomplished, comparison will substantially advance the field of political communication research. Particularly the generalization and contextualization of existing theories and the construction of new theories will profit from it.

The future of comparative political communication research, however, is determined by the actual work of researchers. Van de Vijer and Leung (2000) divide researchers into "sojourners" and "natives." They define the latter as a small circle of colleagues specializing in comparison. These researchers concentrate mainly on the macroconcepts of system and culture, innovative evaluation methods, multimethod designs, and theory building. Yet, the direction of research will be defined by the booming group of sojourners. Although the primary expertise of these investigators is in another content domain, increasing academic exchange and the internationalization of the objects under study will prompt them to carry out projects in comparative research. Because of its rapid growth, this group will be responsible for the majority of cross-cultural publications. Sojourners are chiefly interested in testing the generalizability of theories and validating their concepts in different national contexts and cultural milieus. We intended this chapter to be mainly an orientation for this group as we see a new imperative regarding the verification of scientific knowledge appear: Go comparative!

REFERENCES

Almond, Gabriel A., and G. Bingham Powell. 1966. *Comparative Politics: A Developmental Approach. An Analytic Study.* Boston: Little Brown & Co.

Almond, Gabriel A., G. Bingham Powell, Kaare Strom, and Russell J. Dalton, eds. 2003. *Comparative Politics Today: A World View. Updated 7th edition.* New York: Longman.

Beck, Ulrich. 2000. *What is Globalization?* Cambridge: Polity.

Blumler, Jay G., and Michael Gurevitch. 1995a. Comparative Research: The Extending Frontier. In Jay G. Blumler and Michael Gurevitch, eds. *The Crisis of Public Communication.* London: Routledge, pp. 73–85.

———. 1995b. The Formation of Campaign Agendas in the United States and Britain. In Jay G. Blumler and Michael Gurevitch, eds. *The Crisis of Public Communication.* London: Routledge, pp. 86–96.

———. 2001. Americanization Reconsidered: UK-US Campaign Communication Comparisons Across Time. In W. Lance Bennett and Robert M. Entman, eds. *Mediated*

Politics. Communication in the Future of Democracy. New York: Cambridge University Press, pp. 380–403.

Blumler, Jay G., Jack M. McLeod, and Karl Erik Rosengren. 1992. An Introduction to Comparative Communication Research. In Jay G. Blumler, Jack M. McLeod, and Karl Erik Rosengren, eds. *Comparatively Speaking: Communication and Culture Across Space and Time*. Newbury Park, CA: Sage, pp. 3–18.

Chan, Joseph Man. 2001. Media, Democracy and Globalization: A Comparative Framework. *Javnost – The Public* 8 (4): 103–18.

Crofts Wiley, Stephen B. 2004. Rethinking Nationality in the Context of Globalization. *Communication Theory* 14 (1): 78–96.

Csikszentmihalyi, Mihaly. 1991. Reflections on the Spiral of Silence. In James A. Anderson, ed. *Communication Yearbook 14*. Newbury Park, CA: Sage, pp. 288–97.

Gunther, Richard and Anthony Mughan. 2000. *Democracy and the Media. A Comparative Perspective*. Cambridge: Cambridge University Press.

Jahn, Detlef. 2002. *The Impact of Globalization on Comparative Analysis*. Paper presented to the 43rd. Annual ISA Convention on "Dissolving Boundaries: The Nexus between Comparative Politics and International Relations," New Orleans, March 24–7.

Jarren, Otfried, and Patrick Donges. 2002. *Politische Kommunikation in der Mediengesellschaft. Eine Einführung*. 2 vols. Wiesbaden, Germany: Westdeutscher Verlag.

Kepplinger, Hans Mathias, Hans-Bernd Brosius, and Joachim Friedrich Staab. 1991. Instrumental Actualization: A Theory of Mediated Conflicts. *European Journal of Communication* 6: 263–90.

Kohn, Melvin L. 1989. Introduction. In Melvin L. Kohn, ed. *Cross-National Research in Sociology*. Newbury Park, CA Sage, pp. 17–31.

Landman, Todd. 2003. *Issues and Methods in Comparative Politics: An Introduction*. Updated 2nd ed. London: Routledge.

Lee, Chin-Chuan, Joseph Man Chan, Zhongdang Pan, and Clement Y. K. So. 2000. National Prisms of a Global Media Event. In James Curran and Michael Gurevitch, eds. *Mass Media and Society*. London: Arnold, pp. 295–309.

Luhmann, Niklas. 1997. Globalization or World Society: How to Conceive of Modern Society? *International Review of Sociology* 7: 67–79.

Mazzoleni, Gianpietro, and Winfried Schulz. 1999. Mediatization of Politics: A Challenge for Democracy? *Political Communication* 16: 247–61.

McLuhan, Marshall. 1962. *The Gutenberg Galaxy*. London: Routledge.

McMichael, Philip. 2000. World-Systems Analysis, Globalization, and Incorporated Comparison. *Journal of World-Systems Research* 3: 668–90. Available on the World Wide Web at http://csf.colorado.edu/jwsr.

Meyer, Thomas. 2002. *Media Democracy. How the Media Colonize Politics*. Cambridge: Polity Press.

Morris, Nancy, and Silvio Waisbord, eds. 2001. *Media and Globalization: Why the State Matters*. Lanham, MD: Rowman & Littlefield.

Norris, Pippa. 2000. *A Virtuous Circle. Political Communications in Postindustrial Societies*. New York: Cambridge.

———. 2002. Campaign Communication. In Lawrence LeDuc, Richard G. Niemi, and Pippa Norris, eds. *Comparing Communication 2. New Challenges in the Study of Elections and Voting*. London: Sage, pp. 127–47.

Pfetsch, Barbara. 1998. Government News Management. In Doris Graber, Denis McQuail, and Pippa Norris, eds. *The Politics of News – The News of Politics*. Washington: CQ Press, pp. 70–93.

————. 2001. Political Communication Culture in the United States and Germany. *Harvard International Journal of Press/Politics* 6: 46–67.

Plasser, Fritz. 2002. *Global Political Campaigning. A Worldwide Analysis of Campaign Professionals and Their Practices*. Westport, CT: Praeger.

Przeworski, Adam, and Teune, Henry. 1970. *The Logic of Comparative Social Inquiry*. Malabar, FL: Krieger.

Semetko, Holli A. 1996. Political Balance on Television. Campaigns in the United States, Britain and Germany. *Harvard International Journal of Press/Politics* 1: 51–71.

Semetko, Holli A., Jay G. Blumler, Michael Gurevitch, and David H. Weaver. 1991. *The Formation of Campaign Agendas. A Comparative Analysis of Party and Media Roles in Recent American and British Elections*. Hillsdale, NJ: Erlbaum Associates.

Semetko, Holli, and Andreina Mandelli. 1997. Setting the Agenda for Cross-National Research: Bringing Values Into the Concept. In Maxwell McCombs, Donald L. Shaw, and David Weaver, eds. *Communication and Democracy. Exploring the Intellectual Frontiers in Agenda-Setting Theory*. Mahwah, NJ: Erlbaum Associates, pp. 195–207.

Shaw, Martin. 1997. The Theoretical Challenge of Global Society. In Annabelle Sreberny-Mohammadi, Dwayne Winseck, Jim McKenna, and Oliver Boyd-Barrett, eds. *Media in Global Context. A Reader*. London: Arnold, pp. 27–36.

Stevenson, Robert L. 1998. The Missing Link in International Communication. In Christina Holtz-Bacha, Helmut Scherer, and Norbert Waldmann, eds. *Wie die Medien die Welt erschaffen und wie die Menschen darin leben*. Wiesbaden, Germany: Westdeutscher Verlag, pp. 143–53.

Swanson, David L., and Paolo Mancini. 1996. Patterns of Modern Election Campaigning and Their Consequences. In David L. Swanson and Paolo Mancini, eds. *Politics, Media and Modern Democracy. An International Study of Innovations in Electoral Campaigning and Their Consequences*. Westport, CT: Praeger, pp. 247–76.

Tomlinson, John. 1999. *Globalization and Culture*. Cambridge: Polity.

Van de Vijver, Fons, and Kwok Leung. 1997. *Methods and Data Analysis for Cross-Cultural Research*. Thousand Oaks, CA: Sage.

————. 2000. Methodological Issues in Psychological Research Culture. *Journal of Cross-Cultural Psychology* 31: 33–51.

Wanta, Wayne, Pu-tsung King, and Maxwell E. McCombs. 1995. A Comparison of Factors Influencing Issue Diversity in the U.S. and Taiwan. *International Journal of Public Opinion Research* 7 (4): 353–65.

Weaver, David, Maxwell McCombs, and Donald Shaw 1998. International Trends in Agenda-Setting Research. In Christina Holtz-Bacha, Helmut Scherer, and Norbert Waldmann, eds. *Wie die Medien die Welt erschaffen und wie die Menschen darin leben*. Wiesbaden, Germany: Westdeutscher Verlag, pp. 189–203.

Author Index

Subject Index

DATE DUE

FEB 0 4 2008			